Computer Aided Fashion Design
Using Gerber Technology

Computer Aided Fashion Design Using Gerber Technology

Jane D. Espinoza-Alvarado

Fairchild Publications, Inc.
New York

Director of Sales and Acquisitions: Dana Meltzer-Berkowitz
Executive Editor: Olga T. Kontzias
Acquisitions Editor: Joseph Miranda
Assistant Acquisitions Editor: Jaclyn Bergeron
Senior Development Editor: Jennifer Crane
Development Editor: Michelle Levy
Art Director: Adam B. Bohannon
Production Manager: Ginger Hillman
Senior Production Editor: Elizabeth Marotta
Copy Editor: Vivian Gomez
Interior Design: Mary Neal Meador
Cover Design: Adam B. Bohannon

Library of Congress Catalog Card Number: 2006940793

ISBN: 978-1-56367-432-7

GST R 133004424

Printed in Canada

TP14

Contents

Extended Contents

Preface

How fast can we get this style to market? We need a new pattern ASAP. Can I get it yesterday? The knockoffs need to be in the stores immediately after Fashion Week. How long for the production?

The above examples are representative of the common culture of the design and manufacturing environments. The world of fashion has always been a competitive one, and there are no signs of this changing in the near future. The constant rush to design and manufacture garments as quickly as possible has pushed technology to new limits.

Computer aided design, commonly referred to as CAD, has progressed enormously and spread widely around the world to keep up with today's global economy and constant scramble for more time. While designing, patternmaking, and manufacturing remain constant as the phases in the creation of a style, the time limits to complete each one of these phases has sped up significantly through the years as a direct result of computerized technology. Gerber Technology, leader of automated software and hardware since the 1960s, offers solutions for companies to remain up to speed with technology and fashion. Their goal is to help designers and patternmakers work as efficiently as possible in an automated environment for a quick turnaround of final designs, garments, and products.

Designing is very exciting and glamorous but also very demanding. To compete, designers currently need to have knowledge not only of colors and design aesthetics or artistic skills, but also of patternmaking and sewing. After all, how good can a design be if it does not work? In addition to these credentials, designers need to have computer skills to create garments accurately and efficiently, as well as the ability to communicate in a work environment that may span continents.

Who Can Use this Book?

Students who aspire to work in the fashion industry will benefit from this book. Fashion designers like to call themselves *visual learners* because they need to see how things work to understand them. After working at a few colleges and universities, it became apparent to me that visual learning is the best approach in teaching students. Since students are at a starting point in their careers and are not yet proficient with the production process, learning a sophisticated program to automate patterns and grading can be overwhelming to them. I found it a challenge and a goal to help them visualize the processes as best as possible, so they could retain the knowledge in the future. The step-by-step procedures, exercises, and review questions in this book are designed to make learning this software as easy and fun as it is to use.

Industry professionals who don't have CAD knowledge may also find this book a useful means of expanding their existing resume qualifications. The step-by-step procedures along with screen shots and drawings of examples in this book should make it easy for beginners to follow. After training and consulting numerous industry professionals not only in the fashion industry, but also in the furniture and transportation and other industrial fabrics industries, I came to understand that continuing production while learning new software is not an easy task. Therefore, professionals who have had CAD training will find this book refreshing when they need to remember what a function does and how it works. Although AccuMark Version 8 is the focus in this book, AccuMark Version 7 users may find this book helpful in advancing their skills in the Version 8 software. (This goes out to all of you who wanted me to stay for another month or two by your side.)

Students and professionals using this book should have basic patternmaking and grading skills. Students, particularly those who do not crack open a book because they think books lack practical information, will find this book handy throughout their schooling. Professionals and graduating students can use this book as a reference guide to thumb through time and time again.

What is Found in this Book?

The book includes the basics to becoming proficient enough to use the Gerber AccuMark software. The version discussed in this book is Version 8, but Version 7 users will find this book helpful too. It is not intended as a book for highly advanced users. The book can be divided into the three following sections:

1. *Chapters 1 through 7*: Setting up a storage area and its basics through the plotting of pieces.

2. *Chapters 8 through 11*: Menus used to manipulate patterns.

3. *Chapter 12*: Making markers.

Chapter 1 helps you learn a little about Gerber Technology and how and where AccuMark software is used. Chapter 2 guides you in setting up a storage area and basic parameter tables, and functions used to get started. Chapter 3 includes commands common with other software and basic to the AccuMark program. Chapter 4 navigates through the process of inputting patterns into the system and saving them. Chapter 5 embodies basic PDS functions that will hold you over until major manipulation of patterns is needed. Chapter 6

helps you set up a model, also known as a cutter's must in the industry. Chapter 7 leads you through plotting pieces that have already been entered. Chapters 8 through 11 encompass many of the common pattern manipulation tasks used in the industry. Finally, Chapter 12 helps you understand the process used to order and create a marker.

What is Not Included in this Book?

Gerber's AccuMark software, while very user-friendly, is quite a sophisticated system. The scope of its capabilities is too large for a basic class semester or quarter, when students are learning production phases as well.

The following topics are therefore not covered:

- Fundamentals of grading
- Alterations
- Matching

Although the concept of grading is not covered, the basics of grading in an automated environment are included. This book is not meant to teach you how to grade, but rather how to apply your knowledge of grading in a computerized setting. Likewise, readers of this book should have basic patternmaking skills. The software is designed to help you use your skills more efficiently.

The software allows users to create alterations. Matching pieces to a fabric or to one another in a marker is another capacity that the software offers. Again, however, these procedures are not covered in this book because they are rather advanced. People who are interested in learning them may look into a training session with Gerber Technology.

The Future of CAD in Fashion

There is so much excitement for what we can accomplish with technology today. I still remember the first time I saw a system plotting. The fact that technology allows me to complete in a fraction of time what took me hours in my dorm room or in a classroom setting was simply shocking to me. I wanted one of my own plotters—yes, in my dorm room! The software included in this book will become even more useful in years to come, with feedback from users. Gerber is constantly using input from their customers to create better software to suit their needs. All the benefits included in the newest systems come from users like you. Aside from this particular software, look for the future of CAD to take us to the printing of our own fabric designs. It is already being done, but the fabric selections will continue to increase. Watch out for 3-D scanning. Presently, the body may be scanned to create a pattern based on your dimensions. This process is becoming highly developed. Virtual draping, also offered by Gerber Technology, allows for the simulation of sewing patterns together. This is very useful in teaching the visual learner and once again, this process will become more advanced in the coming years. The future of CAD looks very appealing.

Acknowledgments

There are countless people to thank for inspiring me to write this book. First, I would like to thank my students, both in the industry and at schools, who kept asking when I was going to write a book on Gerber. Thank you for the inspiration. I hope it will help ease the resistance often experienced while learning the software.

Thanks go to many people at Gerber Technology. Dave Walls, thank you for welcoming me to Gerber Technology. Kanani Mahelona, my first trainer, you always made everything look easy and understandable. Janell Copello-Hall, thanks for showing me the angles I had for writing this book and for your great listening skills. Kathy Vilade, your kind suggestion to beta test and excitement for the software kept me enthusiastic. Debbie Marconi, thank you for your support. Mary McFadden, you were always so sweet and kind to listen to my needs while writing and always offered a helping hand. Sue Carrier, you were just amazingly quick. Thank you for your phone support. To all of you, I am grateful for your help.

Thanks go to all those at Fairchild Publications for the belief and the help in the creation and production of this book. Olga Kontzias, executive editor, and Joseph Miranda, acquisitions editor: you were the first to believe in this book; thank you. Michelle Levy, development editor, thank you for keeping the book on schedule, for picking up the pieces, for tying up loose ends, and for all your suggestions to bring life to this book. Adam Bohannon, creative art director, words cannot thank you enough for your support with the art and with the help in trying to make creating the visual program easier on both ends, especially mine.

Family and friends can truly be a backbone. Thanks for all the encouraging e-mails and phone calls. To my adored siblings, Vanessa, Jill, Cheryl, and Albert, thank you for always keeping my dreams alive; the Mighty Espinozas are my best friends. To my parents, words cannot thank you enough for your unconditional love and support in everything I do. You are the reason I accomplished what I have today. I am sure letting me go to Texas was tough, but I came back and look at the results. I love you both. To my wonderful children, Raquel and Evan, your smiles and chuckles make my every day shine. I am blessed to have you both in my life to love. Dare to dream and reach for the stars! Last and foremost, to my husband Alfredo, you are my very best friend, my mentor, my confidante, my safe harbor. Thank you for your support through this lengthy process filled with busy days and nights. It means the world to me that you believe in me and my goals and dreams. I love you.

CHAPTER ONE

What Is Gerber Technology?

Objective

This chapter helps you to understand what Gerber Technology is and how it is used in the fashion industry. Many times students simply do not comprehend the scope of what this program can do for them in school and once they start working in the fashion industry. As students, you should be aware of the technology available in the fashion industry and stay updated with today's trends so you can better market your credentials.

How Gerber Technology Originated

Gerber Garment Technology, now known as Gerber Technology, was established in 1968 by H. Joseph Gerber. Gerber was born in Austria in 1924 and developed an interest in technology by the age of eight. While a student at the Rensselaer Polytechnic Institute, Gerber created a method to scale distances between points and soon created Gerber Scientific Instruments in 1948. Twenty years later, in 1968, while continuing to build a great reputation in manufacturing automation systems, he founded Gerber Garment Technology. It developed the world's first automated cutting machine for cloth. This event fundamentally changed the apparel industry worldwide. Since Gerber Garment Technology became immersed in more than just the apparel industry, Gerber changed the company's name to Gerber Technology so it would better reflect its products and stance in the sewn-products industry. Gerber Technology is a subsidiary of its parent company, Gerber Scientific, Inc. Its symbol on the New York Stock Exchange is GRB.

How Is Gerber Technology Used in the Fashion Industry?

Gerber Technology creates computer aided design systems, also commonly referred to as CAD. Gerber is known as a leading supplier in high technology and solutions. The company develops hardware and software to automate pattern design, grading, and marker making—the area in which this book concentrates. However, Gerber Technology develops other products as well. For example, Vision Fashion Studio is a program that helps you with the realistic visualization and presentation of collections, catalogs, and storyboards. Gerber Technology also offers a product data management program named WebPDM that allows you to organize specs, materials, costing, and sourcing. Also available is a line that automates the spreading, handling, and cutting of fabrics, which enables your design concepts to go from ideas to wearable garments.

Gerber Technology is used in the apparel, furniture, transportation, industrial fabrics, and composites industries. If it is a sewn product, it is likely to be created on a Gerber system. Gerber has more than ten thousand customers, including Liz Claiborne, Gap, and Jones New York, to name a few. Banana Republic, Levi's, OshKosh B'Gosh, Ralph Lauren, and Tommy Hilfiger garments are being produced on Gerber systems as well. The list goes beyond apparel; it includes the upholstery in airplane seats or in boats. Think about all the products that need to be sewn and require a pattern, and you may notice that the bed sheets, sofas, lounge chairs, office chairs, curtains, and table cloths around your homes fall into this category.

This book covers the Pattern Design, Marker Making, and AccuMark Explorer programs. Together, these programs are known as the AccuMark system, but they open as three separate applications. The three programs are connected, meaning they share data.

AccuMark Explorer allows you to manage your data. You use this application to create storage areas, and you may copy, move, and delete files same as you would on Microsoft Explorer. AccuMark also allows you to manage models/ styles, grade rules, piece annotation, and plotting preferences. The shortcut menu, accessed by right-clicking on a file in AccuMark Explorer, is similar to the shortcut menu in Microsoft Windows. There are many convenient commands in this menu that allow you to open various AccuMark functions. For example, the shortcut menu for a model lets you open it up in Pattern Design or view it through the Model Editor. Explorer makes it more efficient to work in the AccuMark system.

Pattern Design System, also known as PDS, is the area where you create pieces. You can create pieces from scratch or digitize them with a digitizing table. You can use a drafting table to draft the piece into the system as well. Drafting and digitizing give you the same result—it lets you place a pattern in the system. The difference between the two is the method and how you visualize your piece as you input it into the system. Pattern Design System permits you to manipulate pieces. For example, you can create darts, pleats, or fullness; add seam allowance; or create facings and fusing from a pattern, and they may all be done as fast as you can move. What might take someone half an hour to do with paper, scissors, and tape, will take you minutes or even seconds to accomplish with Pattern Design System. PDS does not make someone a patternmaker, but it does help a patternmaker work more efficiently. Therefore, students must learn the basics of patternmaking first.

AccuMark, the marker making program, is where you lay out patterns to be cut on fabric. Many students try to maximize the use of fabric due to fabric costs or time constraints. This is the same situation for companies, except it is on a greater scale because saving one inch may save hundreds of dollars when you deal with much more than one or two yards. How many times have you laid out a pattern again and again, having to take out the pins or move the weights that you used, to get the most out of your fabric? AccuMark marker making makes laying out pattern pieces much easier. There are no pins or weights with which to deal, just you and the computer screen. Since you slide pattern pieces into or out of the marker, it is sometimes said that marker makers are good with puzzles or that making markers is similar to playing a game of Tetris. You can start a marker from scratch, or you can modify an existing marker until you reach your ideal (Fabric Utilization Goal). You can rotate, flip, and even buffer pieces to protect them. This program improves productivity by eliminating repetitive tasks, and it therefore allows a marker maker to be much more efficient in the same manner PDS helps patternmakers.

What Is the Overall Process?

When students or new users first see an AccuMark system, they are impressed with its capabilities. When they have to learn how to work in a computer aided environment and leave the scissors, scotch tape, and measuring tape behind, they can become overwhelmed. It takes some time to adjust to working in this environment. The system is very user-friendly. To complete a function, users need to simply follow the prompts on the screen. Once users are comfortable with the system and realize how easy and efficient it is to get work done, they never want to go back to manual pattern or marker making. Gerber Technology is a customer-driven company; most of the numerous functions available are developed according to customer requests.

The process begins with the creation of a storage area where all data is kept. Using a drafting table or a digitizing table, users input pattern pieces into the system. The pattern may be viewed and manipulated in PDS. You may also create a pattern from scratch in PDS. Grade rules are created in AccuMark Explorer and assigned in Pattern Design. You can also use AccuMark Explorer to create a model (or style), customized tables to determine the layout preferences for your pattern pieces and fabric, and an order a marker. The marker is then ready to be made in AccuMark Marker Making and pattern pieces or markers may be plotted through AccuMark Explorer. This is simply an overview of the process and is discussed in greater detail later in the book.

Is Gerber Technology Widely Used?

Gerber Technology is widely used in the industry. Computer aided design is a skill that many employers are now looking for in job candidates in the fashion and other sewn-goods industries. Gerber Technology's worldwide headquarters is located in Tolland, Connecticut. Gerber hardware and software is currently used in more than 115 countries, and there are more than 10,000 customers. More than 500 colleges and universities in about 60 countries use Gerber. A history of more than 35 years proves that it is not only a strong and solid company, but also an innovator in the fashion industry.

CHAPTER TWO

Get Started:

Set Up Parameter Tables in AccuMark Explorer

Objective

This chapter covers the basic setup in AccuMark Explorer so you can then begin drafting pieces, making markers, or manipulating patterns. It also discusses how to create storage areas, which is similar to the way you create folders in Microsoft Windows. The chapter includes a few tables where you can set up parameters within storage areas, including notches, grading method, and the measurement system. Although these may seem like petty tasks, they are part of a normal working day for an industry professional.

The Gerber Launch Pad, usually located on the desktop, will also be reviewed. This launch pad allows you to quickly access other programs, tables, or editors in the AccuMark software suite. Managing data (e.g., moving and copying files) is also covered in this chapter.

This chapter allows you to gain the following skills:

- Use the Gerber Launch Pad
- Open AccuMark Explorer
- Set up storage areas
- Work with the User Environment Table
- Work with the Notch Table
- Copy files
- Move files
- Delete files
- Find files

Use the Gerber Launch Pad

The **Gerber Launch Pad** allows you to start a program, table, or editor, or other processing forms. If you need to start the patternmaking process, select the first radio button labeled **Pattern Processing, Digitizing, PDS,** as seen in Figure 2.1. The areas related to the title are displayed as icons. For example, you can use the Pattern Design icon, shown in Figure 2.2, to link to the Pattern Design program so you can manipulate pattern pieces.

Open AccuMark Explorer

AccuMark Explorer is the application used to manage your data. Use this program when you create a storage area or need to copy, move, and delete files. It may also be used to open tables and editors that are frequently used, such as Model

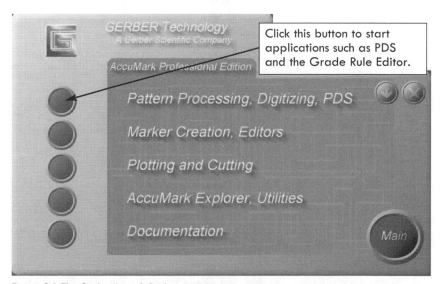

Figure 2.1 The Gerber Launch Pad main menu.

Editors used to create styles, or a Piece Plot Order used to plot pieces.

AccuMark Explorer may be opened in several ways: the Gerber Launch Pad, a desktop shortcut icon, or Start on the Windows task bar.

Open AccuMark Explorer using the Gerber Launch Pad as follows:

1. Using the Gerber Launch Pad, select the fourth button, labeled **Accumark Explorer, Utilities.**

2. Select the **Accumark Explorer** icon.

Open AccuMark Explorer using a desktop icon as follows:

1. Double click on the shortcut icon named **AccuMark Explorer.**

Open AccuMark Explorer using Start on the window's task bar (see Figure 2.3), as follows:

1. Click Start on the Windows task bar.

2. Select **All Programs> AccuMark V8>AccuMark Explorer, Utilities>AccuMark Explorer.**

What Is a Storage Area?

A **storage area** is used to store your pieces, markers, and general piece information. It may be a folder that holds information for a particular designer or manufacturer. The contents of one storage area will not interfere with the contents of another storage area, since they are considered separate folders. Tables, such as the User Environment, Notch, and Model Editor, are created under each storage area. These and other tables included in a storage area are discussed later (see Figure 2.4).

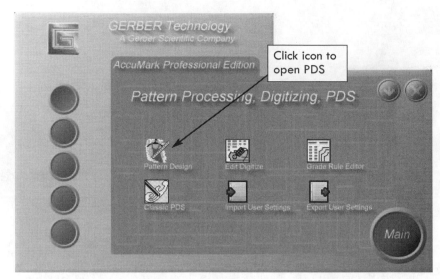

Figure 2.2 The Pattern Design icon in the Launch Pad menu.

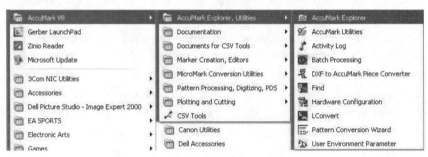

Figure 2.3 Start menu selections to open AccuMark Explorer.

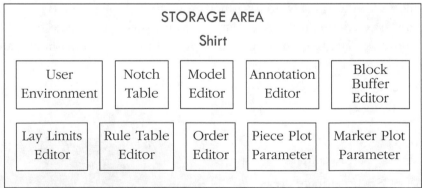

Figure 2.4 Tables and editors found in a storage area.

You should name storage areas in a way that facilitates finding a garment. The system will hold as many storage areas as your hard drive allows. Each storage area name may contain up to eight characters. You cannot use spaces, or symbols such as slashes, ampersands, or parentheses. The hyphen or underscore may be used to substitute for spaces. Below are a couple of examples used in the industry to name storage areas.

Example 1: Designers as customers

Designer name	Storage area name
Liz Claiborne	Liz or LC
Ralph Lauren	Ralph or RL
Versace	Versace

Example 2: A company with garment-type storage areas

When a company manufactures for only one major customer, such as Jones New York, the garments may be separated into storage areas of their own. Since everything manufactured is solely for Jones New York in this example, there is no need for a storage area named Jones New York. Storage area names will instead be specific garment pieces, such as: Jackets, Skirts, Pants, and Suits.

Create a Storage Area

Use the following steps to create a storage area:

1. Open **AccuMark Explorer.**

2. Select device C with the left mouse button, which highlights it in blue. Look at the left side of the AccuMark Explorer window, as shown in Figure 2.5.

3. Select **File>New.** This option will not be available if device C is not selected.

4. Select **Storage Area.** A window labeled **New Storage Area** appears, where you can enter a new storage area name.

5. Type in a name for the storage area. Click **OK** when you are done. The new storage area will appear to the left of AccuMark Explorer under device C and to the right side of it under Contents of C (see Figure 2.6).

Note: If the storage area does not appear, press the F5 key on the keyboard to update the screen.

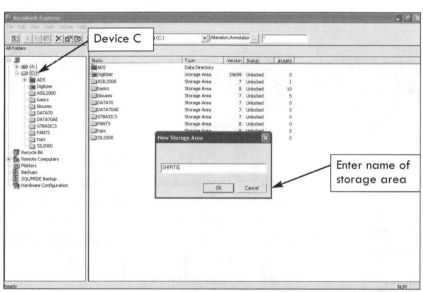

Figure 2.5 Entering a new storage area name.

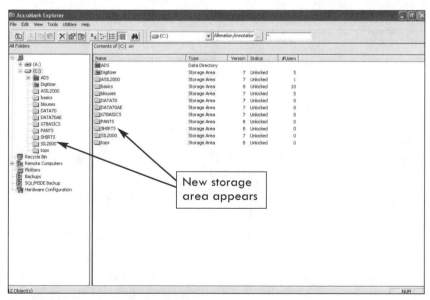

Figure 2.6 New storage area displayed.

User Environment Table

Each time you create a storage area, you also create a **User Environment Table,** by default named P-User Environment. You should not change the name unless more than one table is needed. All tables and editors, such as the Notch Table, refer to this table for storage area parameters. For example, this table determines if a person is working in inches or centimeters. This is the *first* table you should customize after creating a storage area.

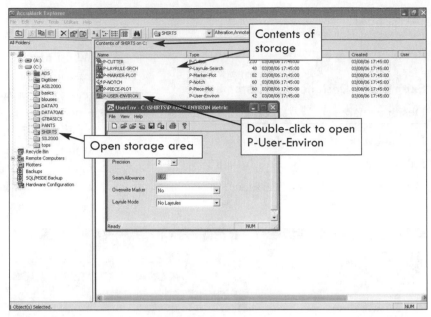

Figure 2.7 User Environment Table displayed.

Open and Customize the User Environment Table

Use the following procedure to open the User Environment Table and set your preferences:

1. Open **AccuMark Explorer**.

2. Double click on the storage area to open it. The contents of the storage area are displayed (see Figure 2.7).

3. Double click on **P-User-Environ** to open the table.

4. Select the **Notation** preference: Metric or Imperial.

> **Metric** is used to work in centimeters/meters.

> **Imperial** is used to work in inches/yards.

5. Select the **Precision** preference: 0, 1, 2, or 3. This determines how many numbers there are after a decimal. Numbers 0 and 1 are rarely used. To get the most precise measurement, use 3. For example: $\frac{1}{8}''$ = 0.13 (2 as the Precision) or 0.125 (3 as the Precision).

6. Select the **Seam Allowance** preference by typing in a number. This is not the same seam allowance that is added around a piece when you create a pattern. When a piece is split during marker making, the seam allowance typed in this field is added to the

split seam so that the piece can be sewn back together. Therefore, the piece remains the same size. For example, when a piece does not fit in the marker, the marker maker splits the piece to place two smaller pieces instead of one large piece.

7. Select **Overwrite Marker** preference: No, Yes, or Prompt. When a marker is processed and has the same name as an existing marker, choosing **No** prevents you from overriding the marker; **Yes** automatically overrides the marker without warning you about the existing marker, which of course erases the old marker; and **Prompt** warns you about the existing marker and allows you to make your choice (see Figure 2.8).

8. Close the window using the **X** at the top right of the window.

9. Select **Yes** when prompted "Save changes to P-User-Environ?" to keep the changes made. It saves in the current storage area as P-User-Environ.

Note: To save under a different name, go to **File> Save As.** Input the new name next to **File Name** and click **Save.**

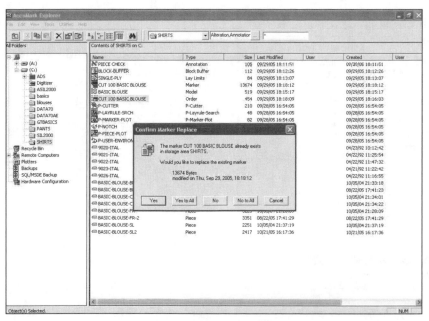

Figure 2.8 Example of Override Marker prompt.

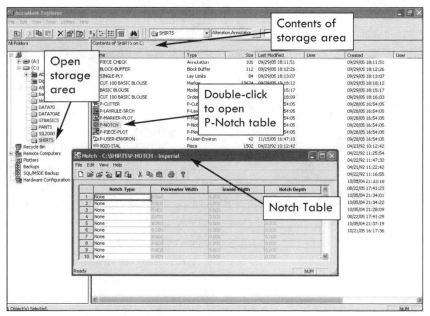

Figure 2.9 Notch Parameter Table displayed.

Notch Table

Notches are used to define seam allowances; show dart, pleat, or gathering locations; and show where one piece matches another. There are six notch types used in the industry. These notches

are known as the Slit Notch, T-Notch, V-Notch, external V-Notch, the Castle/Clicker Notch, and the external Castle/Clicker notch. The slit and V-notch are commonly used in the fashion industry and in schools.

The **Notch Table** is used to set up the types of notches you wish to use. Up to 99 notches may be created per table. Customize at least one notch table per storage area. It is not recommended to change the table name "P-Notch" unless an additional table is needed.

Open and Customize the Notch Table

Use the following procedure to open the Notch Table and set up your preferences:

1. Open **AccuMark Explorer.**

2. Double click on the storage area to open it. The contents of the storage area are displayed, as shown in Figure 2.9.

3. Double click on **P-Notch** to open the Notch Table.

4. Left click on the arrow in row 1, under **Notch Type,** to activate the drop-down menu, and select the notch type you want to create.

   Note: Notch number 1 is usually the most used notch, number 2 is second most used, and so on.

5. Fill in the notch size in the field(s). **Perimeter Width, Inside Width,** and/or **Notch Depth** will light up depending on the notch you choose.

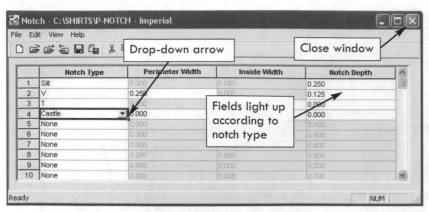

Figure 2.10 Notch size and type entered in Notch Parameter Table.

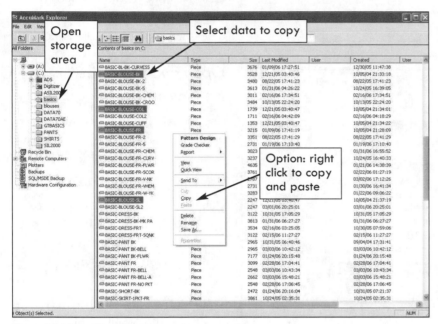

Figure 2.11 Data files selected to copy.

For example, when you select a slit notch, only the **Notch Depth** column lights up (see Figure 2.10).

6. Follow steps 4 and 5 for row 2 and beyond if you need to set up additional notches.

7. Close the window using the **X** at the top right of the window.

8. Click **Yes** when prompted to "Save changes to P-Notch?" to keep the changes made. It saves in the current storage area as P-Notch.

Note: To save under a different name, go to **File>Save As.** Input the new name next to **File name** and click **Save.**

Copy Files

There are several ways to copy data from one place to another. The following process allows you to copy a file from one storage area to another. To copy from more than one storage area to several storage areas at once, see the section entitled Copy Data.

1. Open **AccuMark Explorer.**

2. Double click to open the storage area from where you are copying. The small yellow folder opens.

3. Left click to select the data you need to copy. They will be highlighted in blue (see Figure 2.11).

4. Copy the data into the destination storage area. Click the highlighted data, hold down the left mouse button, and, keeping it held down, drag the data to the destination storage area. Release the button. This is known as a *click and drag* technique. To verify that your data copied, open the destination folder. If the data already exist in that folder, you will see a prompt like this: The data item SHIRT-BK already exists in storage area C:SHIRTS. Would you like to replace the existing data item? Click **Yes** to override or **No** to not override.

Note: In step 3, you can also select the file you want to copy, right click your mouse, and select **Copy.** Place the cursor over the destination storage area, right click your mouse, and select **Paste.**

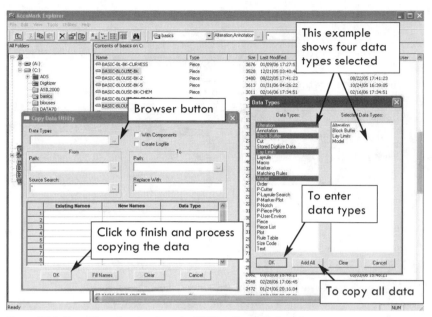

Figure 2.12 Copy Data function from the Utilities Menu displayed.

Utilities Menu

The Utilities menu is used to copy or move data from one or more storage areas to another. It may also be used to delete items from one or more storage areas at a time.

Copy Data

The **Copy Data** process in the Utilities menu allows one or more data files to be copied to several storage areas. It also allows users to copy from multiple storage areas to another group of storage areas. For example, copy a Notch Table from a master storage area to all other storage areas so that you do not have to customize it every time.

Data going into the new storage area(s) may also be renamed when copied using this option. For example, a Lay Limits Editor originally named Single-Ply may be copied into a new storage area with the name Single-Ply-2-Way, as demonstrated later in the procedure for this function. Additionally, a pattern copied from a preproduction storage area that doesn't have a style number, such as Blouse-Front, may be copied to a production storage area with a style number, such as 4300 Blouse-Front.

A **browse button** is seen in many tables or editors in the AccuMark program. It is used to open what is generally known as a lookup window in AccuMark. This lookup window displays data items available for selection. For example, when selecting a storage area from which to copy, the lookup window contains all the available storage areas from which to select. The browse button is commonly located at the right of a data field.

Procedure to copy data

1. Open **AccuMark Explorer>Utilities>Copy.**

2. Click the browse button under the **Data Types** field, which displays the **Data Types** window. Select the data type you want to copy, or click **Add All** to copy everything from the storage area. Click **OK** to enter the data to copy (see Figure 2.12).

3. Check the box next to **With Components** if you would like to copy the components of a file. For example, pieces are components of a model. To copy the model and the pieces, check this box. The Order Editor is also a table that contains components because it includes a Model Editor, Annotation Editor, and so on.

4. Check the box next to **Create Logfile** if you would like the system to create a file that contains a record of what was copied for future reference.

5. In the **From–Path** field, click the browse button to view and select the storage area(s) from which to copy. Click **OK** to enter the storage area(s). The example in Figure 2.13 shows two selected storage areas.

6. In the **Source Search** field, click the browse button to display the **Data Items** window. Select the data items you want to copy, or click the **Select All** button to select all the data items listed. Click **OK** to enter the selected data to copy. Data is entered into the **Existing Names** and **New Names** columns as seen in Figure 2.14. To rename an item in the new storage area, type it in under the **New Names** column. For example, the Lay Limits table named Single-Ply will be named Single-Ply-2 Way when it is copied into the selected storage areas—in this case, the Blouses and Pants storage areas.

7. In the **To–Path** field, click the browse button to select the storage area(s) that you are copying into. Click **OK** to enter the storage area(s).

8. Click **OK** to finish the process.

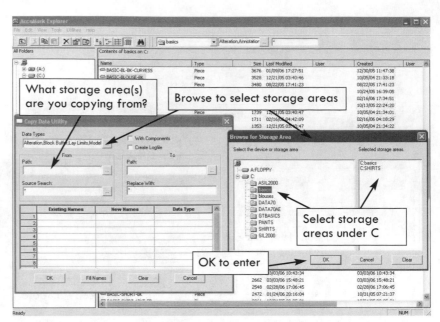

Figure 2.13 Storage areas are selected to copy from.

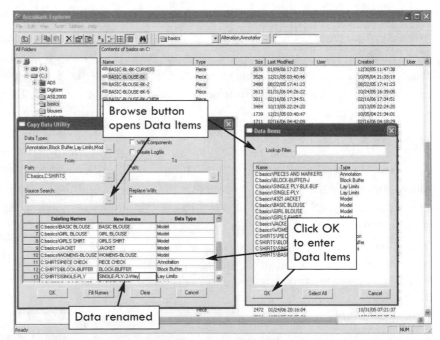

Figure 2.14 Data Items window opened to select data to copy.

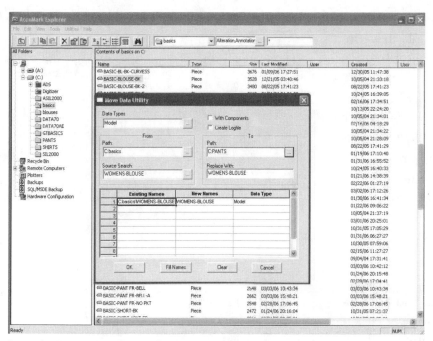

Figure 2.15 Move Data function from the Utilities menu displayed.

Move Data

The **Move Data** function is quite similar to Copy Data. The difference is that data is moved out of a storage area(s) to another storage area(s), rather than being duplicated. For example, if several pieces were saved under the wrong storage area, Move Data allows you to take it out of the wrong storage area and save it in the correct one.

Procedure to move data

1. Open **AccuMark Explorer>Utilities>Move.**

2. Click the browse button in the **Data Types** field, which displays the **Data Types** window. Select the data type you want to move, or click **Add All** to move everything from the storage area. Click **OK** to enter the data to move.

3. Check the box next to **With Components** if you would like to move the components of a file.

4. Check the box next to **Create Logfile** if you would like the system to create a file that contains a record of what was moved for future reference.

5. In the **From–Path** field, click the browse button to view and select the storage area(s) from

which to move. Click **OK** to enter the storage area(s). The example in Figure 2.15 shows C:BASICS as the selected storage area.

6. In the **Source Search** field, click the browse button to display the **Data Items** window. Select the data items you want to move, or click the **Select All** button to select all the data items listed. Click **OK** to enter the selected data to move. Data may be renamed under the **New Names** column at this point.

7. In the **To–Path** field, click the browse button to select the storage area(s) into which to move the data. Click **OK** to enter the storage area(s).

8. Click **OK** to finish the process.

Delete Data

Delete Data is used to delete data items from one or several storage areas at once. You can also right click on the files you wish to delete and select **Delete.** Deleted items regardless of the process used go to the **Recycling Bin,** where you can restore them, if necessary. Please note that this will not work if the properties of the Recycling Bin are set to permanently delete files.

Procedure to delete data

1. Open **AccuMark Explorer>Utilities>Delete.**

2. Click the browse button under the **Data Types** field, which displays the **Data Types** window. Select the data type you want to delete, or click **Add All** to delete everything from the storage area. Click **OK** to enter the data to delete.

3. Check the box next to **With Components** if you would like to delete the components of a file. Be careful not to delete files you need to keep, especially if the Recycling Bin properties are set to delete files permanently.

4. Check the box next to **Create Logfile** if you would like the system to create a file that contains a record of what was deleted for future reference.

5. In the **Paths** field, click the browser button to view and select the storage area(s) from which to delete. Click **OK** to enter the storage area(s).

6. In the **Data Item Search** field, click the browse button to display the **Data Items** window. Select the data items you want to delete, or click the **Select All** button to select all the data items listed. Click **OK** to enter the selected data to delete.

7. Click **OK** to finish the process.

Note: To delete an entire storage area, and not simply certain contents in it, it is easiest to right click over the storage area and select **Delete** while in AccuMark Explorer.

AccuMark Find

AccuMark Find, also known simply as **Find,** is used to locate files in the AccuMark program. You can search by various options, including Name and Location, Date Modified, User, or Advanced.

For example, if you saved a piece and did not notice the storage area into which it was saved, Find allows you to look into all storage areas at once instead of looking for it in each storage area one at a time. It is similar to the Search function in Microsoft Windows. This option can also be accessed from the Gerber Launch Pad: Click on the fourth RADIO button, titled AccuMark Explorer, Utilities.

1. Open **AccuMark Explorer>Tools>Find.**

2. Select the **Name and Location** tab.

3. In the **Named** field, type the name of the file for which you need to search.

4. In the **Look In** field, click the browse button to select the storage areas in which you will search for the named file.

5. Click **Find Now** to search. You see the process as the program searches for the file and then you see the results displayed.

Note: Select the other tabs—**Date Modified, User,** and **Advanced**—to narrow the search.

Test Your Knowledge

Fill in the blanks for the following statements:

1. _____ is the program used to manage data such as moving, deleting, and copying files.
2. Pieces, markers, tables, and editors are saved in a _____.
3. All tables and editors refer to the _____ for storage area parameters.
4. To copy and rename several files, use _____ in the Utilities menu.
5. Data files that are deleted are sent to the _____.
6. To copy a model and all the pieces that belong to that model, check off the box titled _____.
7. To work with the most exact measurement, select _____ as the Precision in the User Environment Table.
8. A storage area may have up to _____ characters.
9. The _____ allows you to start a program such as PDS or AccuMark Explorer.
10. There are _____ notch types used in the industry.

Test Your Skills

The following exercise will allow you to practice the procedures discussed in this chapter:

1. Create two storage areas. Name one TEST1 and the other TEST2, both preceded with your initials. (e.g., NS-TEST1).
2. Copy some pieces from storage area DATA70 to storage area TEST1 using the click and drag technique.
3. Using the Copy function, copy all your pieces into storage area TEST2, but rename the pieces.
4. Using the Move function, move two of your pieces from storage area TEST2.
5. Using AccuMark Find, search for a piece you renamed.
6. Delete the two pieces you moved into TEST1 using the right-click menu.
7. Using the Copy function, copy the model LADIES-BLOUSE from storage area DATA70 to TEST2. Check off the With Components box.
8. Using the Delete function, delete the model LADIES-BLOUSE from TEST 2. Do not check off the With Components box.
9. Delete storage areas TEST1 and TEST2 by right-clicking over each and selecting Delete in AccuMark Explorer.

CHAPTER THREE

Navigating Through PDS

Objective

This chapter introduces you to some basic management options in PDS. While some of the features are similar to those of a word processing program, there are many other beneficial options for users in the PDS work environment. For example, you can open and plot a style using the File menu. You can view and edit point, line, or piece information using the Edit menu. There are options in the View menu that allow you to view points, rule numbers, or notch types on a pattern. The Measure menu offers several options so you can measure a piece accurately, such as measuring from the highest point of a shoulder to the hem or displaying the length of an armhole. After reading this chapter, it becomes clear how the functions covered help a great deal during working sessions. You will also find that it is much more efficient to use hotkeys whenever possible. This chapter serves as an excellent reference on which you can rely until you master the functions.

This chapter allows you to gain the following skills:

- Work with the File menu
- Work with the Edit menu
- Work with the View menu
- Work with the Measure menu

File Menu

The File menu has many options that may already be familiar to most computer users, such as opening, closing, or saving files. However, some of the functions are unique to AccuMark and are very helpful during your work sessions. For example, you can access and edit a Notch Table without opening AccuMark Explorer.

New

When you first open PDS, it opens a window with which you may work automatically. This function also opens an additional window within PDS. Figure 3.1 shows two active work areas listed under the Window menu. You may alternate

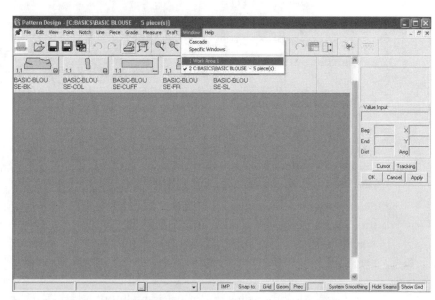

Figure 3.1 Window Menu displayed.

between these work areas/windows. As you can see, Work Area 1 does not have any models open, but it may have pieces that are open. The other window, titled C:BASICS\BASIC-BLOUSE-5 piece(s), shows the model BASIC BLOUSE, located in the storage area BASICS, which has five pieces that are open.

Open

Open lets you open existing pieces, models, or lists in the PDS work area so you can manipulate or review them. Open is the second option listed in the File menu.

Procedure to open a file

1. Select **File>Open.** The **Open** window appears.

2. In the **Look in** field, select the storage area where the pieces or models are located by activating the drop-down menu.

3. In the **Files of type** field, select AccuMark Piece or AccuMark Model by using the drop-down menu to view either pieces or models.

> **AccuMark Piece** lists pieces in the selected storage area.

> **AccuMark Model** lists models in the selected storage area.

Figure 3.2 illustrates AccuMark pieces listed under storage area BASICS.

4. Select the files you want to open by clicking on them with the left mouse button. The **File name** field displays the name of the file you select. If you selected more than one file to open, only the first one you selected will be displayed; the other files are open as well, but they are layered beneath the one on-screen.

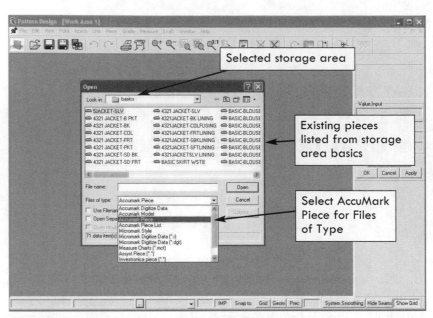

Figure 3.2 Open function used to open pieces.

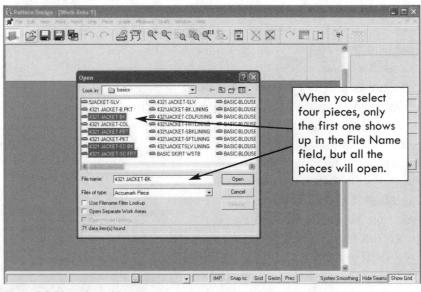

Figure 3.3 Files selected to open.

Note: You can select groups of files at the same time by clicking on the first file with the left mouse button, which highlights it, holding down the Shift key, and clicking the last file in the group with the left mouse button. If you want to open a group of files that are not listed in one group, hold down the Ctrl key and click on each file with the left button, as shown in Figure 3.3.

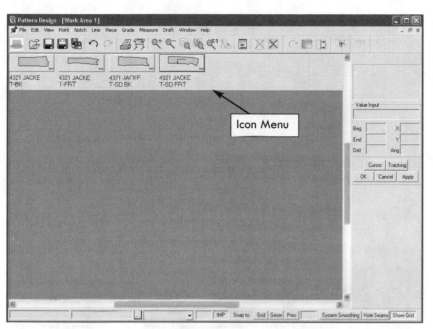

Figure 3.4 Pieces selected are opened in Icon Menu.

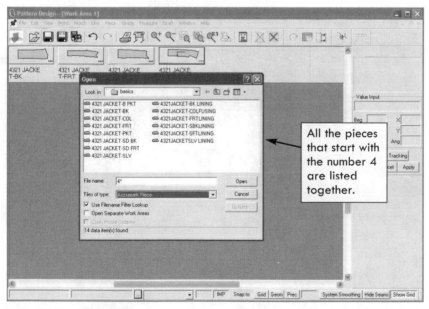

Figure 3.5 Use of Filter Lookup.

5. Click **Open.** Your files open, and files, or pieces, are displayed in the icon menu (see Figure 3.4).

Additional Options

Use Filename Filter Lookup This option may be used to filter out certain files beginning or ending with a particular number or letter. For example, in Figure 3.5, we filtered out all the pieces in the storage area that started with the number 4, by typing in 4* in the File name field. The asterisk represents the remaining part of each file name.

Open Separate Work Areas This option may be used to open each file in its own separate work area or window. For example, in Figure 3.6, two models are opened in their own work areas. This prevents confusion when you have to manipulate complicated styles.

Close

This option lets you close out of any work area in PDS that is open and in use.

Procedure to close a file

1. Select **File>Close.** All the open windows, whether they are opened pieces or models, close.

Close Style/Model

This option lets you close specific models and all their pieces, if you have more than one model open and you don't want to close out of all them.

Procedure for Close Style/Model

1. Select **File>Close Style/Model**. A window appears.

2. Click on the models you want to close with the left mouse button.

3. Click **OK**. The models you selected close (see Figure 3.7).

Save

The Save function lets you to save a piece or model automatically to the selection set up in the Preference/Options window, which is discussed on page 24.

Procedure to save a piece

1. Select **File>Save.**

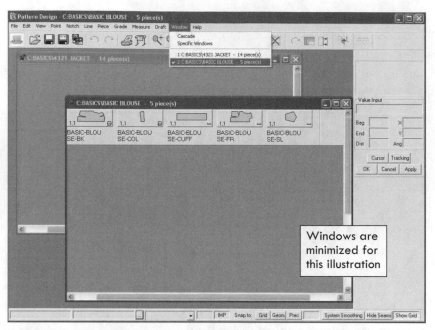

Figure 3.6 Models opened in separate work areas.

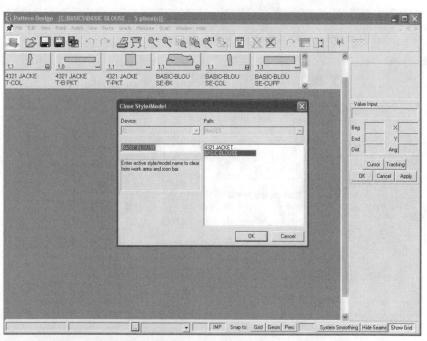

Figure 3.7 Closing a Style/Model.

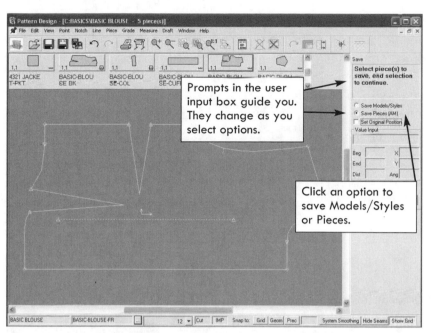

Figure 3.8 Saving pieces with the Save function.

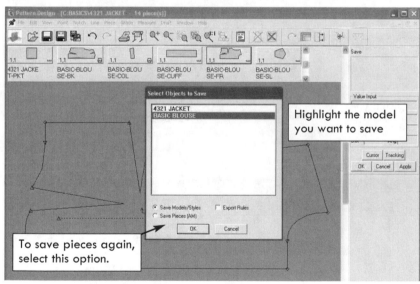

Figure 3.9 Selection of model to save.

2. The user input box, which is an option that can be turned on or off by the user, states, "Select piece(s) to save, end selection to continue." The prompt appears when you select **Save Pieces (AM).** The (AM) identifies this option as one used by AccuMark users (see Figure 3.8).

3. Click on the piece(s) you want to save with the left mouse button, which highlights the piece(s) in red.

4. Right click and select **OK** to finish saving the pieces.

When a prompt states, "end the selection to continue," make a selection with the left mouse button, right click, and select **OK** to proceed.

Note: When you edit a piece, part of it appears in blue. After you save it, the entire piece appears in white. These are default colors.

Save Models/Styles

This option lets you save every piece that belongs to one model.

Procedure to save a model

1. Select **File>Save.**

2. The user input box states, "Select piece(s) to save, end selection to continue." Select the option **Save Models/Styles** (see Figure 3.8). The **Select Objects to Save** window appears (see Figure 3.9). Click on the model you want to save with the left mouse button.

3. Click **OK** to finish and to save the pieces.

Note: To go back to saving pieces, just select **Save Pieces (AM)** in the **Select Objects to Save** window.

Remember that when you use the Save function, pieces or models are automatically saved according to the preferences set up in the Preference/Options window (see Figure 3.10).

There are two options from which to choose in the **Data Stored To** field as defined below.

- If you select **Default Area,** then you save the pieces or models in the storage area you selected in PDS.

- If you select **Retrieved Area,** then you save the pieces or models in the storage area from where you opened them originally.

Save As

The Save As function lets you save a piece or model but, contrary to the Save function, this option lets you choose the storage area in which you want to save the piece or model. Beginners should use this option. When you save a model using this function, all the pieces that belong to it are saved under their piece names.

Procedure to Save As

1. Select **File>Save As.**

2. A user input box states: "Select the piece to Save As."

   Note: As in the Save function, you have the option to save pieces or models. Click on the pieces you want to save with the left mouse button; the pieces turn red. If you want to save a model or style, click on the model so it is highlighted (see Figure 3.8).

3. Right click and select **OK.**

4. The **Save As** window appears (see Figure 3.11). In the **Save in** field, select the storage area into which you want to save the piece or model. In the **File name** field, type in the name of the piece or model, if it is not already correct.

5. Click **Save** to finish.

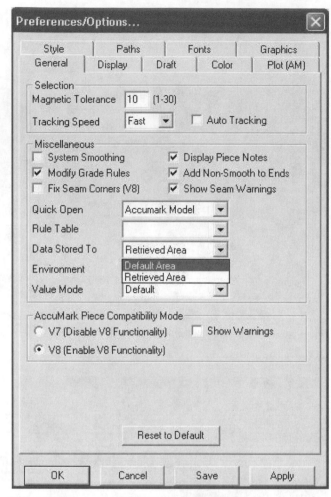

Figure 3.10 Preferences/Options window displayed.

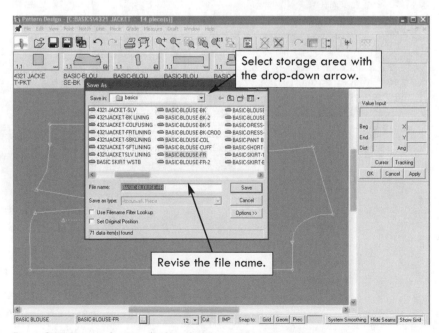

Figure 3.11 Save As function displayed while saving a piece.

Note: Before completing step 4, if the **Options** button is clicked, you may also type in the Piece Category and Piece Description. If you opt to save the category and description data by using the Options button instead of using the Edit Piece Info function, it saves you a step (see Figure 3.12).

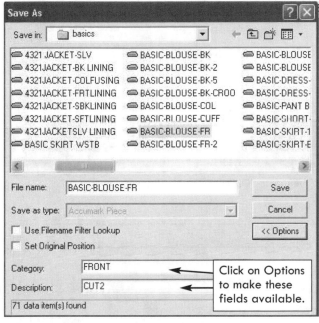

Figure 3.12 Options displays Category and Description fields.

Edit Parameter Notch

This function allows you to access the Notch Table in PDS without having to open it in AccuMark Explorer.

Procedure to edit the parameter of a notch

1. Select **File>Edit Parameter>Notch.** The Notch Table appears (see Figure 3.13). Review or make any necessary measurement or notch type changes for the notches.

2. Click on the **X** at the top right-hand corner of the screen to close the window. If you made any changes, the system will ask you if you want to save the changes. If you didn't make any changes, no prompt will appear and the window will just close.

Print

This function lets you print the pieces on the screen to the printer of your choice.

Print Preview

This function lets you preview how whatever you have open on screen will look when it prints out. You can select **Print** directly from the Print Preview window.

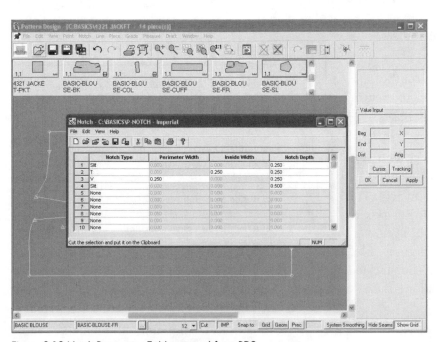

Figure 3.13 Notch Parameter Table opened from PDS.

Plot Preferences/ Options Plot Tab

The Plot option lets you plot pieces from PDS in the plotter and generally lets you do it true to size. Pieces are plotted according to the selections you make in the Plot tab of the Preferences/Options function shown in Figure 3.14. Therefore, you should set it up before using the Plot function in PDS. If a table such as the Piece Plot Parameter Table or the Annotation Table does not exist, you will get an error message when you attempt to plot.

The Preferences/Options function is found in the PDS View menu. The tables discussed in this section are expanded upon in Chapter 7.

Procedure to open and set up the Plot tab in Preferences/Options

1. Select **View>Preferences/Options.**

2. Select the **Plot (AM)** tab.

3. In the **Piece Plot Parameter Table** field, select the table that the system needs to reference so it can plot pieces and models. This table includes items such as the size of the piece and sizes to use when plotting.

4. In the **Annotation Table** field, select the Annotation Editor for the system to reference. This table includes wording and symbols inside or outside of the piece.

5. Check the box next to **Plot Form** so you can view a window that allows you to place pieces as you want them before you plot. This is much like a miniature marker. If this box is unchecked, the Plotter window will not be available and the pieces will be plotted according to the stacking option. The stacking option determines if pieces plot along the width or length of the paper.

6. In the **Stacking** field, select Yes or No (see Figure 3.15).

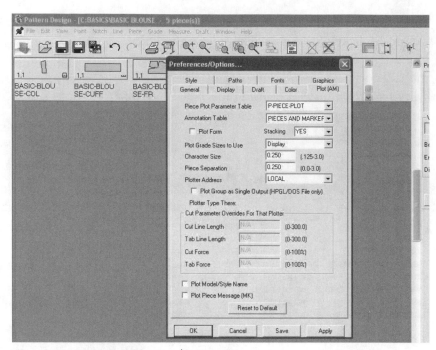

Figure 3.14 Plot tab for Preferences/Options.

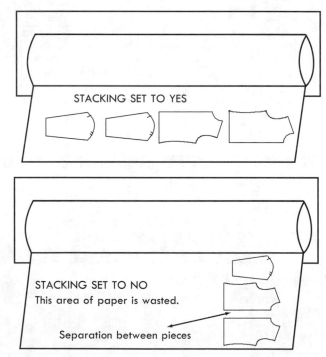

Figure 3.15 Stacking pieces option illustrated.

Yes is used to plot pieces along the width of the plotter paper, which wastes less paper.

No is used to plot along the length of the plotter paper.

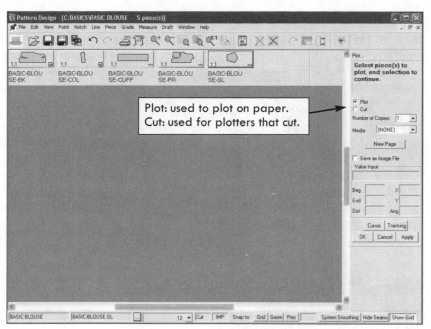

Figure 3.16 Plot function in PDS.

7. In the **Plot Grade Sizes to Use** field, select Display or Parameter Table. **Display** plots the piece at the size shown on-screen. **Parameter Table** plots the piece at the size determined by the table you select in the Piece Plot Parameter Table field.

8. In the **Character Size** field, enter an amount to determine the character or font size for any annotation you make on the pieces.

9. In the **Piece Separation** field, enter an amount to determine how far apart the pieces will be placed from one another on the paper (see Figure 3.15).

10. In the **Plotter Address** field, select the plotter you use to plot. Generally, this is set to **LOCAL.**

11. Check the box next to **Plot Model/Style Name** to plot the Model/Style name.

12. Click **Save** to save the settings.

13. Click **Apply** to apply the selected settings to the working session.

14. Click **OK** to close the Preferences/Options window.

After you review and/or set up the Preference/Options Plot tab, you may plot pieces. Pieces will plot according to the preferences set in that tab.

Procedure to plot

1. Place the pieces you want to plot into the work area (see Figure 3.16).

2. Select **File>Plot.**

3. In the **Number of copies** field, select the number of copies you want to plot.

4. A user input box states: "Select piece(s) to plot, end selection to continue." Left click to select the piece(s), which highlights them in red.

5. Right click and select **OK.** The selected pieces are sent to the plotter; make sure the plotter is set online.

Exit

Exit closes the PDS window and ends the working session. If you did not save pieces prior to this step, a prompt appears that lets you cancel exiting and save the pieces that you need to save.

Edit Menu

The Edit menu has options that let you edit point, line, or piece information along with other beneficial functions such as Undo and Redo.

Undo

Undo lets you go back one step. You may undo multiple times until you restore the piece to the version you desire. When you undo a function, its name is listed next to the Undo function in the View drop-down menu.

Redo

Redo allows you to redo a step that you undid. When you redo a function, its name is listed next to the Redo function in the View drop-down menu.

Edit Point Info

Edit Point Info lets you review or alter point information, such as point numbers, grade rules, or point attributes. To use this function, a piece must be on-screen.

An option labeled **Enable** (see Figure 3.17) is available when you are in Edit Point Info mode. When it is activated, the **Track** button is available. The Track button is used to track points one by one on the pattern. The system stops momentarily at each point clockwise around the piece and displays each point's information. To select a point while tracking, click on the **Stop** button to display that point's information.

Procedure for Edit Point Info

1. Select **Edit>Edit Point Info**. The **Tracking Information** window appears on-screen.

2. The user input box states: "Select point(s) with left button." Left click on the points for which you need to change information. This action will highlight them in red.

   Note: If you select more than one point, all the points will receive the same information that you input into the fields.

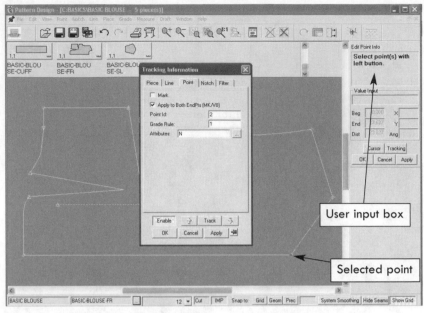

Figure 3.17 Edit Point Info fields displayed.

3. In the **Point ID** field, you may enter a reference point number. When a piece is first drafted into the system, each point has a reference number attached to it. You can leave the number alone or change it if you are using an Alteration Table. You use the Alteration Table and Size Code Table to create sizes in addition to a regular size line. For example, pants may be available in sizes 34S (short), 34R (regular), and 34L (long).

4. In the **Grade Rule** field, enter the grade rule number to grade a piece at the selected point. Grade rules are growth amounts applied to points on a pattern to create smaller and larger sizes from a base size. The grade rule number referenced comes from the Rule Table applied to the piece.

5. Check the box next to **Apply to Both End Pts (MK/V8)** to apply a grade rule to both points on a line. The end point of each line is the beginning of one line as well as the end of another line.

6. In the **Attributes** field, click on the browser button to select an attribute and add it to a point. For example, the "N" shown in Figure 3.17 stands for *Non-Smoothing*. By applying

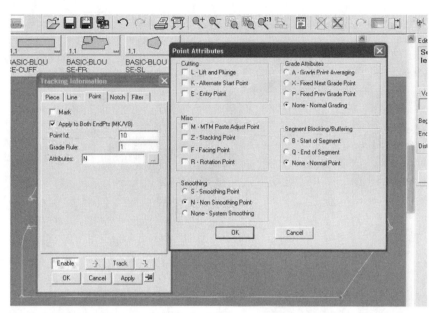

Figure 3.18 Point Attributes options displayed.

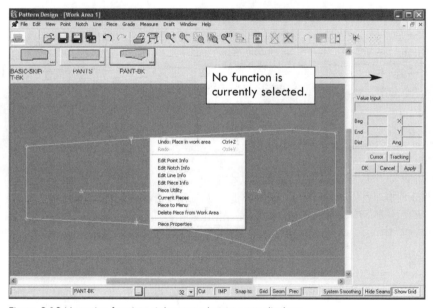

Figure 3.19 No active function; right mouse button menu displays.

"N" to this point, it ensures the corner will be a sharp one rather than curved. Available attributes are displayed in the **Point Attributes** window (see Figure 3.18).

7. Check the box next to **Mark** to place an X on the point selected. This lets you mark an intermediate point without having to display the points with the Intermediate or All Points functions. Unlike intermediate points, end points cannot accept mark points.

8. Click **Apply** to apply the new changes.

9. Click **OK** to close the window.

10. Save the piece to keep your changes permanently.

You may also access the Edit Point Info option by right clicking while out of a function and selecting Edit Point Info (see Figure 3.19).

Edit Notch Info

Edit Notch Info lets you review or alter notches. As in the Edit Point Info function, you are able to track notches for this function.

Procedure for Edit Notch Info

1. Select **Edit>Edit Notch Info.** The **Tracking Information** window appears on-screen (see Figure 3.20).

2. A user input box states: "Select notch(es) for editing." Left click to select notches for which you need to change information, which highlights the notch in red.

   Note: If you select more than one notch, all the notches will receive the same information that you input into the fields.

3. In the **Type** field, select the notch type by activating the drop-down menu. Reference the Notch Parameter Table from the storage area in which the piece is stored for notch measurement.

4. In the **Angle** field, type in the new angle for the notch. The notch is always perpendicular to the point on which it is when you first create it. If you desire a new angle, type the measurement in this field.

5. In the **Point ID** field, type in the new point number if you need to make a change. The point number is used to add or edit alteration rules or matching points in a plaid pattern.

6. The **Grade Rule (V8)** field in Version 8 lets you enter a grade rule, which lets you control the notch movement as you grade the piece.

7. In the **Notch Position on Seam** option, select from the available choices to determine how the notch should lie on the seam allowance. Beginners should always choose Perpendicular.

8. Click **Apply>OK.**

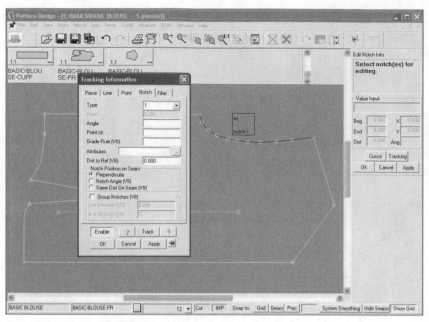

Figure 3.20 Edit Notch Info fields displayed.

9. Save the piece to keep your changes permanently.

Remember, you may also access the Edit Notch Info option by right clicking the mouse button while out of a function and selecting Edit Notch Info.

Edit Line Info

Edit Line Info lets you review or alter line labels or names. Line names are used to distinguish one line from another in certain procedures. They may consist of letters, numbers, or both and can have a maximum of 10 characters. To use this function, a piece must be on-screen. As in the Edit Point Info function, you are able to track lines for this function.

Lines created in the system automatically get line labels. Any lines that do not make up the perimeter of the piece are considered internal lines. They may be labeled letters A to Z or numbers 0 to 16 and 100 to 32000. Numbers 0 to 16 are normally used to match pieces.

The system also has certain labels that are created by default or have a fixed use. For example, a grain line is labeled "G0" and an internal line, when first created, is labeled an "I." Since a grain line will

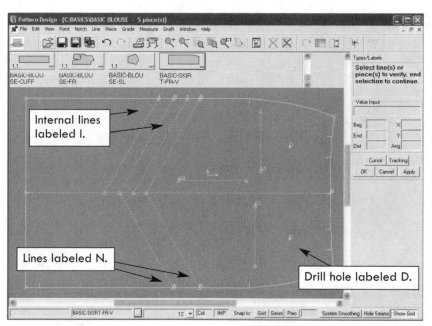

Figure 3.21 Examples of internal lines.

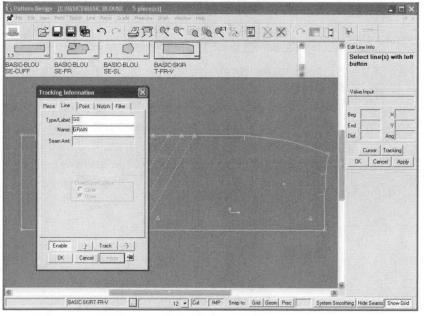

Figure 3.22 Edit Line Info fields display info for selected line.

always have this label, it is considered a fixed label. You can change a grain line's label only if there is an alternate grain line. However, you can change an internal line's label to some other label, as long as it is unused, if it was labeled "I."

Internal lines labeled 0 to 16, 100 to 14999, and A to M (except D) do not mirror, which means these lines are not repeated on the opposite side of a mirrored garment. Internal lines labeled 15000 to 32000 and N to Z (except P) do mirror, which means these lines do repeat on the opposite side of the garment. An unfolded mirrored piece illustrates this concept (see Figure 3.21).

Procedure for Edit Line Info

1. Select **Edit>Edit Line Info.** The **Tracking Information** window appears (see Figure 3.22).

2. A user input box states: "Select line(s) with left button." Left click on the lines for which you need to change information, which highlights them in red.

   Note: If you select more than one, all the lines will receive the same information that you input into the fields.

3. In the **Type/Label** field, type a label for the line.

4. In the **Name** field, type a name for the line.

5. Click **Apply>OK.**

6. Save the piece to keep your changes permanently.

Remember, you can also access the Edit Line Info option by right clicking the mouse button while out of a function and selecting Edit Line Info.

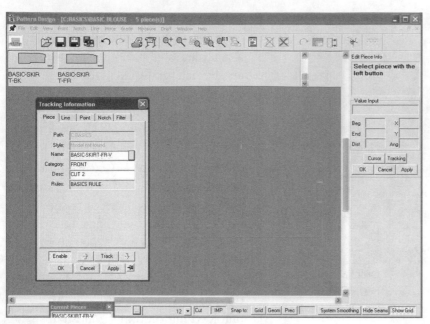

Figure 3.23 Edit Piece Info fields display for the selected piece.

Edit Piece Info

You can use Edit Piece Info to review or change piece information, such as the Descriptive Data. Descriptive Data is discussed in further detail in Chapter 4.

Procedure for Edit Piece Info

1. Select **Edit>Edit Piece Info.** The **Tracking Information** window appears on-screen.

2. A user input box states: "Select piece with the left button." Left click to select the piece and edit information, which highlights the piece in red (see Figure 3.23).

3. The **Path** field, although grayed out, shows the storage area in which the piece is saved.

4. The **Style** field, also grayed out, shows to which style/model the piece belongs, if you opened the piece as part of a model.

5. In the **Name** field, type in the piece name. You cannot leave this field blank and are allowed a maximum of 20 characters per piece name, which may consist of letters, numbers, or both. A piece name is usually a combination of the style/model name and the type of pattern piece; for example, 4200 Side Front, where "4200" is the style and "Side Front" is the type of pattern piece.

6. In the **Category** field, type in the category of the piece. You cannot leave this field blank. You have a 20-character limit, but the name may consist of letters, numbers, or both; for example, Side Front.

7. In the **Description** field, type in descriptive information about the piece. This is an optional field that lets you input any extra information about a piece, such as the number of pieces to be cut; for example, Cut 2. You have a 20-character limit, but the name may consist of letters, numbers, or both.

8. Click **Apply>OK.**

9. Save the piece to keep your changes permanently.

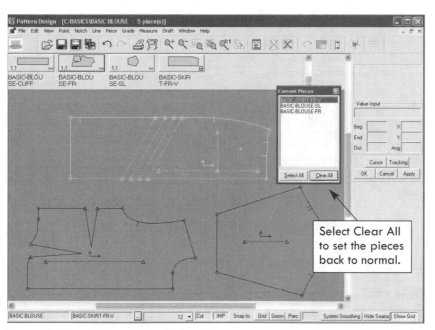

Figure 3.24 Current Pieces option displayed.

Current Pieces

When there are several pieces open on-screen, the Current Pieces function lets you select either just one piece or more than one on which to work. Pieces that are not selected will not be able to be manipulated.

Procedure for Current Pieces

1. Select **Edit>Current Pieces.** The **Current Pieces** window appears on-screen, listing the names of all the open pieces (see Figure 3.24).

2. Click on the names of the pieces on which you want to work for the session. The selected pieces are highlighted and you are able to work on them as long as they are set as current pieces.

Note: If you are done working on a piece and no longer want to consider it a current piece, click the **Clear All** button in the window on-screen.

Select All

There are some functions that let you select more than one piece and apply that function to all the pieces on-screen at once. For example, if you need to apply the same shrinkage amount to all of the pieces on-screen, just click on **Select All.** An easier way to use Select All in this and similar scenarios is to right click your mouse to access the menu and choose Select All.

Clear All

This function clears all the pieces on-screen so they are no longer selected; the pieces will no longer be highlighted in red.

Delete Pieces from the Work Area

When used from the Edit menu, this function clears all pieces from the work area at one time. F10 is a hotkey that performs the same function. This function does not delete pattern pieces from the system, but rather from the screen display.

Procedure to Delete Pieces from the Work Area one at a time

1. Place the mouse over a piece to highlight it. The piece will be highlighted in white if you haven't changed the system color defaults.

2. Right click and select **Delete Piece from Work Area**. Notice how the function name is not plural: Only the highlighted piece is deleted.

View Menu

The View menu has options that let you display notch types, grading information, and point information.

Zoom–Zoom In

Zoom In gives lets you zoom in closer to a part of a piece. The hotkey for Zoom In is F7.

Procedure to zoom in

1. Select **View>Zoom In.**

2. A user input box states: "Press to select one corner, press again to select other corner." Use the left mouse button to click on one corner. Release and click on a second corner. Release to see a square enclosure around the area in which you will zoom. The area you squared off is zoomed in (see Figure 3.25).

Zoom–Zoom Out

Zoom Out gives lets you zoom out of a piece that you have zoomed into by the same number of times you zoomed in originally. The hotkey for this function is F8.

Zoom–Full Scale

Full Scale lets you see each piece on-screen in its entirety. For example, if you cannot see an entire piece within the screen, this function lets you do it. The hotkey for this function is F3.

Zoom–Zoom to Selected

This option lets you do a quick zoom on a highlighted piece. The selected piece is shown as large as possible within the screen. This is useful when you are working on several pieces and you decide you want to look at one pattern more closely. The hotkey for this function is F4.

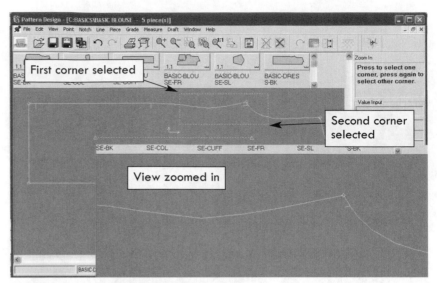

Figure 3.25 Zoomed view of side seam.

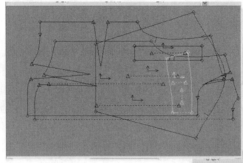

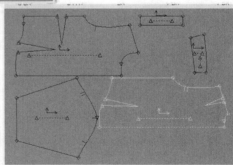

Figure 3.26 F2 key used to separate pieces in work area.

Zoom–1:1

The 1:1 function displays the piece on-screen true to size (in inches).

Zoom–Separate Pieces

When pieces on the screen are on top of one an other, this function separates the pieces within the screen so you can work on them individually (see Figure 3.26). The hotkey for this function is F2.

Point–All Points

The All Points option displays all the points that exist on a piece. Once you are out of this function, the points are no longer displayed. This function comes in handy if there are unnecessary points you need to delete on a piece.

Procedure for All Points

1. Select **View>Points>All Points.**

2. A user input box states: "Select piece(s) to verify, end selection to continue." Left click to select the pieces, which highlights them in red.

3. Right click and select **OK** to display the Points.

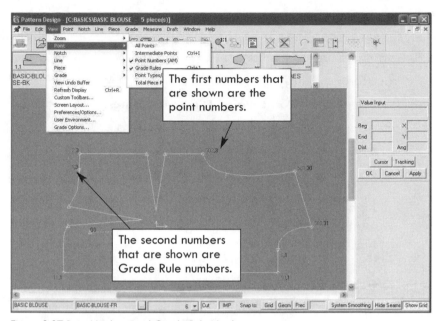

Figure 3.27 Point Numbers and Grade Rule Numbers.

Point–Intermediate Points

The Point–Intermediate Points function displays all the intermediate points on a piece, but they remain displayed even after you are out of this function—you have to turn them off. This function may be used to display points so that you can decide which points to delete later. It may also be used while performing functions from the Modify Points menu. For example, displaying points may help you to better visualize and have more control while manipulating a pattern.

Procedure for Intermediate Points

1. Select **View>Points>Intermediate Points.**

2. A user input box states: "Select piece(s) to verify, end selection to continue." Left click to select pieces, which highlights them in red.

3. Right click and select **OK** to display the points.

Note: To turn off the points, just repeat the function.

Point–Point Numbers (AM)

The Point–Point Numbers (AM) function lets you display point numbers, also known as Point ID. When you first draft a piece into the system, each point has a number attached to it as a reference. You can leave the reference number alone or

change it with the Edit Point Info function if you are using an Alteration Table. Use the Alteration of Table and Size Code Tables to create sizes in addition to a regular size line. For example, pants may be available in sizes 34S (short), 34R (regular), and 34L (long).

Procedure to display Point Numbers

1. Select **View>Points>Intermediate Points> Point Numbers (AM).** The point numbers are turned on as shown in Figure 3.27.

Note: To turn off the point numbers, uncheck the option.

Point–Grade Rules

The Point-Grade Rules function lets you display the grade rule numbers (see Figure 3.27). This allows you to see the numbers all at once rather than checking each point individually, which, of course, makes more efficient use of your time.

Point–Point Types/Attributes

The Point-Point Types/Attributes function lets you display Point Attributes on pieces. This is an easy way to view a piece's attributes and make sure, for example, that it's not curving where it should not be curving. See the Edit Point Info section on page

26 for a more in-depth discussion of Point Attributes. They include attributes such as Smoothing and Non-smoothing.

Procedure to display attributes

1. Select **View>Point>Point Types/Attributes.**

2. A user input box states: "Select piece(s) or point(s) to verify, end selection to continue." Left click to select pieces, which highlights the pieces or points in red.

3. Right click and select **OK** to display point attributes. Once you exit the function, they turn off.

Notch–Types

The Types option, under the Notch submenu, displays the type of notch on the piece. It is a great way for you to view all notch types at the same time and make sure they are correct.

Procedure to view notch types

1. Select **View>Notch>Types.**

2. A user input box states: "Select piece(s) or notch(es) to verify, end selection to continue." Left click to select pieces, which highlights them in red.

3. Right click and select **OK** to display the notch types.

Notch–Shapes

The Shapes option, also under the Notch submenu, displays the notch shape on the piece. Normally, the system displays all notches as slit notches by default. This is a good way for you to view all notch shapes at the same time and make sure they are correct. For example, a V-notch will display as an actual v-shaped notch.

Procedure to view notch shapes

1. Select **View>Notch>Shapes.** The notch shapes are displayed.

Line–Hide/Ignore

There are three selections under Hide/Ignore. They include Perimeter, Internals, and Reset. The purpose of this menu is to let you hide or ignore certain lines so you can concentrate on the rest of the piece. For example, when there are numerous internal lines on a piece, it may become confusing to work on it. Therefore, hiding the internals makes the working session easier to view.

Procedure for Hide/Ignore Perimeter or Internal Lines

1. Select **View>Line>Hide/Ignore>Perimeter** or **View>Line>Hide/Ignore>Internal Lines.**

2. A user input box states: "Select line(s) to hide, end selection to continue." Left click to select the line(s),which highlights them in red.

3. Right click and select **OK** to hide the lines.

Procedure for Reset Hidden Perimeter or Internal Lines

1. Select **View>Line>Hide/Ignore>Reset.**

2. A user input box states: "Select piece(s) to restore, end selection to continue." Left click to select piece(s), which highlights the piece(s) in red.

3. Right click and select **OK** to display the lines.

Piece–Seam Amounts

This view function lets you verify seam allowance amounts. It comes in handy when you forget the seam allowance you entered for a pattern or to view what another patternmaker may have entered. Each seam has its seam allowance amount displayed for that line. Seam amounts stay on until you turn them off.

Procedure to view seam amounts

1. Select **View>Piece>Seam Amounts.**

2. A user input box states: "Select line(s) or piece(s) to display seam amounts, end selection to continue." Left click to select lines or pieces, which highlights them in red.

3. Right click and select **OK** to display Seam amounts. If you want to turn them off, repeat the function.

Grade–Show All Sizes

The Show All Sizes function lets you display all the graded sizes on a pattern piece (see Figure 3.28). This is commonly used to view how a pattern is graded throughout all the available sizes.

Procedure to show all sizes

1. Select **View>Grade>Show All Sizes.**

2. A user input box states: "Select piece(s) to display nest, end selection to continue." Left click to select pieces, which highlights the pieces in red.

3. Right click and select **OK** to display the pieces with graded sizes as a nest.

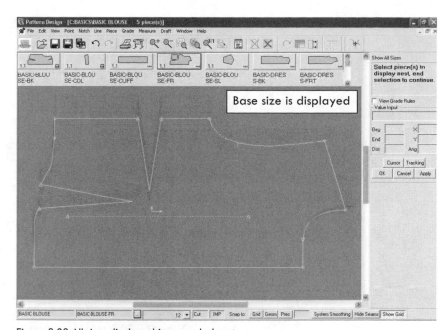

Figure 3.28 All sizes displayed in a graded nest.

Grade–Show Selected Sizes

The Grade–Show Selected Sizes function lets you select specific sizes to view in addition to the base size. For example, Figure 3.29 shows sizes 2 and 10 in addition to the base size. This option is useful when you want to make sure sizes are grading accurately and their proportions are correct.

Procedure to show selected sizes

1. Select **View>Grade>Show Selected Sizes.**

2. A user input box states: "Select piece(s), end selection to continue." Left click to select the pieces, which highlights the pieces in red.

3. Right click and select **OK** to display the **Show Selected Sizes** window and select available sizes.

4. Select the sizes you want to view from the window and click **OK** to proceed. The pieces are displayed with the selected sizes in a nest.

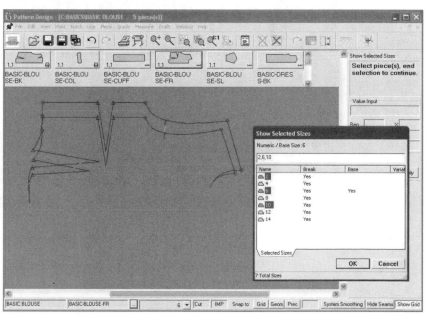

Figure 3.29 Selected sizes displayed.

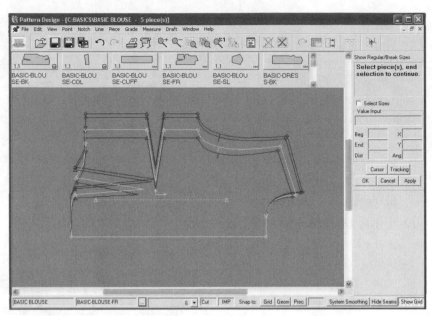

Figure 3.30 Break sizes displayed.

Grade–Show Regular/Break Sizes

The Grade–Show Regular/Break Sizes function displays the break sizes that are determined in the Rule Table Editor and are applied to the pattern piece. A **break size** is the size where the grade rule changes to a different amount. For example, the piece in Figure 3.30 has a base size of 6. Sizes 6 to 12 grade the same amount, let us say ¼". Sizes 12 to 14 grade to ½"; therefore, size 12 is considered a break size. This function makes it easy to see where a pattern changes in growth.

Procedure to show regular/break sizes

1. Select **View>Grade>Show Regular/Break Sizes.**

2. A user input box states: "Select piece(s), end selection to continue." Left click to select pieces, which highlights the pieces in red.

3. Right click and select **OK** to display the pieces with break sizes.

Grade–Clear Nest

The Grade–Clear Nest function clears the graded nest displayed after you use the functions from the Grade submenu in the View menu.

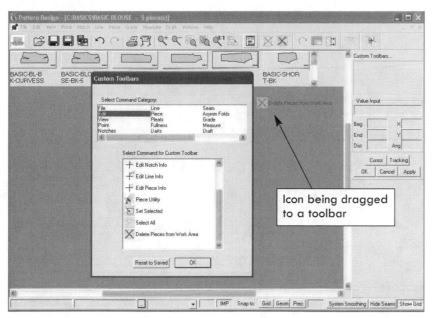

Figure 3.31 Selected icon function dragged into the toolbar.

Refresh Display

The Refresh Display function clears the screen of any superfluous data fragments left behind after you use a function. Pressing Ctrl + R on your keyboard is a shortcut that gives you the same result.

Custom Toolbars

You can set up the toolbar to include icons for functions most used by a PDS user to make your working session as efficient as possible.

Procedure to set up a custom toolbar

1. Select **View>Custom Toolbars.** The **Custom Toolbars** window appears and shows the main menus within PDS (see Figure 3.31).

2. Select the menu you want and click on an icon from within the displayed window. You'll find the menu's functions and its icons under **Select command for custom toolbar.**

3. With the left mouse button, click and drag the icon you want. Release the icon when it's in the spot you want. Once you do this step, you can use the icons for the functions without having to go through the drop down menus.

Note: To delete an icon from the toolbar, right click over the icon and click **OK** when you see the "Delete this toolbar icon?" prompt.

PDS Hotkeys and Keyboard Shortcuts

F2:	Separate Pieces
F3:	Full Scale
F4:	Zoom to Selected
F7:	Zoom In
F8:	Zooms out
F10:	Delete Pieces from the Work area
Shift + Left mouse button:	Allows you to select multiple data items by highlighting the first and last data items in a list. All data items in between are highlighted.
Ctrl + Left mouse button:	Allows you to select multiple data items in no particular order by clicking on each.

Screen Layout

The Screen Layout function lets you select what the PDS window environment will display. When you open this function, notice the number of options from which you can choose. Check or select only those you wish to display on-screen. For display purposes, most options are selected in Figure 3.32 to illustrate them. Under normal circumstances, you wouldn't select all the options selected in Figure 3.32, since the work area becomes smaller when there are numerous options selected.

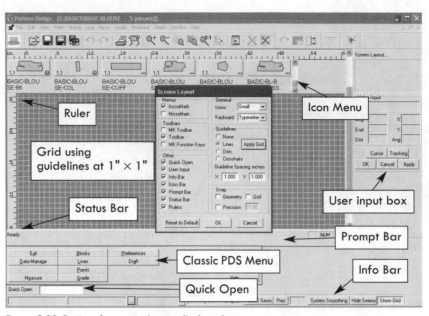

Figure 3.32 Options for screen layout displayed.

Procedure to customize screen layout

1. Select **View>Screen Layout.** The **Screen Layout** window appears with options.

2. Check the box next to each preferred option from the **Menus** area so they will be on-screen.

    AccuMark displays the Classic PDS functions. Users who are up-to-date with the Windows-based version usually do not check off this option.

    MicroMark displays the MicroMark menu for MicroMark users.

3. Check the box next to each preferred option from the **Toolbars** area so they will be on-screen.

    The **MK Toolbar** displays the MK toolbar for MicroMark users.

    The **Toolbar** displays the AccuMark toolbar for AccuMark users.

    MK Function Keys displays MK function keys for MicroMark users.

4. Check the box next to each preferred option from the **Other** area so they will be on-screen.

    The **Quick Open** option lets you input the name of a file to open it up quickly, rather than going to File>Open or using the Open icon.

The **user input** box sits at the far right side of the screen and prompts you when you are using PDS functions. This box is integrated into the software and appears when a function is used even if it is not checked.

The **Info Bar** is located near the bottom of the screen by default and contains useful information about whatever piece you have on-screen, such as its name and available sizes. It displays whether Imperial or Metric notation is being used. It also gives you access to other options, such as Snap to Grid, Snap to Geometry, Snap to Precision, System Smoothing, Hide Seams; and Show Grid. Snap to Grid makes the cursor jump to the closest dot, line, or crosshair displayed on-screen. Snap to Geometry makes the cursor jump to the closest point on a piece. Snap to Precision moves a line or point by the amount set in the Precision area of the Screen Layout function. System Smoothing applies smoothing to pieces and shows how a piece will actually plot. Hide Seams hides seam allowance that exists on a pattern, which results in a cleaner looking pattern. Show Grid displays a grid on-screen

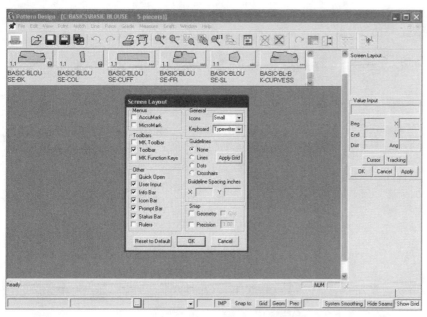

Figure 3.33 The more common screen layout displayed.

as guidelines, dots, or crosshairs for use when aligning pieces.

The **Icon Bar** houses the pattern piece icons as you open them. If it is not checked, icons are not available.

The **Prompt Bar** displays the prompts for functions that are in use, much as the user input box. Do not check this if you have already selected the user input box.

The **Status Bar** notifies you if the system is ready to continue with a function.

The **Rulers** option displays a ruler for reference using the notation you selected.

5. Check the box next to each preferred option from the **General** area so they will show on-screen.

The **Icons** option has three sizes available: small, medium, and large.

The **Keyboard** option has two selections: Typewrite, which customizes the keyboard for AccuMark users, and Alphabetic, which customizes the keyboard for MicroMark users.

6. Check the box next to the preferred option from the **Guidelines** area. Select the type

of guidelines you would like to see displayed on-screen when the grid is in use. Selections include **None, Lines, Dots,** and **Crosshairs.**

7. In the **Guideline Spacing Inches** area, type in the amount for each X and/or Y to space out the guidelines you selected in the Guidelines area.

8. Click **OK** to close the window and apply the changes.

Figure 3.33 displays more common Screen Layout selections. Notice that every selection is not checked off.

Preferences/Options

The Preferences/Options menu has several tabs designated for different areas such as the display of pieces and color preferences. Basic options will be discussed in this section.

Each tab has the options OK, Cancel, Save, and Apply available at the bottom of the window. Apply applies the selections to the working session. Save applies and saves the selections for the working session and current storage area. Cancel cancels any selections that you made while the tab or window was open. OK closes the Preferences/Options window.

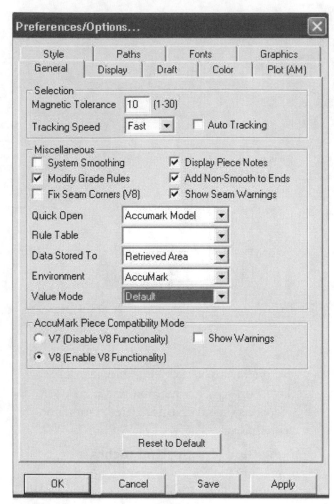

Figure 3.34 General tab for Preferences/Options.

The Reset to Default button in each window returns all the selections to the system defaults.

Preferences/Options–General Tab

The General Tab in Preferences/Options contains selections for the general work environment (see Figure 3.34). Remember that these are your personal preferences for your working environment. Since a correct set of preferences may not exist globally, there are recommendations usually set up per company or commonly used as stated within the described selections below.

Procedure to set general tab selections

1. Select **View>Preferences/Options.** The **Preference/Options** window appears on-screen.

2. Select the **General** tab and select the options to customize your work area.

3. Make your selections for the **Selection** area.

   The **Magnetic Tolerance** option determines how close the cursor needs to get to a point, line, or piece on-screen before highlighting it. The lower the number, the closer the cursor needs to get to the point, line, or piece. Ten is the system default and a good average for most users.

   Choose the **Auto Tracking** option when you want to enable tracking as the cursor moves along a line.

   The **Tracking Speed** option has three speeds for auto tracking: slow, medium, or fast.

4. Make your selections for the **Miscellaneous** area.

   Choose the **System Smoothing** option to view lines on-screen as they would plot out in a plotter. This is a great way to see if wide angles meant to have sharp corners are curving and in need of an "N" attribute. Attributes are discussed in the Edit Point Info section of this chapter on page 26. The default for this option is checked to apply system smoothing.

If the Info Bar was selected as a Screen Layout option, then System Smoothing may be toggled on and off from there as well.

Choose the **Modify Grade Rules** option if you want grade rules to be updated automatically when you make changes to a piece. For example, if you add a tapered pleat, the system updates the grade rules and adds an asterisk next to grade rules to denote that they have changed within the piece.

Choose the **Display Piece Notes** option if you want annotation displayed with pieces. For example, annotation may be a special note on the piece that shows where the pattern needs to be gathered.

Choose the **Add Non-Smooth to Ends** option so that non-smooth, "N," attributes are applied to the endpoints of perimeter lines. This will ensure that corners stay sharp rather than curved if the angle is wide.

The **Quick Open** option has three selections available: AccuMark List, AccuMark Model, and AccuMark Piece. If Quick Open is selected in the Screen Layout option, then this area determines whether the name you type in the field is quickly opening a list, model, or piece.

The **Rule Table** option is used to select the rule table you want to apply to the pieces when you create them with functions such as Rectangle, Collar, Skirt, or drafting in a new piece.

The **Data Stored to** option lists two available selections: Retrieved Area and Default Area. For example, let's say you selected "Retrieved Area" for this field. The default storage area in Pattern Design is "ABC" and a piece is opened from storage area "XYZ." When you save a piece using the Save function, it saves into storage area "ABC" because that is the storage area from which it was retrieved when you

opened it originally. This option was discussed in the Save section of this chapter on page 20.

The **Environment** opiton lists two available selections: AccuMark and MicroMark. AccuMark users should select AccuMark.

The **Value Mode** option is available in most functions to plug in a measurement or a specific value. Long time AccuMark users recognize this as a popup. For example, when you create a rectangle, you can click the **Cursor** button to toggle to **Value** and activate the **Value Input** field. This is known as Value Mode. It is used to enter the size, width, and/or height. The Value button toggles from Value to Cursor. If you use the Cursor Mode, you opt to create a rectangle visually with no specific measurements.

The following are the three selections available for Value Mode:

- **Default** keeps whichever mode was last used—Value or Cursor.

- **Classic AM PDS** changes back to Cursor Mode after you finish working in Value Mode.

- **Reset to Cursor** changes back to Cursor Mode after you use the Value Mode and exit the function.

5. Make your selections for the **AccuMark Piece Compatibility Mode** area: V7 (Disable V8 Functionality) and V8 (Enable V7 Functionality).

V7 (Disable V8 Functionality) may be selected by experienced AccuMark users who work with both versions and are trying to move all their data from Version 7 to Version 8.

V8 (Enable V7 Functionality) is the option that new users select. Version 8 has some options available that Version 7 does not include such as the Tangent notch function.

6. Click **Apply>Save>OK.**

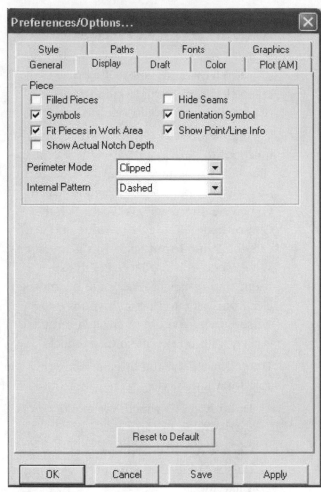

Figure 3.35 Display tab for Preferences/Options.

Preferences/Options–Display Tab

The Display tab in Preferences/Options offers several choices for pattern pieces displayed in the PDS screen work area (see Figure 3.35).

Procedure to set display tab selections

1. Select **View>Preferences/Options.** The **Preferences/Options** window appears on-screen.

2. Select the **Display** tab and select the display preferences.

3. Check the box next to **Filled Pieces** to fill in the pattern pieces with a color. The default color is similar to mustard yellow. You can change the color in the Color tab of the Preferences/Options function. Look for Fabric Type field and select the color of your choice.

   If you do not check this box off, a color will not display inside the piece. The piece will display as a wire frame.

4. Check the box next to **Symbols** to display the geometric symbols that represent endpoints and graded points. Symbols are in the shapes of triangles and diamonds. It is recommended that you select this option.

5. Check the box next to **Fit Pieces in Work Area** so that the pieces you bring into the PDS work area will all fit within the screen. It is recommended that you select this option.

6. Check the box next to **Show Actual Notch Depth** so that the actual notch depth is displayed. For example, a ¼" notch will display with an actual ¼" depth. All notches, by default, display as slit notches of the same size.

7. Check the box next to **Hide Seams** if you do not want the seam allowance on patterns to show. If you opted to display the Info Bar for the screen layout, Hide Seams is also available as a toggle button to turn seams on or off.

8. Check the box next to **Orientation Symbol** if you want the orientation symbol to display inside a piece. The orientation symbol helps you to view or remember the direction in which you drafted the pattern pieces into the system. It is recommended that you select this option.

9. Click **Apply>Save>OK.**

Test Your Display Tab Skills

Use the following steps to practice using the display tab:

1. Bring a piece into the work area.
2. Check options on and off and click Apply to view how your choices affect the display.
3. Select Fit Pieces in Work Area, click Apply, and then click OK to close the window. Click and drag another piece into the workarea to see how it fits into the screen.
4. Open the Preferences/Options Display tab again and deselect the Fit Pieces in Work Area option. Click Apply and then OK to close the window. Click and drag another piece into the screen. Notice how the scale of the screen does not change to fit the piece within the workarea.
5. To view the effects of Hide Seams, check the box and add seam allowance to a piece. Note how the seam allowance does not show.
6. Open the Preference/Options Display tab again and uncheck Hide Seams. Note that the seam allowance on the piece is now visible.

Preferences/Options—Color Tab

The Color tab lets you change the system defaults and customize the colors used in PDS. For example, you can change the base size color or the color of all the other graded sizes. All you have to do is look for the area that you want to change (see Figure 3.36). For example, you may want to fill your pieces in with a different color than the default mustard yellow. The option to change this preference is labeled Fabric Type. The button above Fabric Type shows the default color selection, and when you press it, more color selections appear from which you can choose.

Procedure to set color tab selections

1. Select **View>Preferences/Options.** The **Preferences/Options** window appears on-screens.

2. Select the **Color** tab and make your selections from the displayed options described below.

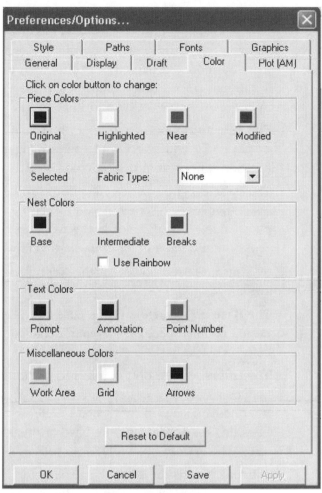

Figure 3.36 Color tab for Preferences/Options.

3. Select your preferred colors for the **Piece Colors** area.

The **Original** option refers to the last saved version of a pattern piece. For example, when you open a piece from a storage area and drag it into the work area, it is the original piece. The system default color is black.

The **Highlighted** option refers to pieces that you highlight during a function. The system default is green.

The **Near** options refers to the color a line, point, or piece changes to when you approach it with the cursor to perform a function. The system default color is black.

The **Modified** option refers to a piece that you have changed or edited—it is modified in some type of way. The part of the piece that you modified may appear on-screen in a different color. Some companies in the industry like to select blue for this option.

The **Selected** option refers to a point, line, or piece that you select while performing a function. The system default color is red.

The **Fabric Type** option refers to the color inside patterns on-screen if you display pieces filled in with color in the work area. The system default color is mustard yellow.

4. Select your preferred colors for the **Nest Colors** area.

The **Base** option refers to the base size of a nested pattern piece. The system default color is black.

The **Intermediate** option refers to the in-between sizes of a nested pattern. Intermediate sizes in this scenario refer to sizes that do not include the base or break sizes. The system default color is yellow.

A **Break Size** is the size where the grade rule amount changes. Note the Breaks button in the Nest Colors area in Figure 3.36. The system default color is dark blue.

5. Select your preferred colors for the **Text Colors** area.

The **Prompt** option refers to the prompts that displays when using a function in the user input box. These are generally at the top right-hand side of the PDS window. Black is recommended for this option.

The **Annotation** option refers to any information or note displayed in a piece. Black or white are recommended for this option.

The **Point Number** option refers to the display of point numbers. The system default color is blue.

6. Select your preferred colors for the **Miscellaneous Colors** area.

The **Work Area** refers to the area or background where your pieces are displayed. The system default color is green.

The **Grid** option refers to the display of a grid.

The **Arrows** option refers to the arrows displayed in several options. For example, arrows are displayed when you use the Rectangle option and use Value Mode to plug in a measurement.

7. Click **Apply>Save>OK.**

Test Your Color Tab Skills

Use the following steps to practice the Color tab options.

1. Bring a piece into the PDS work area.
2. Change the colors in each area, and click Apply to view changes.
3. To view nest colors, go to the View>Grade>Show All Sizes. Open the Preferences/Options Color tab, and change the colors in this section to see the difference. Select Rainbow to view all the sizes in a variety of colors.

Preferences/Options–Plot Tab

The Plot tab was discussed earlier in this chapter in the File menu section under the Plot area on page 24.

Preferences/Options–Paths Tab

The Paths tab is the area where you select the default storage area. This means that every time you open a window in PDS, this storage area will be referenced for certain tables. For example, when you create notches in PDS, it will reference this storage area's Notch Parameter Table. Likewise, when you edit or add grade rules, the Rule Table Editor that is referenced will be from the default storage area.

There are three available areas in the Paths tab. AccuMark users will make selections only from the area labeled AccuMark Storage Area.

Figure 3.37 Paths tab for Preferences/Options.

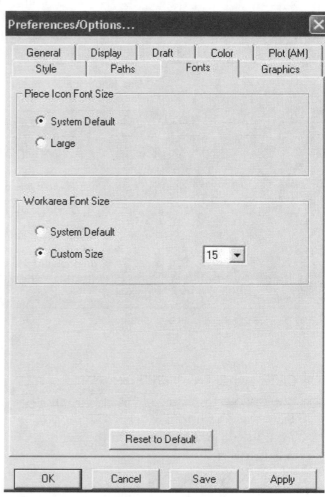

Figure 3.38 Fonts tab for Preferences/Options.

Procedure to set paths tab selections

1. Select **View>Preferences/Options.** The **Preferences/Options** window appears on-screen (see Figure 3.37).

2. Select the **Paths** tab.

3. In the **Device** field, select C from the drop-down menu.

4. In the **Storage Area** field, select the storage area that you would like to set up as the default.

5. Click **Save** to select the storage area as the default, or click **Apply** to select the storage area for the working session in which you are working only.

6. Click **OK** to exit the window.

Preferences/Options—Fonts Tab

The Fonts tab lets you select the Piece Icon Font Size and Work Area Font size. The piece icons are displayed when you open pattern pieces. The font size in the workarea refers to the font size of grade rule numbers, line labels, and measurements that are displayed.

Procedure to set fonts tab selections

1. Select **View>Preferences/Options.** The **Preferences/Options** window appears on-screen (see Figure 3.38).

2. Select the **Fonts** tab.

3. In the **Piece Icon Font Size** area, select from two options: System Default or Large.

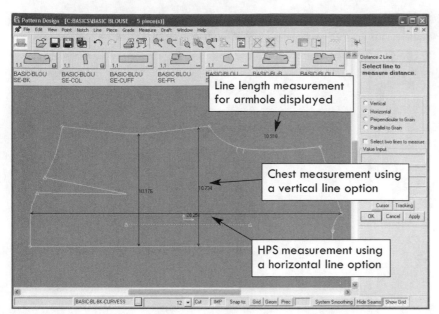

Figure 3.39 Distance 2Line and Line Lengths displayed.

4. Under **Work Area Font Size,** select from two options: System Default or Custom Size. If you select Custom Size, choose the size from the drop-down menu to the right of this field.

5. Click **Apply>Save>OK.**

User Environment

The User Environment function makes the User Environment Table available within PDS so you can make changes or simply review the table. As a reminder, this table sets the measurement system, decimal precision, and grade option you use throughout a selected storage area.

Grade Options

The Grade Options function makes available the three grading method selections. These methods include Small-Large Incremental, Base Up-Down Incremental, and Base Up-Down Cumulative.

Measure Menu

The Measure menu has several options to measure a piece, such as measuring a line or the distance between two lines.

Line Length

Line Length measures the length of a line from one endpoint to the next. The measurement is taken along the shape of the line. It is the fastest way to measure a line segment. You would use this function if, for example, you need to measure an armhole, an arm length, a side seam, or an inseam (see Figure 3.39).

Procedure to measure a line

1. Select **Measure>Line Length.**

2. A user input box states: "Select line(s) to measure, end selection to continue." Left click to select lines, which highlights them in red.

3. Right click and select **OK** to display the line measurement both next to the measured line and in the **Dist** field in the user input box.

Distance 2Line

The Distance 2Line function measures the distance between two lines as shown in Figure 3.39. This is a great way to measure specs such as the Chest, Waist, and High Point Shoulder.

Procedure to measure the distance between two lines

1. Select **Measure>Line Length.**

2. Select **Vertical** or **Horizontal** to set the line direction. See the user input box.

3. A user input box states: "Select line to measure distance." Select one of the two lines that you are measuring to/from with the left mouse button.

4. A gliding line appears. As the line moves, the measurement changes. Left click to stabilize the line, and read its measurement.

Note: You may perform a popup to set the line at a specific location, such as 1" below the armhole for a chest measurement. To perform a popup, press both the left and right mouse buttons and release both at the same time.

Perimeter 2Pt/Measure Along Piece

The Measure Along Piece function measures the distance from one point to another along the shape of the line. The two points you select do not have to be endpoints. For example, use this to measure the width of a pleat or a dart (see Figure 3.40).

Procedure to measure the distance between two points along the perimeter

1. Select **Measure>Perimeter 2pt/Measure Along Piece.**

2. A user input box states: "Select first point to measure perimeter distance." Left click to select a point.

3. Another user input box states: "Select second point to measure perimeter distance." Left click to select a point. The measurement is displayed on-screen and in the Dist field of the user input box.

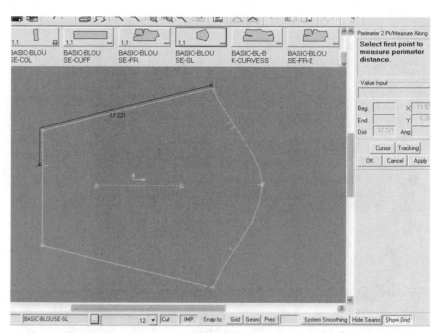

Figure 3.40 Perimeter 2Pt used on a sleeve.

Distance to Notch/Measure Along Piece

The Distance to Notch function measures the distance from an endpoint to a notch as well as between the notches. This helps you to determine if the notches are in the correct places along the seam (see Figure 3.41).

Procedure for Distance to Notch

1. Select **Measure>Distance to Notch/Measure Along Piece.**

2. A user input box states: "Select the portion of a line between notches or between a notch and the end of a line to be measured." Left click to select a portion of the line and display its measurement.

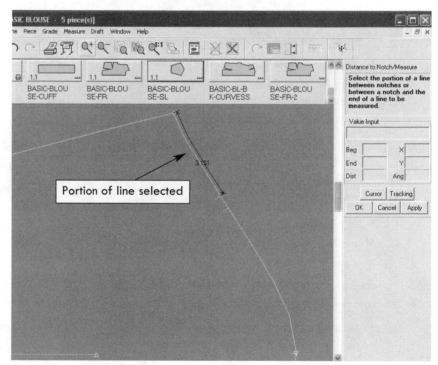

Figure 3.41 Distance is measured from one end of a sleeve cap to a notch.

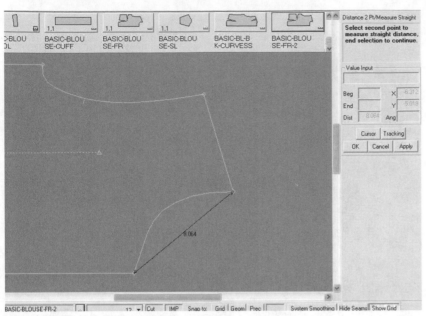

Figure 3.42 Neck is measured using Distance 2Pt.

Distance 2Pt/Measure Straight

The Distance 2Pt/Measure Straight function measures the straight distance from one point to another. Think of it as stretching a string from one point to another. This function comes in handy when you are measuring an armhole straight spec. The function may also be used to determine specs such as the front or back neck drop or neck width.

Procedure for Distance 2Pt/Measure Straight

1. Select **Measure>Distance 2pt/Measure Straight.**

2. A user input box states: "Select first point to measure straight distance." Left click to select the point from which you are measuring.

3. Another user input box states: "Select second point to measure straight distance, end selection to continue." Left click to select the point to which you are measuring. The straight measurement is displayed on the screen.

Note: The user input box displays the X and Y measurements as well. The X serves as a neck drop spec and the Y serves as a neck width spec in Figure 3.42.

Piece Perimeter

The Piece Perimeter function measures a piece along the whole perimeter. You can sometimes use this measurement when calculating cutting time or to pay a cutter by the amount they cut per day.

Procedure to determine the perimeter of a piece

1. Select **Measure>Piece Perimeter.**

2. A user input box states: "Select pieces to measure perimeter, end selection to continue." Left click to select pieces, which highlights them in red.

3. Right click and select **OK** to display the Piece Perimeter.

Piece Area

The Piece Area function measures the area of a piece.You can sometimes use this measurement for costing pieces or to pay a cutter by the area they cut in a day.

Procedure to determine the area of a piece

1. Select **Measure>Piece Area.**

2. A user input box states: "Select pieces to measure area, end selection to continue." Left

click to select pieces, which highlights them in red.

3. Right click and select **OK** to display the Piece Area around the center of the piece.

Angle

Angle displays the angle between two adjacent lines (lines that are next to each other and form a corner). You might use this function to verify that certain areas are squared, such as the armhole and side seam corner of a bodice.

Procedure to measure an angle

1. Select **Measure>Angle.**

2. A user input box states: "Select two lines to measure angle." Left click to select each line.

3. The angle is displayed in the **Ang** field of the user input box.

Clear Measurements

The Clear Measurements function clears the measurements from the screen after you have used one of the Measure menu functions. For example, after you display several measurements, it may become confusing to see so many numbers in the work area. Clearing them makes the work area easier on the eye. To display all measurements again, select the measurement functions you previously used to display them originally.

Hide/Show Measurements

The Hide Show Measurements function hides or displays measurements that have been taken using the selected functions in the Measure menu. For example, if you used Line Length you can use this option to hide or display the measurement of the line, therefore, you won't erase the measurement until you use the Clear Measurements function.

Procedure for Hide/Show Measurements

1. Select **Measure>Hide/Show Measurements.**

2. Left click to select the piece, which hides or displays the measurements.

Test Your Knowledge

Fill in the blanks.

1. If you want to open a model in PDS, make sure the "File of Type" is set to
   _____.

2. If you want to save a piece in a storage area other than the one in which
   it is already saved, then select the option _____.

3. Before plotting pieces, you should make sure the correct tables and
   preferences are set in the _____ in Preferences/Options.

4. If you would like to open more than one model, each in its own screen,
   select the option _____ in the Open function.

5. To make the best use of the plotter paper when plotting, select the
   _____ option in the Plot tab of Preferences/Options.

6. To change point information, such as a Grade Rule or Point Attribute, use
   the _____ function.

7. Descriptive Data such as the Piece Name or Category may be modified in
   the _____ function.

8. If an angle is wide and it curves when you apply System Smoothing, you
   need to change the point _____ to an "N" for non-smoothing.

9. The hotkey for separating pieces on-screen is _____.

10. Point ID is also known as a _____.

11. The quickest way to measure a line from one endpoint to another is to use
    the _____ function.

12. A good way to measure specs, such as a waist or chest, is the
    _____ function.

13. Some corners, such as the one where an armhole and side seam intersect,
    need to be squared. To make sure this corner is 90 degrees, use the
    function _____.

14. Select a storage area as the default area in the _____ of
    Preferences/Options.

15. Items displayed in the PDS work area, such as the ruler, may be selected
    by using the _____ option.

True or False

1. When using the Save function, a piece or model will be saved into a
   storage area according to the Preferences/Options set up in the field
   Data Stored to. TRUE or FALSE

2. Pieces can be sent to the plotter from PDS. TRUE or FALSE

3. The Notch Parameter Table cannot be accessed through PDS. TRUE or
   FALSE

4. Functions such as Edit Point Info, Edit Line Info, and Edit Piece Info may
   also be accessed with the right mouse button while performing a function.
   TRUE or FALSE

5. The Perimeter 2Pt/Along the Line Function measures along the shape or
   curve of a line rather than straight. TRUE or FALSE

Test Your Skills

Every AccuMark Gerber system has at least one sample storage area available with sample data, such as pieces, models, and rule tables. The best known storage area is DATA70. Use this storage area to practice the functions discussed in this chapter, or create a new storage area and copy the data from DATA70 into it.

1. Go to View>Screen Layout. Check options on and off to view the changes on-screen.
2. Go to File>Open. Select a model from the DATA70 storage area.
3. Go to File>Open. Select several pieces from the DATA70 storage area. Check the Open Separate Work Areas option to open each piece in separate workareas.
4. a. Select the window with the model you opened in Step 2; look at the window's drop-down menus.
   b. Now select File>Close Style/Model to close the model.
5. a. Select a window with one of the pieces you opened in Step 3.
   b. Select File>Close.
6. a. Select another window with one of the pieces that are opened.
   b. Select Edit Piece Info to view the piece information.
   c. Change the piece name to a name of your choice. For example, change the name Ladies-Blouse Fr to 123-Shirt Front.
   d. Go to File>Save As. Save the piece with the new name under storage area DATA70 or the storage area you created.
7. a. Select the new piece you saved in the previous step and select Edit Point Info to view point information.
   b. Change the Attribute on the armhole and side seam corner from an N to an S. Select OK.
   c. Apply System Smoothing displayed on the Info Bar at the bottom of the PDS screen. Note how the piece curves outward due to the attribute that was modified. If the Info Bar is not displayed, you did not select it as an option in the Screen Layout function.
   d. Change the attribute back to an N.
8. Using the same piece from Step 7, select Edit Line Info and select the grain line to view the line information.
9. Close out of all the remaining windows that are open. Open the model in DATA70 or the storage area you created again.

10. a. Bring several pieces into the workarea.
    b. Press the hotkey F2 to Separate Pieces on-screen.
    c. Highlight one piece and press the F4 hotkey to Zoom in on the Selected Piece.
    d. Press the F3 hotkey to view Full Scale.
    e. Press the F7 hotkey and Zoom In on a part of the piece.
    f. Press the F8 hotkey to Zoom Out.
    g. Press the F10 hotkey to Delete All Pieces from the Work/Area.
11. Select a piece to bring into the workarea and select the different functions in the Point submenu from the View menu.
12. Using the same piece from the previous step, try the functions in the Notch submenu of the View menu.
13. Select the Line Function from the View menu and try the Hide/Ignore Functions.
14. Add seam allowance to a piece on-screen. Follow these steps:
    a. Piece>Seam>Define/Add Seam.
    b. Left click to select the piece.
    c. Right click and select OK.
    d. Type in ½" in the Value Input field in the user input box, and press Enter on the keyboard.
    e. Go to View>Piece>Seam Amount. Proceed with the function to view seam allowance amount.
15. Select another piece to bring to the screen, and try the different functions in the Grade submenu from the View menu.
16. Select Custom Toolbars from the View menu and drag an icon into the toolbar. Then try deleting the icon you added.
17. Try the Measure menu functions on a piece of your choice. Think about measurements you truly need to create a pattern. For example, you can measure the Center Front with the Line Length function. To measure a notch from the beginning of the seam to where it is placed, use the Distance to Notch or Perimeter 2Pt function. To measure the High Point Shoulder or the waist, use the Distance 2line function.

CHAPTER FOUR

Drafting Pattern Pieces Using Pattern Design System

Objective

Drafting is the process you use to input pattern pieces into the system so you may manipulate them the same way you would manually. For example, you may add notches, darts, pleats, fullness, and seam allowance and manipulate them in a computerized environment.

Most companies have slopers or patterns on oak tag or Mylar for all their styles. These slopers are used to draft the patterns into the system. After you input patterns, you may manipulate them in the system as you would manually. Although you can create patterns from scratch on the system, this chapter focuses on how to input existing patterns by using the drafting method. When you see a knowledgeable person draft a pattern piece, it appears to be very simple. The fact is that it *is* quite simple, once you learn how to do it. After you finish reading this chapter and practice a little, you will see just how simple drafting is for you.

This chapter allows you to gain skills in the following areas:

- Overall drafting process
- Symbols
- Descriptive Data
- Descriptive Data naming rules
- Input Descriptive Data in PDS
- Drafting patterns into the system
- Rules to follow for drafting
- Drafting methods
- Line/Curve drafting procedure

- Making a piece a valid AccuMark piece
- Draft Trace
- Create pieces
- Save a piece in PDS
- Open pieces or models to view in Icon menu

Overview of the Drafting Process

The following is a brief outline of the drafting process so you can get an idea of the big picture, since there are so many details. A detailed procedure is described on page 57.

1. Decide what the Descriptive Data will be.

2. Open PDS.

3. Make sure the piece is on the table; use masking tape for paper patterns and push pins for fabric ones.

4. Select a storage area in which to place the patterns. Use the View>Preferences/Options> Paths tab.

5. Select the Draft Scale function. See Step 2 in the Line/Curve Drafting procedure section on page 58.

6. Select a drafting method: Line/Curve or Sketch Piece.

7. Start drafting the piece in a clockwise direction.

8. Make the pattern piece a valid AccuMark piece by selecting either the Draft Trace or Create Piece function.

9. Input Descriptive Data, including Piece Name, Category, and Description by selecting the Edit Piece Info function. See Step 3 on page 56

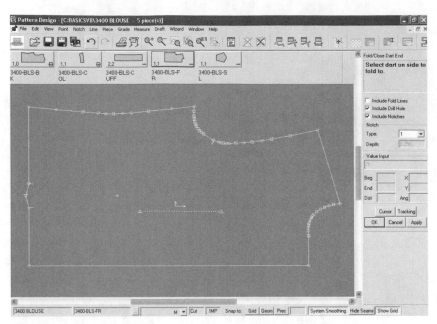

Figure 4.1 Symbols are displayed on a pattern piece in the PDS work area.

require you to use several options that are covered throughout the book. Always save a pattern piece after making any changes you wish to keep.

12. Save a backup copy on a floppy, CD or USB flash drive.

Symbols

Symbols help define point and line segments and appear on pattern pieces that have already been drafted (see Figure 4.1).

These symbols are used to easily view line segments and grading points on patterns. Each symbol has a specific meaning (see Figure 4.2).

Descriptive Data

Every pattern piece has Descriptive Data entered along with it when it is saved. The Piece Name, Piece Category, and Piece Description are collectively referred to as Descriptive Data. Each pattern piece has to have a Piece Name and a Piece Category, but the Piece Description is optional.

and the Line/Curve Drafting Procedure section on page 58.

10. Save the pattern using the Save As function. See Step 18 in the Line/Curve Drafting Procedure section on page 58.

11. Clean up the pattern piece: Straighten lines, soften curves, and so on. This step may

Definitions of Symbols Displayed on Patterns

◇ A diamond shape represents an end point with grading.
An end point represents the beginning or end of a line segment.

△ A triangle represents an end point without grading.
It represents the beginning or end of a line segment.

▽ An upside-down triangle represents an intermediate point with grading.
Intermediate points are found between the beginning and end of a line segment.

▢ A square represents an intermediate point without grading.
These points exist between the beginning and the end of a line segment.

○ A circle represents a system-generated intermediate point without grading.
These points may not be deleted or added.
They are only seen when System Smoothing is turned on.

↱ This symbol is an Orientation symbol.
It represents the direction the pattern was input into the system.

Figure 4.2 Symbols displayed on pattern pieces are defined.

Descriptive Data Naming Rules

- Be consistent. If you abbreviate a word in the Piece Name, then abbreviate it consistently and in the same manner throughout. For example, use either "Frt" or "Fr" for a front; don't use both within a storage area.

- Labeling a Piece Category as "Blouse" does not say what type of piece it is, such as a front or back. Keep your Piece Category labels (whether they are abbreviations or not) consistent with the Piece Name. For example, if the Piece Name is "3400 Sd Frt," the Piece Category should be "Sd Frt." You can also abbreviate in all Piece Names and spell out all Piece Categories.

- Write the Piece Name and Category information onto each pattern piece you manually created. You can also write the information on index cards and tape them onto each pattern (see Figure 4.3).

Defining Descriptive Data

Descriptive Data comprises Piece Name, Piece Category, and Piece Description, each of which is described below.

Piece Name

A Piece Name is commonly composed by combining the model/style name and the type of pattern piece. Figure 4.3 shows an example of two front pattern pieces, whose name is made up of the style number "1230" and the type of pattern piece "Side Front." The following are some points to keep in mind when creating a Piece Name:

- Use a model/style name plus the type of pattern piece.

- Two patterns in the same storage area may not have the same name.

- It is mandatory to have a Piece Name.

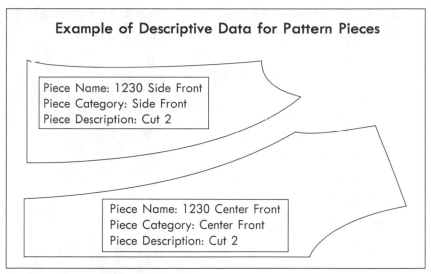

Figure 4.3 Example of Descriptive Data for a front pattern.

- Keep your abbreviations consistent.

- You are allowed to use up to 20 characters, and you can use letters and numbers.

- You can include spaces and dashes, but you cannot use symbols such as ( ), /, [ ], #, or @.

Piece Category

A Piece Category is used to define the type of pattern it is, such as a side or a center front. The following are some points to keep in mind when creating a Piece Category:

- Incorporate the type of pattern piece in the Piece Category.

- Two patterns in a model may not have the same category.

- It is mandatory to have a Piece Category.

- Keep your abbreviations consistent.

- You are allowed to use up to 20 characters, and you can use letters and numbers.

- You can include spaces and dashes, but you cannot use symbols such as ( ), /, [ ], #, or @.

Piece Description

A Piece Description lets you input additional information about a pattern piece. For example, Figure 4.3 shows how a cut number is used in the description field. The following are some points to keep in mind when creating a Piece Description:

- Include any additional information that may serve as a useful reference.

- You can use the same description on other patterns.

- Creating a Piece Description is optional.

- You are allowed to use up to 20 characters, and you can use letters and numbers.

- You can include spaces and dashes, but you cannot use symbols such as ( ), /, [ ], #, or @.

How to Input Descriptive Data in PDS

You should take the following steps when you are done drafting a piece:

1. Make sure a function is not currently active.

2. Right click anywhere in the PDS work area, which activates a menu.

3. Select **Edit Piece Info** (see Figure 4.4). The **Tracking Information** window appears (see Figure 4.5), but the fields are shaded gray.

4. A user input box states: "Select piece with the left button." Left click to select the piece, which highlights it in red. Notice how the fields in the **Tracking Information** window are no longer grayed out.

5. Left click in the field so you can edit it. Repeat the step for all the fields you need to edit.

6. Click **Apply>OK** to enter the piece information.

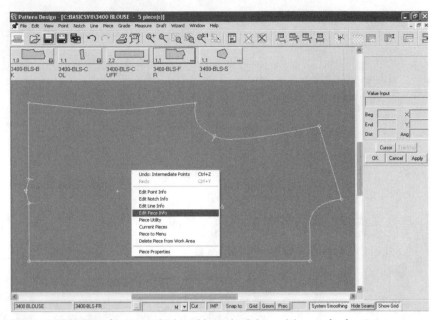

Figure 4.4 Edit Piece function is displayed by right clicking while out of a function.

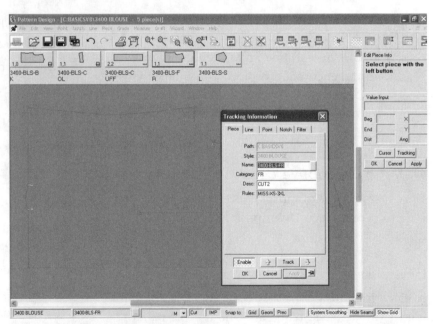

Figure 4.5 Selected piece is shown and the Piece Name field is highlighted for input.

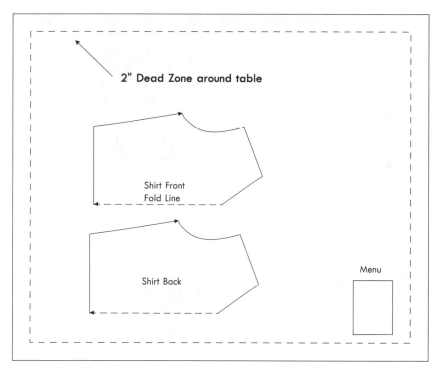

Figure 4.6 Simulation of pattern pieces laid out on a drafting table.

Drafting Patterns into the System

Drafting is the method you use to enter pattern pieces into the system. There are a few rules you need to follow and a couple of methods from which you can select. The following sections will take you through the drafting process.

Rules to Follow When Drafting

- Always draft in a clockwise direction.

- There is a 2-inch dead zone around the whole table. Do not place your patterns in this zone, or they will not fit entirely on-screen.

- When drafting the pieces, make sure they face the same direction, so all necks should face same side.

- If you are working with paper patterns, use masking tape or place it under rehealable plastic. If you are working with fabric patterns, you can use push pins on the existing plastic. The plastic will reheal itself after the push pins are taken out.

- You can draft existing patterns (such as those on oak tag, brown or white paper,

Mylar, or fabric) into the system.

- If the pattern has a fold line, place it at the bottom (see Figure 4.6).

- Never place metal on the table, including keys, the metal rings in binders, and rulers.

- Use your mouse or the pen/stylus. If you use the pen/stylus, then flip the mouse over to avoid flickering on-screen.

- Follow the prompts in the user input box at the top right-hand side of the PDS screen.

- Always start working at the bottom left or right of a pattern piece.

Drafting Methods

You can also draft existing patterns (such as those made on oak tag, brown or white paper, Mylar, or fabric) by using a drafting table. There are two techniques that you can use.

Line/Curve Technique

The Line/Curve method is widely used in the industry because it is the most accurate way to draft a piece into the system. You select points on a pattern piece that is displayed on a drafting table, and the system connects the points to create the shape of the pattern, much like a connect the dots drawing.

Sketch Technique

The Sketch method is used to trace around hard patterns with the pen/stylus such as those made out of Mylar or oak tag. Better? This method is only as accurate as the pattern piece you have cut out. Therefore, if this pattern piece has bumps, the piece you draft using the method will also have the bumps. It is highly recommended that you cut patterns as carefully as possible, although you can always clean up the piece later. The Sketch technique is a quick way to get patterns into the system.

Line/Curve Drafting Procedure

When you draft a pattern into the system, you draft in the piece's perimeter, or outline, first. After you draft the perimeter, you can add drill holes for darts or add reference locations to the piece. As you follow the prompts, notice the one that asks you to select the piece to add to because this is when you enter grain lines, drill holes, and add extra lines. Draft some pattern pieces into the system using the Line/Curve Method as explained below. In this function, left click is the equivalent of pressing down the pen/stylus or clicking the left mouse button. Right click is the equivalent of pressing down the button on the side of the pen/stylus or clicking the right mouse button.

1. Place some piece(s) on the table.

2. Select **Draft>Draft Scale,** which makes the drafting table and PDS screen the same ratio/size.

3. Select **Line/Curve.**

4. Right click and select **Create Draft Piece** (see Figure 4.7).

5. A user input box states: "Press stylus down to select points of line." Press down with the pen/stylus on a point at the bottom left or right of the pattern to start drafting the piece. Continue selecting points around the piece in

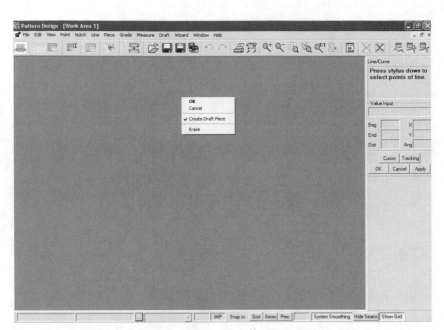

Figure 4.7 Select Create Draft Piece during the Line/Curve function to draft a new piece.

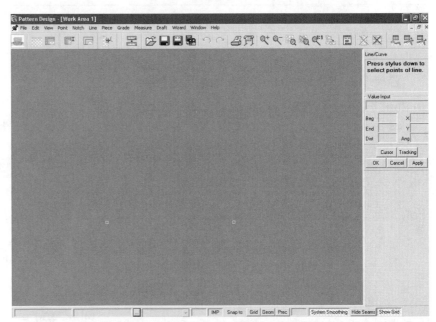

Figure 4.8 Points are selected on the pattern on the drafting table and seen on the PDS screen.

a clockwise direction. The Center Front line is being drafted first in Figure 4.8.

6. Right click the mouse button and select **OK** to connect the points with a line and/or at the corners. You can also change the mode from straight point to curve point and vice versa.

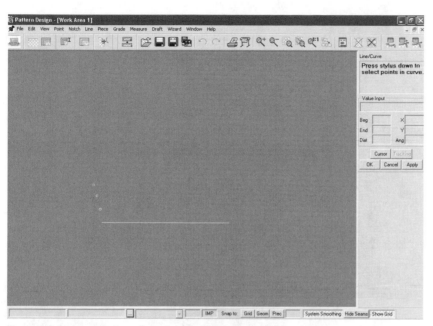

Figure 4.9 Curve mode is used to place curve points along a curved line.

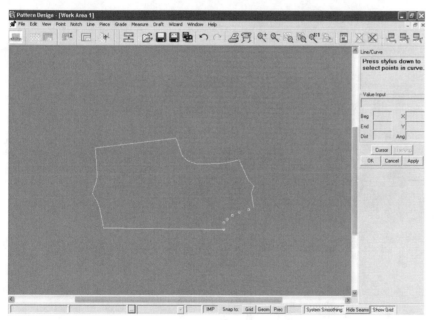

Figure 4.10 Curve points are used for neckline; perimeter is closed when the last point meets the first point.

For smoother, curved lines, always try to use the curve mode (see Figure 4.9).

Keep drafting clockwise all the way to the point where you started. This is the only place where you place one point on top of another. The perimeter or outline of the piece is now finished (see Figure 4.10).

Note: Remember to put down points at the notch locations for darts only. You can add seam notches later, if necessary. To erase any unwanted points, right click and select **Erase** before you right click to connect the points.

7. Right click and select **OK** with the left mouse button (see Figure 4.11).

8. Right click and uncheck **Create a Draft Piece.**

9. A user input box states: "Select piece to add line/curve." Left click to select the piece to which you'll add the line or curve. You may add a grain line now.

10. Draft the grain line. Press down the pen/stylus to select the grain line from the left to the right point (see Figure 4.12). You draft only two points for a grain line. To add additional lines or points to the piece, continue to the next step. If you don't need additional points or lines, right click, select **OK,** right click, and select **Cancel.** Go to step 15 on page 62.

Note: If you draft a grain line from right to left it flips the piece.

11. Right click and select **OK.**

12. A user input box states: "Select the piece to add line/curve" again. You can add points, such as drill holes, or additional lines, at this point. Left click to select the piece to which to add a point or line, which highlights it in red.

13. A user input box states: "Press stylus down to select points of line." To add drill holes, press

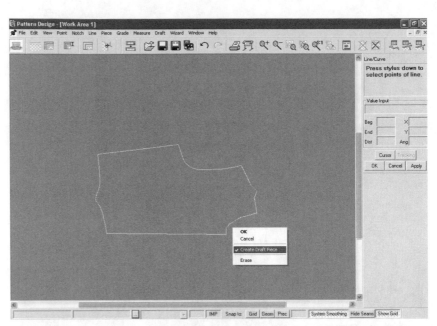

Figure 4.11 Piece perimeter is ended by selecting OK option. De-select Create Draft Piece to add to pattern.

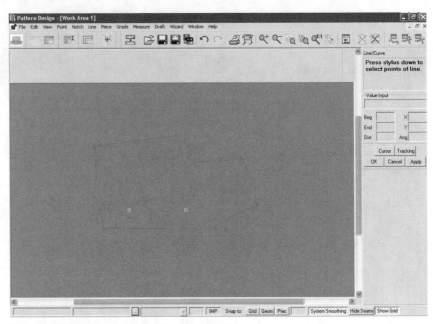

Figure 4.12 Grain line is drafted from left to right on the selected piece.

down the pen/stylus in the middle of the drill hole. Right click and select **OK** (see Figure 4.13). If there is more than one drill hole, repeat steps 11 to 13. When you are done adding drill holes, select **OK** and right click and select **Cancel.**

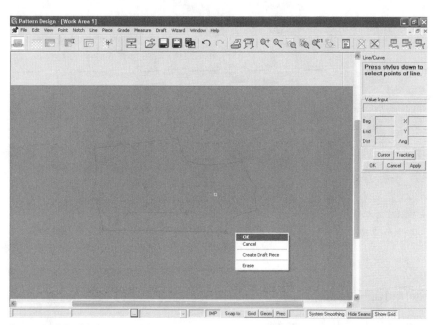

Figure 4.13 Drill holes are added one at a time so they do not connect. Select OK between points.

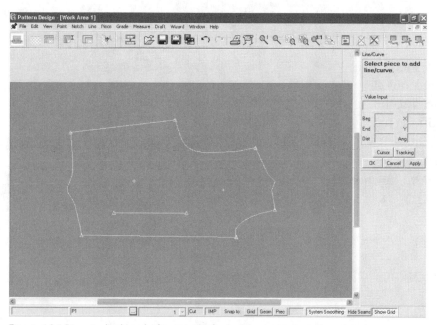

Figure 4.14 Piece is displayed after it is drafted, without an orientation symbol.

Note: Draft each drill hole one at a time so they do not connect to form a line.

14. The piece is now drafted. Notice it does not have an orientation symbol yet (see Figure 4.14) because you must first convert it into a Valid AccuMark Piece.

15. Select **Draft** from the functions toolbar.

16. Select the **Draft Trace** or **Create Piece** function (see Figure 4.15). Draft Trace is recommended for beginners and is discussed in detail below.

17. Input the Descriptive Data for the piece. Exit out of any current function by right clicking until the user input box is empty. Right click and select Edit Piece Info. Refer to the section entitled "How to Input Descriptive Data in PDS" on page 56.

18. Save the piece using the **Save As** function (see Figure 4.16). The piece is now drafted.

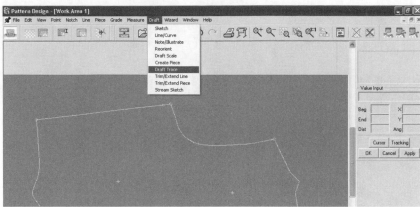

Figure 4.15 Draft Menu is displayed, including Draft Trace and Create Piece functions.

Making the Piece a Valid AccuMark Piece

If you make a piece a Valid AccuMark Piece, you can manipulate it with all the PDS functions. If you don't convert a pattern piece into a Valid AccuMark Piece, then you are limited to certain PDS functions when manipulating a pattern. To convert a piece into a Valid AccuMark Piece use either the Draft Trace or Create Piece function.

Draft Trace

Draft Trace lets you select specific lines. You can ignore unwanted lines or points when using this method. Follow the steps below when using Draft Trace.

1. Select **Draft>Draft Trace** (see Figure 4.17).

2. A user input box states: "Select the perimeter lines to trace, end selection to continue." Left click to create the outline of the pattern piece in a clockwise direction, which highlights the lines in (see Figure 4.18).

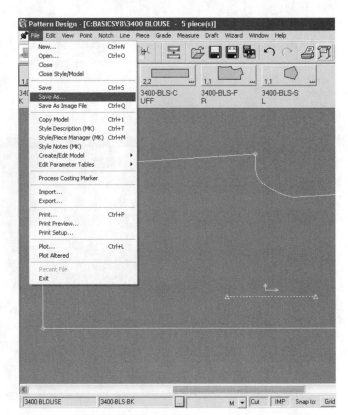

Figure 4.16 Save As function in the File menu is displayed.

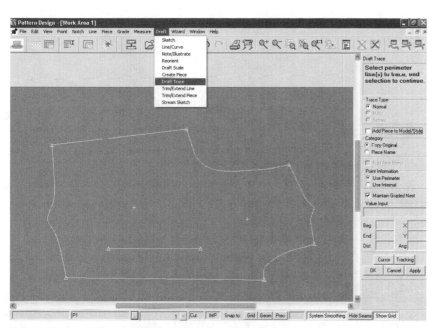

Figure 4.17 Draft Trace function is displayed in the Draft menu.

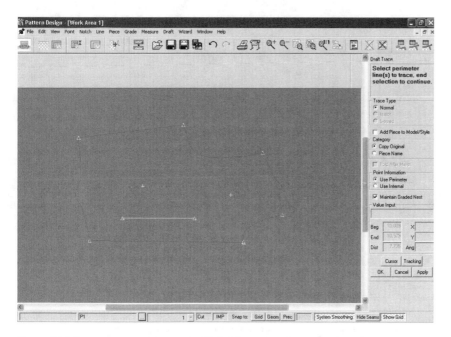

Figure 4.18 Piece perimeter lines are highlighted in red as they are selected.

3. A user input box states: "Select grain line to trace (first will become primary)" (see Figure 4.19). Left click to select the main grain line first, which highlights it in red. Right click and select **OK.** Select any alternate grain lines next. For example, an alternate grain line for grading a lapel on a tailored jacket may exist.

4. A user input box states: "Select internal line(s) and point(s) to trace, end selection to continue." Left click to select any points or lines that you need to include in the drafted piece (see Figure 4.20). If there are no lines or points to select, right click and select **OK.**

5. Move the mouse to separate the piece displays (see Figure 4.21). Left click to set down the piece on-screen.

6. A user input box states: "Enter piece name." Enter the Piece Name and click **OK** or press **Enter** on the keyboard. The piece is now a Valid AccuMark Piece.

7. Right click and select **Cancel** to exit option. Right click and select **Delete Piece from Work Area** (see Figure 4.22) to delete the old draft piece.

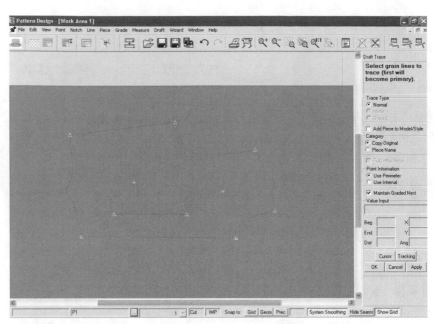

Figure 4.19 Grain line is highlighted in red after it has been selected as the primary grain line.

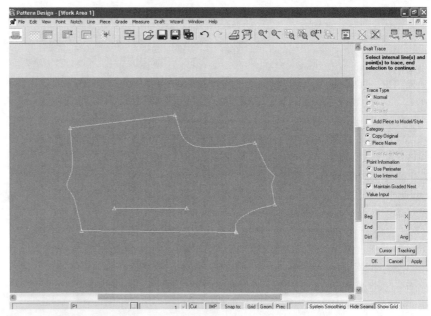

Figure 4.20 Points are selected to add to the drafted piece.

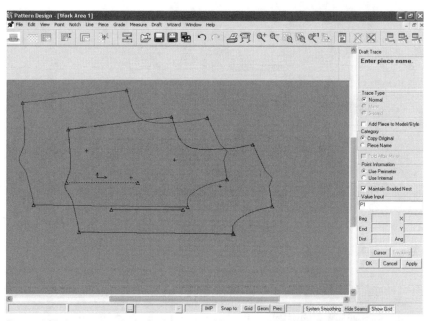

Figure 4.21 A new piece is drafted from an old piece and you must input a name.

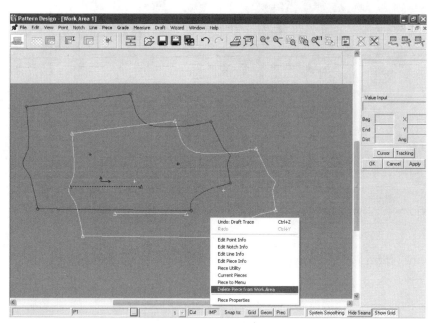

Figure 4.22 Delete Piece from Work Area is used to erase the unwanted draft piece from the screen.

Create Piece

Create Piece lets you select all perimeter lines at once when selecting the piece. If your lines do not connect, a "Line Order Failure" prompt occurs and you might consider using Draft Trace instead. If you need to combine two pieces use the Draft Trace function instead. Follow the steps below when using Create Piece.

1. Select **Draft>Create Piece** (see Figure 4.23).

2. A user input box states: "Select piece to create." Left click to select the piece.

3. A user input box states: "Select Grain lines, first will become primary." Left click to select the main grain line and continue left clicking to select additional lines. Right click if you want the system to create one for you.

   Note: If the piece is off grain, the grain line will be off grain too.

4. A user input box states "Select lines to become internal lines." Left click to select lines such as drill holes or additional annotation lines. If you don't need to select any, go to the next step.

5. Right click and select **OK.**

6. A user input box states: "Enter Piece Name." Input name in the user input box under **Value Input.** Click **OK** or press **Enter** on the keyboard. The piece is now a Valid AccuMark Piece.

How to Save a Piece in PDS

Always save a pattern piece after you create or draft it, or after you have edited it. Saving the piece

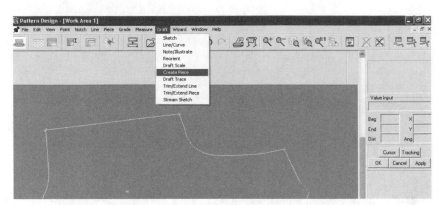

Figure 4.23 Create Piece is found in the Draft menu.

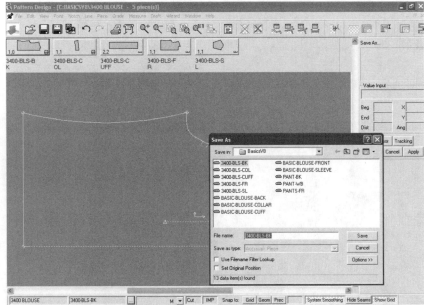

Figure 4.24 Save As window appears when a piece is selected to be saved

allows you to store it in a storage area for later use.

Procedure to save a piece

1. Select **File>Save As.**

2. A user input box states: "Select the piece to Save As." Left click to select the piece and save it.

3. The **Save As** window appears (see Figure 4.24). Select the storage area in which you want to save it by using the drop-down menu in the **Save In** field. Enter the name of the piece in the **File Name** field.

4. Click **Save** to finish.

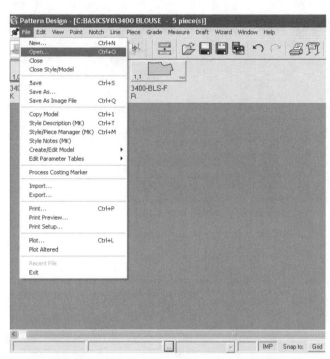

Figure 4.25 The Open function to bring pieces to the Icon menu is found in the File menu.

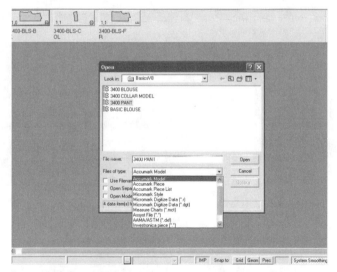

Figure 4.26 Open window appears so you can select models or pieces from a storage area.

Opening Pieces or Models to View in the Icon Menu

You can open pieces or models to manipulate them or confirm that data has been input properly. Follow the steps below when opening a model or piece in PDS:

1. Select File.

2. Select Open or click the yellow Open folder icon (see Figure 4.25).

3. The Open window appears. Use the drop-down menu in the Look In field to select a storage area from which to open pieces or models (see Figure 4.26). Use the drop-down menu in the File of Type field to select a

Drafting Pattern Pieces Using Pattern Design System

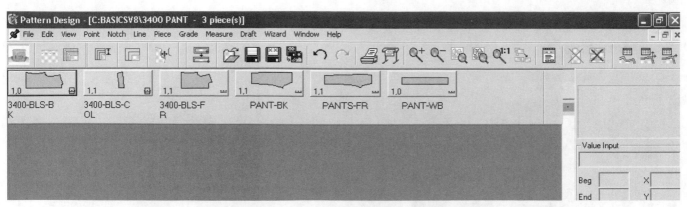

Figure 4.27 Icon menu with pieces opened.

model or piece to open. Select **AccuMark Model** to list models from which you can select. Select **AccuMark Piece** to list pieces from which you can select.

4. Select pieces or models from the listed items. Click **Open** to open the pieces or models; they open in the Icon menu (see Figure 4.27).

Key Terms

Create Piece: Function used to make a piece a Valid AccuMark Piece. It does not let you select individual perimeter and internal lines nor internal points, but rather all perimeter lines at the same time. You must clear intersection of all lines and have no gaps for this function to work successfully.

Descriptive Data: Comprises Piece Name, Piece Category, and Piece Description. Each piece you save requires its own Piece Name and Piece Category. The Piece Description field is optional.

Draft Scale: Function that makes the table surface and on-screen display the same proportion

Draft Trace: Function used to make a piece a Valid AccuMark Piece. It lets you select perimeter and internal lines, internal points, and grain lines.

Drafting: Procedure that allows you to input pattern pieces into the system for future pattern manipulation and plotting.

Edit Piece Info: Function used to input Descriptive data for a piece.

Line/Curve: Method of drafting commonly used in the industry. It allows you to enter the perimeter and internals of a pattern piece made from paper, fabric, or oak tag by placing points down, which turn into line segments. It resembles a connect-the-dots drawing.

Pen/stylus: Device used to draft in pieces. If configured, it may be used as an alternative to the mouse for some functions.

Sketch: Method of drafting that utilizes the pen/stylus as a pencil tool to trace a pattern. It is commonly used with patterns made out of oak tag or Mylar and may be used to sketch patterns by hand.

Symbols: Geometry that helps define point and line segments. They show up after you have drafted a piece or on a piece that you have opened from a storage area. They are in the shape of a squares, diamonds, triangles, or upside-down triangles.

Valid AccuMark Piece: If a piece is not made into a Valid AccuMark Piece, the functions available for you to manipulate a pattern are limited. Use Draft Trace or Create Piece to convert a draft piece into a Valid AccuMark Piece.

Test Your Knowledge

Fill in the blanks for the following review questions.

1. Two ways to make a piece a Valid AccuMark Piece are _____ and _____.
2. Which one of the two methods to create a Valid AccuMark Piece is recommended for beginners?
3. Name the different methods of drafting.
4. Describe the symbols that appear on a piece.
5. Draft Scale makes the _____ and the _____ the same proportion.
6. Identify the mandatory Descriptive Data on a piece.
7. How many characters can each area of Descriptive Data contain?
8. Which drafting method is most commonly used in the industry? Why?
9. After drafting a piece into the system, why is it necessary to make the piece a Valid AccuMark Piece?
10. Why should you not place a piece in the 2-inch Dead Zone of the drafting table?

Test Your Skills

1. Select a basic sloper to draft, such as a bodice. Establish proper grain lines.
2. Give each piece Descriptive Data. You may use index cards or write data directly onto each pattern for easy access.
3. Save each piece into the storage area of your choice or in the DATA70 storage area.
4. Open pattern pieces to confirm they are saved properly.

Note: You may use a fabric pattern instead of a basic sloper for the above exercise, such as a knockoff garment. The beginning drafter will need this to be a fabric pattern that can lay totally flat on the table. You may tape or pin it down on the table or place it underneath rehealable plastic.

CHAPTER FIVE

Basic Cleanup Functions in PDS That Follow Drafting

Objective

This chapter teaches you how to clean up pieces after you draft them into the system. This includes simple tasks, such as making straight lines and placing patterns on the fold. More advanced tasks to manipulate patterns are discussed in chapters 8–10.

This chapter allows you to gain skills in the following areas:

- Intermediate Points
- Align Points
- Add Notches
- Mirror Piece
- Fold Mirror
- Unfold Mirror
- Open Mirror
- Define/Add Seam
- Swap Sew/Cut
- Delete Points
- Combine/Merge Lines
- Split Lines
- Create Rectangle

Intermediate Points

The Intermediate Points function is available in the View menu. It allows you to display all the points of a piece on-screen, including end, intermediate, and grading points. Smooth points are

also shown if you select System Smoothing in the toolbar at the bottom of the PDS screen.

Intermediate Points is just like the All Points function (Chapter 3), except that the points remain displayed until you turn them off, so that you may work on other functions while they are visible (see Figure 5.1).

Use Intermediate Points when

- you need to view and select points to delete.
- you need to modify points using functions such as Move Smooth or Move Pt Line/Slide.

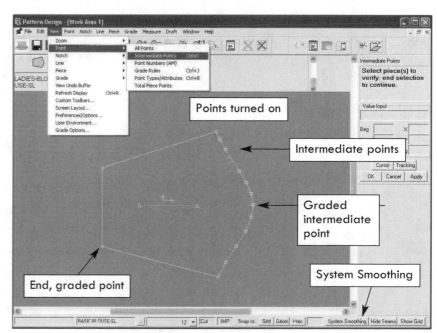

Figure 5.1 Sleeve pattern with intermediate points turned on.

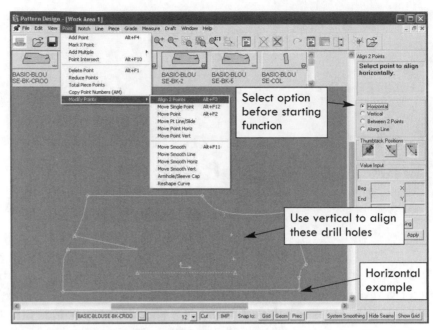

Figure 5.2 Drill holes and center front points need to be aligned.

Procedure for Intermediate Points

1. Select **View>Points>Intermediate Points.**

2. A user input box states: "Select piece(s) to verify, end selection to continue." Left click to select the pieces which highlights them in red.

3. Right click and select **OK** to display all points.

Note: If you want to turn off the points so they are no longer displayed, follow the same steps again. The symbols used to represent points are discussed in Chapter 4.

Align 2 Points

Align 2 Points is used to align one point to another. Think of it as trying to line up a group of children in a single-file.

Use Align 2 Points when

- you need to fix a crooked line. After you draft a piece into the system, you may notice that it isn't straight, even though you drafted in only two points. This error usually occurs because when you place points during the drafting process, one point may have ended up slightly below or above the point at the other end (see Figure 5.2).

Note: The center back of a basic skirt is usually straight and has notches for zipper placement. When using the Align 2 Points function, you may notice that the line is not straight when you align the waist point with the hem point. If this happens, just align the notches, as well.

- you need to align drill holes or other points used for pattern placement purposes. Figure 5.2 shows an example of drill holes used for pocket placement that need to be aligned.

Procedure to align points

1. Select **Points>Modify Points>Align 2 Points.**

2. Select one of the four options in the user input box.

   Horizontal is used to align one point to another horizontally—a horizontal line.

   Vertical is used to align one point to another vertically—a vertical line.

   Between 2 Points is used to align a point to two other points.

   Along Line is used to move a point along another line.

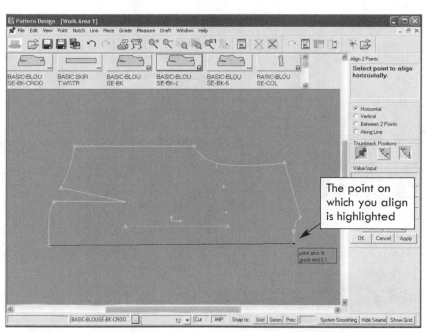

Figure 5.3 Bodice illustrating point to align horizontally

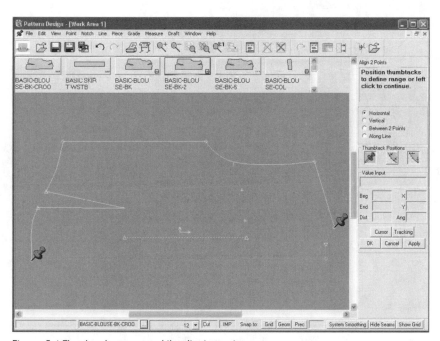

Figure 5.4 Thumbtacks appear while aligning points.

3. A user input box states: "Select point to align horizontally." With the left mouse button click and drag to the point you want to move until it is highlighted and release the button (see Figure 5.3).

Note: Remember that it is generally wise to work with more fabric than you need since it is better to cut away excess than to add fabric. So select the point that will make the piece wider or longer.

4. A user input box states: "Position thumbtacks to define range or left click to continue." Left click to accept the thumbtack location or to move the thumbtacks (see Figure 5.4).

Place the mouse over a thumbtack so the plus sign becomes an asterisk.

Press the left mouse button to pick up the thumbtack.

Move the mouse to the location in which you want to place the thumbtack.

Left click to set the thumbtack in place.

5. A user input box states: "Select the reference point." Left click to select a reference point. This is the point you need to align with the point you selected in Step 3 (see Figure 5.5).

6. The points are aligned, and in this case, the line is straight.

Note: If the line is not straight, then you just need to align or delete other points in the line.

Adding Notches

As discussed in Chapter 2, notches are used for seam allowance, darts, pleats, and gathering. When using the Add Notch function, the Notch Table—from where the piece originates—serves as the reference for the notch type. For example, if Notch 1 in the Notch Table is a V-notch, then a V-notch will plot, when you select Notch 1 as the Notch Type.

Procedure to add a notch

1. Select **Notch>Add Notch.**

2. Select the Notch Type by using the drop-down menu next to **Type** under **Notch** (see Figure 5.6).

3. A user input box states: "Indicate the notch position." Select the location/point where you would like to create a notch with the left mouse button and release it to add the notch.

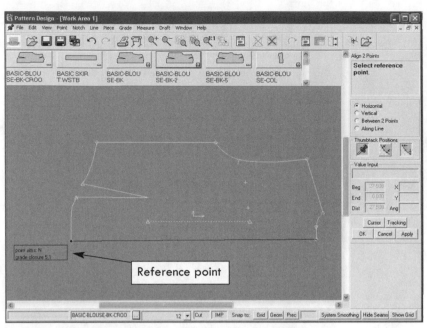

Figure 5.5 Reference point selected in aligning points of a bodice.

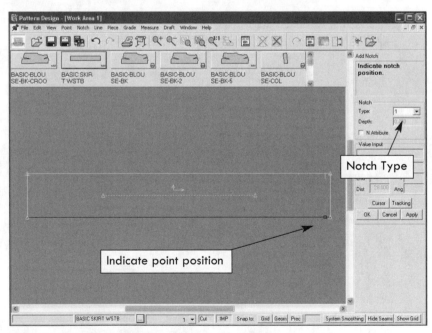

Figure 5.6 Notch position is indicated on a waistband.

Procedure to Add Notch at a specific location

1. Select **Notch>Add Notch.**

2. Select the Notch Type.

3. A user input box states: "Indicate the notch position." To add the notch to the line you want, hold the left and right mouse buttons

down at the same time and then release them both. This technique is known as a **popup.**

4. The **Beg** and **End** fields in the user input box light up (see Figure 5.7). Select either Beg or End and type in the measurement for the notch placement. An arrow lights up according to the field you highlighted.

5. Click **OK** or hit **Enter** on the keyboard. The notch is added at the specified measurement.

Note: In step 4, if you right click and select **Midpoint** from the menu, you may select a line to which you will add a notch, and it will be placed in the middle of the line. This option may be used in other functions as well.

Angled Notch

When you create a notch, the notch is perpendicular, or 90 degrees, to the point you selected. Sometimes you need to show a notch at a different angle, and the Angled Notch function allows you to change the angle.

You may use this function to add a notch as well as change the angle of an existing notch. Make sure to select an existing notch by highlighting the point and reading the point information box that lights up. If you do not select a notch, and simply select a location, then you'll add a new notch that you may angle at the same time, thereby making this function a combination of the Add Notch and Angled Notch functions.

Use Angled Notch when

- you need to direct a notch toward a dart point/apex.
- you need to match the angle of a seam where the corner is not squared.

Procedure to angle notches

1. Select **Notch>Angled Notch** (see Figure 5.8).

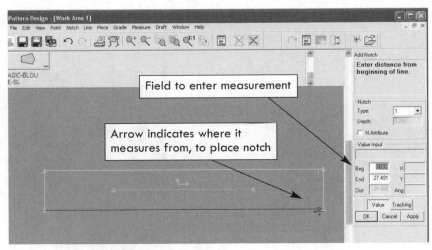

Figure 5.7 Enter distance to add a notch.

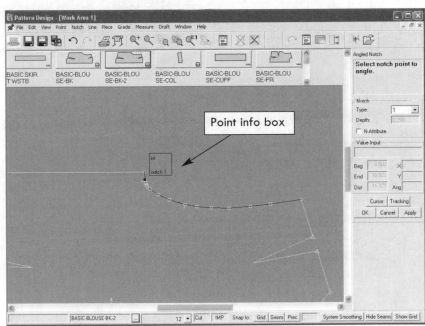

Figure 5.8 Notch point to angle is selected.

2. Select Notch Type.

Note: If you are changing the angle of an existing type 2 notch, and the notch type is set to 1, then the type 2 notch will change to a type 1.

3. A user input box states: "Select notch point to angle." Click and drag with the left mouse button to select the point and release. Read the point information box to ensure you selected the notch point.

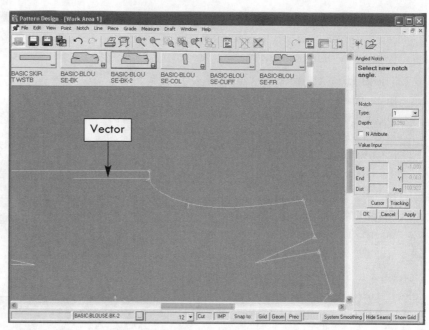

Figure 5.9 Vector is used to select angle of notch.

4. A vector, controlled by the mouse, is active to let you set the notch angle (see Figure 5.9).

5. A user input states: "Select new notch angle." Left click to set the angle.

Mirror Piece

The Mirror Piece function is used to place a piece "on the fold." A basic skirt front is an example of a piece that is mirrored. When manipulating a mirrored piece, always work with it while it is folded so that it remains symmetrical on both sides. A curved seam is not typically mirrored.

While performing this function, you have the option to either fold the piece after it is mirrored or leave it unfolded. Fold the piece after you mirror it so you can continue to manipulate it while keeping the modifications symmetrical, or simply save it in the next step, and the system folds it automatically. Patternmakers opt to leave pieces unfolded when they want to make sure the fold location has the correct shape. For example, when you fold the center front of a skirt, you leave the piece unfolded to make sure the waistline retains the proper shape.

Procedure for Mirror Piece

    1. Select **Piece>Mirror Piece.**

2. Select options in the user input box first.

3. In the **Fold Options** area, check the box next to **Fold after Mirror** to fold the pattern piece after you mirror it.

4. In the **Notch Mirror Line** area, customize each option to your preference.

Select **None** if you do not want any notches on the mirror line. If you select this option, you should not select any other options in this area.

The **Notches (AM)** option lets you choose from two possible locations on a mirrored line: Single End and Both Ends. Select **Single End** when you need to notch only one end of the mirror line. The system will prompt you to select the preferred end if you select this option. Select **Both Ends** when you need to notch both ends of the mirror line.

5. In the **Notch Type** area, select the notch type by activating the drop-down menu. This area is available only if you have selected to notch the mirror line.

6. A user input box states: "Select mirror line on piece(s) to mirror, end selection to continue."

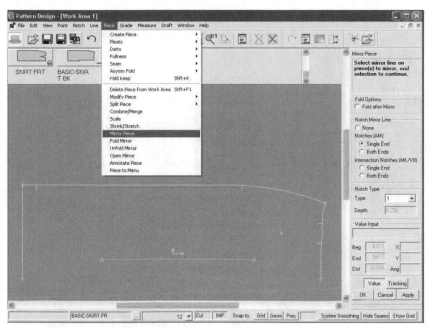

Figure 5.10 Line selected for a fold on mirrored piece.

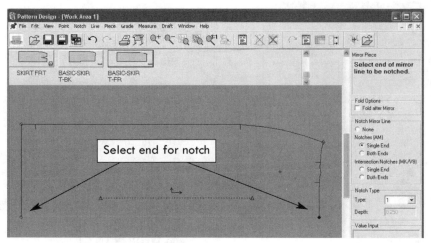

Figure 5.11 Select point to receive notch.

Left click to select a line, which highlights it in red (see Figure 5.10).

7. Right click and select **OK** to mirror the piece. The dashed line represents the mirrored line.

   Note: If you are adding notches to the mirrored line on a single end, continue to the next step.

8. A user input box states: "Select end of mirror line to be notched." Left click to select the point at the end of the line that needs to be notched (see Figure 5.11).

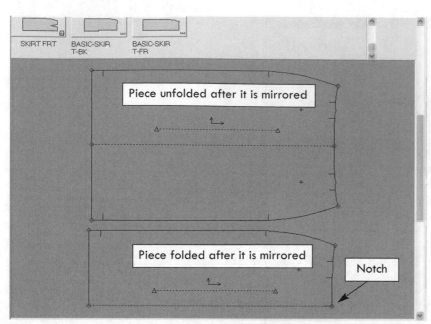

Figure 5.12 Mirrored piece displayed unfolded and folded.

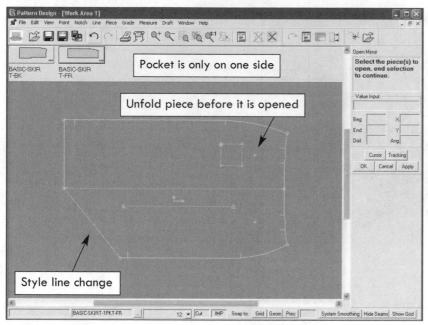

Figure 5.13 Example of a skirt opened with Open Mirror.

The piece is mirrored with a notch. The dashed line represents the mirrored line. Figure 5.12 shows a mirrored skirt, an example of a piece that is folded and unfolded after it has been mirrored.

Fold Mirror

The Fold Mirror function is used to fold a mirrored piece that has been unfolded. Use this function when you need to manipulate further and you want to keep the pattern symmetrical.

Procedure for Fold Mirror

1. Select **Piece>Fold Mirror.**

2. A user input box states: "Select piece(s) to fold, end selection to continue." Left click to select the pieces. Which highlights them in red.

3. Right click button and select **OK** to fold the piece.

Unfold Mirror

The Unfold Mirror function is used to unfold a pattern that was folded. Use the Unfold Mirror function to make sure seam lines, such as necklines or waistbands, are shaped properly.

Procedure for Unfold Mirror

1. Select **Piece>Unfold Mirror.**

2. A user input box states: "Select mirrored piece(s) to unfold, end selection to continue." Left click to select the pieces, which highlights them in red.

3. Right click button and select **OK** to unfold the piece.

Open Mirror

The Open Mirror function is not the same as the Unfold Mirror function. A piece that has been opened cannot be folded or unfolded and is, therefore, not considered an "on the fold" pattern.

Use Open Mirror when

- you are working on a pattern that is primarily symmetrical with the exception of a pocket on one side.

- you are working on a piece that is mostly the same on both sides but you want to make a style line change (see Figure 5.13).

Procedure for Open Mirror

1. Select **Piece>Open Mirror.**

2. A user input box states: "Select the piece to open, end selection to continue." Left click to select the piece, which highlights it in red.

3. Right click and select **OK** to open the piece.

Note: If the piece is folded before you perform the Open Mirror function, the piece will appear folded and the mirror line will appear as a solid line. You cannot unfold the same piece.

Define/Add Seam

Seam allowance is added to a pattern after it is created. The Define/Add Seam function lets you add seam allowance to a pattern piece, as you would manually, with a C-Thru ruler. For fastest results, select all the lines on one piece, or even several pieces, to add the same amount of seam allowance at the same time.

Procedure for Define/Add Seam

1. Select **Piece>Seam>Define/Add Seam.**

2. Select your preference from the user input box.

Manual Even lets you keep the seam allowance parallel to the cut line at the same amount from the beginning to the end of the line. This is the most commonly used option.

Manual Uneven lets you make the seam allowance one width at one end of the line and another width at the other end (see Figure 5.14).

3. A user input box states: "Select line(s) or piece(s) for seam allowance, end selection to continue." Left click to select lines or pieces, which highlights them in red. You may select more than one line on a piece and more than one piece at a time.

4. Right click and select **OK** (see Figure 5.15).

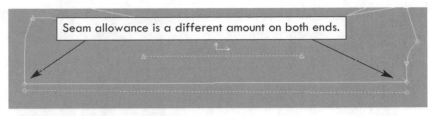

Figure 5.14 Example of uneven seam allowance.

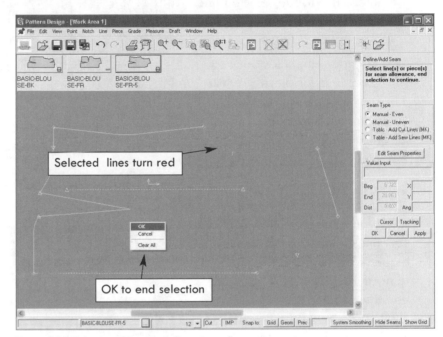

Figure 5.15 Selection of lines to define seam allowance.

5. A user input box states: "Enter seam allowance amount." Enter the seam allowance you want to add to the piece in the **Value Input** field (see Figure 5.16).

6. Click **OK** to add seam allowance to the selected lines or pieces (see Figure 5.17).

7. The function restarts so you can add seam allowance to other lines or pieces, repeat step If you are done adding seam allowance, go to the next step.

8. Right click and select **Cancel.**

Swap Sew/Cut

After you add seam allowance, the sew lines appear on the outside of the pattern. To finish the pattern, perform the Swap Sew/Cut function after adding the seam allowance so that the cut line is outside the piece and the sew line is inside.

If you are done adding seam allowance and applying the Swap Sew/Cut function and you still need to manipulate the piece, use the Swap Sew/Cut function to swap the sew lines back to the outside of the piece.

Procedure for Swap Sew/Cut

1. Select **Piece>Seam>Swap Sew/Cut.**

2. A user input box states: "Select piece(s) to swap sew/cut, end selection to continue." Left click to select the piece, which highlights it in red (see Figure 5.18).

3. Right click and select **OK** to swap the lines (see Figure 5.19).

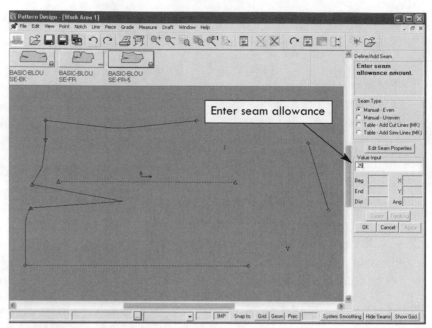

Figure 5.16 Seam amount entered for seam allowance.

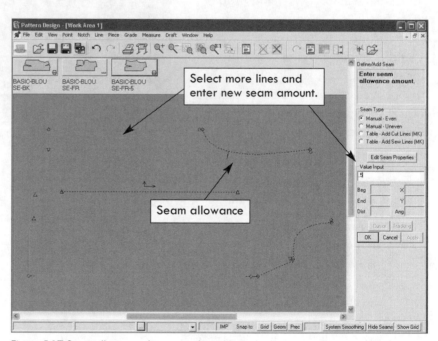

Figure 5.17 Seam allowance shown on selected lines.

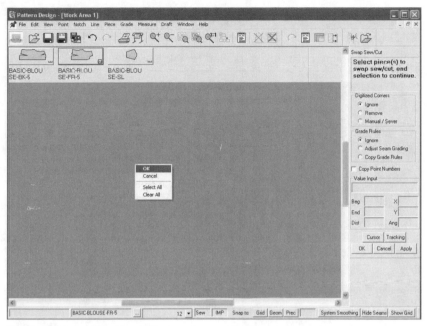

Figure 5.18 Seam allowance is displayed around bodice.

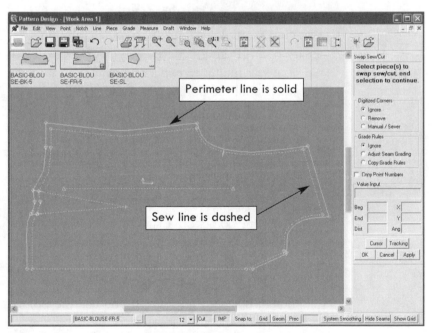

Figure 5.19 Swap/Sew Cut completed on a bodice.

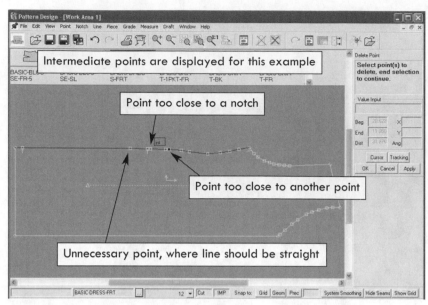

Figure 5.20 Point is selected for deletion.

Delete Point

Use the Delete Point function to delete any unnecessary points from a pattern. You can select individual points or multiple points by creating a marquee box around all the points you want to delete.

Use the Delete Point function when

- there is a superfluous amount of points.

- a point is right next to a notch point. Having a point right next to a V-notch may cause the notch to close considerably (see Figure 5.20).

- there are points on a straight line. There is no need for points on a line that should be straight unless it is a notch.

- you have used **Delete Notch** to delete a notch, but not the point. If you use the point where the notch is located to form a curve, then do not delete the point.

Procedure to delete points

1. Select **Point>Delete Point.**

2. A user input box states: "Select point(s) to delete, end selection to continue." Left click to select the point, which highlights them in red. To create a marquee box around a group of points you want to delete, do the following:

a. left click right outside of the points and release.

b. move the mouse pointer. Control the size of the box with the mouse.

c. left click again to finish the box and enclose the points, you want to delete.

3. Right click and select **OK** to delete the points.

Combine/Merge Lines

The Combine/Merge function is used to make two or more line segments form one solid line. Lines that you want to combine or merge should be next to each other. A line segment endpoint is represented by a triangle or a diamond shape.

Use Combine/Merge when

- lines such as the hem on the shorts in Figure 5.21, should be one line segment so that you can manipulate it as one line. For example, to lengthen or shorten a hem line, you would need to merge it.

- internal line segments that were copied from another pattern as separate lines need to be one continuous style line (see Figure 5.21) is an example of a style line.

Procedure to combine/merge lines

1. Select **Line>Modify Line>Combine/Merge.**

2. A user input box states: "Select line(s) to merge, if internals select near beginning points, end selection to continue." Left click to select perimeter lines, which highlights them in red.

3. Right click and select **OK** to merge the lines (see Figure 5.22).

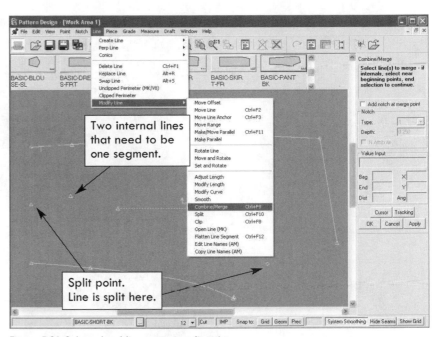

Figure 5.21 Selected red lines contain split points.

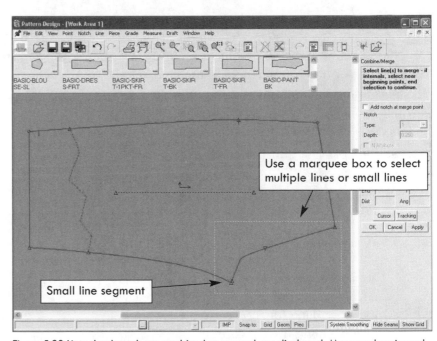

Figure 5.22 Lines that have been combined or merged are displayed. Marquee box is used.

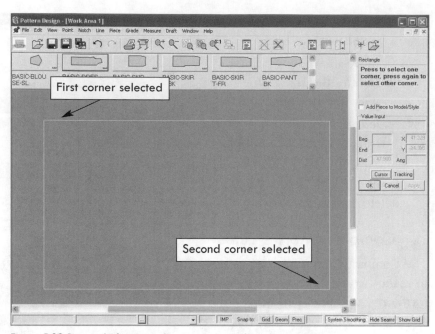

Figure 5.23 Rectangle function indicating corners selected.

Split Line

The Split Line function is sometimes known as the opposite of the Combine/Merge function since it splits a line segment into one or more line segments. When a line is split, a triangle or a diamond shape is displayed.

Use the Split Line function when

- you want to split the corners of a pattern to separate the line segments. Corners of patterns are normally split.

- you want to isolate a line segment to perform another function. For example, when you create a circle, you may wish to split a part of the circle. You can then copy the split area with the Copy Line function to create an armhole or a neckline on a bodice.

Procedure for Split Line

1. Select **Line>Modify Line>Split.**

2. A user input box states: "Select point to split line." Left click to select the location or point to split the line. Perform a **popup** to enter an exact location for the split. To perform a popup, hold down the left and right mouse buttons at the same time over the line you want to split and release both.

Rectangle

The Rectangle function is used to create rectangle or square patterns.

Use the Rectangle function when

- you need to create waistbands.

- you need to create pockets.

- you need to create a piece from scratch, as when using the flat patternmaking technique.

- you need to create any other square or rectangular patterns, such as table cloths, placemats, and pillows.

Procedure to create a rectangle

1. Select **Piece>Create Piece>Rectangle.**

2. A user input box states: "Press to select one corner, press again to select other corner" (see Figure 5.23). To create the corners, do the following:

   a. Press down the left mouse button and release to create the first one.

   b. Move the mouse to adjust the shape of the rectangle.

   c. Left click again to create the other corner and then the entire rectangle.

3. A user input box states: "Enter piece name." Type the piece name in the area that is highlighted (see Figure 5.24).

Note: Next you should save the piece, add Descriptive Data, and continue any further pattern manipulation.

Procedure to create a rectangle with measurements

1. Select **Piece>Create Piece>Rectangle.**

2. A user input box states: "Press to select one corner, press again to select other corner." Press down the left mouse button and release to create the first corner.

3. Press **Cursor** in the user input box or use the popup technique to change from cursor mode to value mode (see Figure 5.25).

   The X, Y, and Dist fields are active in the **Value Input** area. X and Y are the fields most commonly used.

   X is the horizontal or length measurement.

   Y is the vertical or width measurement.

   Dist is the diagonal distance from one corner to the other.

4. Enter the measurements and click **OK** to create the rectangle.

5. A user input box states: "Enter piece name." Type the piece name in the area that is highlighted and click **OK.**

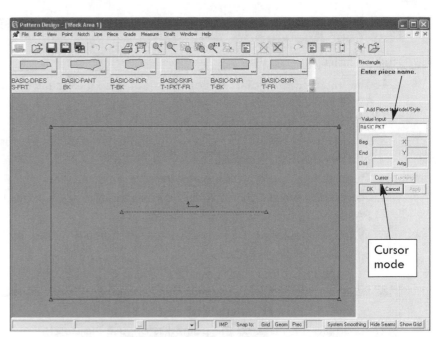

Figure 5.24 Enter a piece name for the Rectangle function.

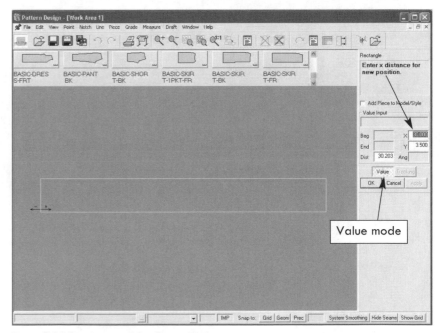

Figure 5.25 Size is entered for the rectangle.

Test Your Knowledge

True or False

1. The Intermediate Points option does not keep the points turned on. TRUE or FALSE

2. Align points may be used to align notches. TRUE or FALSE

3. To perform a popup, press down both the left and right mouse buttons and release. TRUE or FALSE

4. The function Angle Notch cannot create a notch. TRUE or FALSE

5. To place a piece "on the fold," you use the Mirror function. TRUE or FALSE

6. When manipulating a mirrored piece, you should work with it while it is unfolded. TRUE or FALSE

7. An "opened" piece may be folded. TRUE or FALSE

8. When adding seam allowance, the Manual Even option keeps the seam parallel to the perimeter. TRUE or FALSE

9. To delete a notch and the point it is on, use the Delete Point function. TRUE or FALSE

10. Most corners on a pattern are merged or intermediate points. TRUE or FALSE

CHAPTER SIX

Set Up Model Editor

Objective

This chapter teaches you how to set up a Model Editor. A Model Editor is the computerized version of a cutter's must. It contains a list of pattern pieces used to create a garment. For example, the Model Editor for a basic skirt includes the front, back, waistband, and fusing for the waistband. So, each one of those couture dresses you plan to create needs a Model Editor. You save each Model Editor under the style name that you are visualizing at this time.

A model is a way to keep styles filed in your system. These models are referred to later for the production of a marker and for the garment's eventual construction. By the end of this chapter, you should understand what a model is, as well as how to create, open, and save it into the system using existing pieces.

This chapter allows you to gain skills in the following areas:

- Define a Model Editor
- Open a Model Editor
- Create a Model Editor
- Save and name a Model Editor

Definition of Model Editor

A Model Editor is equivalent to a cutter's must, the only difference being that it is created as a form on Gerber software. All pattern pieces used to create a style are included in a Model Editor. These pattern pieces may include self, lining, fusing, and contrast pieces.

You should create a Model Editor for each *garment*, not each *pattern piece*. For example, a Model Editor for a jacket would include front and back patterns, a sleeve, a collar, and pocket patterns as well as any lining and fusing used for its construction. A Model Editor would not be created for each pattern piece such as the sleeve or a collar; otherwise, there would be countless Model Editors.

The **browse button** allows you to view and select pieces that you have already input and saved into the system. It's a small square at the far right of a field when the field is selected. When you use the browse button, it's known as a **lookup,** which is why it's best to fill in the Model Editor after you create pieces to prevent any spelling errors.

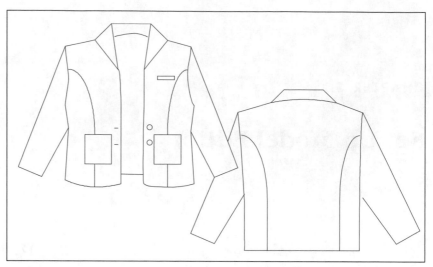

Figure 6.1 Front and back view of a jacket.

Cutter's Must

Style: 4321 Jacket
Fabric: Wool   Color: Navy
Description: Navy sports jacket

SELF:	
4321 Jacket Front	2
4321 Jacket Side Front	2
4321 Jacket Back	2
4321 Jacket Side Back	2
4321 Jacket Sleeve	2
4321 Jacket Collar	2
4321 Jacket Pocket	2
4321 Jacket Breast Pocket	1

LINING:	
4321 Jacket Front Lining	2
4321 Jacket Side Front Lining	2
4321 Jacket Back Lining	2
4321 Jacket Side Back Lining	2
4321 Jacket Sleeve Lining	2

NOTIONS:
2-$\frac{3}{4}$" Buttons

FUSING:	
4321 Jacket Collar	2

Figure 6.2 "Cutter's Must" example used for the jacket in Figure 6.1.

A technical drawing of a jacket is seen in Figure 6.1. The Cutter's Must seen in Figure 6.2 displays all the pieces needed to create the jacket, which is included in the Model Editor.

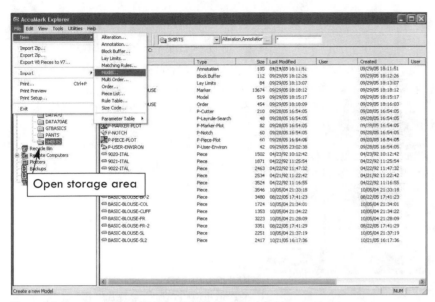

Figure 6.3 Opening a Model Editor using the AccuMark Explorer program.

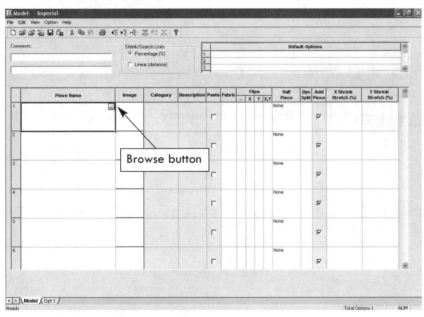

Figure 6.4 Display of a blank Model Editor.

How to Open a Model Editor

A Model Editor may be opened in several ways. Two possible ways are through the AccuMark Explorer or from the Gerber Launch Pad. To open a Model Editor from AccuMark Explorer, follow the steps below (see Figure 6.3):

1. Open **AccuMark Explorer.**

2. Select the storage area where you will create and store the Model Editor. Look under device "C." Left click on the storage area to select.

3. Select **File>New>Model.**

4. The Model Editor opens (see Figure 6.4), so you can fill it in and save it.

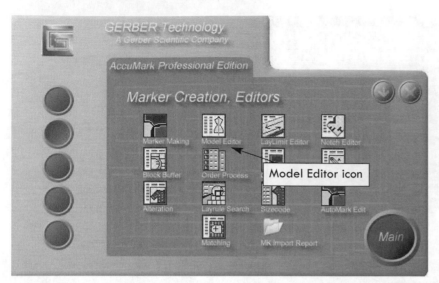

Figure 6.5 The Model Editor may be opened using the Gerber Launch Pad.

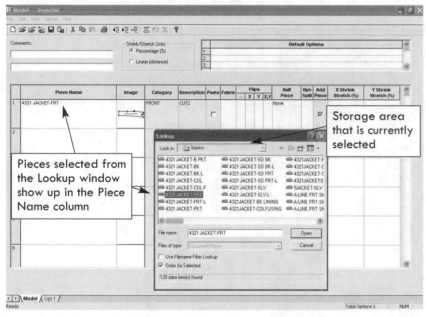

Figure 6.6 Lookup window is used for selection of pieces in the Model Editor.

To open a Model Editor from the Gerber Launch Pad, follow the steps below.

1. Go to the **Gerber Launch Pad.**

2. Select the second radio button labeled **Marker Creation, Editors.**

3. Double click on the **Model Editor** icon (see Figure 6.5) to open it.

How to Create a Model Editor

After you open the Model Editor, you can fill in the appropriate fields. Every column in the Model Editor does not have to be filled out, unless it is needed for company information or proper processing of a marker. For example, while the "Piece Name," "- ," and "X" or "Y" columns are needed to complete a Model Editor, other areas such as "Half Piece," "Dyn Split," "X and/or Y Shrink Stretch" are options that may or may not be needed according to the marker layout circumstances. To hide a column that you do not need to display, right click on the field under the column you wish to hide, and select the option Hide Column from the menu. The jacket in Figure 6.1 is the style used to create a Model Editor for this section.

Comments Use this area for any extra information about the model, such as spec number or button or zipper sizes. You are allowed up to 40 characters.

Piece Name Starting with row 1, select the browse button. This button brings up a window labeled **Lookup** with the pieces that currently exist in the storage area selected (see Figure 6.6). Left click to select the pieces that you want to include in the Model Editor. Click **Open** to enter the pieces in the rows under the Piece Name column.

Note: You can select more than one pattern piece at a time. Holding down the Shift key on the keyboard while clicking with the left mouse button lets you select a group of pieces. Holding down the Ctrl key while clicking the left mouse button lets you select scattered pieces.

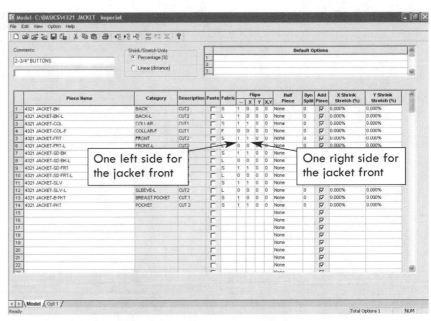

Figure 6.7 A Model Editor is completed for the jacket shown in Figure 6.1.

Image This column displays an image of the pattern piece selected in the Piece Name column. It is a tool that helps you make sure the correct piece is saved with the proper name.

Category This column displays the category of the pattern piece selected in the Piece Name column. You can use this column to make sure two pattern pieces in the model do not have the same Piece Category. If two pattern pieces have the same Piece Category, there will be an error when you process the model for a marker. If this happens, change the category of one of the pattern pieces using Edit Piece Info. When you right click in the Piece Name column, a menu appears that makes available the option Edit Piece Info and lets you change the pattern piece's category.

Description This column displays the description of the pattern piece selected in the Piece Name column. Use this column to make sure you have input any other necessary information for this pattern piece.

Fabric Input the fabric that each pattern is made from into this column. One letter *or* one number may be used to represent each fabric type. It is also commonly known in the fashion industry as a fabric code. The Image col-

umn in Figure 6.7 is hidden so all the pattern pieces are displayed. The following fabric codes are entered:

S is used for self fabric.

L is used for lining fabric.

F is used for fusing fabric.

When you order a marker for this model, you may select the fabric in the Order Editor (see Figure 6.8). For example, if you are laying out lining fabric for the jacket in Figure 6.7, then you input an "L" into the Fabric Type field and the system lays out only the pieces that have an L next to them. You may use up to four fabric codes to represent a fabric. For example, the jacket-front may be cut out in red and sometimes in blue. You may use "R" for red and "B" for blue; therefore, you would input "RB" next to the Jacket-front, under the fabric column of the Model Editor. You can customize the codes to suit your company needs.

- - Column The "- -" stands for "As Digitized." Ask yourself: "How many pieces do I need for this pattern as it was digitized?" Remember that the piece you digitize/draft into the system is considered a left side. Most of the time, at least one will be needed in this column. Some like

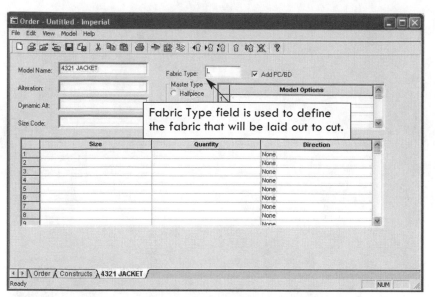

Figure 6.8 View of the Fabric Type and Add PC/BD options in Order Editor

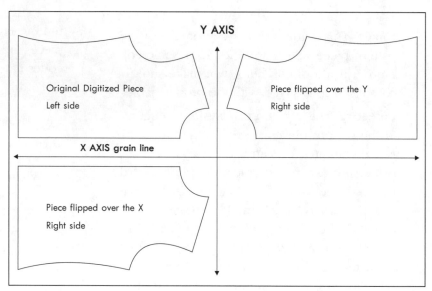

Figure 6.9 An original piece is displayed along with flips on the X and Y axis.

to think of this as the left column. For example, in Figure 6.7, one piece is needed for the jacket-back. Left or right does not matter in this case because the back is on the fold. The jacket-front needs one piece for the left. The right side is input under the "X" column.

X Column This column represents the pieces needed for the opposite side. Some like to think of this as the right column. Since most patterns in the apparel industry are laid along

the X axis or along the grain, the "- -" column and the "X" column are most commonly used together.

Figure 6.9 illustrates both the original piece and the piece flipped over the X axis. If you place a number under the Y column instead of the X column, the piece shows up in a marker as shown in Figure 6.9.

Y Column This column, like the "X" column, represents the number of pieces that are

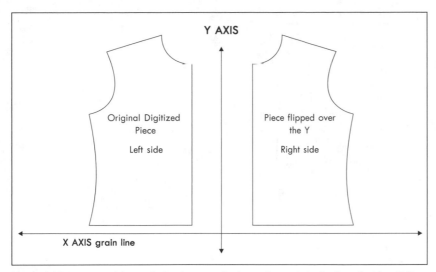

Figure 6.10 An original piece drafted perpendicular to the grain is displayed with a Y flip.

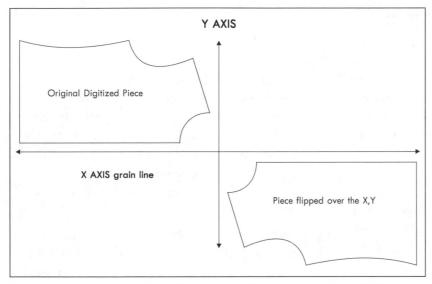

Figure 6.11 A piece drafted along with the grain is displayed along with an X,Y flip.

needed for the opposite side. This column is usually used when patterns are laid perpendicular or against the grain (see Figure 6.10). Garments that fall into this category may include dancewear, due to their tendency to stretch.

If you lay out pattern pieces as seen in Figure 6.10, then you need to fill in the "- -" and "Y" columns, which makes this column the one with the right side pieces.

Note: Typically, either the "X" or "Y" column is filled out along with the "- -" column, as shown in the Model Editor in Figure 6.8.

X, Y Column This column represents a piece that has been flipped over the X axis, and then flipped over the Y axis (see Figure 6.11). Although this column is not commonly used in the apparel industry, other industries, such as the automotive industry, may find this column useful.

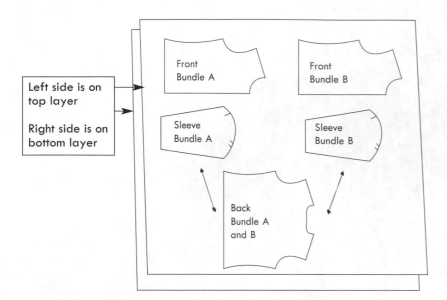

Figure 6.12 A back pattern is displayed half pieced with two bundles.

Half Piece Half piecing allows two bundles of the same size to share one piece. For instance, Figure 6.12 shows how two bundles would share one shirt-back. Each bundle makes one garment. There are two layers of fabric laid out. When you cut out the front and sleeve patterns, you get a left side from the top layer and a right side from the bottom layer. If you lay out a back for each, there would be four backs when only two are needed. Therefore, when this back is half pieced, the top layer back will sew to bundle A and the bottom layer back will sew to bundle B.

There are three options for the Half Piece field.

None: No half piecing will occur. This is the default option.

Same dir: Half piecing will occur if the bundles are laid out in the same direction. The piece will be laid out in the direction of the bundles.

Any dir: A piece will be half pieced regardless of the bundle direction.

Dyn Split This column determines the number of times a piece is allowed to be cut dur-

ing marker making; use numbers 0 to 9 in this field.

Have you ever noticed a seam in the back of a swimsuit bottom or a circular skirt? This seam is an example of a Dynamic Split. The pattern may have been split during marker making to make it fit inside the marker and save fabric.

Add Piece This column is checked off by default. During marker making, it allows this piece to be added in addition to the ordered pieces. A whole model/bundle may be added to the marker if all the pieces are checked off.

When all pieces ordered are placed in a marker and there are spaces that could be filled in with extra pieces, use Add Piece. These extra pieces may be pieces on which sewing operators commonly make errors, such as collars. Since it is easier to start sewing a piece from scratch versus taking it apart, these extra collars come in handy when one is sewn incorrectly. Many of us wish we had had an extra collar cut out the first time we sewed a collar onto a shirt.

Note: Add Pc/Bundle in the Order Editor must checked to activate the Add Piece option in

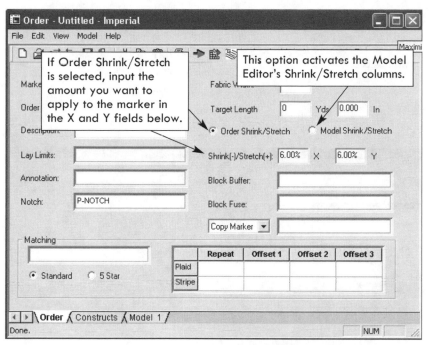

Figure 6.13 The Order Editor lists the option to activate the shrink/stretch function from the Model Editor.

the Model Editor. If it is not checked, you will not be able to add a piece or bundle during marker making.

X Shrink Stretch (%) Input the amount each piece shrinks or stretches in the X direction in this column. To add 5 percent input +5. To take away 5 percent, input −5. Each piece can have different shrink and stretch amounts.

Y Shrink Stretch (%) Input the amount each piece shrinks or stretches in the Y direction in this column. To add 5 percent input +5. To take away 5 percent, input −5. Each piece may have different shrink and stretch amounts.

As stated earlier, the shrink and stretch columns in the Model Editor allow you to have more control of the shrink and stretch per piece. The Order Editor has two options for shrink and stretch: **Order Shrink/Stretch** and **Model Shrink/Stretch** (see Figure 6.13). The Model Editor's shrink/stretch option is activated by selecting Model Shrink/Stretch in the Order Editor. Selecting Order Shrink/Stretch gives all pieces in a marker the same shrink and stretch amount.

How to Name and Save the Model Editor

After you create the Model Editor, you must save it.

To save the Model Editor:

1. Select **File>Save As** (see Figure 6.14).

2. The **Save As** window appears (see Figure 6.15).

3. Type in the name of the model in the File Name field. Every company has a procedure on how to name pattern pieces and the models they create. As discussed in the section titled Descriptive Data in Chapter 4, every pattern Piece Name is usually preceded with a style name or number. For example, in this chapter, the style number 4321 was used with every pattern piece. Since patterns tend to look similar at times, using a style number or name will help to differentiate one piece from another. Therefore, pattern 4321 Jacket-Front will not be mixed up with pattern 4500 Jacket-Front.

The Model Editor's name is usually created using this style name or number. The model in Figure 6.15 is named 4321 Jacket. This model includes all the pattern pieces, preceded by style number 4321, used to create the jacket. Although using this naming convention helps to prevent errors in the cutting room, there are times when other pattern pieces from another model may be used to create a model. For example, pattern 4500 Jacket-Sleeve may replace 4321 Jacket-Sleeve because it is a short sleeve. We do recommend, however, that you make a copy of 4500 Jacket-Sleeve and rename it 4321 Jacket-Sh-Sleeve.

4. Click **Save** to finish.

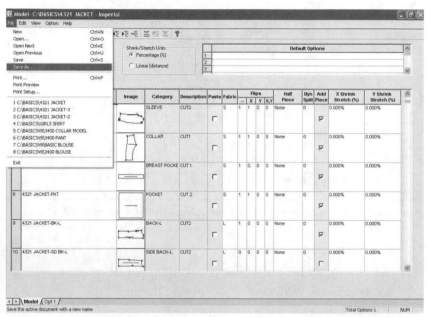

Figure 6.14 A Model Editor is saved using the Save As function located in the File menu.

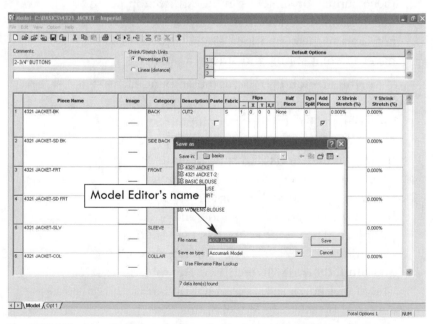

Figure 6.15 The Save As window appears when saving a Model Editor.

Test Your Knowledge

Select the correct answer from the word bank.

Word Bank

X	As digitized
True	Dynamic Split
False	1
4	Y
Half piecing	Cutter's Must

1. The Model Editor is most like a manual _____.
2. You can place up to _____ fabric codes per piece in the Model Editor.
3. All pattern pieces, in all fabric types, may be placed in the Model Editor. _____.
4. The "- -" column stands for _____ and is usually considered a left side.
5. Usually, there is at least _____ piece ordered under the "- -" column.
6. If a pattern is laid along the grain, it is on the _____ axis.
7. If a pattern is laid perpendicular to the grain or at a 90-degree angle, it is on the _____ axis.
8. When two bundles share one piece, it is known as _____.
9. Half piecing may occur when you use bundles that are different sizes. _____.
10. The _____ option allows a piece to be split during marker making.

Test Your Skills

1. Create a Model Editor using the pieces you created and drafted/digitized in Chapter 4.
2. Name the Model Editor according to the piece names that were used to save each piece. For example, if the piece names were "JEU-Front," and "JEU-Back," the Model may be named "JEU-Shirt."

CHAPTER SEVEN

Plotting

Objective

Plotting is the process used to print out pattern pieces or markers on paper using a plotter. You use a printer to print and a plotter to plot, yet in the end, the result is a printout of an item. The difference is that a plotter has a larger printing area and lets you plot patterns that are true to size. Although you can refer to plotting as "printing out a pattern," it is technically correct to refer to the printing of pattern pieces on a plotter as plotting. Therefore, this term is used throughout the chapter and text at large.

During the first stages of pattern creation, plotting is often used to confirm that the proportions and design of a pattern are accurate. Patterns are also repeatedly plotted to ensure that revisions are correct and other sizes are grading properly. Prior to plotting pieces, you need to set up several tables/editors for the system to reference, establish plotter settings, and set the plotter online so it is ready to receive the pattern pieces to plot. This chapter covers the process to plot pattern pieces. You will be able to plot patterns as individual pieces, as models in single sizes, or in a nest. Additionally, you should have the knowledge to plot patterns using the Gerber Launch Pad, AccuMark Explorer, or PDS. Please remember that not all functions available within the tables/editors are discussed in this chapter due to the limited amount of available class time and advanced level of the material.

This chapter allows you to gain skills in the following areas:

- The steps you need to know before you can plot pattern pieces
- How to work with the Annotation Editor
- How to work with a Piece Plot Parameter Table
- How to work with a Piece Plot Order
- Learn how to access the Piece Plot Order to plot pieces

What You Need Before You Can Plot Pattern Pieces

If you are ready to plot a pattern, it means that you have already drafted and digitized the pattern pieces so they exist in the storage area. There are three tables/editors that you must complete before you can plot a pattern on a plotter. You can complete and save the first two listed tables/editors with a file name for when you plot pieces again. You can save multiple versions of each one of these tables/editors to meet different company specifications. The third table listed is the actual order that is used to transmit the information to the plotter.

- *Annotation Editor:* Form used to determine the information, known as annotation, that plots in each piece.
- *Piece Plot Parameter Table:* Form used to determine how a piece will plot, including orientation, point and/or grade numbers, and scale.
- *Piece Plot Order:* The order that states the pieces or model to plot, sizes, annotation size, and plot location.

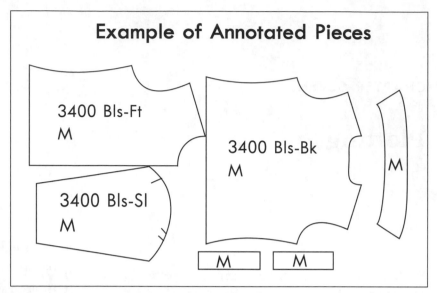

Figure 7.1 Example of annotated pieces.

Once you complete these tables/editors, you may process plotting from the Gerber Launch Pad, AccuMark Explorer, or PDS. The plotter needs to be placed online, meaning made ready for patterns to actually plot. Since there are several types of plotters available, you will need to refer to the plotter instructions or speak with your instructor to get proper plotter setup. The next sections of this chapter guide you through opening, completing, and saving these tables to process pieces or models to plot.

Annotation Editor

The Annotation Editor is used to determine what information will plot inside each piece when plotted (see Figure 7.1). This information is known as **annotation** and it may be a model name, a piece name, or the size, which may be quite beneficial to patternmakers. During the beginning stages of pattern creation, you may plot a pattern several times and continually revise it. The pattern workroom tends to be interrupted constantly—industry professionals who read this book can definitely relate. Because of these interruptions, it may become confusing to keep track of the last revision you made, especially when other similar styles are plotted at the same time. Therefore, certain information plotted inside of a piece, such as the name, can be rather important for a patternmaker or anyone plotting patterns.

Since patternmakers are mainly the ones who plot pattern pieces, the information they include in an Annotation Editor suits their needs. When the pattern goes into production, a whole other set of hands, including patternmakers, handle patterns and therefore you need to plot additional or different information in each piece, which requires that you set up another Annotation Editor. It is common for a company to set up an Annotation Editor for piece plotting and another for marker plotting. It is important to understand that it is not recommended to set up one Annotation Editor per model, but rather to set it up per storage area or per groups of models.

Opening the Annotation Editor

There are several ways to open an Annotation Editor, but the two fastest and most common ways are through the Gerber Launch Pad or AccuMark Explorer. Both processes are described in the following section.

Opening an Annotation Editor using the Gerber Launch Pad

1. Open the **Gerber Launch Pad.**

2. Select the second radio button: **Marker Creation, Editors.**

3. Double click on the **Annotation Editor** icon (see Figure 7.2) to display the Annotation Editor.

Figure 7.2 You may open the Annotation Editor using the Gerber Launch Pad.

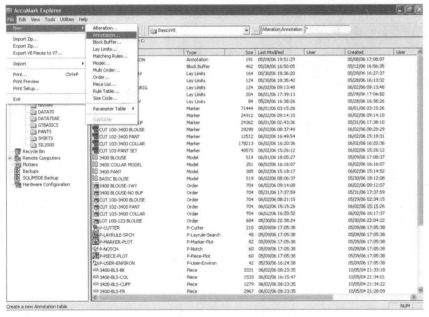

Figure 7.3 You may open the Annotation Editor using AccuMark Explorer.

Opening an Annotation Editor using AccuMark Explorer

1. Open **Accumark Explorer.**

2. Left click to highlight and select the storage area into which you will create and save the Annotation Editor.

3. Select **File>New>Annotation** to display the Annotation Editor (see Figure 7.3).

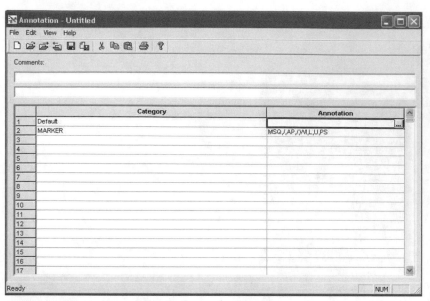

Figure 7.4 Blank Annotation Editor.

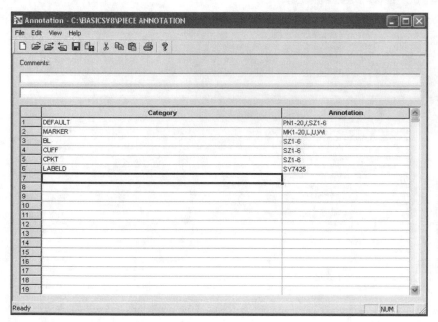

Figure 7.5 Example of an Annotation Editor that is filled out.

same functions. Place the mouse over the icons to display the names of the icons' functions.

Now let's look at the main body of the Annotation Editor, including the **Comments, Category,** and **Annotation** columns. The information entered in this table should be set up to reflect a company's annotation preferences. For example, when plotting pieces, a company may decide that they want only the piece name and size plotted inside each piece. The available preferences are displayed in a separate window when the **browse button**, used to view available data items from which to select, is activated. The browse button is the small square with three dots shown in the first row, second column under the title Annotation.

Figure 7.5 shows a completed Annotation Editor. Notice that the marker line information is different from the default marker line information displayed in Figure 7.4. This is presented to demonstrate that the default information may be changed to suit a company's needs. The following fields in the Annotation Editor are described below, as are how they may be completed. The manner in which you select preferences or annotations is detailed under "Annotation" further below. First, you must understand the meaning of each line that you may set up.

Completing the Annotation Editor

Figure 7.4 shows a blank Annotation Editor. There are four drop-down menus at the top titled File, Edit, View, and Help. These menus include common commands such as toolbar selections, open, save, print, copy, cut, and paste. The icons directly below these menus give you quick access to the

Comments

Use the Comments field to enter any information about the Annotation Editor that you need for reference, as a reminder of something, or as general information. (For example, the comment may state that the Annotation Editor is only used for models with reference points.)

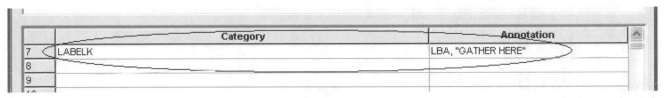

	Category	Annotation
7	LABELK	LBA, "GATHER HERE"
8		
9		

Figure 7.6 Annotation Editor stating any line labeled K will plot Gather Here.

Category

The category of pattern pieces is listed in the Category column. The information listed in the Annotation column is applied to pattern pieces with the category listed in the same row. For example, look at the third row in Figure 7.5 and notice that it lists category "BL," which in this case represents a belt loop. Now notice that to its right, in the Annotation column, it states "SZ1-6." This means that the size of the pattern will plot on any pattern piece with the category "BL" when this table is used. The information selected in the "Default" row is applied to all pieces being plotted, so in this case, pieces with the category "BL" can be referred to as an exception to that rule.

Annotation for labeled points or lines may also be listed under the Category column. For example, the sixth row in Figure 7.5 lists the category "LABELD." Any point or line labeled "D" will have the annotation in the right-hand column plotted. Drill holes are commonly labeled "D" for drill hole, so we recommend that you keep labeling consistent in the Annotation Editor. Since drill holes are usually symbols, such as plus signs or asterisks, there is specific annotation available for them, which is discussed later.

Marker annotation may also be listed in the Category column as seen in Figure 7.5. Marker annotation plots along with a marker when it is plotted and is sometimes referred to as a heading for the marker. This annotation usually includes the marker name, model, length, and width, but once again, this is determined by each company's needs.

The following is a synopsis of what is usually listed in the Category column.

- *Default:* The information selected and listed in the Annotation column in this row applies to all pieces. Think of Default as "the rule" for what annotation plots inside of each piece. Any exceptions should be listed on their own rows.

- *Marker:* The information selected and listed in the Annotation column of this row will only plot when a marker is plotted. If individual pieces that are not in a marker are plotted, this line will be ignored.

- *LabelX:* Replace the "x" with a letter to represent a line or point with that label. If you created a line in a pattern piece for annotation purposes, you may list it in a similar manner. For example, let us say that a line labeled "K" is used to plot the annotation "Gather Here." This line would be set up as shown in Figure 7.6.

- *Category of patterns:* List the category of pieces that are exceptions to the information listed in the Default row. For example, Figure 7.5 lists BL (Belt Loop), CUFF, and CPKT (coin pocket) as categories that you should not plot with the information selected in the Default row. This is commonly done when the information listed in the Default row will not be able to plot within the perimeter lines of a pattern piece and overflow outside the piece because of its small size. Therefore, according to Figure 7.5, any pattern piece with one of these categories will plot only the size. Remember, it is important that you label categories consistently throughout storage areas.

Annotation

Use this column to select the information you need to plot in each piece. This information may

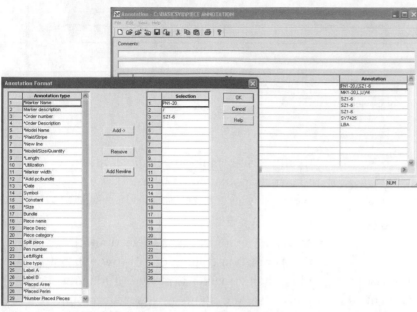

Figure 7.7 The Annotation Format window appears when the browse button is activated.

be referred to as annotation preferences. Each row under the Annotation column displays a browse button when you select the field by left clicking on it once. The browse button, the small square with three dots, displays on the right-hand side of the field. Click the browse button when it appears to display the **Annotation Format** window (see Figure 7.7).

The Annotation Format window is divided into two columns, the Annotation type column and the Selection column. Annotation preferences are selected as follows:

1. Left click on the data item/annotation preference to select it from the **Annotation type** column.

2. Left click on the **Add** button between the two columns to add the data item you selected to the first row of the **Selection** column.

Annotation preferences may be deleted as follows:

1. Left click on the data item/annotation preference to delete it from the **Selection** column.

2. Left click on the **Remove** button between the two columns to delete the data item you selected.

Information plotted in a piece may be plotted on different lines. For example, if the annotation for pieces needs to include a piece name, a model name, and the size, each on a different line, then follow the process below.

1. Left click on **Piece Name** in the Annotation Type column.

2. Click **Add>Add New Line.**

3. Left click on **Model Name** in the Annotation Type column.

4. Click **Add>Add New Line.**

5. Left click on **Size** in the Annotation Type column.

6. Click the **Add** button.

7. Click **OK** to enter information in the editor. Once you go through this procedure, annotation preferences are set up.

There are five available symbols to use when representing a drill hole or other point of reference. The symbol selections are displayed when you select Symbol from the Annotation Type column or the drop-down menu (see Figure 7.8). These symbols include an asterisk, a plus sign, a circle, a square, and a diamond.

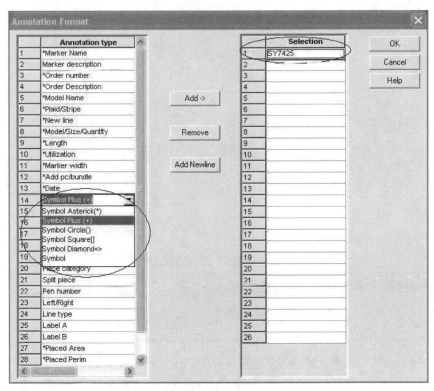

Figure 7.8 Symbol is selected for a drill hole.

The process to set up a drill hole with a plus sign symbol that is ¼" in size is described below.

1. Type in the label name under the Category column of the Annotation Editor first. For example, for a drill hole labeled D, we would type "LABELD" in one row.

2. Left click on the field in the Annotation column in the same row where you typed LABELD. Left click the browse button that appears on the right-hand side of the field to open the Annotation Format window.

3. Select **Symbol** from the Annotation Type column of the Annotation Format window. Click the drop-down menu that appears to the right of the field. Notice the five available symbols listed.

4. Select the symbols you want, in our case the plus sign.

5. Click the **Add** button to add the symbol under the Selection column. It is displayed as SY7425. Click **OK** to enter the information in the editor.

Note: SY represents that it is a symbol, 74 represents the code for the plus sign, and 25 represents and is equivalent to .25 (¼") in size. The code number is entered automatically by the system according to the selection. If you need to change the size, for example, to ½", then change the last two numbers to 50, without a decimal. The highest number that may be input is 99. One quarter of an inch is quite common in the fashion industry.

Saving the Annotation Editor

As with any table, editor, or form that you need to keep, when you complete the Annotation Editor, you need to save it. Save the Annotation Editor by following the steps below.

1. Select the **File>Save As.**

2. The **Save As** window appears. Select the storage area into which you want to save from the Save In field at the top of the window, if the storage area you want is not already shown. Name the editor in the File Name field.

3. Click **Save** when you are done.

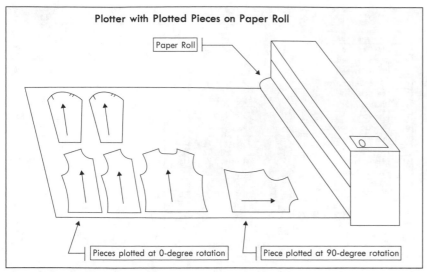

Plotter with Plotted Pieces on Paper Roll

Paper Roll

Pieces plotted at 0-degree rotation

Piece plotted at 90-degree rotation

Figure 7.9 Pieces plotted on a plotter.

Test Your Annotation Editor Skills

Use the following information to set up an Annotation Editor in your selected storage area. Try to save all Test Your Skills editors or tables you create into one storage area so that it will be easy to view everything you have created. The answers are demonstrated in figures at the end of the chapter, so you can really test yourself.

1. The Annotation Editor will be named Piece Annotation.
2. All pieces will have the Piece Name, Piece Description, and Size information plotted on a different line.
3. Leave the Marker line alone for this setup.
4. All pieces with the category COL will have only the size plotted.
5. All pieces with the category CUFF will have only the size plotted.
6. All pieces with the category WPKT (welt pockets), will have only the size plotted.
7. All pieces with the category PKT will have the Piece Category and size plotted, each on a different line.
8. All drill holes labeled D will have an asterisk symbol, ¼" in size.

Piece Plot Parameter Table

After you set up the Annotation Editor, you can set up the Piece Plot Parameter Table, although it really does not matter which one you do first. The Piece Plot Parameter Table is used to set up the parameters that will determine how a piece plots, including orientation, point and/or grade numbers, and scale among other selections. For example, you can plot pieces in quarter scale or smaller so you can place them in a binder for reference.

One Piece Plot Parameter Table should be set up for every plotting situation that is needed, not per model or style. For example, one table may be used to plot pieces in a graded nest and another may be used to plot out sizes individually. The following sections review how to open, complete, and save the Piece Plot Parameter Table. Figure 7.9 displays some pattern pieces plotted on plotter paper.

Opening the Piece Plot Parameter Table

Like opening an Annotation Editor, there are several ways to open a Piece Plot Parameter Table, but the two fastest and most common ways are through the Gerber Launch Pad or AccuMark Explorer.

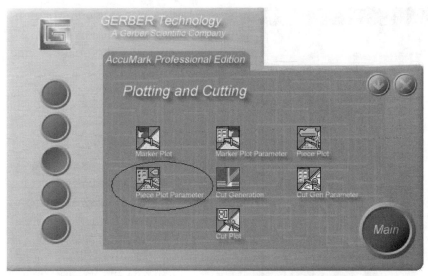

Figure 7.10 You may open the Piece Plot Parameter Table using the Gerber Launch Pad.

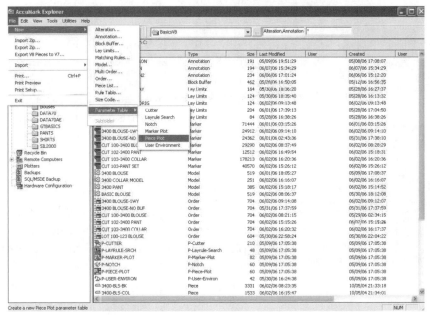

Figure 7.11 You may open the Piece Plot Parameter Table using AccuMark Explorer.

Opening a Piece Plot Parameter Table using the Gerber Launch Pad

1. Open the **Gerber Launch Pad.**

2. Select the third ratio button: **Plotting and Cutting.**

3. Double click on the **Piece Plot Parameter** icon (see Figure 7.10) to display the Piece Plot Parameter Table.

Opening a Piece Plot Parameter Table using AccuMark Explorer

1. Open **AccuMark Explorer.**

2. Select the storage area where you want to create and save the Piece Plot Parameter Table from the yellow folders under device C.

3. Select **File>New>Parameter Table>Piece Plot** to display the Piece Plot Parameter Table (see Figure 7.11).

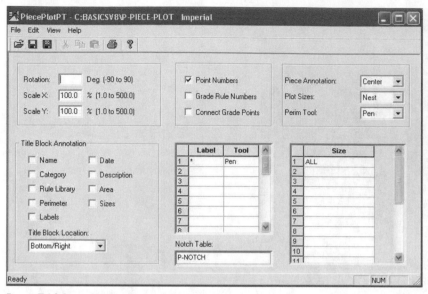

Figure 7.12 Piece Plot Parameter Table is displayed.

The X and Y Directions on a Pattern Piece

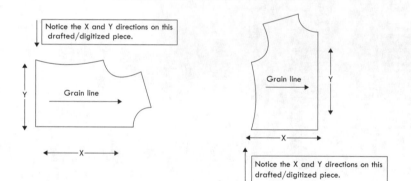

Figure 7.13 The X and Y directions on a piece are determined by a piece's original orientation.

Completing the Piece Plot Parameter Table

When you plot pieces, the Piece Plot Parameter Table gives you different options from which to choose (see Figure 7.12).

The options are described below. The items in parentheses represent the range that you may enter.

Rotation-Deg (-90 to 90)

Use this field to enter the rotation direction in which pattern pieces should plot. For example, go back to Figure 7.9 to see pieces displayed plotted in 0-degree rotation, which is equivalent to how the patterns were digitized, and one piece dis-

played plotted at a 90-degree rotation. Pieces are sometimes rotated to save fabric. Since patterns are being plotted on paper, the grain line is not an issue. If you plot on fabric, then you want to rotate pieces to save fabric.

Scale X- % (1.0 to 500.0)

Enter the size the piece should plot in for the X axis. Enter 100 percent to plot the piece true to size. Any amount higher than 100 percent plots the piece larger in the X axis. Any amount lower than 100 percent plots the piece smaller in the X axis. Figure 7.13 helps you to determine the X axis according to how your pieces are drafted or digitized into the system.

Note: Entering 100 percent for both the X and Y fields yields a true-to-size pattern piece. Use a number from 10 to 20 percent for both the X and Y fields to plot patterns in a small scale if you need to create a log of patterns in a book.

Scale Y- % (1.0 to 500.0)

Enter the size the piece should plot in for the Y axis. Enter 100 percent to plot the piece true to size. Any amount higher than 100 percent plots the piece larger in the Y axis. Any amount lower than 100 percent plots the piece smaller in the Y axis. Figure 7.13 helps you to determine the Y axis according to how your piece is drafted or digitized into the system.

Note: Entering 100 percent for both the X and Y fields yields a true-to-size proportioned pattern piece.

Point Numbers

Check this box to plot the point numbers along with the pattern pieces. As previously discussed, point numbers are sequential reference points automatically created by the system on end points and grade points when the piece is drafted or digitized. They may be used to tell the order in which a piece was entered or the numbers may be changed to act as special point numbers referenced for alterations or matching. This option is helpful when you plot pieces that contain alteration numbers that you want to make sure are accurate.

Grade Rule Numbers

Check this box to plot the grade rule numbers along with pattern pieces. This option is helpful when plotting a graded nest and making sure the grade rule numbers are accurate.

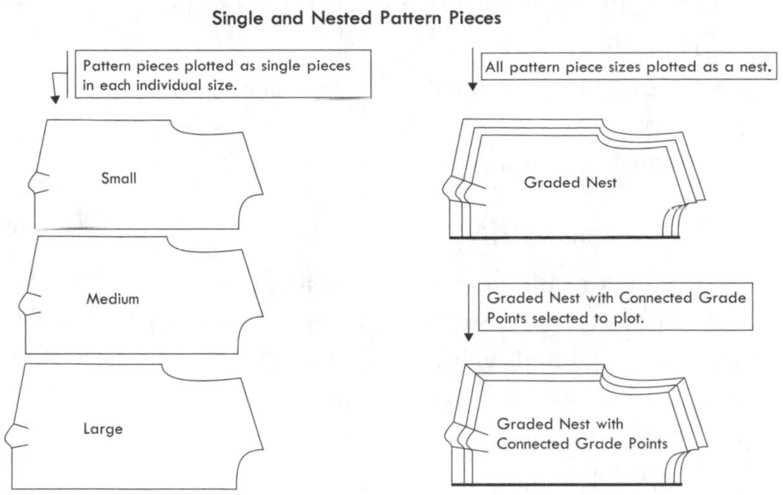

Figure 7.14 Single and nested pattern pieces are displayed.

Connect Grade Points

Check this box to create a line from the smallest to the largest size at each grade point. Figure 7.14 shows a graded nest with this option selected. It is helpful when measuring the growth in a graded nest.

Piece Annotation

Determine where annotation should be placed on a piece by selecting from the two available listed options. Students commonly write pattern information along the grain line and therefore may prefer the Grain option, but both are commonly used in the fashion industry.

- *Center:* Plots annotation in the center of the piece
- *Grain:* Plots annotation along the piece's grain line

Plot Sizes

Determine if pieces should plot out separately in each size or as a nest. See Figure 7.14 for an example of the two available options.

- *Nest:* Plots pattern pieces in a nest. This is used to check the grading on a piece.
- *Single:* Plot pattern pieces in single sizes to cut a sample or to view proportions and changes you've made.

Perim Tool

There are some plotters that are set up to cut pieces out of fabric or paper with a built in plotter knife. Most plotters, however, are used to plot pattern pieces on paper with the plotter pen. There are two options available for this field.

- *Pen:* Select this option to plot pieces with a pen and thereby draw the patterns.
- *Knife:* Select this option to cut pattern pieces if you have a plotter with a knife set in place and ready to cut.

Notch Table

The system references the listed notch table when plotting the piece. The table named "Notch Parameter Table" is selected by default. If the Notch Parameter Table was not filled out, the notches in pattern pieces will not plot.

Size

Select the sizes that should plot when you use this Piece Plot Parameter Table. The five options are listed below.

- *All:* Plots all available sizes for pattern pieces.
- *Smallest:* Plots the smallest size available for pattern pieces.
- *Largest:* Plots the largest size available for pattern pieces.

- *Base:* Plots the base size of each pattern piece plotted.
- *Breaks:* Plots the break sizes for each pattern piece plotted. The break sizes are the sizes where the grading amount changes.

Title Block Annotation

Use this area to plot annotation outside of the plotted pattern piece. Select the box next to each item that is to be plotted with each pattern. This is a great tool to use when you are creating a book log of patterns.

- *Name:* Plots the Piece Name
- *Category:* Plots the Piece Category
- *Rule Library:* Plots the grade rule table applied to the pattern piece
- *Perimeter:* Plots the perimeter measurement of the pattern piece
- *Labels:* Plots the label names with each line
- *Date:* Plots the date
- *Description:* Plots the Piece Description
- *Area:* Plots the area measurement of the pattern piece
- *Sizes:* Plots the sizes for the pattern pieces

Title Block Location

Select from the four listed options for the location where the Title Block Annotation will be plotted on a pattern piece. Make a selection in this field only if you decide to use Title Block Annotation.

- *Bottom/Right*
- *Bottom/Left*
- *Top/Right*
- *Top/Left*

Saving the Piece Plot Parameter Table

After you complete the Piece Plot Parameter Table, you need to save it.

1. Select **File>Save As.**
2. The **Save As** window appears. Select the storage area into which you want to save it from the Save In field at the top of the window, if

the storage area you want is not already shown. Name the editor in the File Name field.

3. Click **Save** when you are done.

Test Your Piece Plot Parameter Table Skills

Use the information listed below to create the following three Piece Plot Parameter Tables. If information is not mentioned as a selection for display, leave the box unchecked. For example, leave Point Numbers unchecked unless it is specifically noted as a preference. Really test yourself; the answers are shown in figures at the end of the chapter.

Piece Plot Parameter Table #1

1. Name this table P-Piece Plot-N50. This allows us to distinguish from the name that pieces plot at half scale and as graded nests.
2. Plot pieces at half scale in the X and Y directions.
3. Have all available sizes plot.
4. Plot sizes in a nest.
5. Plot the annotation along the grain line.
6. Plot pieces without a rotation.
7. Plot grade rules.

Piece Plot Parameter Table #2

1. Name this table P-Piece Plot-S100. This allows us to distinguish from the name that pieces plot in true size and sizes the plot separately.
2. Plot pieces at full scale, true to size.
3. Have all available sizes plot.
4. Plot sizes individually.
5. Plot the annotation in the center of the piece.
6. Plot pieces without a rotation.

Piece Plot Parameter Table #3

1. Name this table P-Piece Plot-N100BRK. This allows us to distinguish from the name that the break sizes of a pattern will plot in true size and as a graded nest in true to size scale.
2. Plot pieces at full scale, true to size.
3. Have all break sizes plot.
4. Plot sizes in a nest.
5. Plot the annotation along the grain line.
6. Plot pieces at a 90-degree rotation.
7. Plot grade rules and point numbers.

Piece Plot Order

The Piece Plot Order is used to select the pattern pieces or models that need to be plotted. The Annotation Editor and Piece Plot Parameter Table of your choice are selected when you place this order. Additionally, plot destination, number of copies, and annotation character size may be selected. The Piece Plot Order is completed every time pattern pieces or models need to be plotted. A Piece Plot Order example is displayed later in the chapter.

Opening the Piece Plot Order

A Piece Plot Order may be opened through the Gerber Launch Pad or AccuMark Explorer, just like the last two tables discussed. Open a Piece Plot Order using either method for the purpose of plotting pieces or models. Plotting pieces and models may also be accomplished through PDS, but the process is slightly different from plotting via the Gerber Launch Pad or AccuMark Explorer. These two processes are described below, while the process from PDS is discussed later in the chapter.

Opening a Piece Plot Order using the Gerber Launch Pad

1. Open the **Gerber Launch Pad.**

2. Select the second radio button: **Plotting And Cutting.**

3. Double click on the **Piece Plot Order** icon (see Figure 7.15) to display the Piece Plot Order.

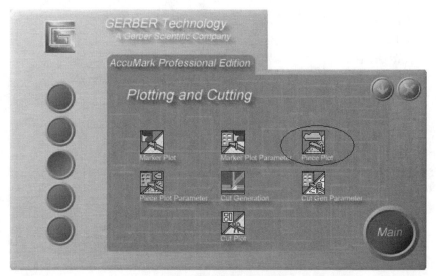

Figure 7.15 You may open a Piece Plot Order using the Gerber Launch Pad.

Opening a Piece Plot Order using
AccuMark Explorer

1. Open **AccuMark Explorer.**

2. Select the storage area where
   the pieces you want to plot
   exist (see Figure 7.16) to display the storage area data
   items.

3. Select the pieces or models to
   plot, which highlights them.

4. Right click on the selected
   items to display a menu.
   Select **Send To>Plotter** to display the Piece Plot Order.

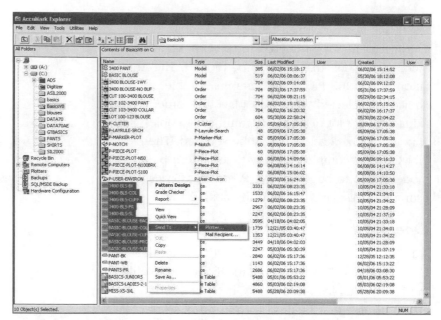

Figure 7.16 You may open a Piece Plot Order using AccuMark Explorer.

Completing the Piece Plot Order

As stated earlier, you must com-
plete the Piece Plot Order each time you are ready
to plot pieces or models. Figure 7.17 shows an
example of a Piece Plot Order when you first open
it. The fields you need to complete are described
in the general order in which you must complete
them. For example, you must select a piece or
model before the Size field displays the available
sizes.

Piece Plot Param

Click the browse button that appears on the right
side of the field when it is selected (see Figure
7.17). A window appears with the available Piece
Plot Parameter Tables. Left click to highlight and
select the table you want the system to reference
when plotting.

Annotation Table

Click the browse button that appears on the right
side of the Annotation Table field when it is
selected. A window appears with the available
Annotation Editors. Select the editor you want the
system to reference when plotting.

Plot As

Following are two options that are available for the
plot as field:

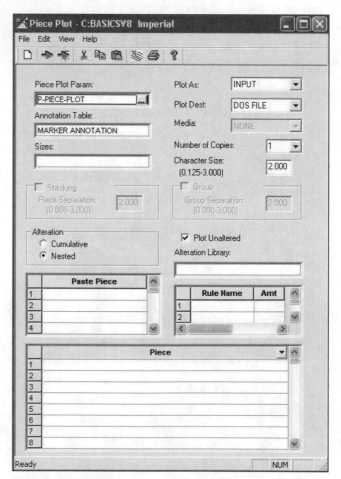

Figure 7.17 Piece Plot Order as it looks when it is first opened.

- *Input:* Select this option so that pieces plot in the original digitized direction.
- *Model:* Select this option so that the left and right sides of pattern pieces are plotted.

Plot Destination

Use this option to designate where the pieces should plot. Sometimes more than one plotter is connected to a system in a company and this option allows you to select which one to use. Since each plotter is given a name, known as a queue name, that name displays as an option.

- *Plotter Queue Name:* Select the plotter in which the patterns will plot.
- *DOS File:* Select this option to save the plot data as a DOS file. This option is not commonly used by students.

Number of Copies

Select the number of copies to plot of the selected pattern pieces by clicking on the drop-down menu.

Character Size: (0.125 to 3.000)

Enter the character size for the annotation that will plot in each piece. The range is displayed in parentheses. It is normal to use .25 (¼").

Piece

Notice the area titled **Piece** at the bottom of the Piece Plot Order in Figure 7.17. The area titled Piece is a title bar for the Piece Plot Order. When the drop-down menu on the right-hand side of the title bar is activated, the three options listed below are available. The option you select becomes the new title for this column and determines whether models, pieces, or lists will be plotted.

- *Piece:* If you select this option, you can choose only pieces from a selected storage area to plot.

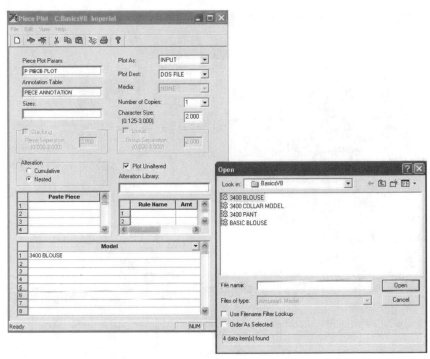

Figure 7.18 Open window displays for model and storage area selection for Piece Plot Order.

- *Model:* If you select this option, you can choose only models from a selected storage area. Figure 7.18 displays this title bar/area set to Model.
- *List:* If you select this option, you can choose only lists from a selected storage area. You may create a piece list to plot pieces that you often plot. A piece list may be created in AccuMark Explorer by selecting **File>New> Piece List.**

After this area/title bar is set up with one of the options stated above, left click on the first row and a browse button appears on the right-hand side of the field. Click the browse button to display the **Open** window. Models may be selected from the storage area of your choice. Multiple models or pieces may be selected and the system will fill each row in the Piece Plot Order with one data item— notice the first row under Model in Figure 7.18.

Size

Select this field to input sizes other than those listed in the Piece Plot Parameter Table to plot. For example, if you selected "All" in the **Size** column of the Piece Plot Parameter Table, and you need to

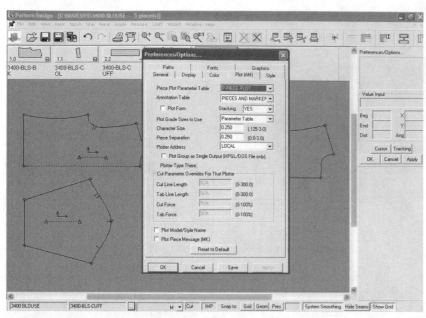

Figure 7.19 Plot (AM) tab preferences are opened in PDS to set plotter preferences.

1. Open **Pattern Design.**
2. Select **View>Preferences/ Options** to display the **Preferences/Options** window.
3. Select the **Plot (AM)** tab (see Figure 7.19).

Notice that the fields are quite similar to those in the Piece Plot Order form we filled out in the last section. The basic fields used are described below.

Piece Plot Parameter Table

Select the Piece Plot Parameter Table for the system to reference.

Annotation Editor

Select the Annotation Editor for the system to reference.

plot only the base size, type in the base size or the word "Base."

Processing the Piece Plot Order

The option to save the Piece Plot Order is not available, although the selections you made the last time you plotted using the Piece Plot Order will display next time you plot (except the models or pieces you selected). After you complete the Piece Plot Order, you need to process it so that the information is sent to the plotter to plot the selected patterns. There are two ways to process the Piece Plot Order:

1. Select **File>Process** to process the order. If the plotter is set online, the pattern pieces will begin to plot.
2. Under the function toolbar that has File, Edit, View, and Help menus, there is an icon toolbar. Use the first arrow icon that points to the right as a quick shortcut to process an order (see Figure 7.18).

Plotting from PDS

Plotting from PDS is easier to understand now that you have learned the principles in the previous section. Plotter preferences should be set up in PDS prior to plotting a piece. To set plotter preferences, follow the procedure below.

Stacking

This option determines how pieces plot across the plotter paper. There are two available options.

- *Yes:* Select this option to stack the pieces across the plotter paper. This choice optimizes the use of plotter paper.
- *No:* Select this option so the pieces will not plot across the paper.

Plot Grade Sizes to Use

Select from the two listed available options.

- *Display:* Select this option to plot the piece with the size displayed on the screen.
- *Parameter Table:* Select this option so that the system refers to the selected Piece Plot Parameter Table in the Plot tab when plotting pattern pieces.

Character Size

Enter the character size for the annotation that plots on each piece.

Piece Separation

Enter the separation that should be allowed between pattern pieces. Separation should be

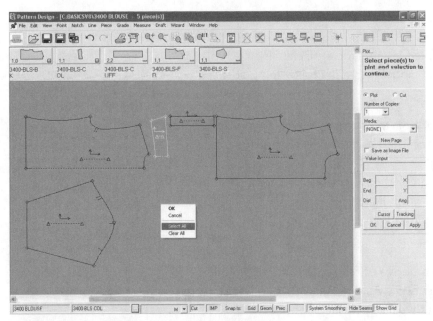

Figure 7.20 Plotting pieces using the Plot function in PDS.

ample when you actually have to cut the pieces
with scissors.

Plotter Address

Select the destination for the pieces to plot, or the
queue name. The option **Local** may be used to
refer to the main plotter used.

When you are finished setting plotter preferences, click **Save** at the bottom of the window to
keep the changes and click **OK** to exit the window. The next time you need to plot, these preferences will already be set up and you do not need
to access them again unless you need to make
changes to the selections.

The next step is to select the pieces to plot and
the Plot function.

1. Bring the pieces or models to plot into the
   PDS Work Area (see Figure 7.20).

2. Select **File>Plot.**

3. A user input box states: "Select piece(s) to
   plot, end selection to continue." Left click to
   select each piece or right click and choose
   Select All to select all the pieces on-screen.

4. Right click to end the selection. The pieces
   should start plotting if the plotter is set online.

Test Your Skills

Refer to the tables and editors you created in this chapter. Determine the tables or editors to use to plot pattern pieces and models using the following guidelines:

Plot #1

1. Select three pattern pieces to plot from your storage area. If you do not have any current pieces, use pieces listed in the DATA70 storage area provided by Gerber Technology.
2. Plot the model at half scale in a graded nest.
3. Annotation should plot along the grain line.
4. Grade rule numbers should plot along with each plotted piece.

Plot #2

1. Plot the same pieces from the plot above at full scale with sizes plotted individually. Plot out only the first two available sizes or smallest sizes, as this gives you the practice without wasting too much paper.
2. Make sure the annotations plot in the center of each piece.

Plot #3

1. Select a model to plot. If you do not have an existing model, use the model "Ladies-Blouse" in DATA70 provided by Gerber Technology.
2. Plot the model at full scale.
3. Plot the break sizes in a nest.
4. Plot grade rule numbers and point numbers.
5. Rotate the patterns by 90 degrees.

The Annotation Editor that should have been completed to finish Test Your Annotation Editor Skills earlier in the chapter should look like the Annotation Editor displayed in Figure 7.21.

The Piece Plot Parameter Tables that you completed for the Test Your Piece Plot Parameter Skills earlier in the chapter should look like the tables displayed in Figures 7.22 to 7.24.

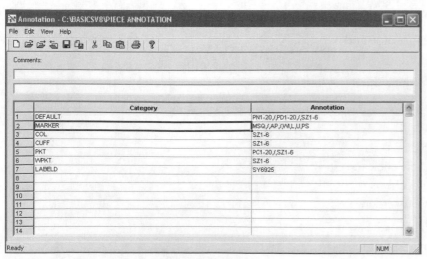

Figure 7.21 Test Your Skills answers for Piece Annotation.

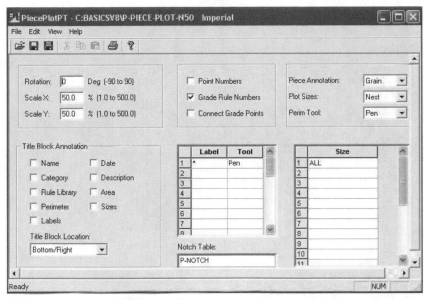

Figure 7.22 Test Your Skills Answer for P-Piece Plot-N50.

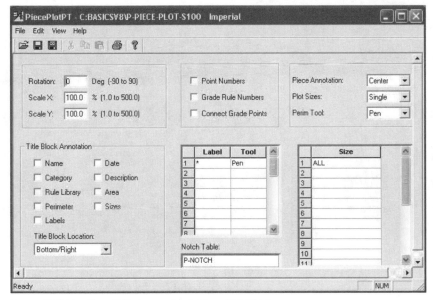

Figure 7.23 Test Your Skills Answer for P-Piece Plot-S100.

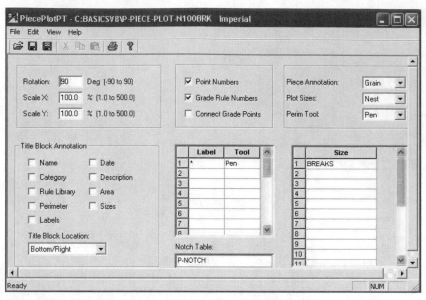

Figure 7.24 Test Your Skills Answer for P-Piece Plot-N100BRK.

CHAPTER EIGHT

Piece Functions in PDS

Objective

This chapter introduces the basic piece functions that are commonly used in the industry, such as creating circles, rectangles, facings, and fusible. The chapter also covers how to add fullness, pleats, and seam allowance; how to manipulate darts; how to change a grain line: and how to flip, rotate, split patterns, and place them on the fold. The chapter does not cover every single function available in this menu.

Measurements are entered in fraction or decimal form. Since most functions will accept either form, you can enter a fraction without having to pull out your calculator each time to figure out the decimal conversion.

Please keep in mind that there are different ways to achieve the same result when you create the examples in this chapter. Furthermore, you may complete the examples by using other functions to reach your desired results.

This chapter allows you to gain skills in the following areas:

- Create Piece menu
- Pleats menu
- Darts menu
- Fullness menu
- Seam menu
- Modify Piece menu
- Split Piece menu
- Delete Piece from the Work Area

- Combine/Merge
- Scale
- Shrink/Stretch
- Mirror Piece
- Fold Mirror
- Unfold Mirror
- Open Mirror
- Annotate Piece
- Piece to menu

Create Piece

The Create Piece menu lets you create pieces such as circles, rectangles, facings, fusible, skirts, and collars.

Rectangle

The Rectangle function creates rectangle or square pattern pieces, and you can enter a length and width for specific measurements. You can also enter a measurement from one corner to the diagonal corner.

Use the Rectangle function when you need to

- create waistbands.
- create pockets.
- start the creation of a piece from a block form.
- create belt loops.

Procedure to create a rectangle

1. Select **Piece>Create Piece>Rectangle.**

2. A user input box states: "Press to select one corner, press again to select other corner." Left click anywhere on the screen and release. Move the mouse and see how the rectangle takes shape as the mouse moves. This creates the first corner. Figure 8.1 shows where we selected our first corner. Press with the left mouse button again to set down the second corner and create the rectangle.

3. Save the piece if you need it for later use.

Note: To enter a value for the rectangle, follow the next procedure instead of Step 2. Press anywhere on the screen with the left mouse button and release. This creates the first corner as shown in Figure 8.1. Move the mouse and see how the rectangle takes shape as the mouse moves.

Click **Cursor** to toggle to **Value** and change to Value Mode, or do a popup (by pressing the left and right mouse buttons at the same time and releasing). Enter values in the X and Y fields.

Circle

The Circle function lets create you a circle by entering a circumference or radius to determine the size or by visually adjusting the size as you create it on-screen. The circle may exist on its own as a pattern or as an internal in an existing piece. This function works the same as the Circle Ctr Rad and Circle Ctr Cirm functions located in the Line menu under Conics (discussed in Chapter 9).

Use the Circle function when you need to

- create circular skirts.
- create hats.
- create circle cutouts.
- create circular designs.
- create designs that may start as circles, such as flowers.

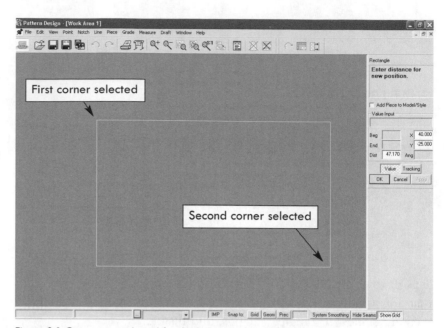

Figure 8.1 Corners are selected for the Rectangle function.

Procedure to create a circle

1. Select **Piece>Create Piece>Circle.**

2. Select your preferences from the user input box.

3. In the **New Piece** area, select from the options described below.

   Name is used to enter a piece name for the circle you are creating. It displays if you check the box next to Create New Piece.

   Create New Piece is used when you want to make a circle for the creation of a pattern on its own. For example, use a circle to create a hat pattern. Leave this option unchecked if you want to create the circle as an internal (for example, you want to create a circular cutout in the back of a dress).

4. In the **Show Center** area, select the type of point you want in the center of the circle.

   None is used to leave the center blank with no point displayed.

   Drill is used to display a drill point (+) in the center of the circle.

Mark is used to display a mark point (X) in the center of the circle.

5. In the **Circle Dimension** area, select the method to create the circle.

> **Radius** is used when you want to create a circle by entering a radius measurement. The radius is measured from the edge of a circle to the center and is considered half the width of a circle.

> **Circumference** is used when you want to create a circle by entering a circumference. The circumference of the circle is the measurement around the outline/perimeter of the circle.

6. A user input box states: "Select center of circle." Left click to select a location/point on the piece or the screen to create a circle. The circle gets larger or smaller with the mouse. If it is not changing, then you are in Value Mode and should be ready to input a measurement. Figure 8.2 displays a point selected on the center back of a dress.

7. A user input box states: "Select radius (or circumference) of circle." According to the selection you made under **Circle Dimension,** enter the radius or circumference in the **Dist** field, which lights up when you perform a popup, or click the **Cursor** button to display **Value.** Click **OK** to enter the value and create the circle.

8. Save the piece if you need it for later use.

Note: The example in Figure 8.2 shows a circle cutout that is being created for a dress. To finish the pattern, you may use the Split function to split the circle and the center front line segments. Splitting the line segments will make it easier for you to trace the pattern with the new circle cutout when you use the Trace function in the Create Piece menu.

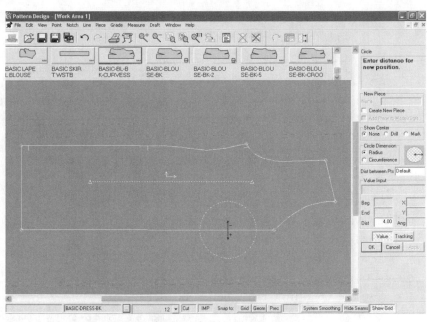

Figure 8.2 Creating a circle in the center of a dress back.

Skirt

The Skirt function is used to create one quarter of the pattern for a circular skirt. Enter the length and total waist of the skirt to create it.

Procedure to create a skirt

1. Select **Piece>Create Piece>Skirt.**

2. A user input box states: "Enter values in fields and click **OK** to create piece." Select the preferences and dimensions in the user input box. See the steps that follow for further explanation.

3. In the **Name** field, enter the name of the skirt that you are going to create.

4. Check the box next to **Show Center Point** to create a point at the center of the skirt. Look at the diagram in the user input box while you are in the function.

5. In the **Dimensions** area, enter the measurements for the two listed fields.

> **Waist** is used to enter the total waist measurement you want for the skirt.

> **Length** is used to enter the length you want for the skirt.

Figure 8.3 shows a skirt with the dimensions of 30" for the waist and 22" for the length.

6. Click **OK** to create the skirt according to the options you selected.

7. Save the piece for later use.

Oval

The Oval function is used to create an oval. Enter a horizontal and a vertical measurement to create the oval (see Figure 8.4).

Use the Oval function when you want to

- create oval cutouts.
- create petal shapes for designs on a garment or pattern shapes.
- create oval shoulder pads.
- create oval patches.
- create table covers.
- create seat covers.
- use part of the oval to help you create another piece—much like using a French curve.

Procedure to create an oval

1. Select **Piece>Create Piece>Oval.**

2. A user input box states: "Enter values in fields and select **OK** to create piece." Select the preferences and dimensions in the user input box. See the steps that follow for further explanation.

3. In the **Name** field, enter the name of the oval you want to create.

4. Check the box next to **Show Center Point** to create a mark point at the center of the oval.

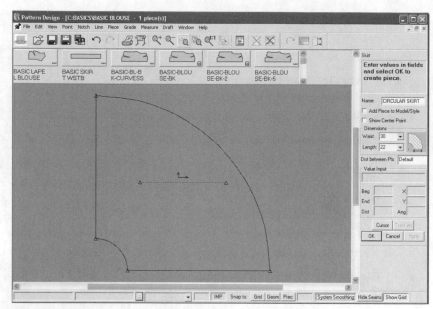

Figure 8.3 Skirt created with the skirt function.

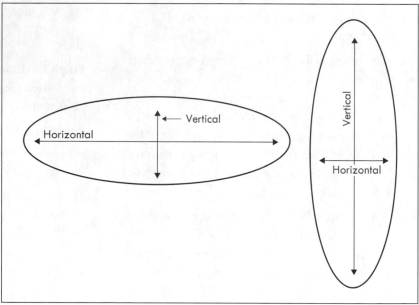

Figure 8.4 Oval directions are illustrated.

5. In the **Dimensions** area, enter the measurements for the two listed fields.

> **Horiz** is used to enter the horizontal measurement of the oval.
>
> **Vert** is used to enter the vertical measurement of the oval.

Figure 8.5 shows an oval with the dimensions of 20" in the horizontal direction and 10" in the vertical direction. Notice the miniature preview that helps you to identify the orientation of your oval.

6. Click **OK** to create the oval according to the options you selected.

7. Save the piece for later use.

Collar

The Collar function is used to create a collar. Enter the dimensions, including collar width, CB to shoulder, shoulder to CF, and line rotation, found in the user input box. CB refers to the center back and CF refers to the center front. When you are done, click OK to create the collar. You may then add seam allowance by selecting Piece> Seam>Define/Add Seam.

Procedure to create a collar

1. Select **Piece>Create Piece>Collar.**

2. A user input box states: "Enter values in fields and click OK to create piece." Select the preferences and dimensions in the user input box. See the steps that follow for further explanation.

3. In the **Name** field, enter the name of the collar you are creating.

4. In the **Dimensions** area, enter the measurements for the options listed.

Collar Width is used to enter the width of the collar.

CB to Shoulder is used to enter the measurement from the center back to the shoulder.

Shoulder to CF is used to enter the measurement from the shoulder to the center front.

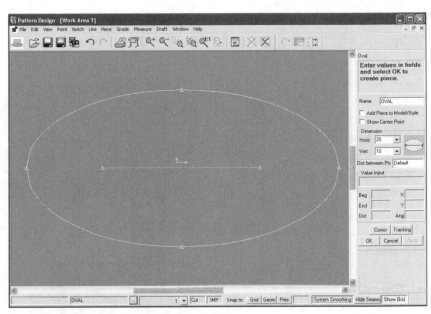

Figure 8.5 Oval created with the Oval function.

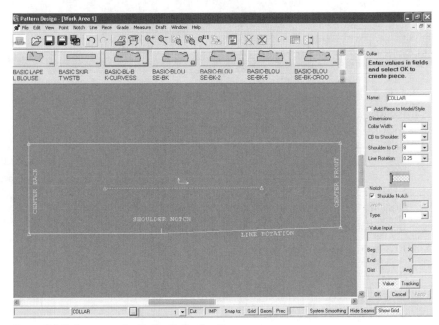

Figure 8.6 Collar created with the Collar function.

Line Rotation is used to enter the amount the line should rotate for the collar from the shoulder to the center front.

Figure 8.6 shows a collar with the dimensions displayed.

5. Click **OK** to create the collar according to the options selected.

6. Save the piece for later use.

Facing

The Facing function is used to create facing for a pattern. There are several options to choose from before you perform this function. You may add seam allowance to the facing piece when it is finished. The allowance is always positive. You can also define the exact length of the line with the Modify Length option.

The **Line Type** you select determines the prompts that will appear during the function. For example, if the piece already has a line that was created to act as a facing line prior to this function, use the line type option Existing Line to select it as the facing line. You could have used options such as Digitized or Offset Even to create a line prior to this function. You may use the Facing or Trace functions to create a facing pattern if you created a line to serve as a facing line; it is simply a matter of preference.

Use the Line Type option labeled Digitized Line to create a facing line within the function. This option works the same as using the Digitized function in the Line menu. Therefore, it is a combination of the Digitized and Facing functions.

Procedure to create a facing

1. Select **Piece>Create Piece>Facing.**

2. Select your preferences from the user input box (see Figure 8.7).

3. Check the box next to **Add Piece to Model/Style** to add the facing piece to a selected model.

4. Check the box next to **Define Seam on Facing Line** to add seam allowance to the facing during the function.

5. Check the box next to **Modify Length** to enter and determine the length of the facing line. This option is available only when you are creating a facing line within the function,

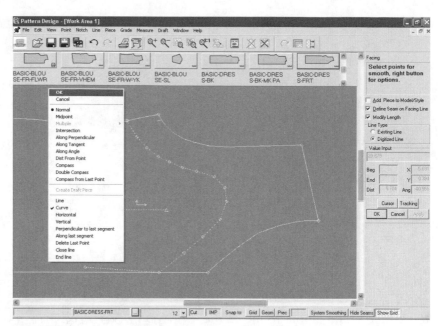

Figure 8.7 Facing line created to build a facing pattern.

which means that you have selected the Line Type option Digitized Line described in the next step.

6. In the Line Type area, select one of the two listed options.

   Existing Line is selected if the line to be used as the facing line already exists on the piece.

   Digitized Line is selected to create a facing line.

7. A user input box states: "Select points for smooth, right button for options." Left click to place points down to create the shape of the facing line. Since Figure 8.7 displays smooth/curve points being placed, the prompt states "points for smooth" rather than "points for straight."

8. Right click and select **OK** to finish creating the line.

9. A user input box states: "Enter amount to adjust length." Enter the measurement to determine the length of the facing line. Click **OK**. This prompt appears because **Modify Length** was selected for this example.

10. A user input box states: "Enter the seam allowance value for the split line." Enter the seam allowance that you want to add the facing pattern. This prompt appears because we selected **Define Seam on Facing Line** for this example. Although not shown here, we entered ½" for this example. The bottom of Figure 8.8 shows the facing with the seam allowance already added.

11. A user input box states: "Select the facing piece." A weight is placed over the side of the piece that is highlighted. Left click to highlight and select the side that you want to create as the facing pattern (see the top area of Figure 8.8).

12. A user input box states: "Enter piece name." Enter the name for the facing. Click **OK** or press **Enter** on the keyboard (see the bottom area of Figure 8.8).

13. Save the new facing piece.

14. The function restarts. Right click and select **Cancel** to exit.

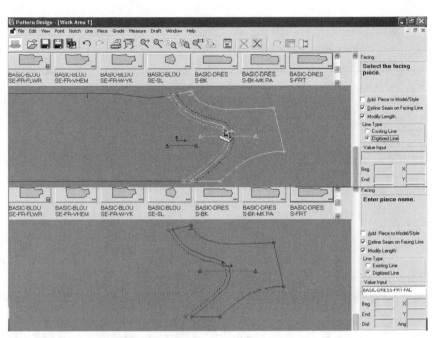

Figure 8.8 Facing is created and named.

Fusible

The Fusible function is used to create the fusing for a garment pattern. The fusible amount entered is always negative since a fusible pattern is usually smaller than the original pattern.

More than one pattern may be selected at the same time to create fusible. Patterns that you select at the same time will receive the same fusible amount. The piece at the left in Figure 8.9 shows a fusing pattern created from the original pattern by reducing it all around the piece. This is the task that you may have heard refered to as "reduce the piece ⅛" all the way around for the fusible."

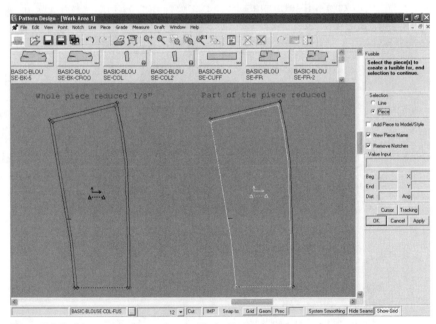

Figure 8.9 Fusible patterns are created with the Fusing function.

If the whole piece does not have to be reduced, specific lines may be selected to be reduced for the fusing pattern. You need to select the Line option for this procedure to be available. The piece at the right in Figure 8.9 displays a fusing pattern created from the original pattern by reducing only two perimeter lines.

Procedure for Fusible

1. Select **Piece>Create Piece>Fusible.**

2. Select your preferences from the user input box.

3. In the **Selection** area, select one of the two listed options.

    Line is used so you can select specific lines or the whole pattern at once. Each line you select turns red.

    Piece lets you select the whole pattern at once.

4. Check the box next to **Add Piece to Model/Style** to add the facing piece to a selected model.

5. Check the box next to **New Piece Name** to allow the created fusible pattern to be named separately. Even if you don't select this option, you can still enter a piece name when you save the piece.

6. Check the box next to **Remove Notches** so that the fusible piece does not contain any notches.

7. A user input box states: "Select the piece(s) to create a fusible for, end selection to continue." Left click to select pieces, which highlights the pieces in red. Right click and select **OK** to end the selection.

8. A user input box states: "Enter the amount the original piece should be reduced when creating the fusible." Enter the amount in the **Value Input** field. Select **OK** or press **Enter** on the keyboard. Although not shown, we entered $-\frac{1}{8}''$ for the examples in Figure 8.9.

9. A user input box states: "Enter piece name." This prompt appears if **New Piece** was selected. Enter the name for the fusible pattern. For example, the information bar shows

that the piece in Figure 8.9 was named Basic Blouse-Col-Fus. The fusible piece is created. The piece is displayed on top of the original piece. Separate the pieces with the F2 hotkey or with the mouse.

10. Save the piece.

Binding

The Binding function is used to create the binding for areas such as armholes, necklines, or hems. Figure 8.10 is a technical drawing of a bodice that has binding in the armholes. Binding is used as a design detail to style a garment, to finish a raw edge, or to reinforce a seam. Figure 8.11 is a photograph of a top with armhole binding. Many times, it is seen in a contrasting color in the areas mentioned above or any seam that needs a clean finish.

Procedure for Binding

1. Select **Piece>Create Piece>Binding.**

2. Select your preferences from the user input box. Notice the options that we have selected for our example in Figure 8.12.

3. In the **Name** field, enter a name for the binding pattern being created.

4. Check the box next to **Add Piece to Model/Style** to add the binding piece to a selected model.

Figure 8.10 Binding is sewn to finish the armholes of this bodice.

Figure 8.11 A top with armhole binding.

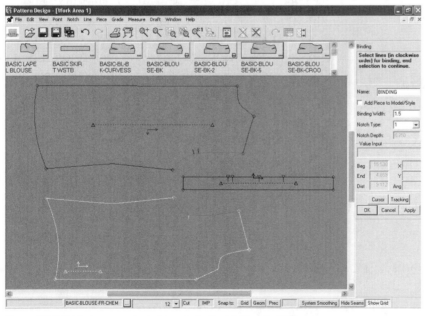

Figure 8.12 Armholes are selected to create the binding shown here.

5. In the **Binding Width** field, enter the width of the binding. The seam allowance may be factored in or may be added later with the Define/Add Seam function.

6. In the **Notch Type** field, select the type of notch you want if a notch is created in the binding pattern. The system will refer to the Notch Parameter Table. Figure 8.12 shows the binding with notches added.

7. A user input box states: "Select lines (in clockwise order) for binding, end selection to continue." Left click to select lines, which highlights them in red. Right click and select **OK** to end the selection. The binding is created and moves along with the mouse. For the example in Figure 8.12, we selected the armholes.

8. Left click to set piece down on the screen.

9. Save the piece.

Copy

The Copy function is used to create a duplicate of the piece displayed on-screen. For example, if you are manipulating a piece and are satisfied with the result but want to manipulate it a little more, then create a copy. You may keep on manipulating the copy and keep the other piece as the piece to revert to if the next steps you take do not give you the results you expected. Sometimes it is easy to forget what point of pattern manipulation was correct, so having a copy of the piece with which you were happy at first is quite helpful.

If you need multiple copies of a saved piece, you do not need to use the Copy function—just bring them down from the icon menu.

The top piece in Figure 8.13 has been manipulated from its original state. The original piece may be seen in the icon menu. Notice that it previously had two darts. The bottom piece in Figure 8.13 is the copy that was further manipulated.

Procedure for Copy

1. Select **Piece>Create Piece>Copy.**

2. Check the box next to **Add Piece to Model/Style** if you want to add the copied piece to a selected model.

3. A user input box states: "Select piece." Left click to select the piece to copy. The new piece moves along with the mouse.

4. Set the piece down on screen with the left button.

5. A user input box states: "Enter piece name." Enter the name of the new piece and select **OK.**

6. Save the piece if you want to keep it.

Extract

The front skirt shown in Figure 8.14 is ready to be created into a skirt pattern that is made up of five pieces. These pieces may be different colors or

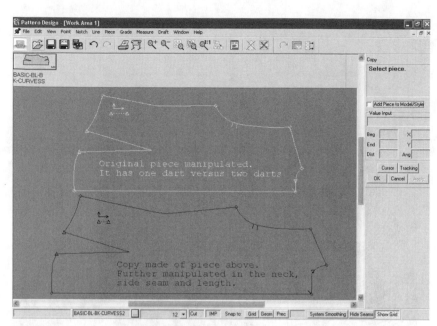

Figure 8.13 The piece is copied to keep the last revision.

simply create stylish seam lines. The style lines have been created to determine where the skirt will be cut or separated. These lines may have been created with functions such as Digitized, 2 Point, or 2 Point-Curve. The style lines shown in Figure 8.14 were created with 2 Point-Curve and the points with Add Point.

The Extract function lets you select a region to extract and essentially traces the region to make it into a piece of its own. Internal lines or points that belong to that region may also be selected to be a part of that pattern, as shown in Figure 8.14, where the piece was extracted along with the points in the region.

Figure 8.14, as well as other figures throughout the book, has been set up to show the different steps involved in the procedure to extract regions. We copied the piece several times to create the illustration. The Trace function may be used instead of this function to get the same results if you prefer to select the lines you want to trace.

Procedure for Extract

1. Select **Piece>Create Piece>Extract.**

2. A user input box states: "Select the Piece to extract regions from." Left click to select the piece.

3. A user input box states: "Select region to extract." Left click to select area to extract. The piece is highlighted in one color and turns to another color when you actually select on your screen; for example, it will change from purple to orange.

4. A user input box states: "Select additional regions adjacent to extracted regions." Left click to select additional regions. If more regions are selected at the same time, they will become a part of the area selected in the step above. The regions must be next to each other as seen in Figure 8.14. Right click and select **OK** to continue.

5. A user input box states: "Enter piece name." Enter the piece name for the extracted region and click **OK.**

6. A user input box states: "Select internal line(s), end selection to continue." Left click to select internal lines or points that need to be added to the extracted region. They turn invisible as you select them. Right click and select **OK** to continue.

Note: If you don't need to select any internal lines, right click and select **OK** to continue.

7. The piece is extracted and moves along with the mouse. Left click to set it down on-screen. A grain line is established at the center of the piece.

8. The function restarts so you can extract more regions. Right click and select **Cancel** if done.

9. Save the extracted pieces. Figure 8.15 illustrates all the regions extracted from the skirt.

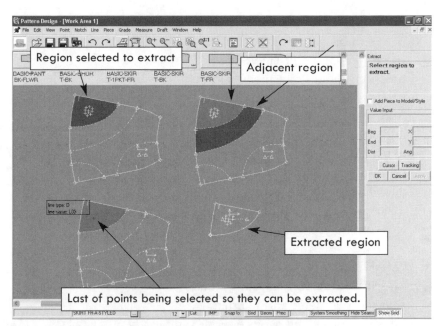

Figure 8.14 Steps showing how a pattern piece is extracted from a skirt.

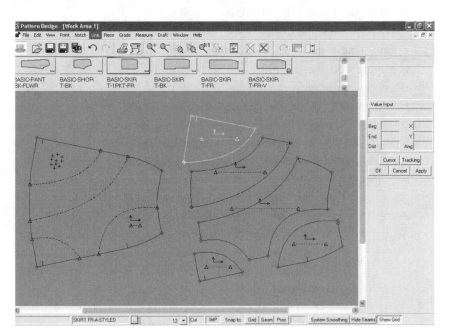

Figure 8.15 All pieces extracted from a skirt.

Note: The new grain lines created may end up going outside of the piece. The Move Pt Line/Slide function in the Point menu can be used to shorten the line. Define/Add Seam may be used next to add seam allowance to the regions extracted. The Swap Sew/Cut function is then used to swap the seam allowance with the perimeter lines. Make sure to save the piece again to keep the changes.

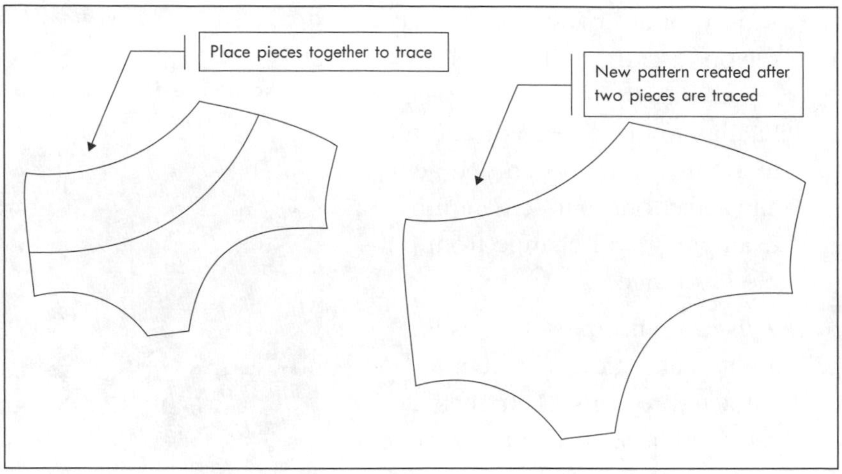

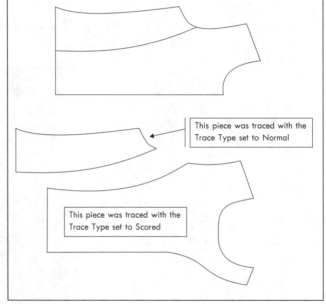

Figure 8.16 Pattern pieces are placed side by side so they can be traced.

Trace

The Trace function is used to trace selected perimeter and internal lines and points on a piece. For example, the regions for the skirt in Figure 8.14 could have been created with the Trace function as well.

You can use more than one piece to trace and create a new piece. For example, two of the patterns created for the skirt in Figure 8.15 may be used to create one piece. Figure 8.16 displays the before and after of two pieces from the skirt in Figure 8.15, placed next to each other to be traced. The Combine/Merge function under the Piece menu can combine these regions as well, but the procedure is different.

Available Options for Trace Function

Trace Type This area has three available options.

- *Normal:* This option is usually used on a piece that is not mirrored, a *closed* piece.

- *Mirror:* Select this option when using a mirrored piece that has a mirror line that needs to remain mirrored. Always select the lines in a clockwise direction from the mirrored line. For example, look at the blouse in Figure 8.17. If you were to trace the center front pattern, you would select the hem first, followed by the princess seam, armhole, shoulder, and neckline.

- *Scored:* Select this option to mirror a part of the piece and add a facing piece at the same time. Figure 8.17 includes an example of a

Figure 8.17 Drawing of a normal piece that is traced versus a scored piece.

scored pattern piece. The procedure using this option is discussed later in this section.

Add Piece to Model/Style: Check this box to add the facing piece to a selected model.

Fold After Mirror: This option is only available when the Mirror option is selected. After a mirrored piece is traced, the new pattern may appear on-screen folded if this box is checked. The piece appears unfolded if this box is not checked.

Maintain Graded Nest: The system tries to maintain and transfer the grading from the original piece to the new traced pattern.

Procedure for Trace using the Normal option in the Trace Type area

1. Select **Piece>Create Piece>Trace.**

2. A user input box states: "Select perimeter line(s) to trace, end selection to continue." Left click to select the lines you need to trace to create the shape of the piece in a *clockwise* direction. Figure 8.18 displays the selected lines to create the side body pattern of a blouse.

3. Right click and select **OK** to end the selection and continue with the function.

4. A user input box states: "Select internal line(s) and point(s) to trace, end selection to continue." Left click to select the lines or points that you need to also trace along with the piece, which highlights them in red. Right click to continue.

   Note: If there are no internals to trace, right click to continue. We did not have any internals to select for the side body in Figure 8.18.

5. The piece is traced and moves along with the mouse. Left click to set down the piece on-screen. A grain line is established at the center of the piece. Figure 8.18 displays the side body pattern that was traced and created.

6. The user input box states: "Enter piece name." For example, although it is not shown, we named this piece Basic-Blouse-Sd-Fr.

7. The function restarts for another piece to be traced. Right click and select **Cancel** if you are done.

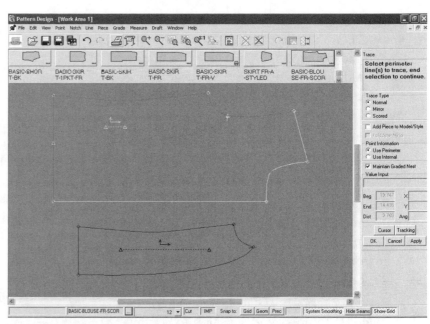

Figure 8.18 Side bodice is traced by using the Normal option.

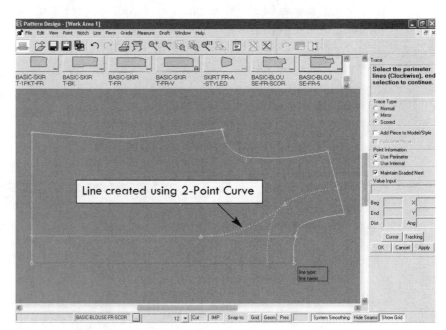

Figure 8.19 A bodice displayed for tracing using the Scored option.

8. Save the traced pieces.

The procedure for tracing a Scored piece is detailed on page 132. Figure 8.19 displays a bodice to be traced with this option. Note that we have created additional necessary lines to trace the piece properly. The Offset Even function was used to create the lines offset from the neckline and center front. Then the 2 Point-Curve function was used to create the shape in the intersection of the two lines. Although these were the functions used for this example, other functions may be used if you prefer.

Procedure for Trace using the Scored option in the Trace Type area

1. Select **Piece>Create Piece>Trace.**

2. A user input box states: "Select the score line." Left click to select the score line. This is the line that will be mirrored. The center front line is selected as the score line in Figure 8.19.

3. A user input box states: "Select perimeter line(s) to trace, end selection to continue." Left click to select the lines you need to trace to create the shape of the piece in a *clockwise* direction. The hem in Figure 8.19 was selected first, followed by the side seam, armhole, shoulder, and neckline.

4. Right click and select **OK** to end the selection and continue with the function.

5. The user input box states: "Select perimeter line to score (Counter Clockwise), end selection to continue." Left click to select the lines that shape the facing to be added. For Figure 8.20, the neckline was selected first, followed by the shoulder, the offset neckline, the curved intersection line, the center front offset, and the hem.

6. Right click and select **OK** to end the selection and continue with the function.

7. The user input box states: "Select internal line(s) and point(s) to trace, end selection to continue." Left click to select the lines or points that you need to also trace along

with the piece, which highlights them in red. Right click to continue.

Note: If there are no internals to trace, right click to continue. We did not have any internals to select for the pattern in Figure 8.20.

8. The piece is traced and moves along with the mouse. Left click to set it down on-screen. A grain line is established at the center of the piece. The pattern at the bottom of Figure 8.20 is the new pattern traced with a facing added.

9. A user input box states: "Enter piece name." For example, although it is not shown, we named this piece Basic-Blouse-Fr. The facing is incorporated into the front piece pattern.

10. The function restarts for another piece to be traced. Right click and select **Cancel** if done.

11. Save the traced pieces.

Note: Since many of the lines now have split points, shown as a diamond shape, the lines should be combined into one line segment using the Combine/Merge function in the Line menu.

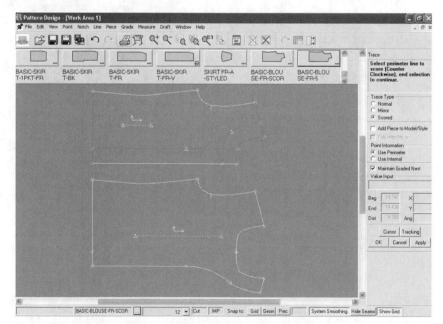

Figure 8.20 A bodice is traced and created with added facing using the Scored option.

Pleats

The Pleats menu gives you the ability to create pleats in various ways. Four options are available for the creation of knife or box pleats as shown in Figure 8.21. Pleats may be used to add fullness or simply for styling. Garments that have been commonly known to contain either knife and/or box pleats include tennis and cheerleading skirts. Figure 8.22 shows a photograph of a tennis skirt with knife pleats.

The functions Knife Pleat and Box Pleat require the piece to have a line digitized prior to using the function to be used as the pleat line. See Figures 8.23 and 8.24. The Variable Pleat and Taper Pleat functions let you digitize a line within the function, to use as a pleat line. Several options and prompts that are used throughout these functions are defined below.

Available Options and Common Prompts in the Pleats Menu

Notching Lines This area has three options for notching preferences on pleat lines.

- *Both:* Select this option so that the system notches both ends of the pleat line.

- *Single:* Select this option and one end of the line may be selected to receive notches.

- *None:* Select this option and no notches will be used.

Notching Folds This area allows you to select which notches you would like to have the system insert. Each function displays a diagram in the user input box that displays the different notch location options.

Notch Type Select the notch type to be used when notches are inserted by activating the drop-down menu.

Half of the underlay This is half of the width or depth of the pleat (see Figure 8.21).

Enter the number of pleats Enter the total number of pleats that the system should create based on the line selected. The Knife Pleat and Box Pleat options will show this prompt.

Slash line from pivot end to open end The pivot end is the end of the line that will not receive any width. For example, when creating fullness at the hem of a straight skirt, the waist is the pivot end and the hem is the open end.

Select location to remain stationary This is the part of the piece that should not move. For example, the side of the piece that is parallel to the grain line, such as a center front, is usually the stationary side chosen to not distort the grain on the pattern.

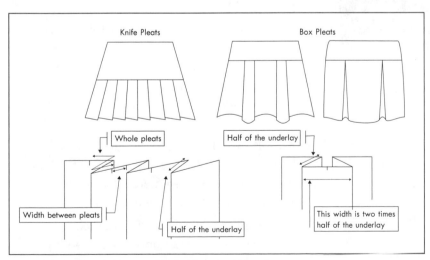

Figure 8.21 Technical drawing of knife pleats and box pleats

Figure 8.22 Photo of a tennis skirt with knife pleats.

Knife Pleat

Knife pleats like the ones shown on the tennis skirt in Figure 8.22 can all face one direction or they may be created to face one another. Figure 8.23 shows a sleeve before and after adding two knife pleats along the length of the sleeve. The line along the center of the sleeve was created with the 2 Point function prior to using the Knife Pleat function. When more than one pleat is created, as in this sleeve, the additional pleats parallel the origi-

nal line created. Create the line to be used as the pleat line according to the direction desired; for example, horizontal, vertical, or at an angle. The underlay entered is applied to both ends of the pleat line. If more than one pleat is created, the distance between the pleats is also the same on both ends of the pleat line.

Procedure to create a knife pleat

1. Create a line to use as the pleat line.

2. Select **Piece>Pleats>Knife Pleat.**

3. Select the **Notching Line** options. We opted to use **Both** in this example to notch both ends of the pleat.

4. Select the **Notching Folds** options. Look at the diagram in the user input box and select the location for the notches desired, as shown in Figure 8.23.

5. Select the **Notch Type** if you are using notches.

6. A user input box states: "Select a pleat line for the knife pleat." Left click to select the pre-digitized line.

7. Right click and select **OK** to continue.

8. A user input box states: "Enter half of the underlay." This is half the width of the total pleat width. We entered ¾" (0.75) for this example. Therefore the total width of our pleat is 1½".

9. A user input box states: "Enter the number of pleats." If more than one pleat is desired, enter it in the **Value Input** field. One is the default. If you need only one, click **OK** and jump to Step 11. We entered two for our sleeve.

10. A user input box states: "Enter distance between pleats." Enter the space between the pleats. Zero may be entered for no distance. We entered 3" for our sleeve.

11. A user input box states: "Select pleat open side." This is the side opposite of the lay side. Left click to select any part of the piece that is considered the open side. Figure 8.23 shows where the open side is located.

12. A user input box states: "Select pleat lay side." The **pleat lay side** is the side of the piece toward which the pleats will lay. Left click to select any part of the piece that is considered the lay side. The pleats are created as shown in Figure 8.23.

13. Save the piece to keep the changes.

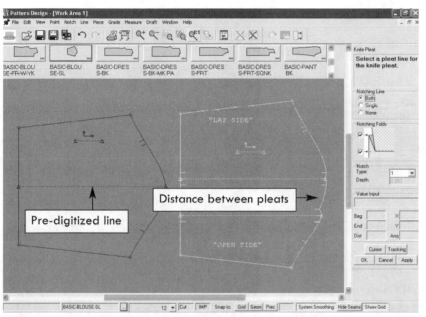

Figure 8.23 Knife pleats are added to a sleeve.

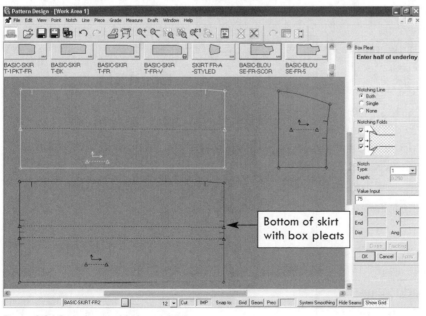

Figure 8.24 Box pleats added to a skirt.

Box Pleat

The Box Pleat function is used to create box pleats or inverted box pleats like the ones shown on the skirts in Figure 8.21. Box pleats are used in many different types of garments, including shirts, pants, and blouses. The pleat commonly seen on the backs of men's dress shirts is a box pleat. The skirt on the left side, under Box Pleats, in Figure 8.21, displays regular box pleats. The skirt on the right side displays inverted box pleats. An inverted box pleat is created in the same way a box pleat is created, but the best way to explain the difference is to say that it is sewn inside out. The detail drawing of the box pleat in Figure 8.21 applies to both regular and inverted pleats.

Figure 8.24 displays a skirt before and after adding a box pleat along the length of the skirt. The skirt created to illustrate this procedure is the one with the regular box pleats shown in Figure 8.21, on the left. Since the skirt has a yoke, we split the skirt first with the option Split on Digitized Line. Then we created the line to be used as the pleat line with the 2-Point function. When more than one pleat is created, the additional pleats are parallel to the original line. Therefore, the pleat line you create should be digitized according to the direction you want; for example, horizontal, vertical, or at an angle. The underlay you enter will be applied to both ends of the pleat line. If you create more than one pleat, the distance between the pleats is also the same on both ends of the pleat line.

Procedure to create a box pleat

1. Create a line to use as the pleat line.

2. Select **Piece>Pleats>Box Pleat.**

3. Select the **Notching Line** options. We opted to use **Both** in this example to notch both ends of the pleat.

4. Select the **Notching Folds** options. Look at the diagram in the user input box and select the location for the notches you want, as seen in Figure 8.24. We have selected all the boxes to place notches on all the folds and where they meet.

5. Select the **Notch Type** if you are using notches.

6. A user input box states: "Select a pleat line for the box pleat." Left click to select the pre-digitized line.

7. Right click and select **OK** to continue.

8. A user input box states: "Enter half of the underlay." This is half the width of the total pleat width. We entered 1" for this example. Therefore, the total width of our pleat is 2".

9. A user input box states: "Enter the number of pleats." If you want more than one pleat, enter it in the **Value Input** field. One is the default. If you need only one, click **OK** to continue and jump to Step 11. We entered one for the skirt in Figure 8.24 and therefore jumped to Step 11.

10. A user input box states: "Enter distance between pleats." Enter the space between the pleats. You may enter zero for no distance.

11. A user input box states: "Select pleat open side." The **pleat open side** is the side opposite of the lay side. Left click to select on any part of the piece that is considered the open side. Refer back to Figure 8.23 for an example of the pleat open side.

12. The pleats are created, as shown in Figure 8.24.

13. Save the piece to keep the changes.

Note: For this example, since the piece was split before creating the pleat, we have to add seam allowance so you can sew the pieces back together. Use the function Define/Add Seam to add seam allowance.

Taper Pleat

Figure 8.25 shows a pair of pants with tapered pleats. A **tapered pleat** has width on one end and none on the other. The pleats on the pant have no width at the waist and width on the pant leg opening and, therefore, go from nothing to 3". The illustrated pleat is a box pleat, but there is a prompt within the function that lets you choose between a box and a knife pleat.

The Taper Pleat function lets you create a pleat line within the function, so you do not have to create a pleat line prior to using this function, as in the Knife Pleat and Box Pleat functions. Since the pleat line is digitized from pivot end to open end, the pleat line on the pant is digitized starting from the waist to the pant leg opening.

Multiple lines may be created for pleat lines within the function. This allows you to place the lines in the necessary direction or angle and one can be different from the other. You can start and end the slash line wherever you think it fits best visually or you can enter a value in the same way you would digitized a line with the Digitized function in the Line menu. For example, the slash line in the pant in Figure 8.26 was created from the

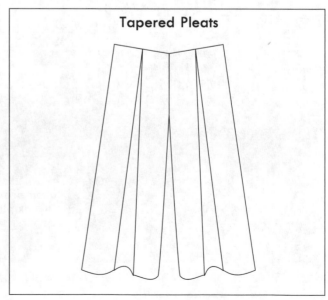

Figure 8.25 Pants created using the Taper Pleat function.

midpoint of the waist to the midpoint of the leg opening.

Refer to the beginning of the pleats section of this chapter for prompts used within this menu of functions.

Procedure to create a tapered pleat

1. Select **Piece>Pleats>Taper Pleat.**

2. A user input box states: "Create a slash line(s) from pivot end to open end." Left click on the line to start the slash line. Left click again to select where to end the line. For example, in Figure 8.26, we created the slash line from the midpoint on the waist to the midpoint of the leg opening.

3. Right click and select **OK** to continue.

4. A user input box states: "Select location to remain stationary." This is the part of the piece that should not move. Repeat this procedure from Step 1 twice to see the difference in selecting stationary lines. First, left click to select the inseam. Second, left click to select the intersection point of the slash line and the waist, as shown in Figure 8.26. This will open the pleat toward both directions and keep it balanced.

5. A user input box states: "Select internal line(s) to move, end selection to continue." The internal line you want to move is the slash line you just created. Right click and select **OK** and the system automatically recognizes this slash line—you won't have to select it with the mouse.

6. A user input box states: "Position piece to create spread." As you move the mouse, watch the piece spread to create the width of the pleat. Left click to set it down on-screen or

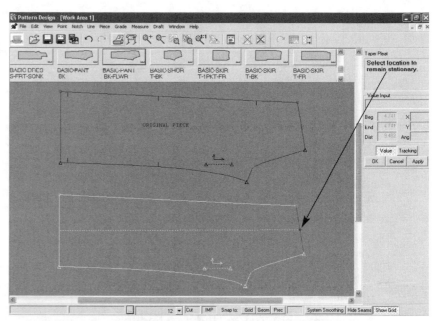

Figure 8.26 A stationary point is selected in the Taper Pleat function.

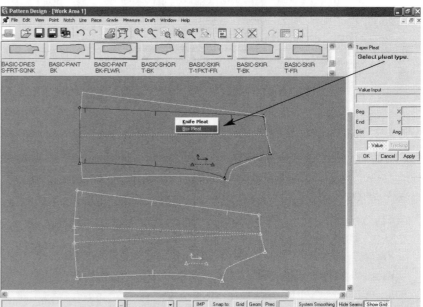

Figure 8.27 The pant is spread while using the Taper Pleat function.

perform a popup to enter a specific measurement. We entered 8" for the pant in this example. Figure 8.27 displays the pant being spread for the pleat creation.

7. A user input box states: "Select pleat type." A small rectangle displays with the options

Knife Pleat and **Box Pleat.** Left click on your selection. If you select a knife pleat, you will be prompted to select the lay side. We selected **Box Pleat.**

8. Select the **Notching Line** options. We opted to use **Single** in this example because we need notches only in the leg opening.

9. Select the **Notching Folds** options. Look at the diagram in the user input box, and select the location for the notches you want. Refer back to Figure 8.24. We have selected all the boxes so we can place notches on all the folds and where they meet.

10. Select the **Notch Type,** if you are using notches.

11. A user input box states: "Indicate line for notch placement." Left click to select the line that will receive the notch. This prompt appears only because we selected the option **Single** for the notching line.

12. Click **OK** in the user input box to accept the options from Steps 10 through 12. The pleat is created as shown on the pant at the bottom of Figure 8.27.

13. Save the piece to keep your changes or save it under a different name.

Variable Pleat

The results from using Variable Pleat could be considered a combination of Knife Pleat or Box Pleat and Taper Pleat. There are two spreads in the garment when you create this type of pleat. The first spread adds width to both ends of the pleat, similar to the spread when you use the Knife Pleat and Box Pleat functions. The second spread works like a Taper Pleat and adds width only to the end of the pleat considered the open end. Figure 8.28 shows a skirt with knife pleats that can be created using this function, although box pleats or one of each might be options you could choose instead, if you were to design this skirt.

The Variable Pleat function lets you create a pleat line within the function so you do not have to create a pleat line prior to using this function as

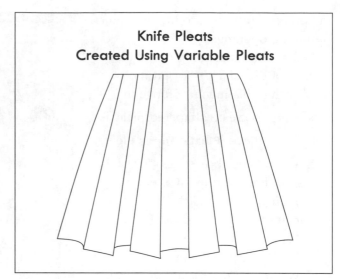

Figure 8.28 Skirt created using the Variable Pleat function.

in the Knife Pleat and Box Pleat functions. Since the pleat line is digitized from pivot end to open end, the pleat line on the skirt in the example is digitized starting from the waist to the hem.

You can create multiple lines for pleat lines within the function. This lets you place the lines in the necessary direction or angle and one pleat line can be different from the other. You can start and end the slash line wherever you think it fits best visually or you can enter a value in the same way you would digitize a line with the Digitized function in the Line menu. For example, the slash lines on the skirt in Figure 8.29 are displayed after we entered 2½" from the center front and side seam to create it.

Refer to the beginning of the pleats section of this chapter for prompts used within this menu of functions.

Procedure to create a variable pleat

1. Select **Piece>Pleats>Variable Pleat.**

2. The user input box states: "Create a slash line(s) from pivot end to open end." Left click on the line to start the slash line. Left click again to end the line. We created two slash lines from the waist to the hem, as seen on the skirt in Figure 8.29.

3. Right click and select **OK** to continue.

4. The user input box states: "Select location to remain stationary." Left click to select a stationary location. This is the part of the piece that should not move. We selected the center front of the skirt in Figure 8.29 so that the grain is not distorted.

5. The user input box states: "Select internal line(s) to move, end selection to continue."

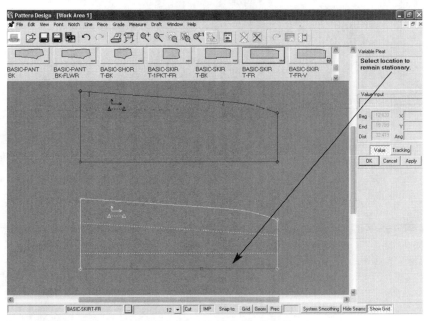

Figure 8.29 A stationary line is selected in the Variable Pleat function.

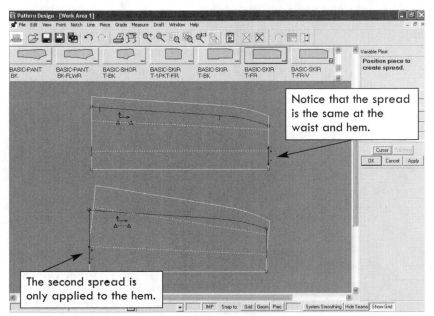

Notice that the spread is the same at the waist and hem.

The second spread is only applied to the hem.

Figure 8.30 A skirt is spread with the Variable Pleat function.

The internal lines you need to move are the slash lines you just created. Right click and select **OK** and the system automatically recognizes the slash lines you created—you won't have to select them.

6. The user input box states: "Position piece to create spread." As you move the mouse, watch the piece spread to create the width of the pleat. Left click to set it down on-screen or perform a popup to enter a specific measurement. This is a parallel move, meaning that you add width or fullness to both ends of the pleat at this point. We entered approximately 1½" for the spread on our skirt. See the skirt at the top in Figure 8.30 to see how the skirt is spread parallel first.

7. The user input box states: "Position piece to create spread." As you move the mouse, watch the piece spread to create the width of the pleat at the open end of the pleat. The pivot end does not spread any more. Left click to set it down on-screen or perform a popup to enter a specific measurement. This move is like the spread used in the Taper Pleat function. See the skirt at the bottom in Figure 8.30 to view how the skirt is spread for the tapered fullness. We entered 5" for this spread.

Note: Since we created two slash lines, Steps 6 and 7 are repeated again.

8. The user input box states: "Select pleat type." A small rectangle appears with the options **Knife Pleat** and **Box**

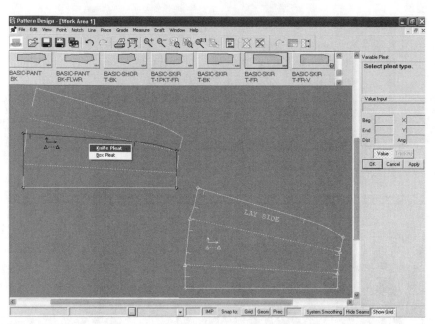

Figure 8.31 Pleat type selections for the Variable Pleat function.

Pleat. Select one with the left mouse button. If you select a knife pleat, you will be prompted to select the lay side. We selected **Knife Pleat** (see Figure 8.31).

9. Select the **Notching Line** options. We opted to use **Both** in this example because we need notches at both ends of the pleat to know how the pleat lays.

10. Select the **Notching Folds** options. Look at the diagram in the user input box and select the location for the notches you want. Refer back to Figure 8.24. We have selected all the boxes so we can place notches on all the folds and where they meet.

11. Select the **Notch Type** if you are using notches.

12. Click **OK** in the user input box to accept options from Steps 9 through 11.

    Note: Since we can select options for two pleat lines, repeat Steps 8 through 12 for this example.

13. The pleats are created, as shown in Figure 8.31.

14. Save the piece to keep your changes or save it under a different name.

Darts

Darts are commonly used to take away excess fabric or fullness to create a better-fitting garment. Sometimes they are used to create a certain look, such as the French dart, which is a deep dart that starts from the side seam of a bodice. Darts come in and out of style, but they are sure to remain as a styling or fitting element in the fashion industry.

The Dart menu has many available functions that let you perform commonly used industry tasks, such as pivoting or rotating darts and distributing or combining darts. "Slash and pivot" or "slash and spread" is a very common phrase that means to move a dart and close another or to combine a dart into another dart. This is the basic procedure used in these functions, so do not let their names throw you off. See Figure 8.32 for some examples of darts as they appear in simple tops and bottoms.

Darts can be manipulated only while they are open. If you use Fold/Close Dart to true up a dart, then you cannot manipulate the dart. Use the Open Dart function to reopen the dart so you can manipulate it again.

Several prompts that are used throughout the Dart menu functions are defined below.

Common Prompts in the Darts Menu

"Select the rotation point location." This is the point you cut to when manipulating a dart manually. It is the point that acts as your pivot point. The rotation point on a basic front is usually the apex of the bust, so it helps if it is digitized when you are a beginner. In other garments, the rotation point lies between the dart being manipulated and the new location. The position at which you place this point determines what the angle of the dart will look like in the end.

"Select hold line." This line is in the part of the garment that you do not want to move. It is the part

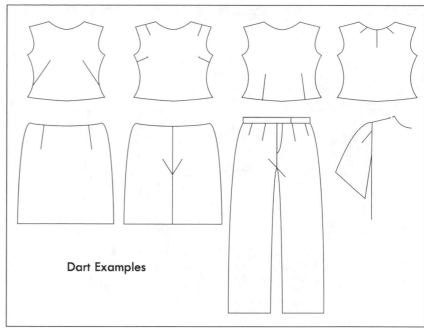

Dart Examples

Figure 8.32 Examples of darts used on garments.

you would tape down when manipulating a dart manually.

"Select opening point." This is the location where you are moving or creating the new dart. Manually, you would draw a line from this point to the rotation point.

"Select new dart apex." The dart apex is the dart depth. It is not referring to the apex of the bust.

Rotate

Rotate is used to pivot an existing dart from one location to another by closing the dart and opening it in a different location. For example, in Figure 8.33, we moved a dart from the hem of the bodice to the shoulder line.

Measurements may be input for some of the steps by performing a popup or clicking **Cursor** to enter Value Mode. For example, you may input the new location for the dart. You can also enter the length of the dart from the seam line from which it starts or enter a specific distance from the selected rotation point.

Procedure for Rotate

1. Select **Piece>Darts>Rotate.**

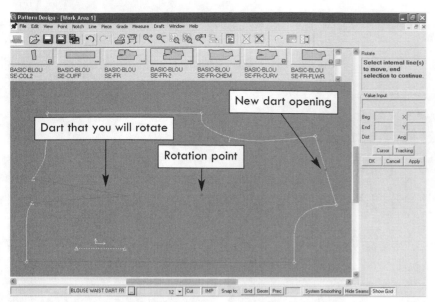

Figure 8.33 Prompt selections defined for the Rotate function.

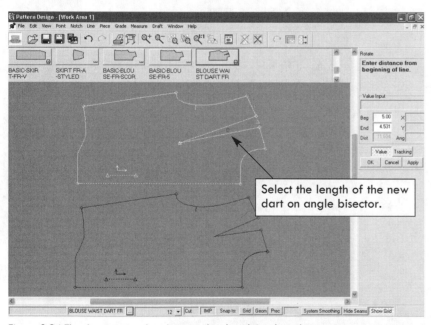

Figure 8.34 The dart is rotated and a new dart length is selected.

4. A user input box states: "Select the hold line." Left click to select the line on the part of the piece that needs to remain stationary. This is the part of the piece that you would tape down if you were doing it manually. We selected the center front in the bodice so that the grain line is not affected.

5. A user input box states: "Select the opening point." Left click to select a point on a perimeter line where the new dart will open, which highlights it in red. You can enter a specific measurement if you perform a popup or if you change to Value Mode. We selected the midpoint of the shoulder in Figure 8.33.

6. A user input box states: "Select internal line(s) to move, end selection to continue." Right click and select **OK** to continue. No line needs to be selected.

7. A user input box states: "Select new dart apex." A red line appears in the center of the dart, which is known as the angle bisector. Left click to select a point along this line or perform a popup or click **Cursor** to change to Value Mode and enter the length or depth of the dart. We entered 5" in the **Beg** field in the user input box for the dart in Figure 8.34. We could have entered a number in the **End** field instead, if we wanted to keep a specific distance from our rotation point, which in this case happens to be our apex/bust point.

8. The dart is created at the new location and the old one is closed, as seen in Figure 8.34.

9. Save the pattern to keep your changes or save it under a different name.

2. The user input box states: "Select dart to rotate." Left click to select the dart, which highlights it in red. Figure 8.33 shows the hem dart we selected.

3. The user input box states: "Select rotation point location." Left click to select a location in the pattern, which highlights it in red. This is the pivot point. We selected the bust point in Figure 8.33.

Distribute/Rotate

Although this function is not next on the menu lineup, we have listed it next because of its similarity to the previous function, Rotate. The Distribute/ Rotate function is used to close part of an existing dart so you can open up a new dart in a different location. Once again, the procedure we commonly know as slash and pivot is the basis for this function. We use the same bodice from the Rotate section so you can note the difference between the two functions. In this section, we take the dart in the hem and distribute part of its width to a new dart.

You can input measurements for some of the steps by performing a popup or clicking **Cursor** to toggle to **Value** and changing to Value Mode. For example, you can enter the new location for the dart. You can also input the length of the dart from the seam line from which it starts or enter a specific distance from the selected rotation point.

Procedure for Distribute/Rotate

1. Select **Piece>Darts>Distribute/Rotate.**

2. The user input box states: "Select dart to distribute." Left click to select the dart, which highlights it in red. Figure 8.35 shows the hem dart we selected.

3. The user input box states: "Select rotation point location." This is the pivot point. Left click to select a location in the pattern, which highlights it in red. We selected the bust point in Figure 8.35.

4. The user input box states: "Select the hold line." Left click to select the line on the part of the piece that needs to remain stationary. This is the part of the piece you would tape down if you were doing it manually. We selected the center front in the bodice in Figure 8.35 so that the grain line is not affected.

5. The user input box states: "Select the opening point." Left click to select a point on a perimeter line where the new dart will open, which highlights it in red. You can enter a specific measurement with a popup or click **Cursor** to toggle to Value Mode. We selected a location on the side seam of the bodice in Figure 8.35.

6. The user input box states: "Enter percentage or fixed measurement to distribute." The width of the dart we selected to distribute appears in the **Value Input** field. Figure 8.35 shows the width of our dart: 2.090.

Enter a percentage to take from the existing dart you selected, such as 50 percent. You can also enter a fixed measurement in inches or centimeters, such as ¾ or 0.75. This amount is taken away from the existing dart. We entered 50 percent so that half of the dart is distributed to create the new dart, as seen in Figure 8.35.

7. A user input box states: "Select internal line(s) to move, end selection to con-

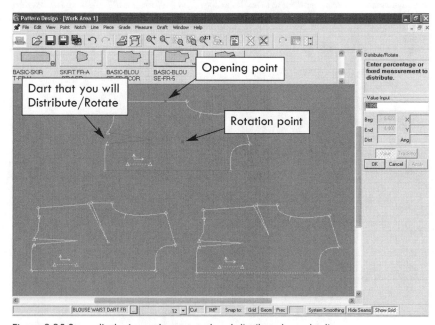

Figure 8.35 Steps displaying a dart rotated and distributed on a bodice.

tinue." Right click and select **OK** to continue. No line needs to be selected.

8. A user input box states: "Select new dart apex." A red line appears in the center of the dart, which is known as the angle bisector. Left click to select a point along this line or perform a popup or change to Value Mode to enter the length or depth of the dart. Notice the angle the dart takes due to the placement of the rotation point.

Although it is not shown, we entered 2" in the **Beg** field in the user input box for the dart in Figure 8.35. We could have entered a number in the **End** field instead if we wanted to enter a distance for the length of the dart.

9. Save the pattern to keep your changes or save it under a different name.

Distribute Same Line

The Distribute Same Line function is used to distribute the partial or whole width of a dart to one or more new darts. The location of the new darts must be on the same line as the existing dart. If you want to distribute to a different line, use the Distribute/Rotate function. The real purpose of this function is to create one or more darts from an existing dart (see Figure 8.36).

When you perform the function, the width of the dart appears with the "Enter percentage or fixed measurement to distribute" prompt. You have a choice to either enter a percentage for the system to take away from the existing dart or you can enter the exact measurement to take away from the dart. When you enter a percentage, you must use the percent sign at the end of the number; for example, 25% not 25. When you enter a fixed measurement, enter it as a fraction or decimal. For example, enter 0.75 or ¾; do not enter the inches symbol.

Let's say we have a dart that is 1" in width. Below are two examples of the math involved when using Distribute Same Line.

Example 1

A. We want to distribute this dart to create two more darts.

B. We enter 0.500 as the fixed measurement to distribute. Remember that the system can convert fractions.

C. The ½" is then distributed to the two new darts. Each dart is therefore ¼" in width. The original dart is now is ½" in width instead of 1".

Example 2

A. We want to distribute this dart to create two more darts to have three equal darts.

B. We enter 66.6% as the percentage to distribute. This means you have taken ⅔ or 66.6% width away from the original dart and now have ⅓ or 33.3% left for the original dart width.

C. The amount 0.666" is taken away from the original dart. The original dart is now 0.334" in width.

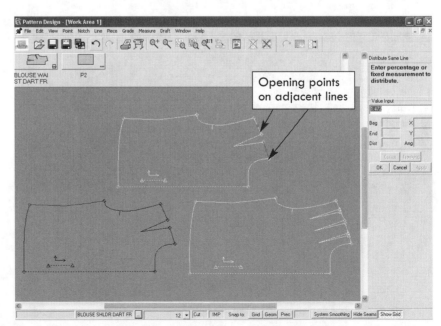

Figure 8.36 Steps displaying Distribute Same Line function used to create three shoulder darts.

D. The 0.666" is divided and distributed to the two new darts. Each dart is therefore 0.333" in width.

Procedure for Distribute Same Line

1. Select **Piece>Darts>Distribute Same Line.**

2. A user input box states: "Select a dart line." Left click to select the dart, which highlights it in red. We selected the shoulder dart on the bodice in Figure 8.36.

3. A user input box states: "Select open points on the adjacent lines for new darts." The adjacent lines are on either side of the dart. Left click on at least one point to select the location for the new darts, which highlights them in red.

4. Right click and select **OK** to continue.

5. The user input box states: "Enter percentage or fixed measurement to distribute." The width of the dart you select to distribute appears in the **Value Input** field. Figure 8.36 shows the width of our dart is 1.472.

   Enter a percentage or a fixed measurement to be taken away from the existing dart. We entered 66.6% for the dart in Figure 8.34. We now have three equal darts created as shown in Figure 8.36. Each one is 33.3% of the width of the original dart width (1.472").

6. Save the pattern to keep your changes or save it under a different name.

Combine Same Line

The Combine Same Line function is sometimes considered the opposite of Distribute/Same Line. It is used to combine two or more darts into one dart. The darts to combine must be on the same line as the dart to be combined to, known as the destination dart. If you wish to combine darts that exist on different lines, then use

the function Combine Different Line. We used the bodice created with Distribute Same Line in Figure 8.36 to perform this function. If the darts on each side of the center dart need to be combined into the center dart, the function has to be repeated twice.

Procedure for Combine Same Line

1. Select **Piece>Darts>Combine Same Line.**

2. The user input box states: "Select destination dart to combine to." Left click to select the dart, which highlights it in red. This dart receives the width of the other darts you select. We selected the middle dart on the shoulder in Figure 8.37.

3. The user input box states: "Select dart to be combined." Left click to select a dart. This dart closes and its width is distributed or combined into the destination dart selected in the previous step. We selected the dart to the left of the center dart in Figure 8.37.

4. Right click and select **OK** to continue. The dart is closed and combined into the destination dart, as shown in Figure 8.37.

5. Save the pattern to keep your changes or save it under a different name.

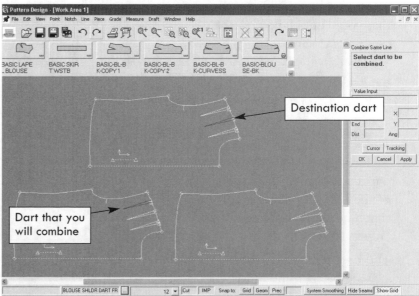

Figure 8.37 Shoulder darts are combined using the function Combine Same Line.

Combine Diff Line

The Combine Diff Line function is sometimes considered the opposite of Distribute/Rotate. It is used to combine two or more darts into one dart. The darts you want to combine must be on different lines. If you wish to combine darts that exist on the same line, use the Combine Same Line function. The bodice we use for the example in Figure 8.38 has a French dart on the side seam and a dart in the armhole. We are going to close the armhole dart and combine its width into the French dart.

Procedure for Combine Diff Line

1. Select **Piece>Darts>Combine Diff Line.**

2. The user input box states: "Select dart to combine." Left click to select the dart, which highlights it in red. This dart closes and its width will be distributed or combined into the destination/target dart selected in Step 5.

3. The user input box states: "Select rotation point location." This is the pivot point. Left click to select a location in the pattern, which highlights it in red. We selected the bust point in Figure 8.38.

4. A user input box states: "Select the hold line." Left click to select the line on the part of the piece that needs to remain stationary. This is the part of the piece that you would tape down if you were doing it manually. We selected the center front of the bodice in Figure 8.38 so that the grain line is not affected.

5. The user input box states: "Select target dart." This is the dart that receives the width of the dart you want to combine and that you selected in Step 2.

6. The user input box states: "Select internal line(s) to move, end selection to con-

tinue." Right click and select **OK** to continue. No line needs to be selected.

7. The user input box states: "Select new dart apex." A red line appears in the center of the dart, which is known as the angle bisector. Left click to select a point along this line, or you can perform a popup or click **Cursor** to toggle to Value Mode and enter the length or depth of the dart. Notice the angle the dart takes due to the placement of the rotation point. We entered 9" for the length of the dart. The width of dart you want to combine is moved into the target dart and a new dart is created, as seen in Figure 8.38.

8. Save the pattern to keep your changes or save it under a different name.

Add Dart

The Add Dart function is used to create a dart on a pattern. You can enter the location, width, and depth of the dart or enter a specific measurement for each using the popup technique or by clicking **Cursor** to toggle to **Value** and change to Value Mode. A dart is created perpendicular to the line on which it is created, but, if needed, you can change

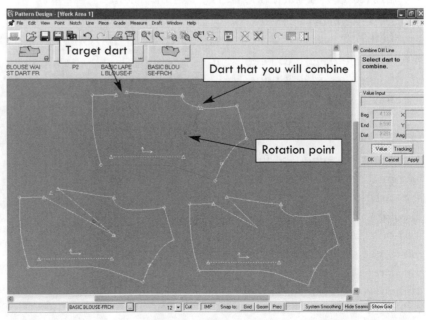

Figure 8.38 The armhold dart combined with the side seam using the Combine Diff Line function.

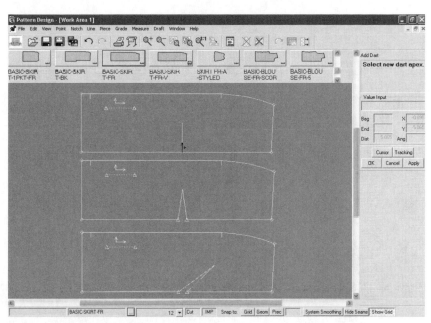

Figure 8.39 Steps displaying a dart added to a skirt and then angled in a different direction.

the angle with a function such as Move Point in the Point menu. We opted to create one of the dart examples shown in Figure 8.32, so we used the Move Point function to change the angle of the dart, as shown in the last stage of Figure 8.39.

Procedure to add darts

1. Select **Piece>Darts>Add Dart.**

2. The user input box states: "Select opening point." Left click to select where you want the new dart to be located. You may enter an exact measurement. We selected our point 15" below the waist on the center front of the skirt displayed in Figure 8.39.

3. The user input box states: "Select new dart apex." We performed a popup and entered 5" in the **Dist** field for our skirt example.

4. The user input box states: "Enter dart width." We entered 1½" for our skirt. The dart is created.

Note: To finish this pattern, the next step is to true the dart with the Fold/Close Dart End function. Then you add seam allowance to the pattern with the Define/Add Seam function. We opted to change the angle of the dart before truing the dart for this example.

Add Dart with Fullness

The Add Dart function discussed in the last section takes away fullness. The Add Dart with Fullness function, alternatively, is used to create a dart while adding fullness to the pattern. You may enter the location, width, and depth of the dart or enter a specific measurement for each by using the popup technique or by clicking **Cursor** to toggle to Value Mode.

Procedure to add dart with fullness

1. Select **Piece>Darts>Add Dart With Fullness.**

2. The user input box states: "Select the dart opening." Left click to select where you want the new dart to be located. You may enter an exact measurement. We selected a point on the waist (see Figure 8.40).

3. The user input box states: "Select a point on a boundary line to slash to." We selected a point on the hem to slash to with the left mouse button, as shown in Figure 8.40. You may enter an exact measurement.

4. The user input box states: "Select location to remain stationary." We selected the center front of the skirt in Figure 8.40. This is the part of the piece that must not move and you would tape down if you were doing it manually.

5. The user input box states: "Select internal line(s) to move, end selection to continue." Right click and select **OK.** The system automatically draws a line from the opening point to the slash point.

6. The user input box states: "Spread the dart opening to the desired dart width." Enter the width for the new dart.

7. The user input box states: "Select new dart apex." Enter the depth or length for the new dart. The dart is created, as seen on the bottom skirt in Figure 8.40.

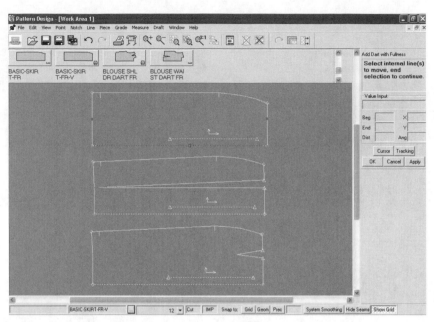

Figure 8.40 A dart added with fullness on a skirt waist.

Note: As in the previous section, Add Dart, to finish this pattern you need to true the dart with the Fold/Close Dart End function. Then you add seam allowance to the pattern using the Define/Add Seam function.

Change Dart Tip

The Change Dart Tip function is used to change the length of a dart. The length is shortened or lengthened by way of the dart tip. The angle of the dart remains the same.

When you establish a new position for the tip in Step 3 of the procedure detailed below, you may perform a popup or change to Value Mode to enter an exact measurement. The **Dist**, **X,** and **Y** fields light up. The number you enter in the Dist field becomes the length of the new dart (see Figure 8.41).

If you choose to fill in the X and Y fields, one field will determine how much to add or take away from the length of the dart. If you enter a number in the other field, it can change the angle of the dart. For example, if -2 is entered in the X field and 1 is entered in the Y field for a dart, the dart will lengthen by 2" and the angle will change by an inch. If you wish to change the angle of the dart, you may also use the Move Point function.

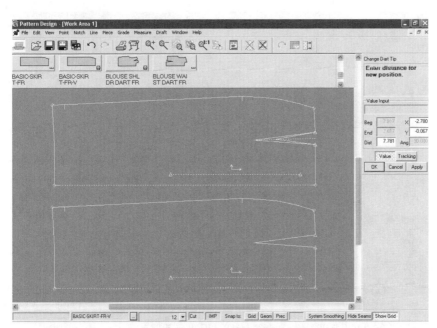

Figure 8.41 The length of a dart is changed using the Change Dart Tip function.

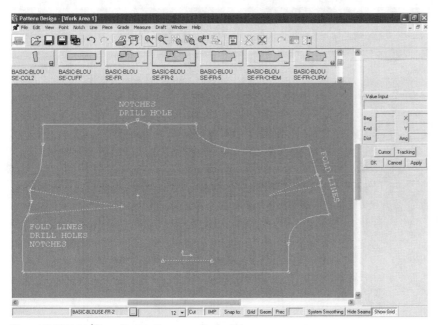

Figure 8.42 Fold/Close Dart options are displayed.

3. The user input box states: "Select a new position for the dart tip." The tip of the dart moves along with the mouse as it moves. Select a new length or perform a popup or change to **Value Mode** to enter the length or depth of the dart. The length of the dart is changed.

Fold/Close Dart End

The Fold/Close Dart End function is used to true up a dart. If you are working manually, then you fold the dart as you would sew it and then you cut the seam line on which it sits to get the correct seam shape.

There are several options available for you when you close the dart. You can include fold lines, drill holes, or notches when you close a dart (see Figure 8.42). A dart may not be manipulated when this function is applied. To manipulate the dart, you must first open it with the Open Dart function discussed in the next section.

Procedure for Fold/Close Dart Tip

1. Select **Piece>Darts>Fold/ Close Dart Tip.**

2. The user input box states: "Select dart on side to fold to." Left click to select a side of the dart.

3. The user input box states: "Enter the distance of drill hole from Apex." This is the distance between the drill hole and the end of the dart. It is usually ½". The dart is folded/closed and, therefore, trued up.

4. You may add seam allowance to your piece. Save the piece to keep your changes.

Procedure for Change Dart Tip

1. Select **Piece>Darts>Change Dart Tip.**

2. The user input box states: "Select a dart line." Left click to select the dart, which temporarily highlights the dart legs. The dart tip moves along with the mouse.

Open Dart

The Open Dart function is used to open a dart that has been folded and closed or trued up. When a dart is open, you may manipulate it.

Procedure to open a dart

1. Select **Piece>Darts>Open Dart.**

2. The user input box states: "Select a closed dart to open." Left click to select the line between the dart legs (see Figure 8.43). The dart is opened.

Smooth

The Smooth function is used to smooth a curved line or a region of a line. For example, after digitizing a garment, some lines such as the armhole, neckline, side seam, or inseam may have bumps. This function may be considered part of cleaning up the piece. This option is also found in the Line menu.

Procedure to smooth lines

1. Select **Piece>Darts>Smooth.**

2. The user input box states: "Select the line to smooth." Left click to select the line to smooth and notice the thumbtacks that appear. The armhole is selected in Figure 8.44.

3. The user input box states: "Position thumbtacks to define range or left click to continue." If the thumbtacks are in the correct position, left click to accept the location and continue. If not, move the thumbtacks to the area you want to change. In Figure 8.44, the thumbtacks are placed

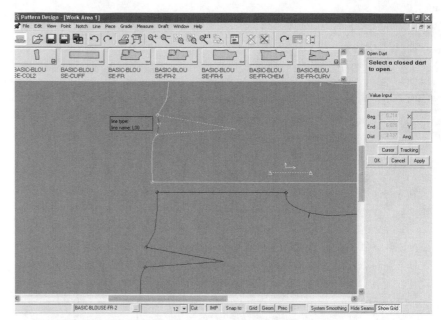

Figure 8.43 A dart is opened using the Open Dart function.

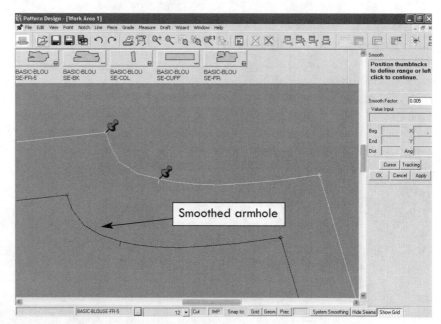

Figure 8.44 Smooth function is used to smooth an armhole.

just outside of the area that needs to be smoothed.

4. The line or range of line is smoothed. Figure 8.44 shows the original armhole and the armhole after it is smoothed. To continue smoothing, left click until the desired smoothness is achieved.

Flatten Line Segment

Just as the name states, the Flatten Line Segment function flattens a line. There are two options that let you delete notches, dart points, or both. For example, a skirt with a curved side seam may be flattened while keeping important notches such as the hip and hem notches. This option is also found in the Line menu.

Procedure to flatten lines

1. Select **Piece>Darts>Flatten Line Segment.**

2. Select your preferences from the user input box.

3. Check the box next to **Delete Notches** to delete the notches on the line to flatten (see Figure 8.45).

4. Check the box next to **Delete Dart Points** to delete the darts on the line you need to flatten. We checked this box in Figure 8.45.

5. The user input box states: "Select line to flatten." Left click to select a line to flatten. The waist on a skirt is selected in Figure 8.45.

6. The user input box states: "Position thumbtacks to define range or left click to continue." If the thumbtacks are in the correct position, left click to accept the location and continue, as shown in Figure 8.45. If not, move the thumbtacks to the area you want to flatten.

7. The line is flattened. Figure 8.45 shows the skirt waist flattened with the darts and notches deleted.

8. The function restarts. Right click and select **Cancel** to exit.

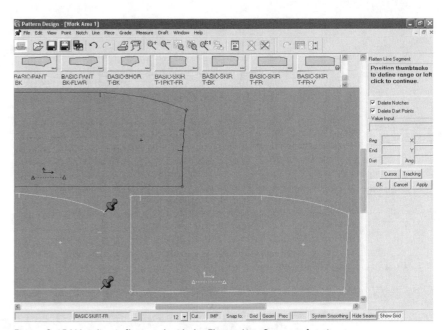

Figure 8.45 Waistline is flattened with the Flatten Line Segment function.

Examples of Garments with Fullness

Figure 8.46 Examples of garments with fullness.

Fullness Menu

The Fullness menu has several options that let you create fullness in garments in various ways. This menu has similar options to the Pleats menu except that there are no notches involved when you create the spread to add fullness. Fullness may be added along the width or length of a garment. A fullness function, such as Parallel Fullness, may be used to add length in the middle of a garment rather than lowering the hem. This may be used to manipulate a garment for a taller or shorter person. Several prompts that are used throughout the Fullness menu functions are defined below.

Common Prompts in the Fullness Menu

"Create a Slash line from pivot end to open end." The pivot end does not receive any width. For example, the slash line for the pants in Figure 8.46 was created from the waist, the pivot end, to the leg opening, the open end.

You may create multiple slash lines. This lets you place the lines in the direction or angle necessary and, furthermore, one could be different from the other. You can start and end the slash line wherever you think it fits best visually or you can enter a value in the same way you digitize a line with the Digitized function in the Line menu. For example, the slash line in the pant in Figure 8.46 may have been created from the midpoint of the waist to the midpoint of the leg opening.

"Select location to remain stationary or select the line to hold." This is the part of the piece that should not move. For example, the side of the piece that is parallel to the grain line, such as a center front, is usually the stationary side chosen to not distort the grain on the pattern. If you are working on this project manually, this is the part you would tape down.

"Select the internal line(s) to move." The internal lines are the slash lines you created. The system automatically recognizes these lines and, therefore, you may right click and select **OK** to continue at this point.

Fullness

Fullness is used to add fullness to a perimeter seam line you select on a garment. For example, the hem of a sleeve or skirt needs four inches of fullness added. Although you do not create slash lines during this function, the system creates one that is not visible. The slash line is created between the middle of the line to slash to and the middle of the line for fullness.

The shirt piece in Figure 8.47 is the bodice shown on the right in Figure 8.46. For this section, we are adding fullness to the top part of the bodice.

Procedure to add fullness

1. Select **Piece>Fullness>Fullness.**

2. The user input box states: "Select line for fullness." Left click to select a line to which you want to add fullness. We selected the Empire seam for the top part of the bodice in Figure 8.47.

3. The user input box states: "Select line to slash to." Left click to select the line to slash to. We selected the shoulder in Figure 8.47.

4. The user input box states: "Select line to hold." Left click to select the line you want to hold stationary. We selected the center front in Figure 8.47.

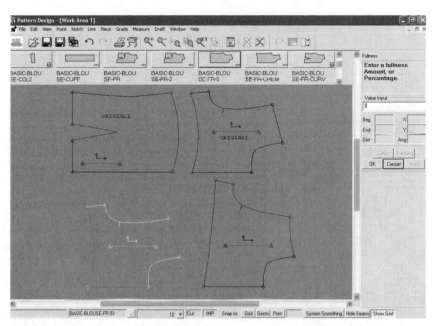

Figure 8.47 Steps showing fullness added to the top bodice with the Fullness function.

5. The user input box states: "Enter a fullness Amount, or Percentage." We entered 3" as shown in Figure 8.47.

6. Add seam allowance to the garment and save it if you want to keep your changes.

Variable Fullness

The Variable Fullness function is a combination of the Parallel Fullness and Tapered Fullness functions. You add parallel fullness first, so you can add the same width to both ends of the slash line you create when spreading the piece. Then you add tapered fullness without adding any further fullness to the *pivot* end of the slash line, while the *open end* of the slash line receives extra fullness.

The skirt illustrated in Figure 8.46 was created from a basic skirt by using the Variable Fullness function. We use this skirt to demonstrate this function in Figure 8.48, which shows the steps in the function. The skirt, as shown at the top left of Figure 8.48, shows how the parallel spread is created. The skirt to its right shows the tapered spread. Since the skirt had two slash lines, we perform the parallel and tapered fullness functions on each line. The final skirt is shown at the bottom of the screen.

Procedure to add variable fullness

1. Select **Piece>Fullness> Variable Fullness.**

2. The user input box states: "Create a slash line(s) from pivot end to open end." Left click to select the line on which to start the slash line. Left click again to select where you want to end the line. We created two slash lines from the waist to the hem in Figure 8.48.

3. Right click and select **OK** to continue.

4. A user input box states: "Select location to remain stationary." This is the part of the piece that should not move and you would tape down if you were doing this manually. Left click to select a stationary location. We selected the center front on our skirt so that the grain line is not distorted.

5. The user input box states: "Select internal line(s) to move, end selection to continue." The internal lines to move are the slash lines created. Right click and select **OK**.

6. The user input box states: "Position piece to create spread." Parallel fullness is first and adds equal fullness to both ends of the slash line—in this case the waist and the hem. Move the mouse to select the amount you want it to spread or enter a value (see Figure 8.48). We used a popup to enter 2" for this spread.

7. The user input box states: "Position piece to create spread." Move the mouse to select the amount you want it to spread or enter a value. Add tapered fullness now. Notice how only the hem, the open end of the slash line, receives fullness for our example. We used a popup and entered 5" for this spread, as shown in Figure 8.48. The skirt has fullness added.

8. Save the piece to keep your changes.

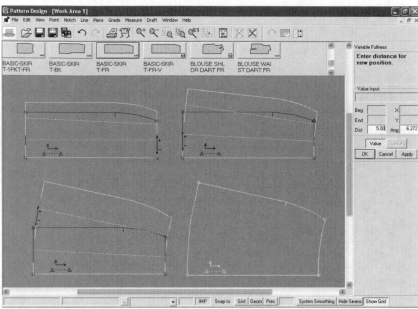

Figure 8.48 Variable Fullness displayed in steps on a skirt.

Note: Since we had two slash lines, Steps 6 and 7 were repeated for the second slash line.

Tapered Fullness

The **Tapered Fullness** function is used when a garment needs to be created with fullness added to only one end of the garment and the other end needs to remain with the same width. The open end of the slash line created is the end that receives the fullness. The process for this function is similar to the Fullness function, except that you may create multiple lines, so there is more control as to where the slash lines are created.

The pant illustrated in Figure 8.46 was created from a basic pant by using the Tapered Fullness function. We use this pant to demonstrate this function in Figure 8.49. Notice that when we were prompted to "select the line to remain stationary," we actually selected the intersection of the slash line and the waist. Selecting this point allows the pant leg to spread toward both directions, as shown in Figure 8.49. You may also select a point versus a line when you are adding fullness to a sleeve.

Procedure to add tapered fullness

1. Select **Piece>Fullness>Tapered Fullness.**

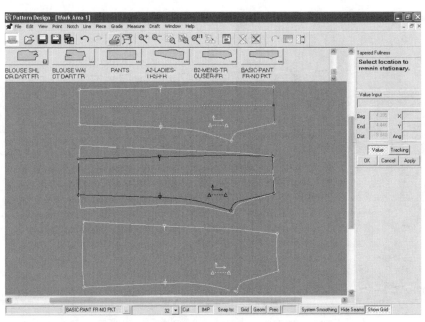

Figure 8.49 Fullness added to a pant hem with the Tapered Fullness function.

2. The user input box states: "Create a slash line(s) from pivot end to open end." Left click to select the line where you want to start the slash line. Left click again to select where you want to end the line. We created the slash line from the waist to the leg opening in Figure 8.49.

3. Right click and select **OK** to continue.

4. The user input box states: "Select location to remain stationary." Left click to select a location. We selected the intersecting point between the slash line and the waist, which makes the pant leg spread in both directions.

5. The user input box states: "Select internal line(s) to move, end selection to continue." Right click and select **OK.**

6. The user input box states: "Position piece to create spread." The spread moves with the mouse, as seen in Figure 8.49. Left click to set the spread in the location you want or enter a measurement. We used a popup and entered 7" for our pant leg spread. The pant leg has fullness added only to the leg opening in this example, as seen on the pant at the bottom of Figure 8.49.

7. Save the piece to keep your changes.

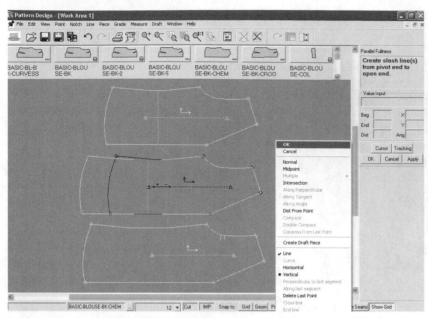

Figure 8.50 Steps displaying rusching on a bodice created with the Parallel Fullness function.

Parallel Fullness

Parallel Fullness is used when you need to add fullness, width, or length to a garment. Equal fullness is added to both ends of the slash lines you create.

Use the Parallel Fullness function when you need to

- add fullness to a skirt so that it may gather at the waist and have the same amount of fullness fall at the hem.

- shorten or lengthen a skirt or bodice.

- create a gathered sleeve that has the same amount of fullness at the cap and sleeve opening.

- add fullness for shirring or rusching.

We will create the bodice with rusching in Figure 8.46. We add length to the bodice in the waist area by adding parallel fullness to gather it for this look. When we create the slash line, we select the Vertical option from the right-click menu so the line can remain straight (see Figure 8.50). This keeps the center front on the grain. Try creating a slash line that is straight and one that isn't to see the difference when the pattern is spread.

Procedure to add parallel fullness

1. Select **Piece>Fullness>Parallel Fullness.**

2. The user input box states: "Create a slash line(s) from pivot end to open end." Left click to select the line where you want to start the slash line. Left click again to select where to end the line. We created the slash line from the side seam to the center front in Figure 8.50.

3. Right click and select **OK** to continue.

4. The user input box states: "Select location to remain stationary." Left click to select a stationary location. We selected the center front of our blouse.

5. The user input box states: "Select internal line(s) to move, end selection to continue." Right click and select **OK.**

6. The user input box states: "Position piece to create spread." The spread moves along with the mouse, as seen in Figure 8.50. Left click to select the location for the spread or enter a specific measurement. We performed a popup and entered 5" as the spread of our blouse for the fullness we wanted so it gathers. The blouse at the bottom in Figure 8.50 shows the added fullness.

7. Save the piece to keep your changes.

Taper Slash-n-Spread

The Taper Slash-n-Spread function is used when you need to add fullness to only one end of a garment but the other end needs to remain the same width. The open end of the slash line created is the end that receives the fullness. The process for this function is similar to the Tapered Fullness function, except that you may use multiple pieces to create the spread through all the patterns at once.

Figure 8.51 shows a sleeve pattern that is constructed with a top and bottom pattern. We placed both pieces next to each other, as if sewn, to perform the Tapered Slash-n-Spread function. Notice that when prompted to select the line to remain stationary, we actually selected the intersection of the slash line and the sleeve cap. Selecting this point allows the sleeve to spread toward both directions, as shown in Figure 8.51, which illustrates all the steps.

Procedure for Taper Slash-n-Spread

1. Select **Piece>Fullness>Taper Slash-n-Spread.**

2. The user input box states: "Select pieces to perform slash and spread." Left click to select the pieces you want to spread.

3. Right click and select **OK.**

4. The user input box states: "Create a slash line(s) from pivot end to open end." Left click to select the line where you want to start the slash line. Left click again to select where to end the line. We created the slash line between the sleeve cap of the top sleeve pattern and the hem of the sleeve of the bottom sleeve pattern in Figure 8.51.

5. Right click and select **OK** to continue.

6. The user input box states: "Select location to remain stationary." Left click to select a stationary location. We selected the intersecting point between the slash line and the sleeve cap (see Figure 8.51).

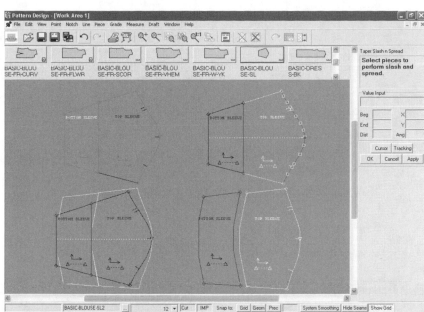

Figure 8.51 Steps displaying fullness added to the sleeve opening with the Taper Slash-n-Spread function.

7. The user input box states: "Select internal line(s) to move, end selection to continue." Right click and select **OK.**

8. The user input box states: "Position piece to create spread." The spread moves along with the mouse, as seen in Figure 8.51. Left click to select the location for the spread or enter a specific measurement. The pattern has tapered fullness added to all the selected pieces. We used a popup and entered 7" for the spread on our sleeve. See the separated sleeve patterns in Figure 8.51.

9. Save the piece to keep your changes.

Parallel Slash-n-Spread

The Parallel Slash-n-Spread function is used when you need to add fullness, width, or length to a garment. You add equal fullness to both ends of the slash lines you created. The process for this function is similar to the Parallel Fullness function, except that you may use multiple pieces to create the spread through all the patterns at once.

Figure 8.52 shows a bodice pattern that is constructed with three front patterns—a side front, middle front, and center front. We placed all three pieces next to one another, as if they were sewn, to perform the Parallel Slash-n-Spread function. We added two inches of length to all three pieces in the waist area.

Procedure for Parallel Slash-n-Spread

1. Select **Piece>Fullness> Parallel Slash-n-Spread.**

2. The user input box states: "Select pieces to perform slash and spread." Left click to select the pieces you want to spread.

3. Right click and select **OK.**

4. The user input box states: "Create a slash line(s) from

pivot end to open end." Left click to select the line where you want to start the slash line. Left click again to select where you want to end the line. We created the slash line between the side seam of the side front and the center front of the center front pattern.

5. Right click and select **OK** to continue.

6. The user input box states: "Select location to remain stationary." Left click to select the side seam.

7. The user input box states: "Select internal line(s) to move, end selection to continue." Right click and select **OK.**

8. The user input box states: "Position piece to create spread." The spread moves along with the mouse, as seen in Figure 8.52. Left click to select the location for the spread or enter a specific measurement. Parallel fullness is now added to all the selected pieces. We used a popup and entered 2" for the spread on our blouse. Our garment is now longer by 2" as shown in the separated patterns in Figure 8.52.

9. Save the piece to keep your changes.

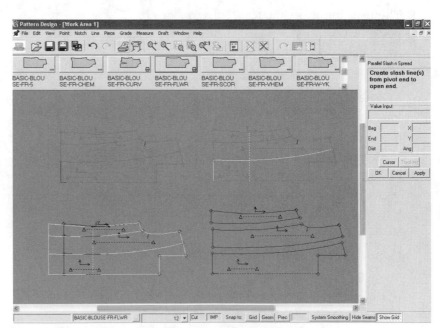

Figure 8.52 Parallel Slash-n-Spread used to lengthen bodice patterns.

Seam

The Seam menu is used to modify patterns with seam allowance, either by adding seam allowance or removing it. Although there are many more options available in this menu, we discuss the three basic ones that you will cover in class.

Define/Add Seam

The Define/Add Seam function is used to add seam allowance to patterns. This is usually the last step in the creation of a garment before saving it in the system.

You may add seam allowance to one or several pattern pieces at a time. If you select several pieces at one time, the amount you enter is applied to all the pieces. You can add seam allowance to individual lines on one or more pieces as well. Once again, all lines that you select at the same time receive the same amount you enter.

Adding seam allowance is always positive since you need to add growth so you can sew the garment together and have it adhere to the spec size you created. Seam allowance may be entered as a negative number; however, doing so usually means that you added the seam allowance while you

were creating the pattern to show where the seam allowance falls on the pattern.

If you enter "0" for a piece that currently has seam allowance, the system will remove it. Keep in mind that if there are seam lines inside the piece, the system deletes only the seam allowance lines, but the seam allowance still remains. To properly take off the seam allowance, use the Swap Sew/Cut function so that the seam allowance lines are on the outside of the piece. Then use Define/Add Seam and enter "0" to remove the seam allowance.

Figure 8.53 shows seam allowance being added to a pattern that was split into three patterns. Assuming the rest of the pattern already has seam allowance, we need to add seam allowance only to the areas that were split. The bodice below this garment shows how a garment may have different seam allowances added to different lines. The seam amounts are shown because we used Seam Amount in the View menu to turn them on for display.

Procedure for Define/Add Seam

1. Select **Piece>Seam>Define/Add Seam.**

2. The user input box states: "Select line(s) or piece(s) for seam allowance, end selection to continue." Left click to select a line or piece, which highlights it in red. See Figure 8.53 to view our selections.

3. Right click and select **OK.**

4. The user input box states: "Enter seam allowance amount." We entered .5 (½") for the bodice in Figure 8.53 and clicked **OK.** The seam allowance is added to selected lines or pieces.

Note: If you add seam allowance to a pattern, the seam is on the outside, as shown in Figure 8.53. The next step would be to use the Swap Sew/Cut function (discussed in the next section of this chapter), and then save the piece.

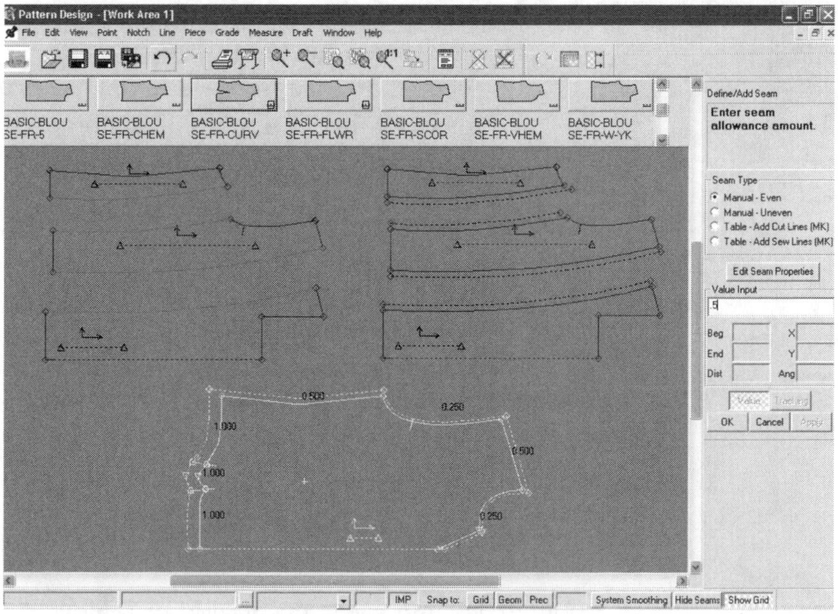

Figure 8.53 Seam allowance added using Define/Add Seam.

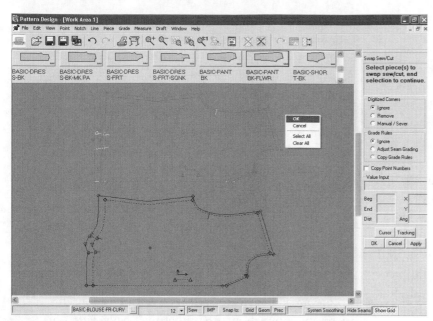

Figure 8.54 Swap Sew/Cut is used to swap the sew and cut lines of a bodice.

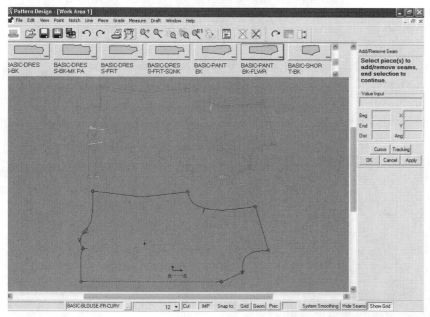

Figure 8.55 Add/Remove Seam is used to hide the seams on this bodice.

Swap Sew/Cut

The Swap Sew/Cut function is used to exchange the sew line with the seam allowance line. This step is usually taken after you have added seam allowance to a piece by using the Define/Add Seam function. Some functions may require the seam allowance to be outside of the piece so you can manipulate the pattern; therefore, use the Swap Sew/Cut function.

Procedure for Swap Sew/Cut

1. Select **Piece>Seam>Swap Sew/Cut.**

2. The user input box states: "Select piece(s) to swap/sew cut, end selection to continue." Left click to select pieces, which highlights them in red (see Figure 8.54).

3. Right click and select **OK** to swap seam allowance with cut lines.

Note: To exchange the lines again, repeat the function.

Add/Remove Seam

The Add/Remove Seam function is used to hide or show existing seam allowance in patterns. It toggles the seam allowance to be added or removed. If you apply this option to a piece, toggle to remove the seam allowance, and apply the Define/Add Seam function, then the seam allowance lines will not show.

Procedure for Add/Remove Seam

1. Select **Piece>Seam>Add/Remove Seam.**

2. The user input box states: "Select piece(s) to add/remove seams, end selection to continue." Left click to select pieces, which highlights them in red (see Figure 8.55).

3. Right click and select **OK** to add or remove seam allowance to the pattern. The blouse at the bottom of Figure 8.55 has the seams hidden.

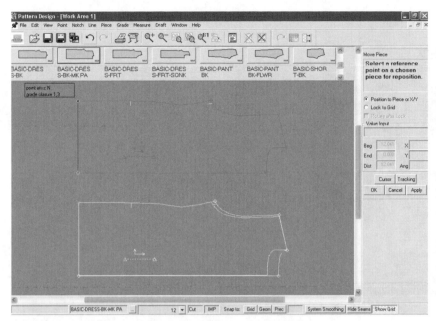

Figure 8.56 Move Piece is used to place one dress on top of another.

Modify Piece

The Modify Piece menu is used to manipulate patterns by flipping, rotating, or changing their grain line. While most of the functions in this menu are discussed, we cover only those functions that you will cover in class.

Move Piece

The Move Piece function is commonly used to move one piece on top of another at a specific point.

Use the Move Piece function when you need to

- view the difference between an original and a modified pattern.
- place pieces next to one another at a target point to trace the pattern.

Figure 8.56 shows a modified piece placed on top of the original piece. Since the hem area was not modified, we selected the point that is intersected by the side seam and hem in the original piece as the reference point. We then selected the same point—the target point—on the modified piece. The modified area in the armhole and neck-

line area is clearly visible now that one piece is on top of the other for comparison.

Procedure to move a piece

1. Select **Piece>Modify Piece>Move Piece.**

2. The user input box states: "Select piece(s) to reposition, end selection to continue." Left click to select the piece, which highlights it in red. See Figure 8.56 to see the dress we selected.

3. Right click and select **OK.**

4. The user input box states: "Select a reference point on a chosen piece for reposition." Left click to select a point on the piece selected in the previous step. See the highlighted point we selected in Figure 8.56 at the hem.

5. The user input box states: "Select a point on target piece. End selection to place. Use value mode to input X/Y distance." We left clicked on the same point on the hem of the modified piece in Figure 8.56.

6. Right click and select **OK** to move the piece.

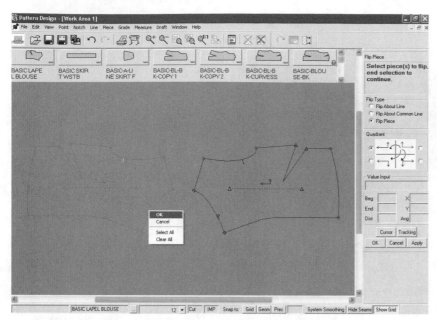

Figure 8.57 Bodice shown in original (left) and flipped position (right).

Flip Piece

This function is used to flip a piece from its original orientation. This is one of the times when keeping the orientation option "on" for the screen layout is useful. The piece can be flipped in four different directions or it may be flipped about, or over, a selected line.

Use the Flip Piece function when the

- piece is digitized in the wrong direction.
- grain line is digitized from right to left and the piece is in the wrong direction.
- direction of a piece needs to match the direction of other pieces in the model.
- piece needs to be prepared to walk against another piece.
- piece needs to be placed in the correct direction for an embroidery, appliqué, or motif for a fabric roll that has been laid out to cut.
- piece needs to be placed in the direction for a nap fabric.
- piece needs to be set up in the correct direction with the "Set and Rotate/Lock" function.

Procedure to flip a piece

1. Select **Piece>Modify Piece>Flip Piece.**

2. Select your preferences from the user input box.

3. In the **Flip Type** area, select from the three available options. We selected **Flip Piece.**

    Flip About Line flips the piece over a selected line.

    Flip About Common Line flips the piece over a selected common line.

    Flip Piece flips the selected piece according to the selection you made in the Quadrant area.

4. In the **Quadrant** area, select the direction in which you want to flip the piece. Look at the small diagram in the user input box to decide in which direction the piece should be flipped. This option may be selected only if the **Flip Piece** option is selected in the previous step.

5. The user input box states: "Select piece(s) to flip, end selection to continue." Left click to select the piece, which highlights it in red. We selected the blouse on the left side in Figure 8.57.

6. Right click and select **OK** to flip piece.

Rotate Piece

This function is used to rotate a piece from its original orientation. Just as with the Flip Piece function, keep the orientation option on for the screen layout. Pattern pieces are rotated in the increment selected in a clockwise or counter clockwise direction.

Use the Rotate Piece function so the

- piece may be rotated at a 45-degree angle to lay it on the bias.
- piece may be rotated at a 90-degree angle to lay it cross grain, such as a collar.
- piece may be rotated at 180 degrees to have it face the other direction.

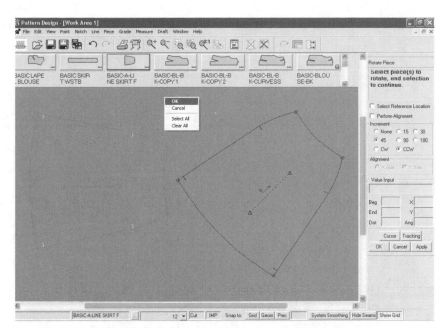

Figure 8.58 Rotate Piece is used to place this skirt on the bias.

Procedure to rotate a piece

1. Select **Piece>Modify Piece>Rotate Piece.**

2. Select your preferences from the user input box.

3. In the **Increment** area, select from the listed options.

    None allows the piece to be freely rotated. You can enter an exact angle by performing a popup or entering Value Mode. You may select either **15, 30, 45, 90, or 180** degrees to rotate a piece.

    CW rotates clockwise.

    CCW rotates counter clockwise.

4. Select the increment to rotate your piece. We selected **45.**

5. Select to rotate clockwise or counter clockwise.

6. The user input box states: "Select piece(s) to rotate, end selection to continue." Left click to select a piece, which highlights it in red. We selected the skirt on the left (see Figure 8.58).

7. Right click and select **OK** to rotate the piece.

Note: To keep the piece in the new rotated direction, realign the grain line with the Realign Grain/Grade Ref function discussed a little later in the chapter. Then save the pattern piece.

Set and Rotate/Lock

The Set and Rotate/Lock function is used to set one piece onto another at a selected point. The function then lets you rotate and place down the piece at a selected location.

Use the Set and Rotate/Lock function when you need to

- trace the pieces to create a new piece.

- use the pieces to create a third piece. In Figure 8.59, we can use the layout of the pieces as shown to create a new sleeve cap.

Procedure for Set and Rotate/Lock

1. Select **Piece>Modify Piece>Set and Rotate/Lock.**

2. The user input box states: "Select match point on target piece." Left click to select a point. The selection will turn red. The target piece is the piece that will remain stationary.

3. The user input box states: "Select match line on target piece." Left click to select the line the set piece will match on the target piece. We selected the shoulder line on the blouse in Figure 8.59.

4. The user input box states: "Select match point on set piece." This point will snap to the point selected on the target piece in Step 2. We selected the same point on the shoulder of the set piece—the back, in this case. It is the same point we selected on the shoulder of the target pattern—in this case, the front.

5. The user input box states: "Select set point on set piece." Select the line on the set piece. This line will join the match line on the target piece. The point selected on the set piece is matched to the point selected on the target piece. The piece rotates around the matched points. We selected the shoulder line for our example.

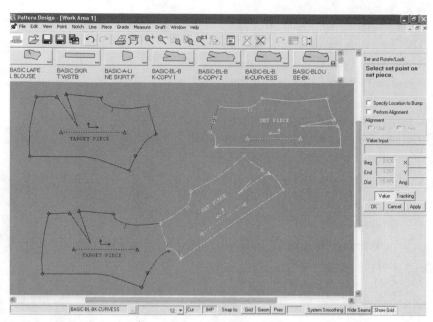

Figure 8.59 Set and Rotate/Lock function is used to match two patterns at the shoulder.

6. The user input box states: "Select set point on set piece." Left click to set down the piece at a desired location. We performed a popup and entered "0" in the **Dist** field so there is no space between the shoulder lines, as seen in Figure 8.59.

Walk Pieces

Pieces are walked in our industry to make sure seams are the same length, will sew properly, and/or that notches fall in the correct location. This function makes it quite nice to walk pieces without having to do it manually. Figure 8.60 shows a sleeve that is ready to be walked along the armhole of the front and back pattern pieces.

You can use this function to perform simple tasks, such as selecting the lines on the stationary pieces as prompted and then selecting the lines on the walk piece. You then move the piece along the seams you selected and see if they walk well or not so you can make any necessary changes. Other than the options **OK, Cancel, Change Direction,** and **Continue Walking,** defined below, no other options are necessary at first. We suggest you wait before until you are comfortable with the basic functionality of the procedure before exploring the right-click menu options.

The **Mobile** piece is the piece that walks. The **Stationary** piece does not move. Several options are available within the Walk Pieces function as described below.

Point Type

Add Mark Adds an "X" point to mark a location when one of the mark options is selected from the right-click menu.

Add Notch Adds a notch point in the location where you stop and one of the mark options is selected from the right-click menu.

Notch Type Select the notch type to add if "Add Notch" is selected.

Right-Click Menu

This menu is available after you select the line on the walk piece by right clicking the mouse (see Figure 8.60.)

OK Used to end or accept a selection.

Cancel Used to Cancel the function.

Change Direction Used to change the direction to walk the piece on the stationary line or the walk line.

Exclude Before Excludes walking from being performed in the region before a point you select.

Exclude After Excludes walking from being performed in the region after a point you select.

Exclude Region Excludes walking from being performed in the region you select.

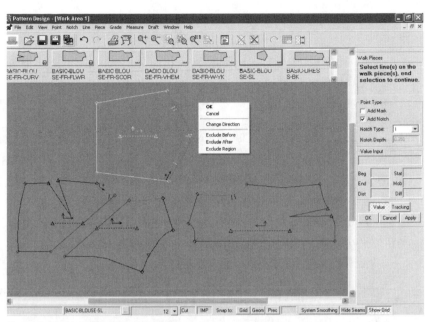

Figure 8.60 Walk Pieces is used to ensure that the selected seams will sew properly.

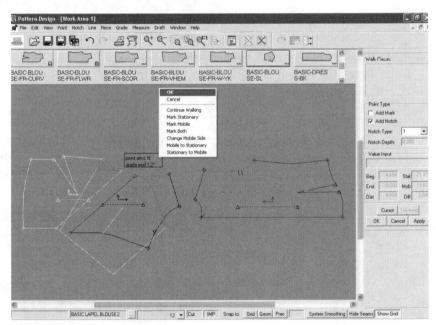

Figure 8.61 Sleeve cap is walked along front and back armholes.

Right-Click Menu

The right-click menu is available after you select the line on the walk piece and the line in the stationary piece by right clicking the mouse (see Figure 8.61).

OK Used to end or accept a selection.

Cancel Used to Cancel the function.

Continue Walking Resumes walking after you have stopped temporarily to use another option or to zoom.

Mark Stationary Marks the stationary piece with the Point Type you selected.

Mark Mobile Marks the moving/walking piece with the Point Type you selected.

Mark Both Marks both the stationary and the mobile pieces with the Point Type you selected.

Change Mobile Side The mobile piece is walked on top of the stationary piece along the inside edge of the seam. Use this option to walk the mobile piece along the outside edge of the seam. The result is the same; only the view is different.

Mobile to Stationary If the lines do not match, this adjusts the endpoint of the seam line being walked so that it matches the endpoint of the stationary piece.

Stationary to Mobile If the lines do not match, this adjusts the endpoint of the seam line of the stationary piece so that it matches the endpoint of the piece being walked.

Procedure for Walk Pieces

1. Select **Piece>Modify Piece>Walk Pieces.**

2. The user input box states: "Select line(s) on the stationary piece(s), end selection to continue." Left click to select lines, which highlights them in red. We selected the armholes of the front and back pieces.

3. Right click and select **OK.**

4. The user input box states: "Select line(s) on the walk piece(s), end selection to continue." Left click to select lines, which highlights them in red. Figure 8.60 shows the sleeve cap we selected. We also opted to change the direction from the right-click menu.

5. Right click and select **OK** to walk the pieces (see Figure 8.61).

Realign Grain/Grade Ref

The Realign Grain/Grade Ref function is used to change the grain line on a piece that has been rotated or flipped from its original digitized direction. It may also be used to simply return the piece to its original digitized direction after you have rotated, flipped, or modified it.

Figure 8.62 shows a skirt that we rotated 45 degrees with the Rotate Piece function because we want to place it on the bias. We have to change the grain line so that it sits in a horizontal, or X axis, position.

Procedure for Realign Grain/Grade Ref

1. Select **Piece>Modify Piece>Realign Grain/Grade Ref.**

2. Select from the two available options in the user input box.

    Realign Piece returns the piece to its original digitized direction.

    Realign Grain/Grade Ref changes the grain line so that it is correct for the new direction or rotation of the piece. We opted to realign the grain, as shown in Figure 8.62.

3. The user input box states: "Select grain line/grade ref to realign." Left click to select a grain line, as shown in Figure 8.62. The grain line changes to the horizontal position and the piece stays in the 45-degree rotation we previously selected. The skirt at the right side of Figure 8.62 displays the realigned grain line.

Note: You need to save for the process to be finalized. If you don't save the piece, it reverts back to its last saved version.

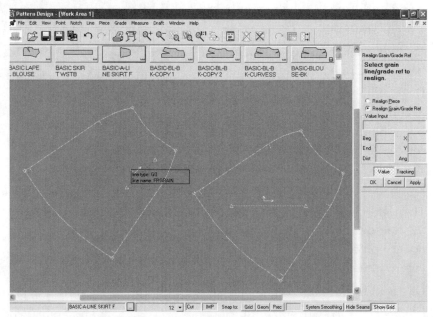

Figure 8.62 Realign Grain/Grade Ref is used to correct a grain line.

Split Piece

The Split Piece menu is used to split pieces in several different ways. All of the functions allow you to delete the original piece from which the new pieces are created and allow you to add seam allowance to the split seam lines within the function.

Garments are commonly created from a master pattern. The split functions give you the flexibility of creating many stylized garments (see Figure 8.63). We use the garments in this figure as examples of each function. Several of the common options available for the Split Piece menu functions are described below.

Available Options in the Split Piece Menu

Add Piece to Model/Style Check this box to add the piece to a selected model.

Delete Original Piece Check this box so the system removes the original piece from the screen. The original piece remains in the storage area from where it was retrieved originally.

Define Seam on Split Line Check this box to add seam allowance to the split lines during the function.

Modify Length Check this box to enter and determine the length of the split line. This option is available only when you use the "Split on Digitized Line" function.

Grading Area See Figure 8.64 for examples of the listed options for this area.

- *Grade Straight:* Grading is not added to the split area, but the original grading is maintained at the endpoints.

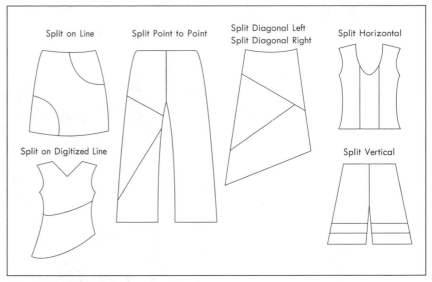

Figure 8.63 Examples of garments with splits.

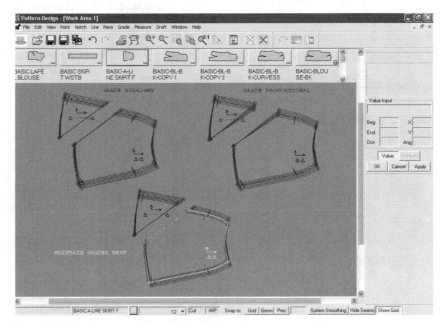

Figure 8.64 Grading options for splitting functions.

- *Grade Proportional:* This option proportionally divides grade rules to the split pieces.

- *Maintain Graded Nest:* Maintains the grade rules for the internal lines at the points where they are split.

Split on Line

A line to be used as a split line needs to be created before using this function. It may be created using numerous functions such as Digitized, 2-Point, or 2-Point-Curve. The Split on Line function allows you to split the pattern along the selected line. The skirt created in Figure 8.65 is also illustrated in Figure 8.63.

Procedure for Split on Line

1. Select **Piece>Split Piece>Split On Line.**

2. Select the options you want in the user input box. See Figure 8.65 to see our selections for this example.

3. A user input box states: "Select splitting line." Left click to select a line, as shown in Figure 8.65. You can select only one at a time.

4. A user input box states: "Enter the seam allowance value for the split line." This prompt appears because we selected the option **Define Seam on Split Line.** We entered .5 (½").

5. A user input box states: "Enter piece name." Enter a name for the piece with the weight on top of it and highlighted in red. We named this piece Skirt Fr-Bt-Panel.

6. A user input box states: "Enter piece name." Enter a name for the next piece with the weight on top of it and highlighted in red. We named this piece Skirt Fr-Mid-Panel.

7. The pieces are split. Move them apart with the mouse.

8. Use Swap Sew/Cut to exchange the seam and cut lines. Save the pieces to keep your changes.

Note: To finish the example in Figure 8.65, continue splitting the next line shown on the pattern.

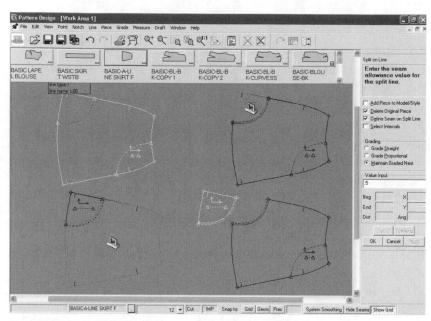

Figure 8.65 Steps displaying a skirt pattern split with Split on Line.

Split on Digitized Line

The Split on Digitized Line function allows you to digitize a line within the function. This line is then used to split the piece. The creation of this line is just like creating a line with the Digitized function under the Line menu. After creating a line and splitting it, the function restarts and you can create another line to further split the piece. The desired location for the split line may be entered by performing a popup or entering Value Mode. The bodice created in Figure 8.66 is illustrated in Figure 8.63.

Procedure for Split on Digitized Line

1. Select **Piece>Split Piece>Split On Digitized Line.**

2. Select options desired in the user input box. See Figure 8.66 to view our selections for this example.

3. The user input box states: "Select first point for line, right button for options." Left click to set the down points and create the shape of the line you desire. We created a curved line from one side seam to the other, so we used the right-click menu to select the Curve option after setting down the first point.

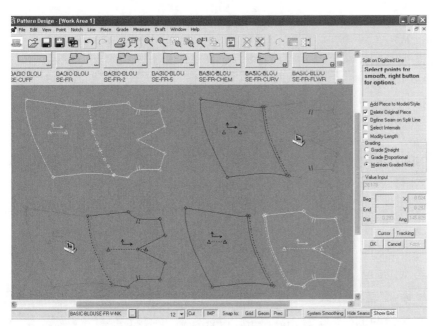

Figure 8.66 An empire bodice created with Split on Digitized Line.

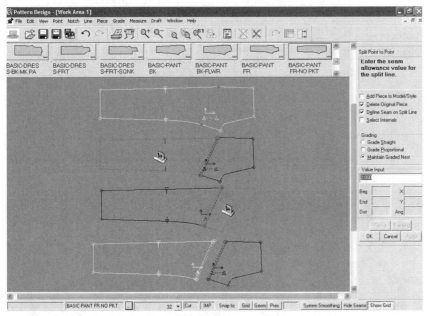

Figure 8.67 Split Point to Point is used to split a pant.

4. Right click and select **OK.**

5. The user input box states: "Enter the seam allowance value for the split line." This prompt appears because we selected the option **Define Seam on Split Line.** We entered ½" for our blouse.

6. A user input box states: "Enter piece name." Enter a name for the piece with the weight on top of it and highlighted in red. We named this piece Bodice-Top-Fr.

7. The user input box states: "Enter piece name." Enter a name for the next piece with the weight on top of it and highlighted in red. We named this piece Bodice-Bot-Fr.

8. The pieces are split. Move them apart with the mouse. See Figure 8.66 to see the split on our blouse.

9. The Use Swap Sew/Cut to exchange the seam and cut lines. Save the pieces to keep your changes.

Split Point to Point

The Split Point to Point function allows you to digitize a line within the function. This line is then used to split the piece. A straight line is created from the first point selected to the second point selected. Therefore, if you wish to create a curved line, this is not the correct function to use. After creating a line and splitting it, the function restarts and you may create another line to further split the piece. Enter the location at which you want your split line to be by performing a popup or entering Value Mode. The pants created in Figure 8.67 are displayed in Figure 8.63.

Procedure for Split Point to Point

1. Select **Piece>Split Piece>Split Point To Point.**

2. Select the options you want in the user input box. See Figure 8.67 to see our selections for this example.

3. The user input box states: "Select first point of split line." Left click to select point. We selected to perform a popup and enter the first point at 10" below the waist on the side seam.

4. The user input box states: "Select second point of split line." Left click to select point. We selected to perform a popup and enter the second point at 6" below the crotch on the inseam.

5. The user input box states: "Enter the seam allowance value for the split line." This prompt appears because we selected the option **Define Seam on Split Line.** We entered ½".

6. The user input box states: "Enter piece name." Enter a name for the piece with the weight on top of it and highlighted in red. We named this piece Pant-Bot-Fr.

7. The user input box states: "Enter piece name." Enter a name for the next piece with the weight on top of it and highlighted in red. We named this piece Pant-Top-Fr.

8. The pieces are split. Move them apart with the mouse. See Figure 8.67 to see the split on our pant leg pattern.

9. Use the Swap Sew/Cut function to exchange the seam and cut lines. Save the pieces to keep your changes.

Split Horizontal

The Split Horizontal function lets you select a point on a perimeter line on which you can create a split line horizontally, in the X axis, across the piece. The created line is a straight horizontal line that is used to split the piece. (If you want to create a curved line, this is not the correct function to use.) After creating a line and splitting it, the function restarts and you may select another point for an addi-

tional horizontal split. You can enter the desired location for the split point by performing a popup or entering Value Mode. A drawing of the bodice created in Figure 8.68 is displayed in Figure 8.63.

Procedure for Split Horizontal

1. Select **Piece>Split Piece>Split Horizontal.**

2. Select the options you want in the user input box. See Figure 8.68 to view our selections for this example.

3. The user input box states: "Select location to place split line." Left click to select point. We selected to perform a popup and enter the split point at 2" from the center front on the neckline as seen in Figure 8.68. The pattern piece temporarily does not show the split line due to the next step.

4. The user input box states: "Enter the seam allowance value for the split line." Enter a seam amount in the **Value Input** field and click **OK.** This prompt appears because we selected the option **Define Seam on Split Line.** We entered ½" and the horizontal split line was created.

5. The user input box states: "Enter piece name." Enter a name for the piece with the weight

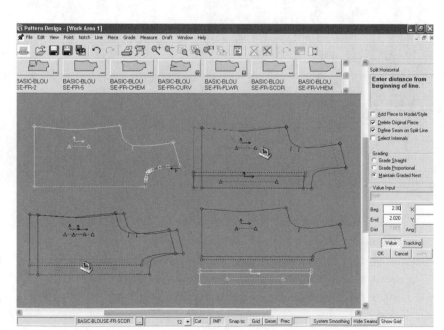

Figure 8.68 Split Horizontal is used to split a bodice along the length.

on top of it and highlighted in red. We named this piece Bodice Sd-Fr.

6. The user input box states: "Enter piece name." Enter a name for the next piece with the weight on top of it and highlighted in red. We named this piece Bodice-Fr.

7. The pieces are split. Move them apart with the mouse. See Figure 8.68 to view the split on our blouse.

8. Use the Swap Sew/Cut function to exchange the seam and cut lines. Save the pieces to keep your changes.

Split Vertical

The Split Vertical function works exactly like the Split Horizontal one except that it splits in the vertical direction. A point is selected on a perimeter line and a split line is created from that point vertically, in the Y axis, across the piece. The created line is a straight vertical line that is used to split the piece. After creating a line and splitting it, the function restarts and you may select another point for an additional vertical split. You may enter the desired location for the split point by performing a popup or entering a Value Mode.

The bottom of the pant legs shown in Figure 8.69 displays how the Split Vertical function can be used to split a pair of pants in a decorative way. The splits lie below the decorative ribbon on each pant leg. We will be using the drawing of the shorts displayed in Figure 8.63 as the example for our procedure in Figure 8.70.

Procedure for Split Vertical

1. Select **Piece>Split Piece>Split Vertical.**

2. Select the options you want in the user input box. See Figure 8.70 to view our selections for this example.

3. The user input box states: "Select location to place split line." Left

click to select point. We performed a popup and entered the split point at 4" from the hem on the side seam, as seen in Figure 8.70.

Figure 8.69 Photo of a pair of pants split vertically on the pant legs.

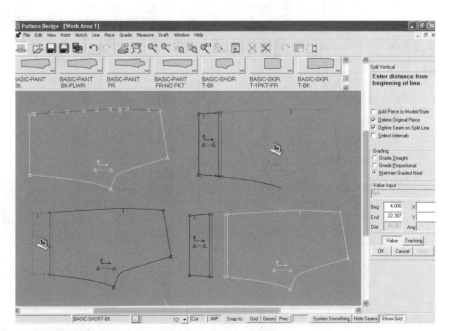

Figure 8.70 Split Vertical is used to split a shorts pattern.

4. The pattern piece temporarily does not show split line because of the next step.

5. The user input box states: "Enter the seam allowance value for the split line." This prompt appears because we selected the option **Define Seam on Split Line.** We entered ½". The vertical split line is created.

6. The user input box states: "Enter piece name." Enter a name for the piece with the weight on top of it and highlighted in red. We named this piece Short-Top-Fr.

7. The user input box states: "Enter piece name." Enter a name for the next piece with the weight on top of it and highlighted in red. See Figure 8.70. We named this piece Short-Bot-Fr.

8. The pieces are split. Move them apart with the mouse. See Figure 8.70 to view the split on our shorts.

9. Use the Swap Sew/Cut function to exchange the seam and cut lines. Save pieces to keep them.

Split Diagonal Left

The Split Diagonal Left function is used to split a piece at a 45-degree angle. The split is created from a selected point toward the *bottom* left of the garment being split. Enter the location you want for the split point by performing a popup or entering the Value Mode. The skirt created in Figure 8.71 is illustrated in Figure 8.63.

Procedure for Split Diagonal Left

1. Select **Piece>Split Piece>Split Diagonal Left.**

2. Select the options you want in the user input box. See Figure 8.71 to view our selections for this example.

3. The user input box states: "Select location to place split line." Left click to select point.

We selected the notch point on the hip in Figure 8.71.

4. The user input box states: "Enter the seam allowance value for the split line." This prompt appears because we selected the option **Define Seam on Split Line.** We entered ½". The split line is created and the garment is split.

5. The user input box states: "Enter piece name." Enter a name for the piece with the weight on top of it and highlighted in red. We named this piece A-line-Skirt-Top-Fr.

6. The user input box states: "Enter piece name." Enter a name for the next piece with the weight on top of it and highlighted in red. We named this piece A-line-Skirt-Bot-Fr.

7. The pieces are split as seen on our skirt in Figure 8.71. Move them apart with the mouse.

8. Use the Swap Sew/Cut function to exchange the seam and cut lines. Save the pieces to keep your changes.

Note: We use the Split Diagonal Right function in the next section to finish the look for this skirt.

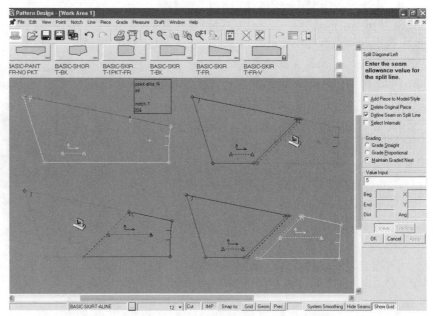

Figure 8.71 Split Diagonal Left is used to create a 45-degree split on a skirt.

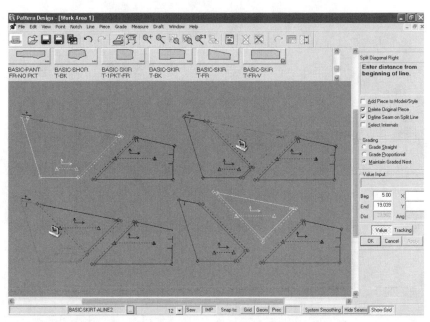

Figure 8.72 Split Diagonal Right is used to split a skirt at a 45-degree angle.

Split Diagonal Right

The Split Diagonal Right function is used to split a piece at a 45-degree angle. The split is created from a selected point toward the *bottom* right of the garment being split. If the point is selected at the bottom of a piece, the line will angle toward the left because the selected point is considered to be in the bottom right location. You may enter the location you want for the split point by performing a popup or entering the Value Mode. We are using the same skirt used as the example for the last section, Split Diagonal Left, to finish the pattern. The skirt created in Figure 8.72 is illustrated in Figure 8.63.

Procedure for Split Diagonal Right

1. Select **Piece>Split Piece>Split Diagonal Right.**

2. Select the options you want in the user input box. See Figure 8.72 to view our selections for this example.

3. The user input box states: "Select location to place split line." Left click to select point. We performed a popup and selected a point 5"

from the hem on the side seam as shown in Figure 8.72.

4. The user input box states: "Enter the seam allowance value for the split line." This prompt appears because we selected the option **Define Seam on Split Line.** We entered ½". The split line is created and the garment is split.

5. The user input box states: "Enter piece name." Enter a name for the piece with the weight on top of it and highlighted in red. We named this piece A-line-Skirt-Mid-Fr.

6. The user input box states: "Enter piece name." Enter a name for the next piece with the weight on top of it and highlighted in red. We named this piece A-line-Skirt-Bot-Fr.

7. The pieces are split. Move them apart with the mouse. See Figure 8.72 to view our skirt split.

8. Use the Swap Sew/Cut function to exchange the seam and cut lines. Save pieces to keep them, making sure to input the correct names.

Combine/Merge

The Combine/Merge function is used to join pattern pieces together. Pieces may be existing patterns or newly created pattern pieces. Figure 8.73 displays a small piece being merged with the remainder of the sleeve pattern. Notice the diagonal internal line that already exists on the pattern. The line is there because this part of the sleeve was previously two pieces and we combined them and used the option Convert Mrg Line to Internal.

There are several grade options and merge line rule options available with this function. We suggest you try out each one of them when you are more familiar with the grading process. Figure 8.73 has Target Pc Grade Ref Line selected so that rules are based on our grain line and are not changed. We have also selected the Remove Rules option so that all rules are removed from the merge lines.

Procedure for Combine/Merge

1. Select **Piece>Combine/Merge.**

2. Select the options you want in the user input box. See Figure 8.73 to view our selections for this example.

3. Check the box next to **Delete Original Piece** so that the system removes the original piece from the screen. The original piece remains in the storage area from where it was retrieved originally.

4. Check the box next to **Convert Mrg Line to Internal** to convert the merge lines into internal lines.

5. Check the box next to **Add Piece to Model/Style** to add the merged pattern piece to a selected model.

6. The user input box states: "Select merge line." Left click to select line. We selected the

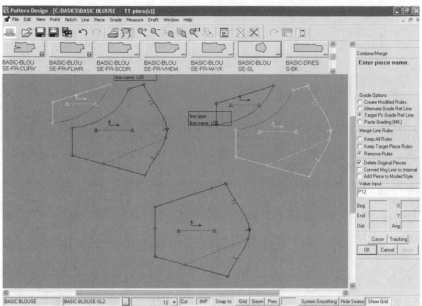

Figure 8.73 Sleeve patterns combined into one pattern using Combine/Merge.

line on the small piece as shown in Figure 8.73.

7. The user input box states: "Select target line." We selected the line on the bigger piece, as shown in Figure 8.73.

8. The user input box states: "Enter piece name." Enter a name for the piece and click **OK** or press Enter on the keyboard.

9. The pieces are merged and the old pieces are deleted from the screen because of the options we selected. See the sleeve at the bottom center of Figure 8.73 to see how the sleeve patterns look once they are merged.

10. Use the Line>Combine/Merge function to merge lines that are split yet should be one continuous line.

11. Save the piece in the correct storage area.

Shrink/Stretch

When you lay out fabric to be cut on a table, the fabric may shrink or stretch. That is why it is common to hear that the fabric needs to be laid out for a couple of hours to settle down. When you place a pattern on fabric and cut it and don't take the

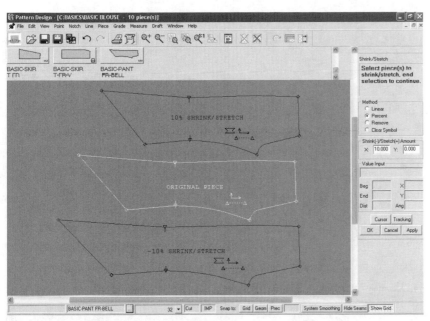

Figure 8.74 Shrink and stretch are applied to a pant.

stretch or shrinkage of the fabric into consideration, the garment may turn out longer, shorter, wider, or narrower than you intended. If the pattern is laid along the grain, this shrink or stretch may also be referred to as shrink/stretch along the X the length or the Y the width.

Figure 8.74 shows the original piece shrunk by 10 percent in the X axis. The piece is shown above the original one so that you can note the difference. The piece below the original was stretched 10 percent. Notice that the piece is longer so that it can shrink back to its normal size.

Procedure for Shrink/Stretch

1. Select **Piece>Shrink/Stretch.**

2. Select the options you want in the user input box first. We selected the percent option and entered a value of 10 for the shrink/stretch amount in the X.

3. The user input box states: "Select piece(s) to shrink/stretch, end selection to continue." Left click to select pieces, which highlights them in red.

4. Right click and select **OK** to shrink or stretch the pieces.

Mirror Piece

The Mirror Piece function is used to place a piece on fold. When manipulating a mirrored piece, such as a skirt front, always work with it while it is folded so that it remains symmetrical on both sides. A curved seam is not commonly mirrored.

While performing this function, you have the option to fold the piece after you mirror it or leave it unfolded. A piece is folded after it is mirrored so you can continue to manipulate it while keeping modifications symmetrical or simply save it. Patternmakers opt to leave it unfolded when they want to make sure the fold location has the correct shape. For example, when the center front of a skirt is folded, the piece is left unfolded to make sure the waistline has the proper shape.

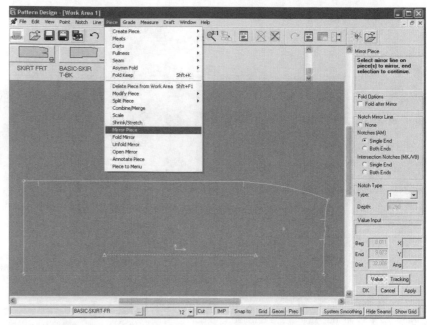

Figure 8.75 Mirror Piece function displayed with a selected mirror line.

Procedure for Mirror Piece

1. Select **Piece>Mirror Piece.**

2. Select the options you want in the user input box first.

3. In the **Fold Options** area, you may check the box next to Fold after Mirror to fold the pattern piece after you mirror it. We opted not to check this box (see Figure 8.75).

4. In the **Notch Mirror Line** area, select each preferred option. **None** is selected if you do not want any notches on the mirror line. If you select this option, you shouldn't select any other options in this area.

   Notches (AM) has two available options for notch location on a mirrored line: **Single End** and **Both Ends.** Select Single End only when one end of the mirror line needs to be notched. The system will prompt you to select the preferred end if you select this option. The Both Ends option will notch both ends of the

mirror line. The (AM) means this option is meant for use by AccuMark users.

5. In the **Notch Type** area, select the notch type by activating the drop-down menu. This area is available only if you have selected to notch the mirror line.

6. The user input box states: "Select mirror line on piece(s) to mirror, end selection to continue." Left click to select a line, which highlights it in red. We selected the center front of the skirt in Figure 8.75.

7. Right click and select **OK** to mirror the piece. The dashed line represents the mirror line.

   Note: If you are adding notches to the mirror line on a single end, continue to the next step.

8. The user input box states: "Select end of mirror line to be notched." Left click to select the point at the end of the line that you need to notch. The piece is mirrored with its notch. The dashed line represents the mirror line. We selected the endpoint on the waist end as shown in Figure 8.76. See the skirt shown at the top of Figure 8.77 to view the piece mirrored and unfolded.

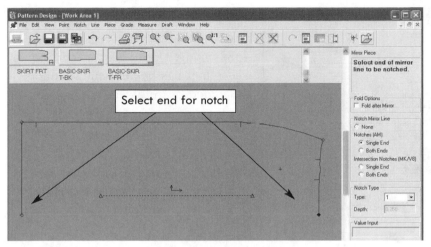

Figure 8.76 Select endpoint to notch on the mirrored piece.

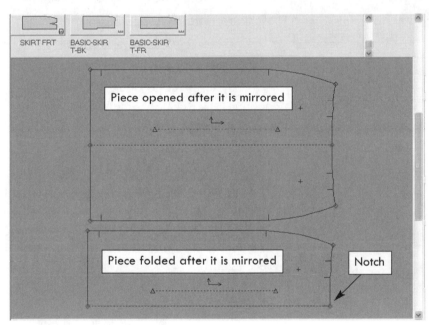

Figure 8.77 Opened and folded mirrored piece.

Fold Mirror

The Fold Mirror function is used to fold a mirrored piece after it is unfolded. Figure 8.77 shows an unfolded skirt pattern. Use this function when you need to further manipulate a piece and you wish to keep the pattern symmetrical.

Procedure for Fold Mirror

1. Select **Piece>Fold Mirror.**

2. The user input box states: "Select piece(s) to fold, end selection to continue." Left click to select pieces, which highlights them in red.

3. Right click with the mouse button and select **OK** to fold the piece as shown in Figure 8.77.

Unfold Mirror

The Unfold Mirror function is used to unfold a pattern that is folded. Use the Unfold Mirror function to make sure seam lines such as necklines or waistbands are shaped properly.

Procedure for Unfold Mirror

1. Select **Piece>Unfold Mirror.**

2. The user input box states: "Select mirrored piece(s) to unfold, end selection to continue." Left click to select pieces, which highlights them in red.

3. Right click the button mouse and select **OK** to unfold the piece. Figure 8.77 includes an example of an unfolded piece.

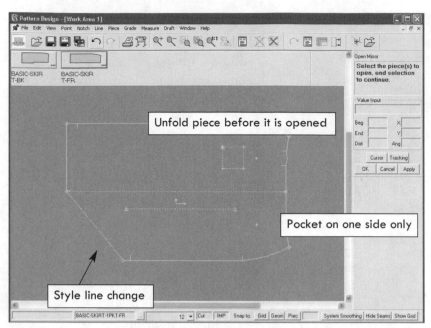

Figure 8.78 Open Mirror is used to open a skirt permanently.

Open Mirror

The Open Mirror function is not the same as the Unfold Mirror function. A piece that has been opened cannot be folded or unfolded. It is not considered an on the fold pattern.

Use the Open Mirror function (see Figure 8.78) on

- a pattern that is primarily symmetrical with the exception of a pocket on one side.

- a piece that is mostly the same on both sides, but for which you want to make a style line change.

Procedure for Open Mirror

1. Select **Piece>Open Mirror.**

2. The user input box states: "Select the piece to open, end selection to continue." Left click to select piece, which highlights it in red.

3. Right click and hit **OK** to open the Piece.

Note: If you fold a piece before performing the Open Mirror function, the piece will appear folded and the mirror line will appear as a solid line. This piece cannot be unfolded. You may go back to Piece>Mirror Piece and mirror the solid line to mirror the piece again.

Annotate Piece

The Annotate Piece function is used to write in pattern instructions or notes in a piece. This annotation may be plotted. You may set the character size, grading, and rotation when you create the annotation. You may copy, delete, move, or rotate existing annotation. Figure 8.79 shows the windows with new annotation and edited annotation. Both windows do not appear at the same time—we created the screen shot in this manner for your reference.

Procedure to create a new annotation on a piece

1. Select **Piece>Annotate Piece.**

2. The user input box states: "Select location for annotation or existing annotation to edit." Left

click to select a location in the piece.

3. The **New Piece Annotation** window displays.

4. Select a character size if you want something other than what the default is.

5. Type in a font rotation to rotate the annotation if you do not want it in the normal horizontal direction. For example, type in 90 to rotate the annotation 90 degrees. The annotation in Figure 8.79 is not rotated.

6. Type in a grade rule to have the annotation grade with the nested sizes.

7. Click **OK** to display the annotation.

Procedure to edit an annotation on a piece

1. Select **Piece>Annotate Piece.**

2. Left click on the annotation. The **Edit Annotation** window displays, as seen in Figure 8.79.

3. Select the option you want. The mouse is automatically attached to the annotation to perform the option.

   Copy Annotation is copied and system prompts to place it in new location.

   Delete Annotation is automatically deleted.

   Move Annotation moves along with the mouse and is ready to be set down on screen with the left mouse button.

   Rotate Annotation freely rotates with the mouse. Set it down on screen with the left mouse button.

Piece to Menu

The Piece to Menu function is used to send an existing piece that has been changed back to the

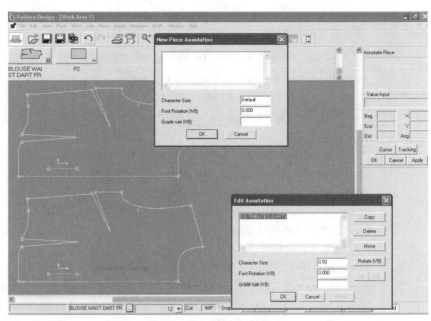

Figure 8.79 Annotation may be added to a piece or edited.

menu. It is also used to send a new piece that has been created to the icon menu. This option may also be accessed by clicking the right button while not in a function.

When sending a modified piece back to the menu, the system states that it already exists in the menu and prompts you to enter a new name for the piece. If the option Overwrite is selected, the piece in the menu will be overwritten. You have to save the piece to keep the changes.

If the piece being sent to the menu is a newly created piece, the system will automatically send it into the icon menu.

Procedure for Piece to Menu

1. Select **Piece>Piece to Menu.**

2. Left click to select piece to be sent to the menu. If it is a new piece, it will automatically be sent to the icon menu. If the piece already exists, continue to the next step.

3. The user input box states: "Piece already in menu. Enter new name." Enter a new name for the piece and click **OK** or check the box next to the Overwrite option to overwrite the existing piece in the icon menu.

Test Your Skills

Select TRUE or FALSE for the following statements:

1. The Combine/Merge function in the Piece Menu combines line segments on a piece. TRUE or FALSE

2. You may place a piece on the fold by using the Mirror Piece function. TRUE or FALSE

3. A mirrored piece that has been modified while it was unfolded may be folded back up. TRUE or FALSE

4. A piece is placed on the fold, mirrored. You wish to unfold it and make a change to the other half that will not be mirrored. The Open Mirror function is used to open the piece so that it is no longer folded. TRUE or FALSE

5. Pattern instructions or notes may be written on a piece using the Annotate Piece function. TRUE or FALSE

6. You may not shrink or stretch a piece's width and length at the same time using the Shrink/Stretch function. TRUE or FALSE

7. After adding a positive seam allowance to a pattern using the Define/Add Seam function, you need to swap the seam allowance and the cut lines with the Swap Sew/Cut function. TRUE or FALSE

8. The Rectangle function may be used to create waistbands and pockets. TRUE or FALSE

9. The Skirt function creates a quarter panel of a circular skirt. TRUE or FALSE

10. You may enter a radius or circumference when creating a circle. TRUE or FALSE

11. A pattern piece needs to have a raw edge finished with binding around the whole neckline, front and back. The Binding function can be used only to create the front neckline binding first and then the back binding. TRUE or FALSE

12. A facing may be created for a piece using the Facing function, but a line must be created prior to using the function. TRUE or FALSE

13. A piece has style lines created in it so that it may be eventually be separated into several pieces. The Extract function may be used to trace a region of the piece and create it as a piece of its own. TRUE or FALSE

14. The Trace function may be used to trace two pieces that are placed next to each other. TRUE or FALSE

15. The length of a dart may not be changed. TRUE or FALSE

16. The angle of a dart may not be changed. TRUE or FALSE

17. A dart may be moved from the side seam to the waist using the Rotate function. TRUE or FALSE

18. A portion of a waist dart may be rotated to the shoulder using the Distribute/Rotate function. TRUE or FALSE

19. When using the dart functions, when you are prompted to enter a new dart apex, it is referring to the new bust point. TRUE or FALSE

20. Two darts, an armhole dart and a side seam dart, may be combined into one dart using the Combine Same Line function. TRUE or FALSE
21. The rotation point used in many of the dart functions is equivalent to the pivot or point you cut to when manipulating a pattern. TRUE or FALSE
22. A dart may be rotated while it is folded. TRUE or FALSE
23. When adding fullness to pieces using the fullness functions, no notches are added. TRUE or FALSE
24. Parallel Fullness may be added to a garment to add length or a styling element such as rusching. TRUE or FALSE
25. You want to add fullness to a sleeve, but you want to add it only to the sleeve cap, so you use the Tapered Fullness function. TRUE or FALSE
26. You need to add fullness only to the hem of a skirt, but you do not need to create any slash lines, so you use the Variable Fullness function. TRUE or FALSE
27. The Split Diagonal Left and Split Diagonal Right functions split a piece at a 90 degree angle. TRUE or FALSE
28. Seam allowance may be added to the whole pattern when using the Split Piece Menu options. TRUE or FALSE
29. Split Point to Point creates a straight line split from the first point to the second point selected. TRUE or FALSE
30. A pre-digitized line does not have to be created before using the Split on Line function. TRUE or FALSE
31. There is no difference between a box pleat and a knife pleat. TRUE or FALSE
32. Half the underlay of a knife or box pleat is half of the total width of the finished pleat. TRUE or FALSE
33. Knife pleats or box pleats may be created with no width on one end and 3 inches on the other end using the Taper Pleat function. TRUE or FALSE
34. A piece that lays along the grain on the X axis needs to be placed on the bias. The "Rotate Piece" function would be used first to rotate the piece in a 45-degree angle. TRUE or FALSE
35. After rotating the piece in the previous question, to keep the piece in this rotation, the grain line must be changed with the Realign Piece/Grade Ref function and saved. TRUE or FALSE

CHAPTER NINE

Line Functions in PDS

Objective

This chapter introduces the basic line functions that are commonly used in the industry, such as creating style lines, moving and extending lines, and replacing lines. Not all functions available in the line menu are discussed in this chapter.

Keep in mind that you may create the examples used in this book with the corresponding functions covered here. Since there are different ways to achieve the same result, you may find that a function may or may not be the most efficient option for a particular example. Furthermore, you may need to complete the examples discussed by using other functions to reach your desired results.

This chapter allows you to gain skills in the following areas:

- Create lines
- Perpendicular lines
- Conics
- Delete lines
- Replace lines
- Swap lines
- Modify lines

Create Line

The Create Line menu gives you the ability to create lines such as style lines, matching reference lines, new perimeter lines, and facings.

Digitized

The Digitized function is used to create internal lines on an existing piece. These internal lines may

be made up of one or more multiple points, although most internal lines are made up of at least two points. Digitized lines may be straight or curved and creating them is similar to drafting a pattern into the system. One-point internals are usually considered drill holes and are commonly used as reference points for pattern placement, such as a back pocket on a jean. The Add Point function is a better option to create one-point internals.

Use the Digitized function when you need

- to create style lines for appliqués.
- to create style lines for gores or yokes.
- lines for matching.
- new perimeter lines.

Figure 9.1 shows a garment with details that could be created using the Digitized function.

Figure 9.1 A flower design may be created with the Digitized function.

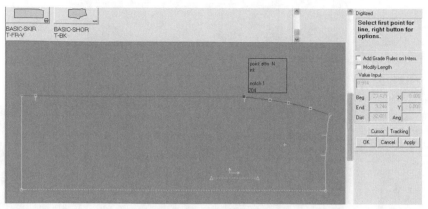

Figure 9.2 Hip point selected as the location to start digitizing.

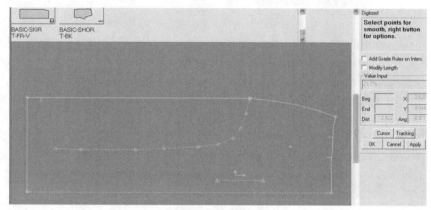

Figure 9.3 Princess seam created with the Digitized function.

Procedure for Digitized

1. Place on-screen the pattern to which you need to add a digitized line.

2. Select **Line>Create Line>Digitized.**

3. A user input box states: "Select first point for line, right button for options." Left click to select the point where you want to start your line. The example in Figure 9.2 shows the hip notch selected as a starting point.

   Note: You may also right click your mouse button to access options such as **Midpoint** to select the middle of a line, or perform a popup to enter a specific measurement for where you want to start and end the line segment.

4. A user input box states: "Select points for straight, right button for options." Continue left clicking to place points and create the shape of the line, just as you do when you originally

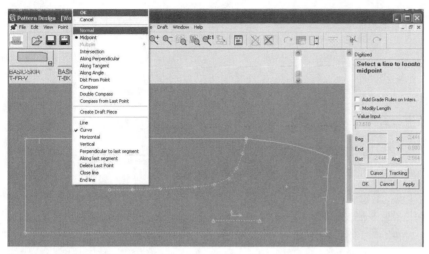

Figure 9.4 Midpoint option available for the Digitized function.

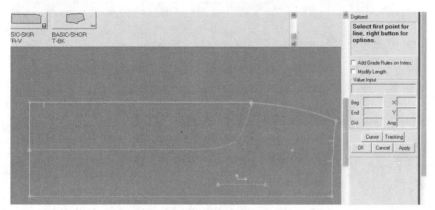

Figure 9.5 Princess seam completed with the Digitized function.

draft in a pattern. It is much like placing points for a connect-the-dots drawing. Figure 9.3 shows a curved seam being created on a skirt. This pattern may be split along this seam to create a better fitting garment or to add style.

Note: Right click to access options, as shown in Figure 9.4. If **Curve** is selected from the right-click menu, the prompt states, "Select points for smooth, right button for options" instead of "Select points for straight, right button for options. . . ."

5. Right click and select **OK** when you are done to create the line (see Figure 9.5).

6. The function restarts for additional lines. If done, select **Cancel** in the user input box or right click and select **Cancel.**

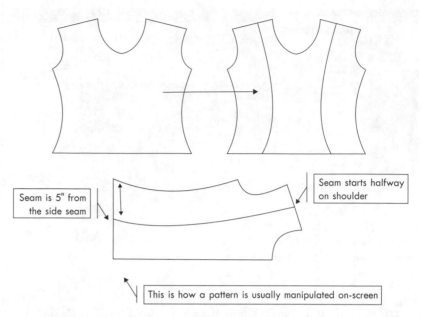

Seam is 5" from the side seam

Seam starts halfway on shoulder

This is how a pattern is usually manipulated on-screen

Figure 9.6 Technical drawing of a princess seam on a bodice.

Test Your Digitized Function Skills

Figure 9.6 shows a garment that had princess seams added with the Digitized function. The technical drawing shown is normally interpreted as a garment with a center front and side fronts sewn to each side. The Digitized function is used to create the initial seams in the pattern and determine where they will be located. The pattern is then cut along the seam with another function, such as Split on Line, and seam allowance is added as well. For this exercise, we simply add the seams so that you are comfortable using the Digitized function.

1. Select a basic top with which to work such as the one shown in Figure 9.6.
2. Select the Digitized function.
3. The user input box states: "Select first point for line, right button for options." Right click and select Midpoint from the right-click menu.
4. The user input box states: "Select a line to locate midpoint."
5. Select the shoulder line.
   Note: If the right-click menu is on top of the line, click elsewhere on the screen and the menu will disappear so you may view the line.

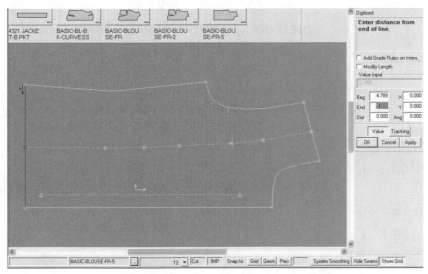

Figure 9.7 Princess seam created with the Digitized function.

6. The right-click menu appears again. Select Normal so you can proceed to place the points.

7. Left click to place points and create the shape of a princess seam similar to the one shown in Figure 9.6.

8. When placing the last point on the hem, perform a popup (by holding down both the left and right mouse buttons and releasing them at the same time).

9. The user input box states: "Enter distance from beginning of line." The Beg and End fields, as well as other fields, are available for measurement input (see Figure 9.7).

10. Highlight the End field and type in 5", as shown in Figure 9.7. Notice that the user input box now states: "Enter distance from end of line." This occurs because in this example we are measuring 5" from the side seam, which is the end of the hem line segment when you move clockwise around the piece. The arrow shown on the screen helps you visualize from where the system will measure the 5".

11. Click **OK** or press **Enter** on the keyboard to enter the measurement.

12. Right click and select **OK** to end the line.

13. Right click and select **Cancel** if you wish to exit the function.

2 Point

The 2 Point function is similar to the Digitized function in that it is used to create internal lines on an existing piece. The difference is that with this function, more than two points may not be used to create internal lines. Furthermore, the internal lines created with this function can be only straight lines, since the system draws a line from the first point to the second point that you select.

Use the 2 Point function when you need to

- create new straight perimeter lines, such as an asymmetrical hem on a skirt or a normal pant, shirt, or skirt hem.
- create straight gore or yoke style lines.
- use the best option for creating match lines.
- see reference lines so you can place one pattern on top of another pattern.

Procedure for the 2-Point function

1. Bring the pattern to which you wish to add a 2-point line into the work area.
2. Select **Line>Create Line>2 Point.**
3. The user input box states: "Select first point for line, right button for options." Left click to select the location to place the first point.

   Note: Remember, as discussed in the Digitized section, you have the option to perform a popup or right click for other options, such as Midpoint.

4. The user input box states: "Select points for straight, right button for options." Left click to select the location for the second point to create a line.

5. The function restarts so you can add more lines. When you are finished, right click and click **Cancel.**

Test Your 2 Point Function Skills

Figure 9.8 shows a garment with a straight yoke that cuts across the waist. It lays 12¾" from the top of the center front. As stated in the Test Your Digitized Function Skills section, you would use the 2 Point function to determine where the seams fall on this pattern. The pattern would then be split with another function such as Split on Line. This exercise shows you how to create the seam, not how to split the pattern.

1. Select a basic top with which to work such as the one shown in Figure 9.8.
2. Select the 2 Point function.
3. The user input box states: "Select first point for line, right button for options."
4. Select the first point anywhere on the center front and perform a popup. Type in 12.75 in the Beg field and select **OK** on the screen or press **Enter** on the keyboard (see Figure 9.9).
5. The user input box states: "Enter value from beginning of line." Do not enter a value at this time. The Value Mode will remain on because you entered the 12.75 value measurement. This occurs because Value

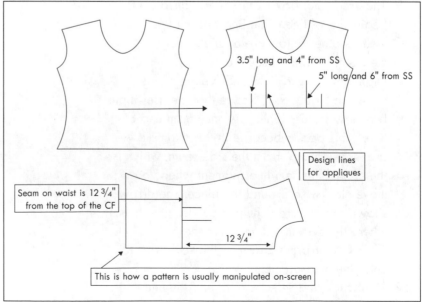

Figure 9.8 Bodice with yoke and style reference lines.

Mode in our Preferences/Options is set to Default, and whichever mode you selected remains selected. Look at the bottom window of Figure 9.9.

6. Click on the word Value in the user input box to unselect it and note that it changes to Cursor mode. When Value is unselected in the User Input box, it changes to Cursor mode and lets you view the line as it is created, but to enter a value, you must switch it back to Value.

7. Right click and select Vertical.

8. Select the side seam line to place the second point to create the waist yoke.

9. The function restarts automatically. Do not exit the function so that we may now create the appliqué lines. If you did exit the function, select it again.

10. The user input box states: "Select first point for line, right button for options." Perform a popup on the new yoke line.

11. Type in 4" in the End field and click **OK.** We are measuring from the side seam (see Figure 9.10).

12. Right click and select Horizontal. Perform a popup.

Note: If you did not right click and select Horizontal in this step, but you still performed a popup, the Dist, X, and Y fields would all light up rather than just the X field. Input 3.5" in the X field for the length and 0 in the Y field so that the line does not angle to achieve the same results. The same applies for Step 16.

13. Only the X field becomes available. Type in 3.5". Look at the bottom window of Figure 9.10.

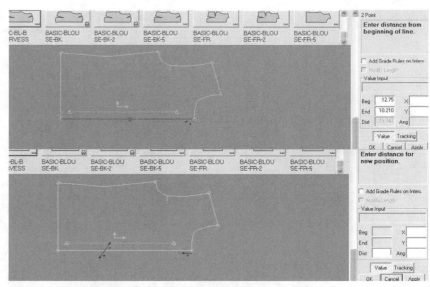

Figure 9.9 Start point is entered to create a 2 point line.

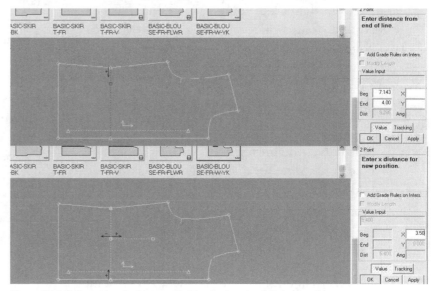

Figure 9.10 Yoke and style line are digitized using the 2 Point function.

14. The user input box states: "Select first point for line, right button for options." Perform a popup on the yoke line.

15. Type in 6" in the End field and click **OK.** We are still measuring from the side seam.

16. Right click and select Horizontal. Perform a popup.

17. In the X field, type in 5" to complete appliqué lines.

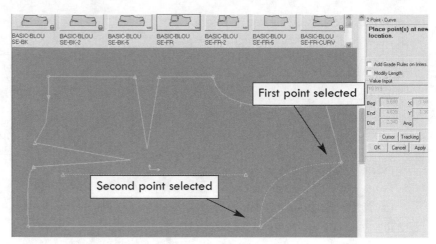

Figure 9.11 A curved neckline is created using the 2 Point-Curve.

2 Point-Curve

The 2 Point-Curve function is very much like 2 Point, except that it lets you create a curved line instead of a straight one. The line created by the two points you select may be manipulated into a curve. An existing piece must be used to perform this function.

Use the 2 Point-Curve function when you need to create

- new curved perimeter lines, such as an armhole, a neckline, or a side seam of a skirt or bodice.
- curved style lines, such as gores and yokes.
- reference lines for appliqués.

Procedure for 2 Point-Curve

1. Place on-screen the pattern to which you want to add a 2 Point-Curve line.

2. Select **Line>Create Line>2 Point-Curve.**

3. The user input box states: "Select first point for line, right button for options." Left click to select a location to place the first point, perform a popup, or right click to get access to options such as **Midpoint.**

4. The user input box states: "Select points for straight, right button for options." Left click to select where you want to place the second point. Perform a popup, right click, or move the mouse to select a location and left click to place the point.

5. The user input box states: "Place point(s) at new location." Move the mouse until you achieve the shape you want. Left click to place down the point on-screen to create the line (see Figure 9.11). You can now change the line into a perimeter line by using the Swap or Replace functions, discussed later in the chapter.

6. The function restarts so you can add more lines. If you are finished, right click and select **Cancel.**

Offset Even

Offset Even creates a line that is offset parallel to a selected line. You may offset multiple lines at the same time. When you offset a line, it shortens or lengthens as you move it, but the system tries to keep the same shape.

Use the Offset Even function when you want to

- create facings for armholes, necklines, or waistlines.
- create additional style line copies.

Procedure for Offset Even

1. Select **Line>Create Line>Offset Even.**

2. Select your preferred options from the user input box.

3. Select either the **Add** or the **Replace** option.

    Add is selected if you want the newly created offset line to be an additional line. It

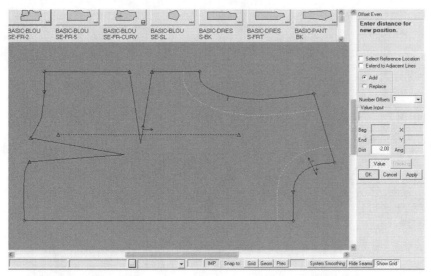

Figure 9.12 Armhole and neckline facings created with the Offset Even function.

appears on-screen as a dashed line (see Figure 9.12). If you select this option, the **Number Offsets** field becomes available. Click the drop-down menu in this field to select the number of offsets you want to create.

Replace is selected if you want the new offset line to replace the original perimeter line.

4. The user input box states: "Select line to offset, end selection to continue." Left click to select the lines to offset, which highlights them in red. Figure 9.12 shows an armhole and a neckline for each of which we will create a facing.

5. The user input box states: "Input the offset amount." As the mouse moves, the new line follows. Notice that the grayed out **Dist** field shows the distance the line is moved away from the original line. Enter a value with a popup or click **Cursor** in the user input box to switch to Value Mode. Figure 9.12 shows how 2" is input to create the facing with a specific width. The offset line is created.

6. To finish creating the facing, use the Facing, Trace, or Split on Line functions.

Offset Uneven

Offset Uneven creates a line that is offset from a selected line. The line may be offset at specific amounts at different locations on the line. For example, a sleeve cap may be changed from 0 at the armhole to ½" at the top of the sleeve cap, described further in the following sections.

Use the Offset Uneven function when you want to

- modify an existing side seam or inseam or to create a new one at a specific distance.

- add a little fullness or length to a sleeve cap.

Procedure for Offset Uneven

1. Select **Line>Create Line>Offset Uneven.**

2. Select your preferred options from the user input box.

3. Select either the **Add** or the **Replace** option.

   Add is selected if you want the newly created offset line to be an additional line. It appears on-screen as a dashed line.

   Replace is selected if you want the new offset line to replace the original perimeter line.

4. Check the box next to **Extend to Adjacent Lines** if you want the offsets extended to meet the lines next to the offset line.

5. A user input box states: "Select point to offset uneven from." Left click to select the point to offset first, which highlights it in red (see Figure 9.13).

6. A user input box states: "Enter offset to move this point." Enter the amount in the

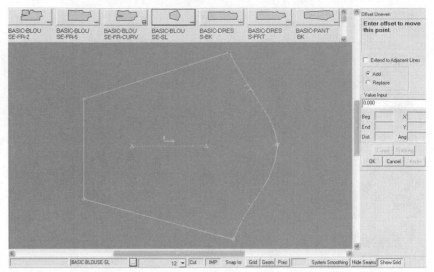

Figure 9.13 Point to offset is selected on sleeve with the Offset Uneven function.

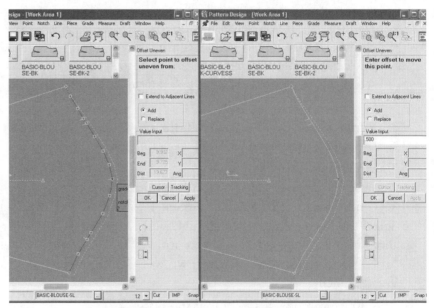

Figure 9.14 Points are offset using the Offset Uneven function.

Value Input field and click **OK** or press **Enter** on the keyboard. Figure 9.13 shows "0" entered.

7. Return to Step 5. The prompt restarts so you can select the next point. The left side of Figure 9.14 displays the point at the top of the sleeve cap as the next selected offset point. The right side of Figure 9.14 displays the input amount to offset the line at this point.

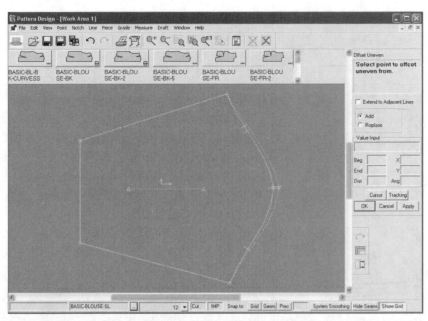

Figure 9.15 New sleeve cap is created with the Offset Uneven function.

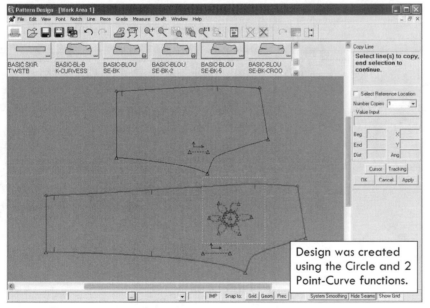

Design was created using the Circle and 2 Point-Curve functions.

Figure 9.16 Marquee box used to copy lines of flower design.

8. Continue selecting a point to move and the amount to offset until you reach the end of the line. Figure 9.15 displays the sleeve cap completed from nothing at one end to ½" at the top of the cap and back to nothing at the other end.

Copy Line

The Copy Line function makes an exact copy of a line. The shape and the length remain the same. You may copy the line to another piece or the same piece.

Use the Copy Line function when you need to

- copy a line from one piece to another, such as a neckline or armhole.

- copy a line, such as a side seam from a front to a back so that they walk well together.

- copy internals from one piece to another.

Procedure for Copy Line

1. Select **Line>Create Line>Copy Line.**

2. In the **Number Copies** field, click the drop-down menu to select the number of copies you want to create of the selected lines.

3. A user input box states: "Select line(s) to copy, end selection to continue." Left click to select the line(s) to copy. Figure 9.16 shows a marquee box being used to select all the lines of the design on a pant. All the lines that need to be copied must be inside the marquee box. To use a marquee box, click and drag with the left mouse button until the lines you want to copy are inside the marquee

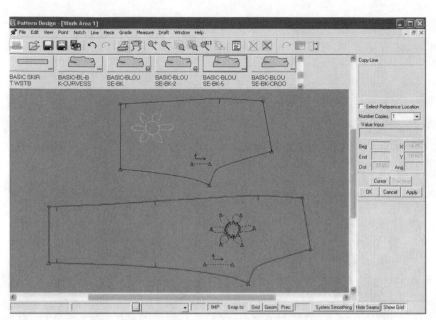

Figure 9.17 Flower design copied onto short with the Copy Line function.

box. Left click again to finish creating the marquee box.

4. A user input box states: "Select the piece(s) to receive the copied line(s), end selection to continue." Left click to select the piece to which you are copying the lines, which highlights the piece in red.

5. Right click and select **OK** to continue. Lines copied move along with the mouse. Left click to place the lines down on-screen. See Figure 9.17 to view the shorts with the lines copied from the pant pattern.

6. The function restarts. Right click and select **Cancel** to exit.

Mirror

Use the Mirror function to create a mirror image of a line. You may mirror multiple lines at the same time. You may use internal or perimeter lines when you perform this function.

Use the Mirror function when you need to

- mirror a line or lines while creating a design. For example, you may want to mirror a design on the front of a skirt from the left side to the right side.

- mirror a line while creating or manipulating a pattern. For example, when creating an off-the-shoulder blouse, if the side seams need to be the same, they may be mirrored.

Procedure for Mirror

1. Select **Line>Create Line>Mirror.**

2. A user input box states: "Select line(s) to mirror, end selection to continue." Left click to select the lines to mirror, which highlights them in red.

3. A user input box states: "Select line to mirror about." Left click to select a line as a guide for the system to mirror the selected lines on the opposite side. The lines are mirrored as seen on the right-hand side of Figure 9.18.

Note: In Figure 9.18, we did not have a line to "mirror about." We created a temporary line using the 2-Point function to accomplish our flower design.

Blend

The Blend function works on a line segment from one end to the other. It is used to create a new line that blends from one endpoint and adds to or subtracts from the garment at the other end point. Figure 9.19 displays a side seam blended to the waist while fullness is added to the hem line.

Procedure for Blend

1. Select **Line>Create Line>Blend.**

2. The user input box states: "Select blend point." Left click to select the point to blend, which highlights it in red.

3. The user input box states: "Move end of basis line." Line moves along with mouse. Perform a

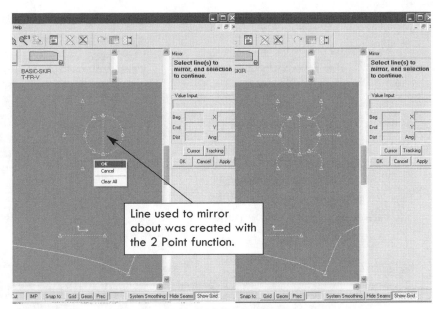

Figure 9.18 Mirror Line is used to mirror lines of a design.

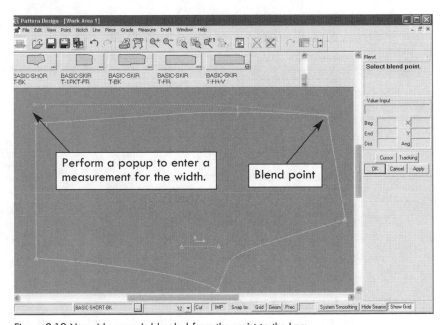

Figure 9.19 New side seam is blended from the waist to the hem.

popup to enter a specific measurement or place down the line with the left mouse button to create a blend line. Use the Swap Line or Replace Line functions to make the blend line a perimeter line. Swap Line would be used for the example in Figure 9.19.

Perp Line

The Perp Line menu is a short name for the Perpendicular Line menu. It is used to create perpendicular lines. It is a useful menu to create patterns from a block pattern or to create new internal lines on an existing pattern to become perimeter lines. It is also used to create matching lines since they usually run parallel or perpendicular to the grain.

Perp On Line

The Perp On Line function is used to create a line perpendicular to a point you selected.

Use the Perp On Line function when you want to

- use the line as a guide while creating a block pattern, such as a neckline or armhole (see Figure 9.20).

- help with the correction of a corner that should be squared at a 90-degree angle, such as an armhole corner.

- create plaid or stripe matching lines. They are normally perpendicular to each other.

Procedure for Perp On Line

1. Select **Line>Perp Line>Perp On Line.**

2. Select your preferences for a half or whole line in the user input box.

> **Half** creates the perpendicular line on one side of the selected point (see Figure 9.21).
>
> **Whole** creates the perpendicular line on both sides of the selected point (see Figure 9.22).

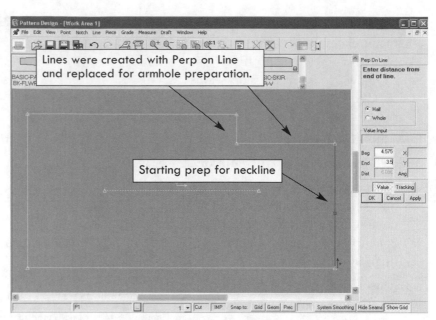

Figure 9.20 Basis for new armhole and neckline created with the Perp on Line function.

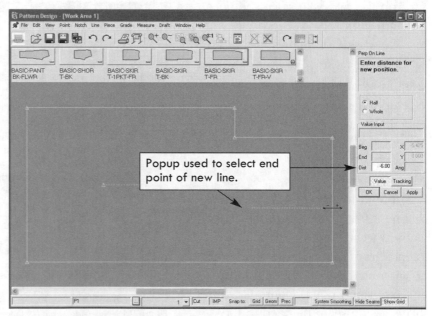

Figure 9.21 Line length is entered in the Perp on Line function.

3. A user input box states: "Select point of intersection." Left click to select the location where the perpendicular line will intersect.

4. A user input box states: "Select end point of new line." Left click to select the length of the line or perform a popup to enter a specific measurement.

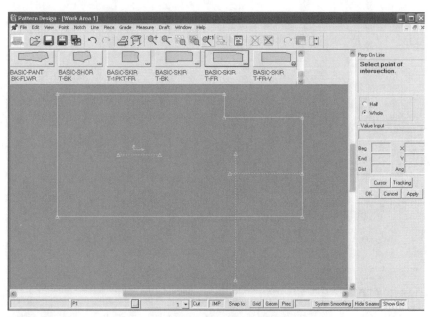

Figure 9.22 Perpendicular lines completed using Perp on Line.

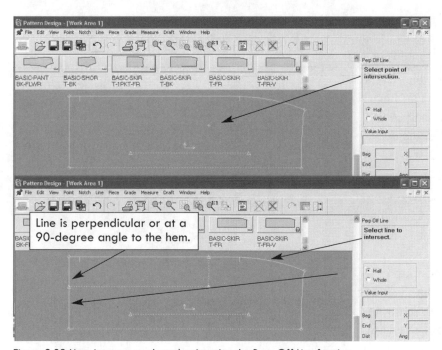

Line is perpendicular or at a 90-degree angle to the hem.

Figure 9.23 Lines intersect a selected point using the Perp Off Line function.

Perp Off Line

The Perp Off Line function allows a point to be selected to intersect a line at a 90-degree angle. The example in Figure 9.23 illustrates a point selected as the meeting point for a perpendicular line toward the hem and another toward the side seam. You may treat these lines as style lines to be cut into separate patterns with a function such as Split on Line, or as reference lines for a detail such as rick rack.

Procedure for Perp Off Line

1. Select **Line>Perp Line>Perp Off Line.**

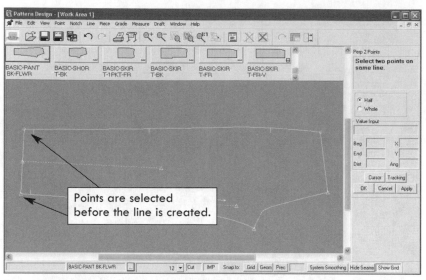

Figure 9.24 A line is created perpendicular to a pant hem.

2. The user input box states: "Select point of intersection." Left click to select the location where the perpendicular line will intersect.

3. The user input box states: "Select line to intersect." Left click to select the line. The line is created perpendicular to the line selected while intersecting the point you selected.

Perp 2 Points

Perp 2 Points creates a line midway between two selected points. The line created is perpendicular to the line segment in which the two points are located. The example in Figure 9.24 shows a garment that is off grain. Since the grain on a pant is normally perpendicular to the hem, a line is being created to take the place of the existing grain line and place the piece in the proper grain direction. This section shows you how to create the line, but for the example mentioned, the next steps include changing the line label of the new line and deleting the existing grain line. You may change the line label by using the Edit Line Info option discussed in Chapter 3 and you may delete the line by using the Delete Line option, discussed later in this chapter.

Use the Perp 2 Points function if you want to

- create a new grain line.
- split a piece and mirror it on the new line.

Procedure for Perp 2 Points

1. Select **Line>Perp Line>Perp 2 Points.**

2. The user input box states: "Select the two points on same line." Left click to select two points on a line.

3. The user input box states: "Select end point of new line." Select the length of the line by performing a popup or by placing it down with the left mouse button without giving a specific measurement.

Conics

The Conics menu is used to create circles and ovals. The circles and ovals created are usually internal lines and therefore an existing piece is needed on-screen to perform most of the functions. These internal lines are used in the fashion industry to create cutouts in the fronts or backs of garments or as reference lines for appliqués such as rhinestones or beads. There are, however, two functions that do allow a circle to be created as a stand-alone pattern piece.

Circle Ctr Rad

Circle Center Radius creates a circle where you may input a radius to determine the circle's size. The circle may exist on its own as a pattern or as

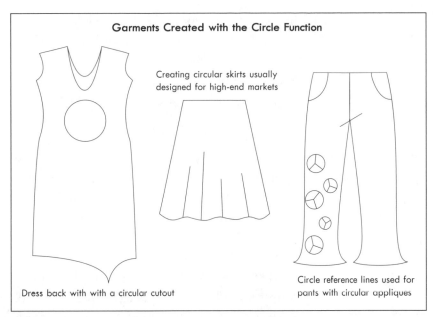

Figure 9.25 Circle function used to create circular designs.

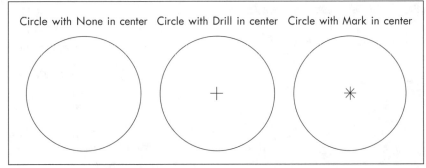

Figure 9.26 Circles illustrating three center options.

an internal line within an existing pattern piece. The circular skirt seen in Figure 9.25 is an example of a garment created using a circle to exist as a pattern of its own. Due to its doughnut-like shape and lack of seams, circular skirts use large amounts of fabric and are commonly made from beautiful fabrics in haute couture. The circular cutout seen on the back of the dress in Figure 9.25 is an example of a circle that was created using a circular internal line. The line was used as a reference line to create the new shape of the pattern. Internal circle lines may also be used as a reference when placing appliqués like the ones on the pants in Figure 9.25. Use the Circle Ctr Rad function when you want to

- create circular skirts.
- create hats.
- create a reference for circle cutouts in pants, dresses, or tops.
- create a reference for circular designs that will be decorated with items like sequins or rhinestones.
- aid in the creation of designs that may start as circles, such as flowers.

Procedure for Circle Ctr Rad

1. Select **Line>Conics>Circle Ctr Rad.**

2. Select your preferences from the user input box.

3. In the **New Piece** area, select from the options described.

   Name is used to enter a piece name for the circle you are creating. It will display if you check the box next to Create New Piece.

   Create New Piece is selected when you want to make a circle for the creation of a pattern on its own. For example, use a circle to create a hat pattern. Leave this option unchecked if you want to create the circle as an internal.

4. In the **Show Center** area, select the type of point you want at the center of the circle (see Figure 9.26).

   None is used to leave the center blank, with no point displayed.

   Drill is used to display a drill point (+) at the center of the circle.

   Mark is used to display a mark point (∗) at the center of the circle.

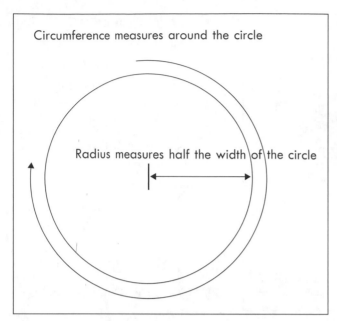

Figure 9.27 Circle with circumference and radius illustrated.

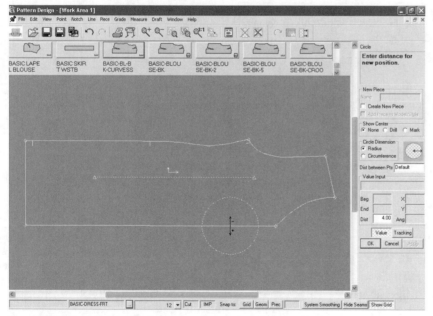

Figure 9.28 Circle Ctr Rad used to create a cutout in a dress back.

5. In the **Circle Dimension** area, select the method to create the circle (see Figure 9.27).

> **Radius** is selected when you want to create a circle by entering a radius measurement. The radius is measured from the edge of a circle to the center and is considered half the width of a circle.

> **Circumference** is selected when you want to create a circle by entering a circumference. The circumference of the circle is the measurement around the perimeter, or outline, of the circle. For example, you could create the pattern for a skirt to include a specific sweep measurement for the hem.

6. A user input box states: "Select center of circle." Left click to select a location/point on the piece or the screen to create the circle. The circle size moves along with the mouse. If it is not moving, then you are in Value Mode and are ready to input a measurement, so see the next step.

7. A user input box states: "Select radius (or circumference) of circle."

> According to the selection you made under **Circle Dimension,** enter the radius or circumference in the **Dist** field, which lights up when you perform a popup or click the **Cursor** button to display **Value.** Click **OK** to enter the value and create the circle (see Figure 9.28).

8. Save the piece if you need it for later use.

Note: The example in Figure 9.28 displays a circle cutout being created for a dress, as is shown in Figure 9.25. To finish the pattern, you can use the Split function, to split line segments, and the Trace function under the Piece menu to trace the new pattern shape.

Circle Ctr Cirm

The Circle Center Circumference function creates a circle where a circumference may be input to determine the size. The circle may exist on its own as a pattern or as an internal in an existing piece. See Figure 9.25 for some examples of what can be done with this function. It is similar to Circle Ctr Rad function. The examples listed under the last section apply to this function as well.

Procedure for Circle Ctr Cirm

1. Select **Line>Conics>Circle Ctr Cirm.**

2. Select your preferences from the user input box (New Piece, Show Center, and Circle Dimension areas).

3. A user input box states: "Select center of circle." Left click to select a point to create a circle. The plus sign in Figure 9.29 represents the center at this point in the procedure. Circle size moves along with the mouse. If it is not moving, then you are in Value Mode and are ready to input a measurement, so see next step.

   Note: To return back to moving the circle along with the mouse, click the **Value** button to toggle it to **Cursor** and place you in cursor mode.

4. A user input box states: "Select circumference of circle." Enter circumference in the **Dist** field as seen in Figure 9.29, which lights up when a popup is performed or click the **Cursor** button is to display the Value Mode and create the circle.

Note: The example in Figure 9.29 displays a circle created for the creation of a circular dress, as shown in Figure 9.25.

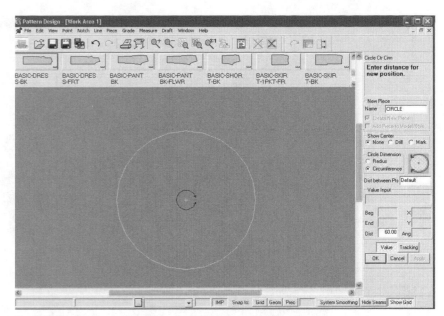

Figure 9.29 Creating a circle with a specified circumference.

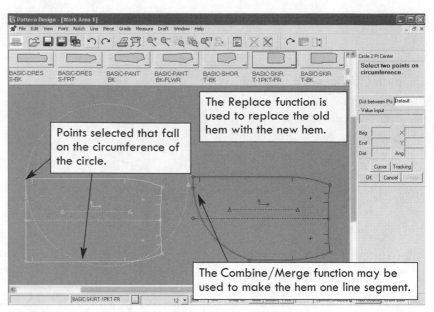

Figure 9.30 Skirt hem is rounded using Circle 2Pt Center.

Circle 2 Pt Center

Circle 2 Point Center creates a circle between two selected points either on a perimeter or an internal line. The selected points do not have to be on a line; they may be inside or outside of the piece. The selected points will fall on the circumference or outline of the circle you create. The created circle becomes an internal in the selected piece placed on-screen.

Use the Circle 2 Pt Center function when you need to

- create a curved hem line that intersects two specified points (see Figure 9.30).
- create an armhole that intersects two specified points.
- create circle cutouts.
- create circular designs.
- create designs that start or include circles, such as flowers.

Procedure for Circle 2 Pt Center

1. Select **Line>Conics>Circle 2 Pt Center.**

2. A user input box states: "Select two points on circumference." Left click to select the two points you want the circle to intersect.

3. The circle moves along with mouse. Set the line down with the left mouse button at the location you want.

Note: To complete the example in Figure 9.30, use the Replace or Swap functions to make the new circle segment the permanent perimeter hem line. You may need to perform other functions, such as Delete and Combine/Merge in the Line menu, to finish cleaning up the piece.

Circle 3 Pt

Circle 3 Point Center creates a circle among three selected points either on a perimeter or an internal line. The selected points do not have to be on a line; they may be inside or outside of the piece. The selected points fall on the circumference or outline of the created circle. The created circle becomes an internal in the selected piece placed on-screen. If the points are laid out almost in a straight line, the circle becomes quite large so it can intersect the points.

Use the Circle 3 Pt function to

- create side seams (see Figure 9.31).
- create an inseam while intersecting three specified points.

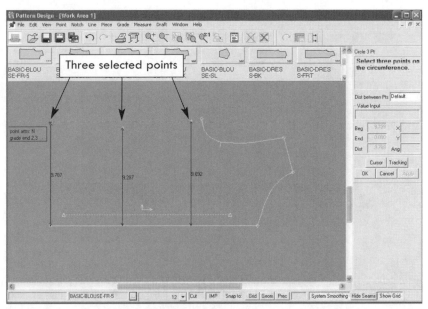

Figure 9.31 Points selected for a circle circumference.

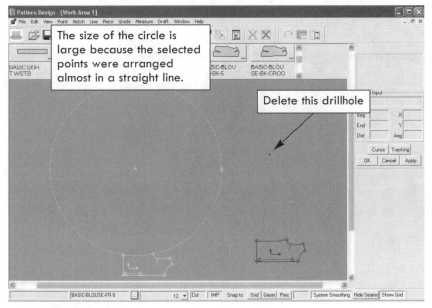

Figure 9.32 Circle created from points selected in Figure 9.31.

- create circle cutouts.
- create circular designs.

Procedure for Circle 3 Pt

1. Select **Line>Conics>Circle 3 Pt.**

2. The user input box states: "Select three points on circumference." Left click to select each of the three points you want the circle

to intersect. Figure 9.31 shows three points selected at measurements assigned to meet specs for the pattern shown. A circle is created with the three points falling on the circumference or outline of the circle. Figure 9.32 shows how large the circle is because of the the selected points.

Note: To complete the example in Figure 9.32, use the Replace or Swap functions to make the new circle segment the permanent perimeter side seam. You may perform other functions, such as Delete in the Line menu, to finish cleaning up the piece. Do not forget to delete the drill hole from the created circle.

Curved Intersection

Use the Curved Intersection function to make a regular corner into a curved or rounded corner. The curved corner may be changed back into a regular corner depending on the option you select in the user input box. The corner must contain an endpoint; if it does not, you need to split it to use the function. After the corner is curved, or rounded, as some industry professionals say, you may merge the lines to turn the new split points into intermediate points.

Use the Curved Intersection function when you need to

- create a rounded corner pocket.
- round out hem corners and create a jacket, such as a cut-away.
- round out lapel corners.
- round out the corners of a design.

Procedure for Curved Intersection

1. Select **Line>Conics>Curved Intersection.**

2. Select your preferences from the user input box.

3. In the **Line Type** area, select from one of the two available options described.

   Perimeter is selected if the line that is being used is a perimeter/boundary line.

   Internal is selected if the line that is being used is an internal line. Make sure the corner contains an end point/split in the corner.

4. In the **Option** area, select from one of the four available options described.

   Add/Change Radius (Mk/V8) is used to curve the corner. Perform a popup or change to Value Mode to enter the distance needed from the corner selected to the curve line. For example, enter 1" if you need to curve the corners at 1" for the specification on a lapel (see Figure 9.33). If you need to change the measurement of a curved corner, you can do so, but only if you didn't sever the corner.

   You may not be able to perform some functions on this type of corner, such as Combine/Merge lines, unless you sever the corner. Some warning messages that you may get are: "Cannot merge a corner line" or "Intersection error(s) on piece ————. Please check this piece and correct the problem." This curved corner may be changed back to a regular corner using the Delete option described below.

   Add Severed also curves the corner like the option above. The difference is that this option severs the corner automatically after it is created. Enter the distance

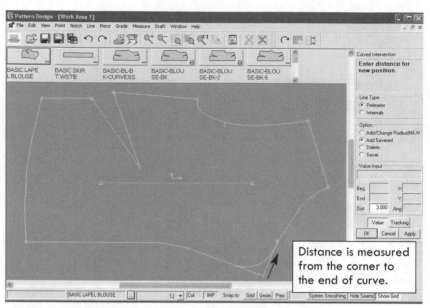

Figure 9.33 Curved Intersection used to curve the corner on a lapel.

needed by changing to Value Mode and entering an amount in the Dist field. This corner may not be changed back to a regular corner using the Delete option described below.

Delete is used to delete a curved corner created using the Add/Change Radius option.

Sever is used to separate or cut a curved corner that is not meant to be changed back to a regular corner. If you sever a corner, the curved corner is permanent. If you want a regular corner again, you have to recreate it.

5. According to the option you select, the following prompts will display:

   "Select a corner to add a curved intersection" (Add/Change Radius)

   "Select a corner to add a severed curved intersection" (Add Severed)

   "Select a perimeter curved intersection to delete" (Delete)

   "Select a perimeter curved intersection to sever" (Sever)

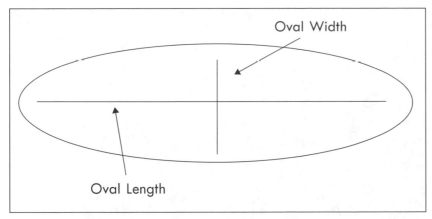

Figure 9.34 Drawing illustrating oval length and width.

Oval Orient

Use the Oval Orient function to create oval shapes. The created oval is an internal line that becomes part of the selected piece on-screen. It may be used for style lines or cutouts, or part of the oval may be split and copied onto another piece to help create a side seam on a skirt. Figure 9.34 displays and defines the width and length of an oval.

Use Oval Orient function to

- create oval cutouts.
- create oval shoulder pads.
- create table covers.
- create seat covers.
- use part of the oval to create another piece.

Procedure for Oval Orient

1. Select **Line>Conics>Oval Orient.**

2. The user input box states: "Select center of oval." Left click to select a location in which to place the oval. A pre-digitized line or point may help you locate a specific area on which to place the oval (see Figure 9.35).

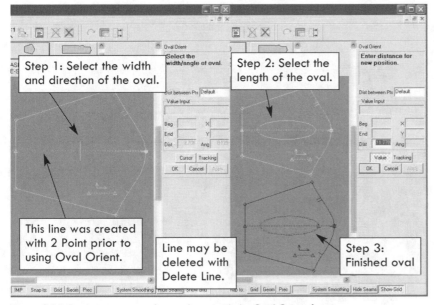

Figure 9.35 Oval cutout created on a sleeve with the Oval Orient function.

"Select two adjacent lines" (Internals) (Only Add Severed is available)

6. Left click to select a corner. The curve moves along with the mouse. Perform a popup or change to Value Mode to enter a measurement or left click to create the curve without a specific measurement. Figure 9.33 displays a regular corner on a lapel that is rounded out with the **Add Severed** option at a 3" distance.

3. The user input box states: "Select the width/angle of the oval." See the left side of Figure 9.35. Enter a width or angle and click **OK.**

4. The user input box states: "Select the length of the oval." The length moves with the mouse. Left click to set down the oval at a desirable length or enter a measurement by performing a popup or changing to Value Mode as seen at the top right of Figure 9.35. At the bottom right of the figure, the created oval is shown.

Delete Line

Delete Line lets you take out unwanted line segments, such as internal lines or points. Perimeter lines and grain lines cannot be deleted. If Delete Line is performed on a curved perimeter line, it will change the line from a curved to a straight line segment, since no pattern can exist without an outline. It is a quick way to delete all intermediate points in a line segment in this scenario.

Procedure for Delete Line

1. Select **Line>Delete Line.**

2. The user input box states: "Select line(s) to delete, end selection to continue." Left click to select the lines, which highlights them in red.

3. Right click and select **OK** to delete the lines.

Replace Line

The Replace Line function lets you exchange a perimeter line for an internal line. The internal line must touch the perimeter outline of the piece in two locations. If the internal does not touch a perimeter line, it must be extended or the function may not work. Figure 9.36 shows a bodice with a V-neck that is being replaced with a square neckline. The square neckline is made up of two lines created using the 2 Point function. Notice that the lines touch the perimeter of the piece in two locations.

Procedure for Replace Line

1. Select **Line>Replace Line.**

2. The user input box states: "Select internal line(s), end selection to continue." Left click to select the internal lines, which highlights them in red. These are the lines you wish to make the new perimeter lines.

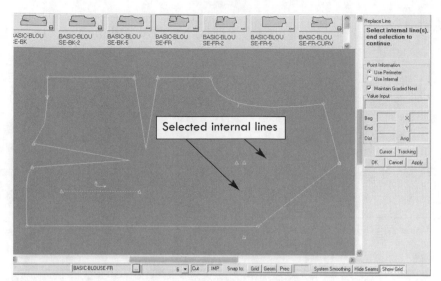

Figure 9.36 V-neck about to be replaced with a square neckline.

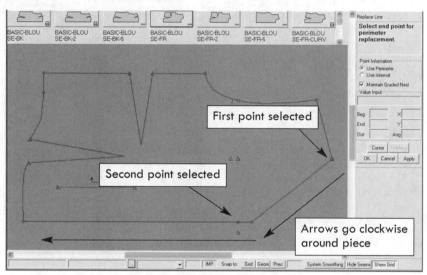

Figure 9.37 First and last points selected in a clockwise sequence.

3. Right click and select **OK** to continue.

4. The user input box states: "Select start point for perimeter replacement." Left click to select the point where the internal line intersects with the perimeter line when moving clockwise on the piece.

5. The user input box states: "Select end point for perimeter replacement." Left click to select the second point where the internal intersects with the perimeter line (see Figure 9.37). The lines are replaced (see Figure 9.38).

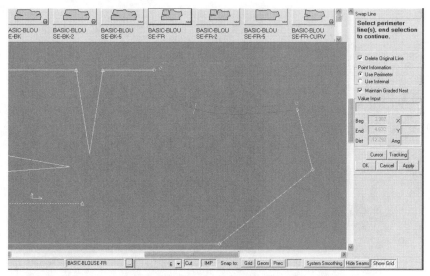

Figure 9.38 Neckline replacement Is completed wIth the Replace LIne functIon.

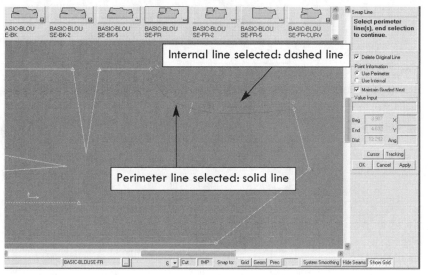

Figure 9.39 Swap Line function used to swap old armhole with new armhole.

Swap Line

The Swap Line function lets you exchange a perimeter line for an internal line. The internal lines do not have to touch the perimeter outline of the piece as they do in the Replace Line function. Figure 9.39 shows a bodice with an armhole being swapped for a new armhole. The new armhole line was created using the Offset Even function, so the new armhole line does not touch the perimeter of the piece—therefore, you need to use the Swap Line function instead of the Replace Line function.

Procedure for Swap Line

1. Select **Line>Swap Line.**

2. The user input box states: "Select internal line(s), end selection to continue." Left click to select the internal lines, which highlights them in red. These are the lines you want to make the new perimeter lines (see Figure 9.39).

3. The user input box states: "Select perimeter line(s), end selection to continue." Left click to select the perimeter lines, which highlights them in red.

   The lines are swapped (see Figure 9.40). The option **Delete Original Line** was selected in this example, so it deleted the original line. If it is not selected, both the original and the new line display. To discard the old line, the Delete Line function would have to be used next.

4. The function restarts. Right click and select **Cancel** if you are done.

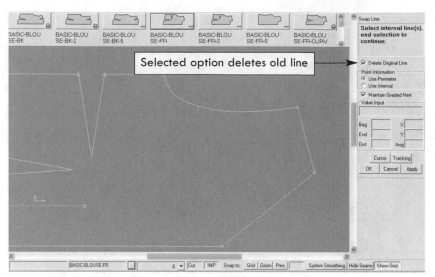

Figure 9.40 Swap Line function illustrating delete line option.

Modify Line

The Modify Line menu is used to manipulate and modify lines on existing pieces. This menu lets you move a hem line to shorten or lengthen a garment, rotate a line to create more fullness, and modify the length of a line or the shape of a curved line. These are only a few examples of the tasks you can accomplish using this menu.

Move Offset

The Move Offset function makes a line parallel to its original position. This function is similar to the Offset Even function in that the line offset stays parallel to the original while trying to maintain the same shape. The Move Offset function does not offer the options to add a line or to make several offsets of the original line. The original line is simply moved to the chosen location in an X or a Y

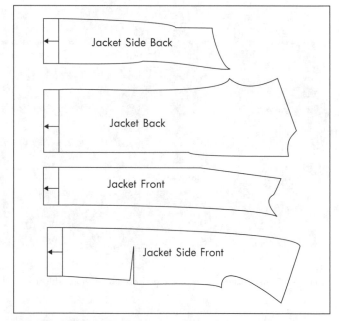

Figure 9.41 Drawing showing how jacket pieces may be lengthened with the Move Offset function.

direction. Try selecting different lines, including curved and straight lines, to note the way this function works. Try it on a grain line too.

Use the Move Offset function to

• lengthen or shorten a garment, as in a pant hem or shirt length. All patterns affected may be changed at the same time. For example, change the length of all jacket panels front, sides, and back to lengthen them (see Figure 9.41).

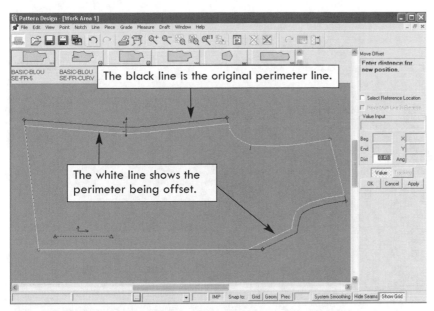

Figure 9.42 A side seam and neck are offset with the Move Offset function.

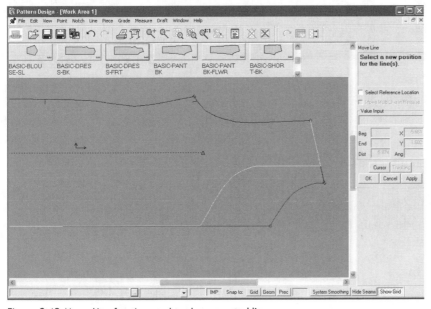

Figure 9.43 Move Line function used to change a neckline.

- add or take away width from a garment side seam or center front.

- add height to a shoulder.

- drop or raise a neckline while changing the shoulder width and neck drop.

- open or close the opening of an armhole while changing the shoulder and side seam.

Procedure for Move Offset

1. Select **Line>Modify Line>Move Offset.**

2. The user input box states: "Select line(s) to offset, end selection to continue." Left click to select the lines to offset, which highlights it in red. Figure 9.42 shows a side seam and neckline selected to offset.

3. The line moves with the mouse.

4. A user input box states: "Input the offset amount." Left click to set the line down. You may also perform a pop-up or change to Value Mode to input a specific amount to offset the selected line. See **Dist** field highlighted in Figure 9.42.

5. The function restarts to enable you to move additional lines. Right click and select **Cancel** to exit the function.

Note: As the lines are offset in Figure 9.42, the shoulder width, neck width and drop, side seam length, armhole opening, and waist and hem widths are changed. Whenever changes are made to a piece, note that other areas of the garment may be affected.

Move Line

The Move Line function moves a line in an X or Y direction. The difference between this function and the Move Offset one may be seen when each is performed on a curved line. The Move Line function can change the shape of the line selected (see Figure 9.43).

More than one line on one pattern or several patterns may be selected to move at the same time. When selecting multiple lines, we recommend that curved lines be the same shape. For example, the side seam of a front and a back garment may be moved at the same time to obtain the same shape. Otherwise, select curved lines individually. For example, change a neckline first, then change the armhole, since they will not move the same way and are not the same shape.

Use the Move Line function to

- lengthen or shorten a garment as in a pant hem or shirt length. All patterns affected may be changed at the same time. For example, change the length of all jacket panels front, sides, and back.

- add or take away width from a garment side seam or center front.

- add height to a shoulder.

- drop or raise a neckline while changing the shoulder width and neck drop.

- open or close the opening of an armhole while changing the shoulder and side seam.

Procedure for Move Line

1. Select **Line>Modify Line>Move Line.**

2. A user input box states: "Select line(s) to move, end selection to continue." Left click to select the lines to move, which highlights them in red.

3. The line moves as the mouse is moved. Figure 9.43 shows a selected neckline being moved.

4. A user input box states: "Select a new position for the line." It is common to set down the line with a left click when it is at the location and is the shape you want, although a specific measurement may also be entered.

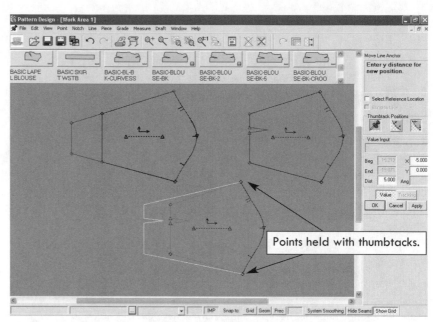

Points held with thumbtacks.

Figure 9.44 A sleeve with different functions applied to it for comparison.

5. The function restarts to move additional lines. Right click and select **Cancel** to exit the function.

Move Line Anchor

The Move Line Anchor function moves a line while holding two other locations in place while not changing the shape or length of the selected line to move. This is especially noticeable on a sleeve or any garment that tapers.

Figure 9.44 shows a sleeve with different functions applied to it for comparison. The sleeve on the top left had the Move Line function applied to it. Notice how the sleeve opening becomes narrower. The hem of the sleeve on the top right could not be moved with the Move Offset function because the dart restricted the move. The sleeve on the bottom has the Move Line Anchor function being performed. Notice how the sleeve opening and dart do not change in size. The adjacent lines do stretch to lengthen the sleeve; the width naturally widens up to the location that was held by thumbtacks.

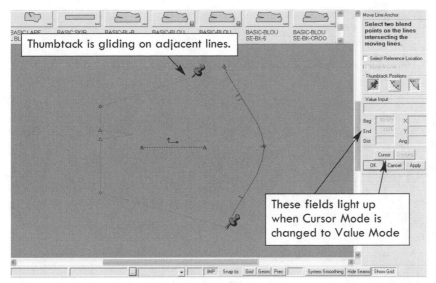

Figure 9.45 Move Line Anchor function illustrating thumbtacks.

Available Options for Move Line Anchor

Thumbtack Positions There are three icons displayed under this option, but the two icons at the right represent available choices. The first box with the thumbtack shows that a selection between these two options will be activated.

- If the first option (the middle box) is selected, the thumbtacks will be placed on the adjacent points, regardless of whether they are intermediate points or endpoints.

- If the second option (the box on the far right) is selected, the thumbtacks will be placed on the adjacent endpoints only—this is the widest range available to move the selected point. The thumbtacks may be moved to select a narrower region.

Use the Move Line Anchor function to

- lengthen or shorten a sleeve while not changing the sleeve opening spec.

- lengthen or shorten a sleeve while not changing size of elements on the pattern such as a dart.

- lengthen or shorten a shirt from the waist without changing the area above the waist, such as the chest spec.

- lengthen or shorten a pant from the top of the waistband or the knee.

Procedure for Move Line Anchor

1. Select **Line>Modify Line>Move Line Anchor.**

2. Select from the two **Thumbtack Positions** in the user input box.

3. A user input box states: "Select perimeter line(s) to move, end selection to continue." Left click to select the lines to move, which highlights them in red. The sleeve opening and dart lines were selected for the example in Figure 9.44. The adjacent lines were not selected.

4. Right click and select **OK** to continue.

5. The user input box states: "Select two blend points on the lines intersecting the moving lines." Thumbtacks are displayed. Left click to accept where the thumbtacks are placed or read further to move them. If the Cursor Mode is active, place the mouse over thumbtack and see how the cursor changes from a plus sign to an asterisk. Press down the left mouse button and release. The thumbtack glides along the line (see Figure 9.45). If Value Mode is active, click on the thumbtack to move it. The **Beg** and **End** fields display so you can enter where you want the thumbtack to be placed.

6. The user input box states: "Move the lines to the new location." Move the line and set it down with the left mouse button or change to Value Mode to enter a measurement. Figure 9.44 displays the X distance moved as –5" to lengthen and the Y field has 0" input to allow for no angle deviation.

7. The function restarts so you can move additional lines. Right click and select **Cancel** to exit the function.

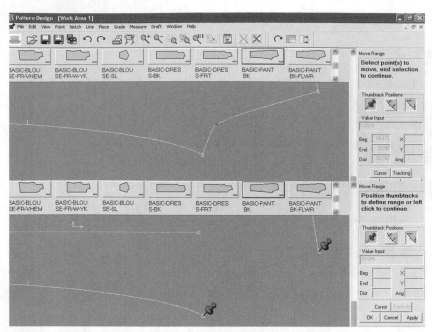

Figure 9.46 Point selection and thumbtacks using the Move Range function.

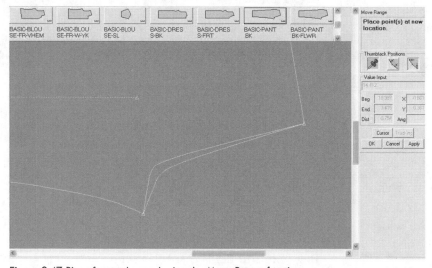

Figure 9.47 Rise of pant changed using the Move Range function.

Move Range

Move Range is used to change the shape of a curved line. Intermediate points within the line are selected and the line is pulled like a rubber band. The area of the line to be reshaped, referred to as the range, may be selected with thumbtacks that display while performing the function. The Move Range function works in the same way that the Move Smooth function works located in the Modify Points menu.

Use the Move Range function to

- change the shape of the rise on a pant.
- change the shape of an armhole curve.
- change the shape of a curved side seam.
- change the shape of any curved style line that contains intermediate points.

Procedure for Move Range

1. Select **Line>Modify Line>Move Range.**

2. Select from the two **Thumbtack Positions** in the user input box.

3. The user input box states: "Select point(s) to move, end selection to continue." Left click to select the points to move, which highlights them in red. See top area of Figure 9.46 to view the point we selected.

4. Right click and select **OK** to continue.

5. The user input box states: "Position thumbtacks to define range or left click to continue." Thumbtacks are displayed. Left click to accept where the thumbtacks are placed or move them, as described in the last section, to select a shorter range within the line. See bottom area of Figure 9.46 to see the thumbtacks located at the widest range possible for this selection.

6. The user input box states: "Place point(s) at new location." The points and the range selected move along with the mouse. Place them down at the desired location with the left mouse button. Figure 9.47 displays the line moved prior to being set down.

7. The function restarts so you can move additional points. Right click and select **Cancel** to exit the function.

Make/Move Parallel

Make/Move Parallel is used to make a line parallel to another line. It may also be used to make a line parallel to the X or Y axis. You may then move the line to another location. This function is a combination of the Make Parallel and Move Line functions.

Use the Make/Move Parallel function to

- make a line, such as the center front or back, parallel to the grain line and then move it in or outside of a pattern.

- make style lines digitized into the system parallel to one another and move them to another location.

Procedure for Make/Move Parallel

1. Select **Line>Modify Line>Make/Move Parallel.**

2. A user input box states: "Select line(s) to move, end selection to continue." Left click to select the lines to move which highlights them in red (see Figure 9.48).

3. Right click and select **OK** to continue.

4. The user input box states: "Select line to use as a guide." Left click to select the line to which you want to make the line parallel. The style line above the line being moved is selected in Figure 9.48.

5. The user input box states: "Select point indicating side to remain stationary." Left click to select the point on the side of the line that should remain stationary. The point on the right side is selected in Figure 9.48.

6. The user input box states: "Move the line to the new location." The line moves as you move the mouse. Set down the line with the

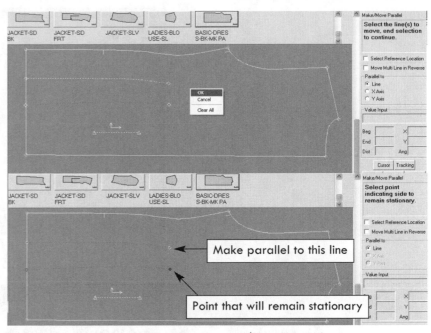

Figure 9.48 Style lines are paralleled with the Make/Move Parallel function.

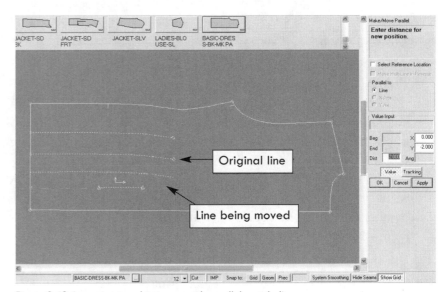

Figure 9.49 Amount entered to move and parallel a style line.

left mouse button or enter a value. The line is made parallel and moved. Figure 9.49 shows the line being moved to the location input into the highlighted fields in the user input box.

7. The function restarts to edit another line. Right click and select **Cancel** to exit.

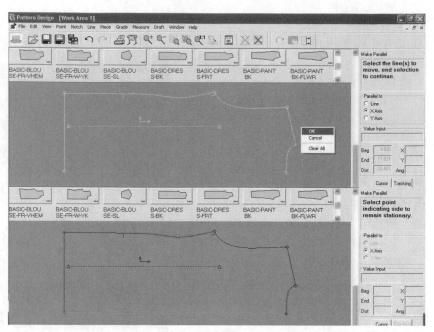

Figure 9.50 Center front set parallel to grain line using the Make Parallel function.

Make Parallel

Make Parallel is used to make a line parallel to another line. It may also be used to make a line parallel to the X or Y axis. The example used in Figure 9.50 has the option under Parallel to set to the X axis. Therefore, the system does not prompt you for a guide line since the X axis is the actual guide. If the option Line was selected, the system would prompt you to select a guide line for the parallel line as in the previous section and in Figure 9.48.

Use the Make Parallel function to

- make a line, such as the center front or back, parallel to the grain line. This is equivalent to making the line parallel to the X axis if the piece is horizontal on the screen or parallel to the Y if it is cross grain.

- make style lines digitized into the system parallel to one another.

Procedure for Make Parallel

1. Select **Line>Modify Line>Make Parallel.**

2. A user input box states: "Select line(s) to move, end selection to continue." Left click to select the lines to make parallel, which highlights them in red. See Figure 9.50 to view our selection.

3. Right click and select **OK** to continue.

4. The user input box states: "Select point indicating side to remain stationary." Left click to select the point on the side of the line that should remain stationary. The line is made parallel. The point at the right end of the pattern is selected in Figure 9.50.

5. The function restarts. Right click and select **Cancel** to exit.

Rotate Line

Rotate Line rotates and changes the angle of a line while using a pivot point. A line is selected to rotate and then a pivot point is selected on the same line. The closer the mouse is to the pivot point, the more control you will have in rotating the line.

Use the Rotate Line function to

- add fullness to a hem and taper at the waist.

- add fullness to the waist and taper at the hem (see Figure 9.51).

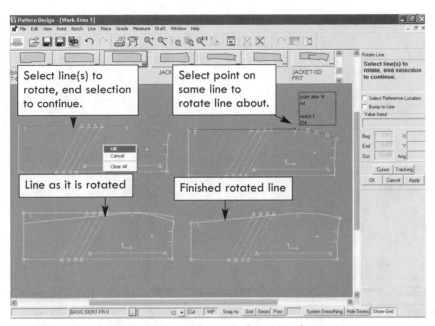

Figure 9.51 Steps show side seam rotated using the Rotate Line function.

- add fullness to any hem and taper on the other end or vice versa.

Procedure for Rotate Line

1. Select **Line>Modify Line>Rotate Line.**

2. The user input box states: "Select line(s) to rotate, end selection to continue." Left click to select the lines to rotate, which highlights them in red. See Figure 9.51 for our line selection.

3. Right click and select **OK** to continue.

4. A user input box states: "Select point on the same line to rotate line about." This is a pivot point. Left click to select a point (see Figure 9.51).

5. The line rotates as you move the mouse. An angle measurement may be input with a popup or by changing to Value Mode. Left click to set down the line. Figure 9.51 displays the side seam of the skirt rotated.

6. The function restarts so you can rotate additional lines. Right click and select **Cancel** to exit.

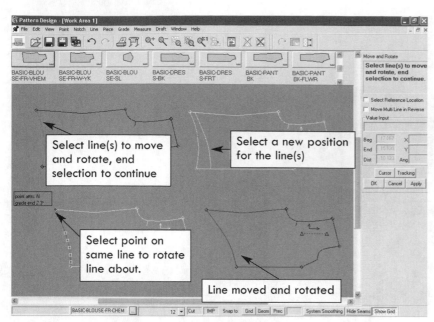

Figure 9.52 Steps show hem moved and rotated with the Move and Rotate function.

Move and Rotate

The Move and Rotate function moves and rotates a line. It is a combination of the Move Line and Rotate Line functions. A line is selected to move and the shape may be changed if it is a curved line. Then a pivot point is selected to rotate the line. The closer the mouse is to the pivot point, the more control you will have in rotating the line.

Use the Move and Rotate function to

- change the shape of a side seam to add full-ness to the hem and taper at the waist on a skirt or a pair of pants.

- change the shape of an armhole and rotate it to raise it at the side seam.

Procedure for Move and Rotate

1. Select **Line>Modify Line>Move and Rotate.**

2. The user input box states: "Select line(s) to move and rotate, end selection to continue." Left click to select the lines, which highlights them in red (see Figure 9.52).

3. Right click and select **OK** to continue.

4. The user input box states: "Select a new position for the line." The line moves along with the mouse. Left click to set down the line at the desired location. The hem is being moved on blouse in Figure 9.52.

5. The user input box states: "Select point on the same line to rotate line about." This is a pivot point. Left click to select a point. See Figure 9.52 to view our selection.

6. The line rotates as the mouse is moved. An angle measurement may be input with a popup or by changing to Value Mode. Left click to set down the line. Figure 9.52 displays the hem moved up; the curve was slightly changed and it was rotated higher at the center front.

7. The function restarts. Right click and select **Cancel** to exit.

Set and Rotate

Set and Rotate is used to set a line onto a piece. It is usually used after a line has been created with a Create Line function such as Digitized or Copy Line. For example, a neckline is copied from one pattern to another. The neckline may then be set onto the receiving pattern with Set and Rotate. Figure 9.53 shows a line that has been copied from another piece and is being set onto the pattern shown.

Procedure for Set and Rotate

1. Select **Line>Modify Line>Set And Rotate.**

2. The user input box states: "Select match point on line to set." Left click to select the point, which highlights it in red.

3. The user input box states: "Select match point on target line." Select the point to match.

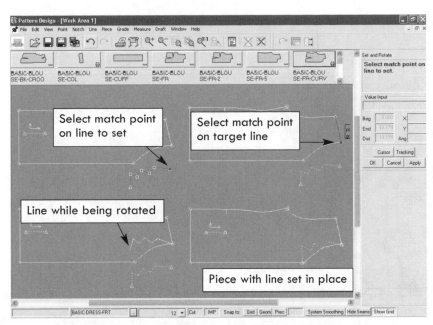

Figure 9.53 Steps show neckline set onto dress using the Set and Rotate function.

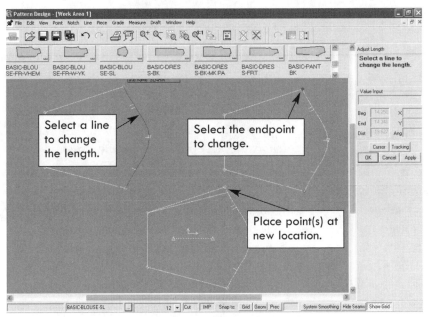

Figure 9.54 Sleeve cap is lengthened using the Adjust Length function.

4. The user input box states: "Select a new position for the line." The line moves along with the mouse. Left click to set down the line at the desired location. The neckline is set on a dress in Figure 9.53.

Note: To finish the pattern in Figure 9.53, use the Replace or Swap function to exchange the lines and delete the original neckline.

Adjust Length

Adjust Length lengthens or shortens a line to meet the measurement a pattern requires. The lines adjacent to the line being changed move according to the adjustment made. For example, use this function to change the length of a sleeve cap.

Procedure for Adjust Length

1. Select **Line>Modify Line>Adjust Length.**

2. The user input box states: "Select a line to change the length." Left click to select the line that needs to be shortened or lengthened. The line will change colors momentarily. The sleeve cap is selected in Figure 9.54.

3. The user input box states: "Select the end point to change." Left click to select the point at the end of the line that you want to move to change the length. The endpoint on the sleeve cap is selected in Figure 9.54.

4. The user input box states: "Place point(s) at new location." The point moves along the line to change as the mouse is moved. Left click to place the point down or enter a specific measurement. Figure 9.54 shows the point selected being moved along the sleeve cap, the line to adjust, to lengthen the length.

5. The function restarts. Right click and select **Cancel** to exit.

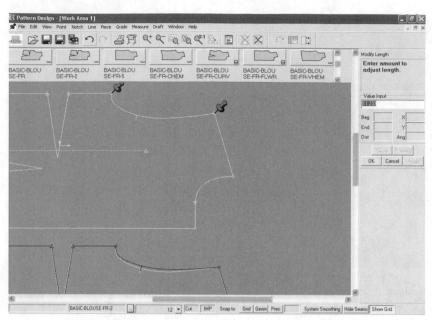

Figure 9.55 Armhole length modified using the Modify Length function.

Modify Length

When following a spec sheet, notice that some lines specify a measurement for line lengths. For example, armhole or neckline circumferences have a certain length so they can fit properly. The Modify Length function shows the actual length of the selected line and allows the user to enter the desired finished amount. If an armhole is 7" but should be 7½", enter 7½" and the system changes the line without moving the hold points selected.

A certain region of a line may be selected to modify the length. The region is selected by placing the thumbtacks that display. While the system tries to keep the line smooth, an excessive amount added or subtracted to the line may result in a distorted line. If this happens, you need to clean up the line by using a function such as Delete Point or Smooth to fix the line according to your needs.

Procedure for Modify Length

1. Select **Line>Modify Line>Modify Length.**

2. The user input box states: "Select a line to change the length." Left click to select the line to change. The line will change colors momentarily and thumbtacks appear. The armhole is selected in Figure 9.55.

3. The user input box states: "Position thumbtacks to define range or left click to continue." If the thumbtacks are in the correct positions, left click to accept the location and continue. If not, move the thumbtacks to the area you want to change. In Figure 9.55, the thumbtacks were accepted at the location shown.

4. The user input box states: "Enter amount to adjust length." The length of the line appears highlighted as shown in Figure 9.55. Type in the total length that the line should be changed to and click **OK** or press **Enter.** For Figure 9.55, we entered 11". The line length is changed. Figure 9.55 shows the original armhole on top of the new armhole to show the difference in length. Notice that the points held with the thumbtacks did not change.

5. The function restarts. Right click and select **Cancel** to exit.

Modify Curve

Modify Curve is quite similar to Move Range and Move Smooth. It is used to change the shape of a curved line. Intermediate points within the line are selected and the line is pulled like a rubber band.

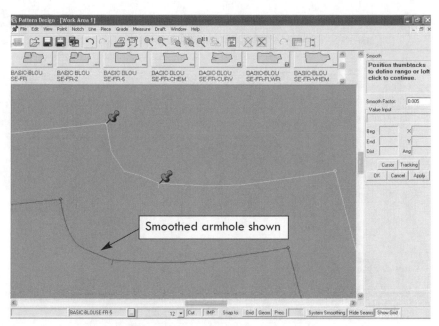

Figure 9.56 Armhole smoothed out using the Smooth function.

The area of the line to be reshaped, referred to as the range, may be selected with thumbtacks that display while performing the function. See the examples listed under the section Move Range for Modify Curve example suggestions.

Procedure for Modify Curve

1. Select **Line>Modify Line>Modify Curve.**

2. The user input box states: "Select point(s) to modify curve, end selection to continue." Left click to select the points to move and thumbtacks appear.

3. The user input box states: "Position thumbtacks to define range or left click to continue." Left click to accept where the thumbtacks are placed or move them to select a different range within the line.

4. The user input box states: "Place point(s) at new location." The points within the range selected move along with the mouse. Place them down at the desired location with the left mouse button. The line is set at new location. Figure 9.47, used in the section Move Range, is also a good example for this section.

5. The function restarts. Right click and select **Cancel** to exit.

Smooth

Smooth is used to smooth a curved line or a region of a line. For example, after digitizing a garment, some lines such as the armhole, neckline, side seam, or inseam may need some smoothing to take out bumps in the line. This may be considered part of the "cleaning up the piece" procedure.

Procedure for Smooth

1. Select **Line>Modify Line>Smooth.**

2. The user input box states: "Select the line to smooth." Left click to select line to smooth and thumbtacks appear. The armhole is selected in Figure 9.56. The view is also zoomed.

3. The user input box states: "Position thumbtacks to define range or left click to continue." If the thumbtacks are in the correct positions, left click to accept the location and continue. If not, move the thumbtacks to the area you want to change. Figure 9.56 shows the thumbtacks placed just outside of the area to smooth. The line or range of line is smoothed. Figure 9.56 displays the original armhole and the armhole after it is smoothed. To continue smoothing, continue left clicking until the desired smoothness is achieved.

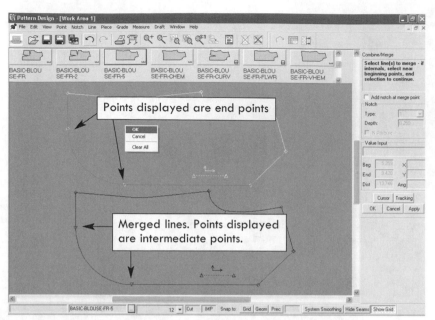

Figure 9.57 Split hem line is combined into one line using the Combine/Merge function.

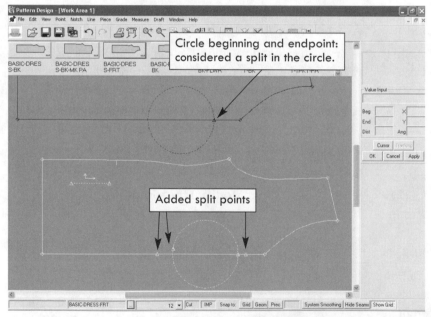

Figure 9.58 Circle and center back are split using the Split function.

Combine/Merge

The Combine/Merge function is used to combine two or more line segments into one line segment. Lines are combined to help perform other functions that include moving, copying, or offsetting lines. There are times that lines are split while per-

forming certain functions. For example, when a corner is curved, the line segment becomes split (see Figure 9.57). Combine/Merge is used to make these segments into one line again.

Use the Combine/Merge function to

- combine lines that were split while performing another function.

- combine lines that you prefer combining after digitizing a pattern.

- combine internal lines that were created as a design with functions such as 2 Point or 2 Point-Curve that later need to be combined.

Procedure for Combine/Merge

1. Select **Line>Modify Line>Combine/Merge.**

2. The user input box states: "Select line(s) to merge—if internals, select near beginning points, end selection to continue." Select at least two lines to combine, which highlights them in red.

3. Right click and select **OK** to continue to combine/merge the lines.

4. The function restarts. Right click and select **OK** to exit.

Split

The Split function can be known as the opposite of the Combine/Merge function. A line segment may be split into more than one line segment with this function. For example, earlier in the chapter, Figure 9.28 displayed a dress with a circle created to form a circle cutout. The piece has to be traced to finish the pattern, but the circle and center back line need to be split so that the system can determine which lines it is tracing. Figure 9.58 shows the circle when it is first created. Below it, the circle is shown split in another location to define the part

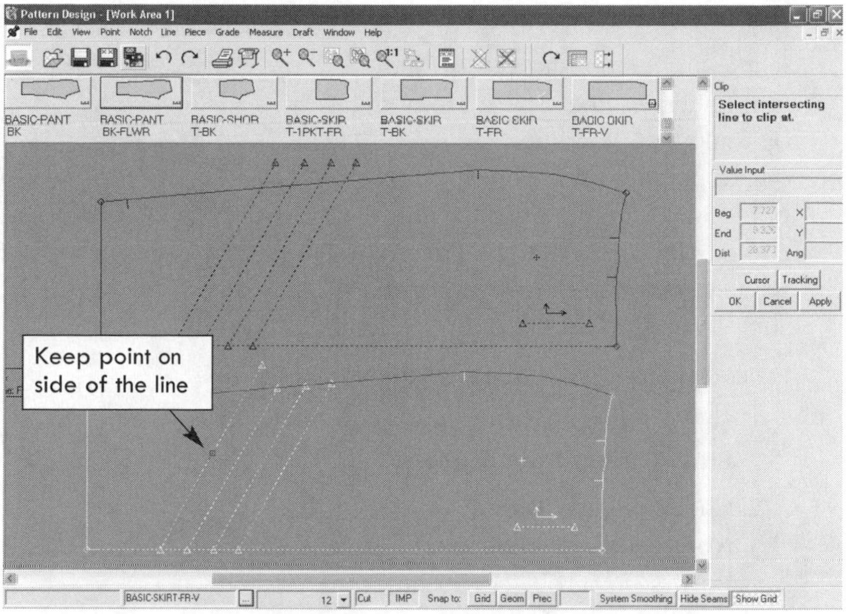

Figure 9.59 Style lines clipped with the Clip function after side seam was rotated.

of the circle to trace later. Notice that the center back of the dress is also split before and after the locations where the circle intersects the center back line. This is also done to define the area that will be traced later with the Trace function under the Create Piece menu.

Use the Split function to

- split a circle or an oval when creating a cutout.

- split a circle or an oval to define an area of the line segment to copy. For example, a part of the oval may be used as a side seam for a skirt.

- split a part of a garment that needs to be traced.

- split at a point where it is preferred to have a split point for manipulation of other functions.

Procedure for Split

1. Select **Line>Modify Line>Split.**

2. The user input box states: "Select point to split line." Left click to select the point where you want to split. The line segment is then split.

3. The function restarts. Right click and select **Cancel** to exit.

Clip

The Clip function is used to cut a line at a location where another line intersects. Earlier in the chapter, in Figure 9.51, a skirt side seam was rotated and the existing style lines remained outside of the pattern. Clip is the function you could use next if you wanted to cut the lines at the side seam so that they remain inside the piece. Figure 9.59 displays the skirt before and after lines are clipped.

Procedure for Clip

1. Select **Line>Modify Line>Clip.**

2. The user input box states: "Select line to clip on side to keep." Left click to select a location anywhere on the line on the side to keep. See the point selected in Figure 9.59.

3. The user input box states: "Select intersecting line to clip at." Left click to select the line that intersects and will cut the line to clip. The side seam is selected in Figure 9.59. Figure 9.59 displays three internal lines that are already clipped and one in the process of being clipped.

4. The function restarts. Right click and select **Cancel** to exit.

Flatten Line Segment

Just as the name states, this function flattens a line. There are two options that allow the user to delete notches, dart points, or both. For example, a skirt with a curved side seam may be flattened while keeping important notches such as the hip and hem notches.

Procedure for Flatten Line Segment

1. Select **Line>Modify Line>Flatten Line Segment.**

2. Check options **Delete Notches** and **Delete Dart Points** on or off. For example, in Figure 9.60 we checked them on to delete the darts and the notches.

3. The user input box states: "Select line to flatten." Left click to select line to flatten. The waist on skirt is selected in Figure 9.60.

4. The user input box states: "Position thumbtacks to define range or left click to continue." If the thumbtacks are in the correct area, left click to accept the location and continue, as shown in Figure 9.60. If not, move the thumbtacks to the area you want to flatten. Figure 9.60 displays the skirt waist flattened with darts and notches deleted.

5. The function restarts. Right click and select **Cancel** to exit.

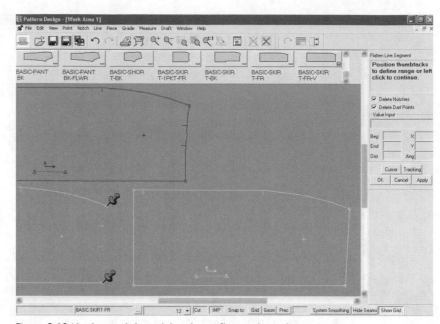

Figure 9.60 Notches and darts deleted on a flattened waistline.

Test Your Knowledge

Select the correct answer from the word bank.

Key Terms

Circle Ctr Cirm	Move Line Anchor
Circle Ctr Rad	Move Offset
Combine/Merge	Offset Even
Copy Line	Offset Uneven
Curved Intersection	Perp Line
Delete Line	Replace Line
Digitized	Set and Rotate
Make Parallel	Smooth
Modify Length	Swap Line
Move and Rotate	2 Point-Curve
Move Line	

1. What function is used to create a line with multiple points? _____

2. The _____ function is a quick way to make a curved line between two selected points, such as an armhole or empire seam.

3. What function can be used to copy an armhole from one piece to another? _____

4. Facings for an armhole or a neckline may be created using the _____ function because it creates lines parallel to the selected lines while allowing a measurement to be entered.

5. The _____ menu is useful to aid in the creation of patterns from a block.

6. Circles may be created as stand-alone patterns or internals using the _____ or the _____ functions.

7. Use the _____ function to erase unwanted lines.

8. Corners on pockets, lapels, or hems may be curved using the _____ function.

9. When exchanging an internal line for a perimeter line, if the internal line touches and intersects the perimeter of the piece in two locations, the _____ function may be used.

10. When exchanging an internal line for a perimeter line, if the internal line does not touch or intersect the perimeter of the piece, the _____ function may be used.

11. When a garment needs to be shortened or lengthened, but the line being moved needs to remain the same length, as in a tapered skirt or sleeve, the _____ function is the best option to use.

12. Consider the following scenario: An armhole needs to be moved to create a slightly larger opening and the shape needs to be changed for design or fit purposes. The angle of the armhole also needs to be changed. What function may be used to perform these changes? _____

13. When several lines need to be combined to create one line, use the
_____ function.

14. A line has been copied from one piece to another. The _____
function may be used to set the line onto the new piece.

15. The _____ function may be used to smooth a section of a
line, such as the hip area of a pant.

16. If a neckline circumference needs to be a specific length, but the endpoints
at the shoulder and center front cannot be moved, the _____
function can be used to enter the exact length needed and the system will
change the length.

17. The grain line needs to be moved from the top right corner of a garment
to the bottom left of a garment, therefore moving in the X and Y
directions. What is the best function to perform this move?
_____

18. What is the best function to offset several points in different amounts, such
as a side seam that needs to go from nothing to ¼" at the waist to ½" at
the hem? _____

19. If a line needs to be moved 1" parallel to the original line, use the
_____ function.

20. What is the best function to make a digitized style line parallel to another
line? _____

CHAPTER TEN

Point Functions in PDS

Objective

This chapter introduces basic point functions that are often used in the industry, such as adding points to show where pockets fall on shirts, adding drill holes for buttonhole placement, moving and sliding points on line segments to create wider or narrower neck openings, or creating tapered waists.

By the end of this chapter, you should be able to manipulate the points within a line to set them down in the correct locations to meet your garment specifications and to create your own styles. Although this menu is all about points and not lines, keep in mind that lines do move and become more flat or curved according to how you manipulate or move the points within a line. Remember that lines are made up of points. Not all the functions available in this menu are discussed in this chapter.

The examples used in this book may be created with the corresponding function discussed in the chapter. Since there are different ways to achieve the same result, however, the function listed may not be the most efficient option for that example. Furthermore, you may need to complete the examples discussed for a function by using additional functions so you can get the results you want.

This chapter allows you to gain skills in the following areas:

- Add Point
- Add Mark X Point
- Add Multiple
- Point Intersect
- Delete Point
- Modify Points menu

Add Point

The Add Point function is used to create and add points to a pattern. You may add points by simply selecting a place to set a point down on the pattern or by entering a location using a reference point. A point added to an existing line is considered an intermediate point and does not appear unless you opt to view the intermediate points in the View menu. A point that is not added to a line will appear as a plus (+) sign and is therefore considered a drill hole and labeled "D" by default by the system.

Use the Add Point function to

- show the placement of a pocket on a shirt, pant, or skirt.
- indicate the bust/apex on a bodice.
- add more points on a line to have more control over it when you manipulate it.

Procedure for Add Point without entering a specific location

1. Select **Point>Add Point.**

2. A user input box states: "Indicate point position." Left click to select where you want to place the point. Place the point inside the pattern and not on the line so you can see the point. Place another point on the line and notice that it is not visible. Select **View>Point>**

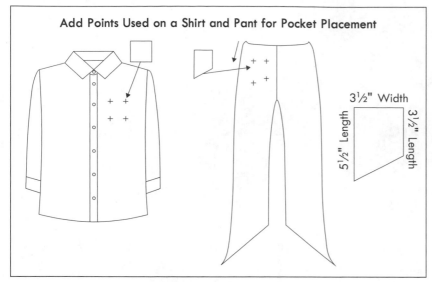

Add Points Used on a Shirt and Pant for Pocket Placement

3½" Width

5½" Length

3½" Length

Figure 10.1 Use the Add Point function to show pocket placement locations.

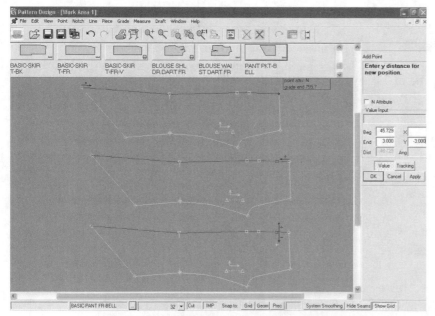

Figure 10.2 Steps using the Add Point function to enter pocket placement location.

Intermediate Points to view the point you added.

Say we want to place a pocket 3" below the waist and 3" in from the side seam on a pair of pants (see Figure 10.1). Since we need to measure 3" below the waist first, the reference point will be the intersection between the waistline and the side seam.

Procedure for Add Point using a reference point and entering a specific location

1. Select **Point>Add Point.**

2. A user input box states: "Indicate point position." Perform a popup to select the point that intersects the waist and the side seam (see Figure 10.2). We entered 3" in the **End** field to measure from the waist. We then entered –3" in the **Y** field to measure from the side seam.

3. The function restarts. Using the new point added to the pant in Step 2, we create the additional point for the pocket placement.

4. A user input box states: "Indicate point position." We select the new point (see Figure 10.3) by performing a popup. Notice the fields that are now available under the **Value Input** area. Since the point is moving in the negative direction along the Y axis, we entered –3" in the **Y** field. We entered 3" because the pocket width is 3½" and we want to hide the points/drillholes with the pocket. The additional point is created.

5. Save the piece to keep your changes. Repeat Step 2 if you want to create additional pocket placement points.

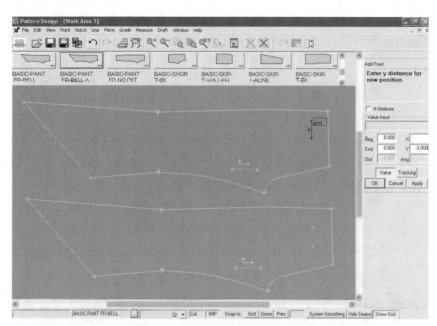

Figure 10.3 Create additional points from an existing point using the Add Point function.

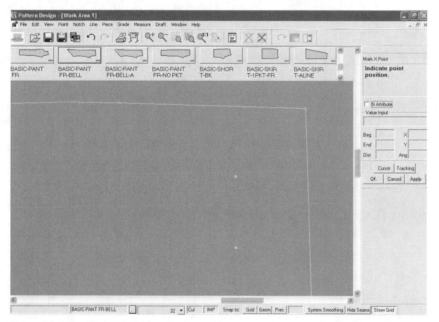

Figure 10.4 The Mark X Point function is used for a pocket placement reference and a hip location.

Mark X Point

The Mark X Point function works in the same way that Add Point works, except that the point you add is not invisible. When adding a point to a line using Mark X Point, the point displays as an X,

while with the Add Point function it is invisible. This point is considered an intermediate point. If you place a point on a piece and not on a line with this function, the point appears as an asterisk, rather than as a plus sign when using the Add Point function. This point is not considered a drill hole; it is labeled "E" by default by the system and may be changed.

Use the Mark X Point function to

- show the placement of a pocket on a shirt, pant, or skirt with points that are not considered drill holes.

- indicate the bust/apex on a bodice with a point that is not considered a drill hole.

- add a visible point on a line as a reference point when manipulating a pattern or creating a new pattern.

Procedure for Mark X Point

1. Select **Point>Mark X Point.**

2. A user input box states: "Indicate point position." Left click to select where you want to place the point. We selected a point on the side seam (see Figure 10.4).

3. We also recreated the pocket placement locations that we created in Figures 10.2 and 10.3. Since we used Mark X point, the points display as asterisks rather than plus signs.

Note: We recreated the pocket placement locations mentioned in Step 3 by entering specific measurements using the popup technique, as we did with the Add Point function.

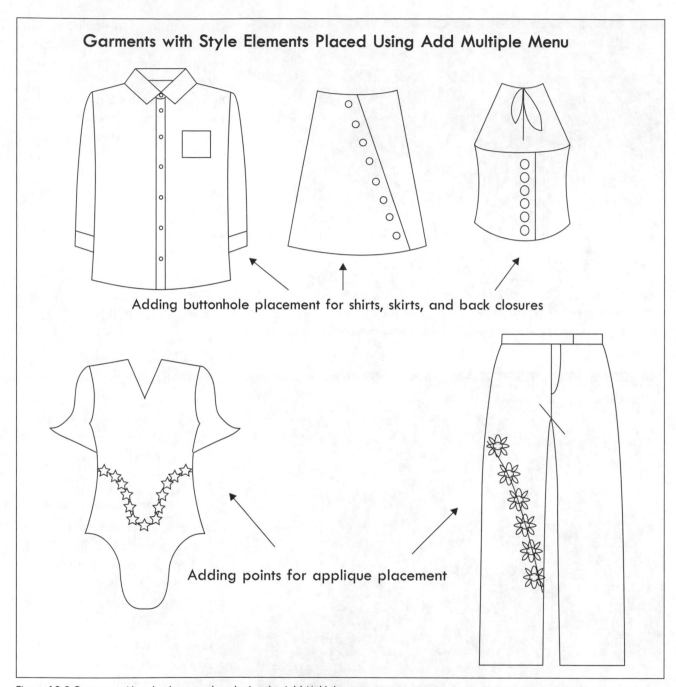

Garments with Style Elements Placed Using Add Multiple Menu

Adding buttonhole placement for shirts, skirts, and back closures

Adding points for applique placement

Figure 10.5 Garments with style elements placed using the Add Multiple menu.

Add Multiple

The Add Multiple menu lets you create points that you may use as reference points for style elements on a pattern, such as a row of flowers or stars (see Figure 10.5). You may also use this menu to determine buttonhole placement on garments such as the shirt, bodice, and skirt shown in Figure

10.5. Additionally, two of the functions in this menu give you the option to select from three types of points—drillholes, mark points, or notches.

You have probably done the math for buttonhole locations on a shirt before. When placing button-hole locations on a shirt, do you dread thinking about how the first button needs to be three quarters of an inch down from the top and six inches from the bottom? That's the easy part! Doing the math to get the buttonholes evenly distributed between two points is the trickier part—but the options in this menu make the task easier. You just have to select the first and last points and input the number of buttonhole locations you need and the system does the math for you.

Add Drills

The Add Drills function comes in handy when approaching garments, such as the collared shirt in Figure 10.5. We will use this shirt as the example for the procedure described below. Select a start point and an endpoint for point placement. Enter the number of points you need between the start point and endpoint so the system can evenly place them within this region in a straight line as though a string were stretched between the two selected points. If you are trying to place points along a curved seam line, the points do not follow the curve of the line. The popup technique or toggling from Cursor to Value Mode let you select the placement for the start and endpoints (see Figure 10.6).

The start point and endpoints in Figure 10.6 were selected from the same location on the skirt to point out the difference. The start point was selected closer to the waist on the skirt.

Ends to Receive Points

None Drill holes are not be placed on the start point or endpoint.

Both Drill holes are placed on the start point and endpoint.

First A drill hole is placed on the start point but not on the endpoint.

Last A drill hole is placed on the endpoint but not on the start point.

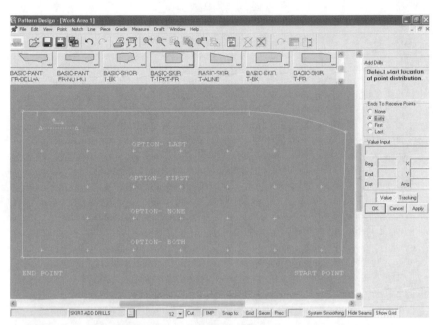

Figure 10.6 Ends to Receive Points option visually defined.

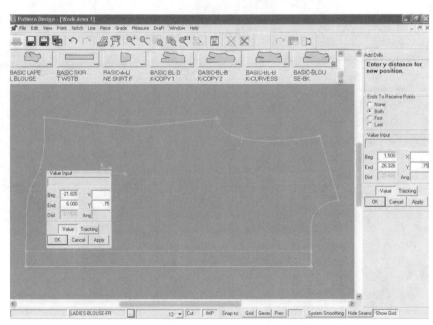

Figure 10.7 Start and endpoints placed at specific locations on a shirt.

Procedure to Add Drills

1. Select **Point>Add Multiple>Add Drills.**

2. Select the option you want from the area **Ends to Receive Points.** We selected **Both** in Figure 10.7 because we want a point placed at the start point and another at the endpoint.

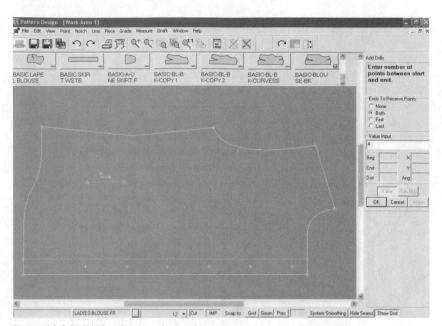

Figure 10.8 Drill holes distributed on a shirt.

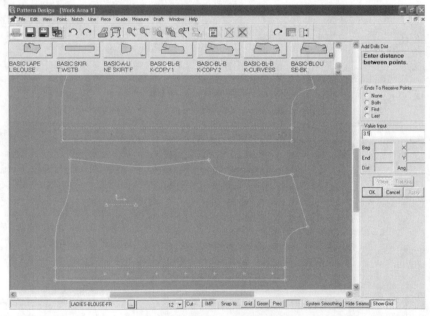

Figure 10.9 Drill holes distributed 3½" apart.

We performed a popup and entered 6" in the **End** field and .75 in the **Y** field so it is aligned with the start point. See the box on the left side of Figure 10.7 for our endpoint value input.

5. A user input box states: "Enter number of points between start and end." Since we wanted a total of six points, we entered 4 in the **Value Input** field (see Figure 10.8). The other two points are placed on the start point and endpoints because we selected the option **Both** in Step 2. Six drill holes are distributed for our shirt example.

Add Drills Dist

In the Add Drills Dist function, you place the distance drill holes will be separated instead of the number of drillholes. For the shirt in Figure 10.8, instead of specifying six drill holes in the system, we could have the system place as many drill holes as it can, 3½ inches apart from one another, between the start point and endpoint. Let's see how that looks when we use this same shirt to explain the procedure for Add Drills Dist.

Procedure for Add Drills Dist

1. Select **Point>Add Multiple>Add Drills Dist.**

2. Select the option you want from the area **Ends to Receive Points.** We selected **First** in Figure 10.9. We want a point placed only at the start point.

3. A user input box states: "Select start location of point distribution." Left click to select a point. We performed a popup and entered 1.5" in the **Beg** field and 0.75 in the **Y** field, as we did for the example in Figure 10.7 in the previous section.

3. A user input box states: "Select start location of point distribution." Left click to select a point. We performed a popup and entered 1.5" in the **Beg** field and .75 in the **Y** field as shown on the right in Figure 10.7.

4. A user input box states: "Select end location of point distribution." Left click to select a point.

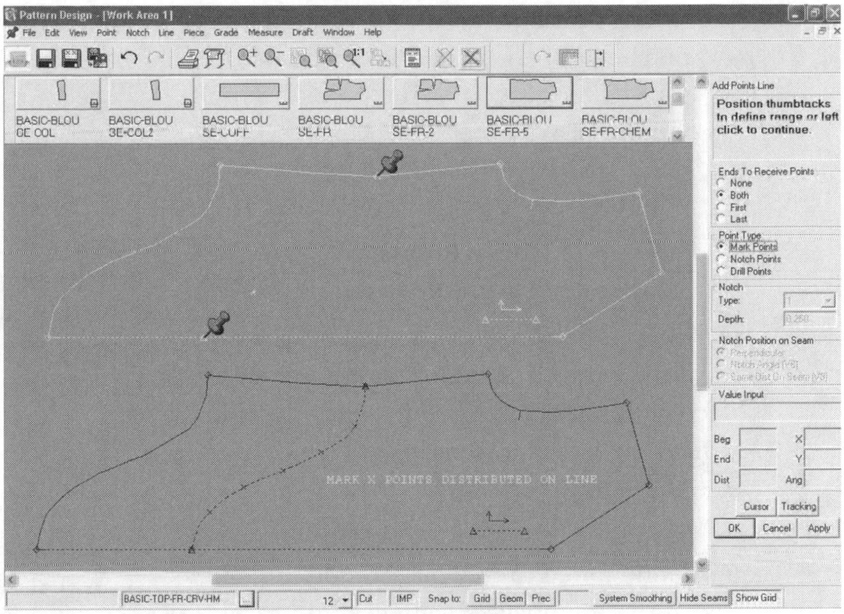

Figure 10.10 Mark X points are shown along a style line.

4. A user input box states: "Select end location of point distribution." Left click to select a point. We performed a popup and entered 6" in the **End** field and 0.75 in the **Y** field, as we did for the example in Figure 10.7 in the previous section.

5. A user input box states: "Enter distance between points." Enter the distance you want between the points. We entered 3.5 in Figure 10.9. The drill holes are distributed at the distance entered. For our example, there are seven drill holes distributed 3.5" apart from one another.

Add Points Line

The Add Points Line function lets you place points along a straight or curved line. The line may be an internal or a perimeter line and must already exist before you may use this function. The points you create may serve as reference points for appliqués, such as the stars on the bodice or the flowers on the pants in Figure 10.5.

There are three points from which to select, including notches, mark points, or drill holes. Sometimes reference points are needed in a curved line formation, but the actual line on which

the points are created is not needed after the points are placed. The line may be deleted only if you use drill points as the point type. If you use notches or mark points, the line must remain or all the points created on it will be erased if you delete the line. The bodice with the stars in Figure 10.5 is the garment we are modifying in Figure 10.10.

Procedure for Add Points Line

1. Select **Point>Add Multiple>Add Points Line.**

2. Select the option desired from the area **Ends to Receive Points** (None, Both, First, Last). We selected **Both** in Figure 10.10 to place points on the start point and endpoint.

3. In the **Point Type** area, select one of the available options.

   Mark Points is used to display points with an X. When you select this type of point, and you delete the line used to add points, then the points are deleted too.

   Drill Points is used to display points as a + sign. When you select this type of point, and you delete the line used to add points, then the points are not deleted.

Notch Points is used to display points as notches. When using this option, make sure to select the notch type in the user input box. When you select this type of point, and you delete the line used to add points, then the points are deleted too.

We selected **Mark Points** for Figure 10.10 as indicated by the X's along the curved line.

4. A user input box states: "Select a line to receive points." Left click to select the line, which highlights it in red. See Figure 10.10 to see the line we selected.

5. A user input box states: "Position thumbtacks to define range or left click to continue." To move the thumbtacks, left click and release on top of the thumbtack and move your pointer to the location you want. Left click again to set it down. Left click one more time to accept the location. Refer to Figure 10.10 to see how thumbtacks appear.

6. A user input box states: "Enter number of points between start and end." Enter the number of points you need minus any points you added to the start point or endpoint. For example, we wanted a total of seven points for the bodice in Figure 10.10, so we entered five because we selected both the start point and endpoint to receive points. The points are evenly distributed along the line.

7. The function restarts. Right click to **Cancel** when you are done.

8. Save the piece to keep your changes.

Add Points LN Dist

The Add Points LN Dist function lets you place points along a straight or curved line. The line may be an internal or a perimeter

line and must already exist before you use the function. The points you create may serve as reference points for studs, rhinestones, sequins, or appliqués, such as the stars on the bodice or the flowers on the pants in Figure 10.5. In this function you enter the distance between the distributed points instead of the actual number of points. The system places as many points as possible, with the distance entered, between the start point and endpoint.

As in the Add Point Line function, there are three points from which to select—notches, mark points, or drill holes. Sometimes reference points are needed in a curved line formation, but the actual line on which the points are created is not needed after the points are placed. You may delete the line only if you use drill points as the point type because a drill point may exist on a pattern on its own without being part of a line. If you use notches or mark points, the line you use must remain or all the points created on it are erased if you delete the line. This happens because notches and mark points are considered intermediate points, and they need to be on a line to exist. The pants with the flowers in Figure 10.5 is the garment we are modifying in Figure 10.11.

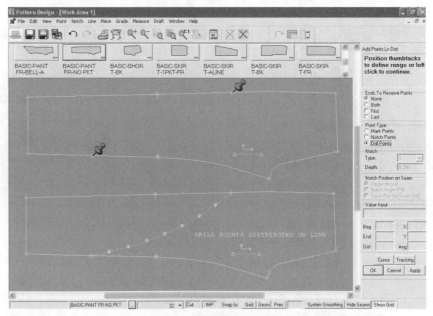

Figure 10.11 Drill points distributed on a pant using the Add Points LN Dist function.

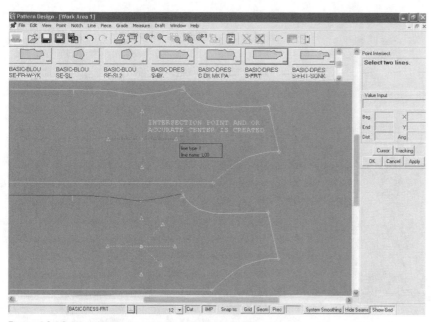

Figure 10.12 Mark X points created to show where lines intersect.

Procedure for Add Points LN Dist

1. Select **Point>Add Multiple>Add Points LN Dist.**

2. Select the option desired from the area **Ends to Receive Points** (None, Both, First, Last). We selected **None** in Figure 10.11.

3. In the **Point Type** area, select one of the available options (Mark Points, Drill Points, Notch Points). We selected **Drill Points** for Figure 10.11.

4. A user input box states: "Select a line to receive points." Left click to select line, which highlights it in red. See Figure 10.11 to see the line we selected.

5. A user input box states: "Position thumbtacks to define range or left click to continue." To move the thumbtacks, left click and release on top of the thumbtack and move the pointer to the location you want. Left click again to set it down. Left click one more time to accept the location.

6. A user input box states: "Enter distance between points." Enter the distance you want between the points distributed. We entered 3" of separation for our example in Figure

10.11 and the system placed seven points along the line.

7. The function restarts. Right click to cancel if you are done.

8. Save the piece to keep your changes.

Point Intersect

When two lines meet or intersect, the point at which they touch is known as the intersection point. This point may not be visible or even exist as a point on either line. The Point Intersect function places a mark point, in the intersection of two lines, as seen on the first dress in Figure 10.12. The Point Intersect function is also used to view and mark the location where one line will intersect another line if it is extended. Figure 10.12 shows a mark point on the side seam where the selected vertical line would intersect the side seam if it were to be extended. Therefore, parallel lines, or lines that will not cross if they are extended, cannot be selected for this function to work properly.

Use the Point Intersect function to

• find the intersection point of two crossing lines.

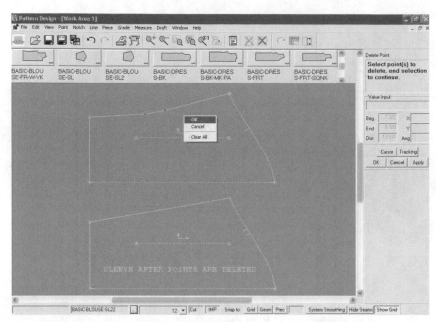

Figure 10.13 Points deleted on a sleeve seam using the Delete Point function.

• find the point where one line will intersect another line if it is extended.

• create the intersection point for a new style line. Figure 10.12 shows how the intersection point is used to create additional lines from an accurate center point.

Procedure for Point Intersect

1. Select **Point>Point Intersect.**

2. A user input box states: "Select two lines." Left click to select the two lines that intersect or would eventually intersect if they were to be extended, which highlights them in red. The mark X point is added. We selected the horizontal and vertical lines on the top dress in Figure 10.12. We then selected the vertical line and the side seam on the dress shown at the bottom of Figure 10.12.

3. The function restarts. Right click to **Cancel** when you are done.

4. Save the piece to keep your changes.

Delete Point

The Delete Point function is used to erase unwanted points from a pattern piece. The point may be an intermediate point along a line, a drill hole, or mark point in a pattern. You cannot delete an endpoint on the perimeter of the piece. If you try to do so, the system simply does not do anything to that point. The two lines that meet at a perimeter endpoint have to be combined or merged for the point to be deleted because it becomes an intermediate point.

Deleting points on a curved line alters the shape of the line. If all the points on a curved line are deleted, the line turns into a straight line. A straight line segment should not have any intermediate points unless they are notch points or mark points. For example, the center back of a basic skirt is a straight line with two notches in the back to represent where the back opening is located.

Procedure for Delete Point

1. Select **Point>Delete Point.**

2. A user input box states: "Select the point(s) to delete, end selection to continue." Left click to select the points, which highlights them in red. Right click to continue and delete the points (see Figure 10.13).

Note: You may delete more than one point using a marquee box. To use a marquee box, left click on the screen to start the box. Move the mouse until the box encloses all the points you want to delete. Left click again to finish the marquee box. Right click to continue.

3. The function restarts. Right click to **Cancel** when you are done.

4. Save the piece to keep your changes.

Modify Points

The Modify Points menu lets you modify points in a pattern. You may move one or more points along a line or in a horizontal or vertical direction to allow for the optimal modification of a pattern. For example, you may drop or raise a neck or armhole or widen or narrow a neck width. You may also lower a hem on one side, while keeping the grain line intact. A point may be aligned to another point to straighten a skewed line or to align one drill hole to another. For example, points may be moved to create a bell bottom on a sleeve or pant. The examples are endless.

It is highly recommend that you leave the intermediate points on while learning the functions for this menu. It is not necessary for them to be on once you have a full understanding of how each function works. It especially helps to see how functions with the word "smooth" work versus the ones without the word smooth in them. For example, the Move Point Horiz function moves a point in a horizontal direction, while keeping the points before it and after it in place. The Move Smooth Horiz function, however, moves a point in a horizontal direction while holding the endpoints before and after it in place. Go to **View>Point>Intermediate Points** and follow the prompts to see the intermediate points on the selected piece.

Remember to always save the pattern pieces at the end of each function if you want to keep the changes. Also keep in mind that modifications may affect other pattern pieces in the garment, so those pieces need to be modified as well to keep the garment well balanced so it can be constructed properly.

Align 2 Points

When you need to draft a basic front skirt with pocket point placements, this function lets you fix crooked pieces. This function lets you fix other issues, such as side seams in skirts that don't fall straight from the hip point or drill holes digitized in for pocket placements that are not aligned. You select a point and move it so it lines up correctly with another point, referred to as the reference point or location to which to align.

The prompts during the procedure appear in the user input box, according to the option you select. For example, if you select the Horizontal option the prompt states: "Select point to align horizontally," but if you select the Vertical option, the prompt states: "Select point to align vertically." See the option descriptions below.

Horizontal

Select this option to move a point on a horizontal line or in a horizontal direction. For example, the center front and side seam of the skirt in Figure 10.14 are horizontal lines that need to be corrected.

Vertical

Select this option to move a point on a vertical line or in a vertical direction. For example, the drill holes for the skirt in Figure 10.14 need to be aligned in a vertical direction. If the hem in Figure 10.14 were crooked, you would use this option to fix it because it is a vertical line.

Between 2 Points

Select this option to move a point that needs to fall in line between two other points. For example, the hem notch in Figure 10.14 needs to align to the hem and the hip notch.

Along Line

Select this option to move a point onto a different line. For example, the drill hole in Figure 10.14 is moved onto a style line so when the pocket is placed, its width will reach from one style line to the next.

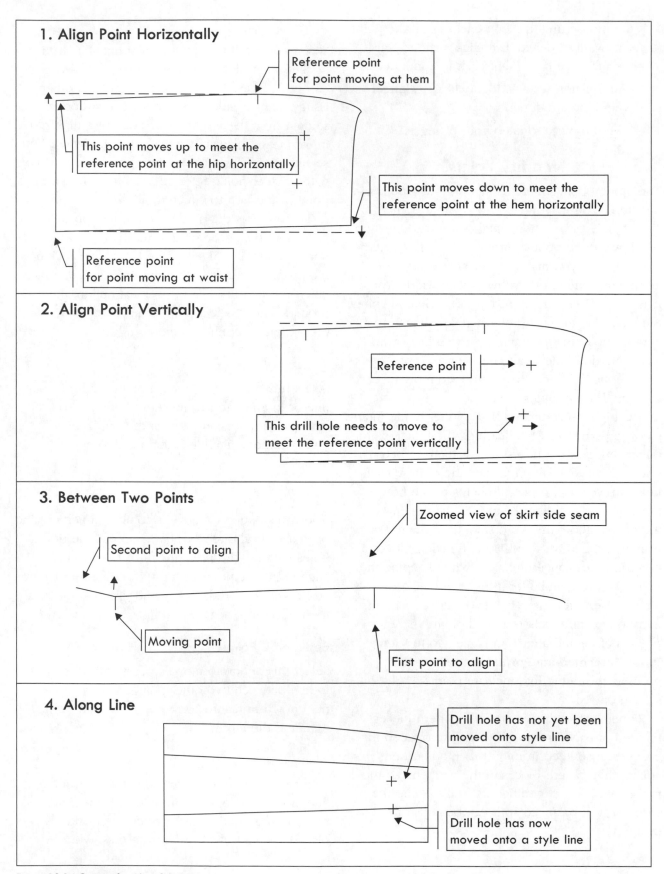

1. Align Point Horizontally

Reference point
for point moving at hem

This point moves up to meet the
reference point at the hip horizontally

This point moves down to meet the
reference point at the hem horizontally

Reference point
for point moving at waist

2. Align Point Vertically

Reference point

This drill hole needs to move to
meet the reference point vertically

3. Between Two Points

Zoomed view of skirt side seam

Second point to align

Moving point

First point to align

4. Along Line

Drill hole has not yet been
moved onto style line

Drill hole has now
moved onto a style line

Figure 10.14 Options for Align 2 Points.

Procedure for Align 2 Points

1. Select **Point>Modify Points> Align 2 Points.**

2. Select the appropriate option for alignment from the user input box. We chose **Horizontal** because we are correcting the center front first.

3. A user input box states: "Select point to align horizontally." Left click to select the point you want to move. We selected the point at the waist (see Figure 10.15). Remember that it is always better to go larger than to go smaller because you can always trim away excess fabric.

4. A user input box states: "Position thumbtacks to define range or left click to continue." Anything on the other side of the thumbtacks (the white lines) will not be affected. We opted to leave the thumbtacks at their locations, so we left clicked to continue and accept the locations. The top right skirt in Figure 10.15 shows the thumbtacks.

5. A user input box states: "Select the reference point." Left click to select the point. This is the point to which the point you selected in Step 3 should line up. The points are aligned. The function restarts for the next area that needs to be aligned. If no other areas need to be aligned, exit the function by right clicking and selecting **Cancel**. We selected the hem point, as shown on the bottom left skirt in Figure 10.15. Since there are more areas to align, we did not cancel the function.

6. Make sure the option selected in the user input box is appropriate for the next align-

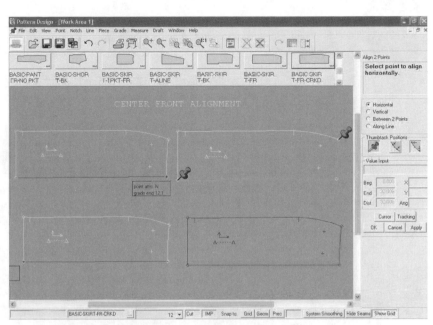

Figure 10.15 Straightening center front with Align 2 Points.

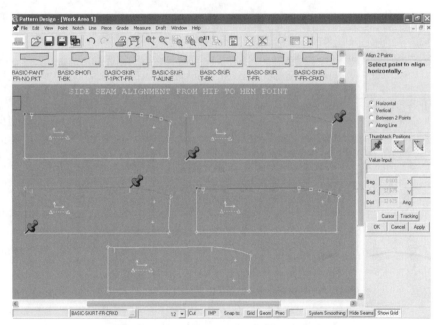

Figure 10.16 Steps shown aligning the side seam hip notch with the hem point.

ment. We chose **Horizontal** because we are aligning the notch point to the hem point so that it falls straight from the notch.

7. A user input box states: "Select point to align horizontally." Left click to select the point to move. We selected the point at the hem (see Figure 10.16).

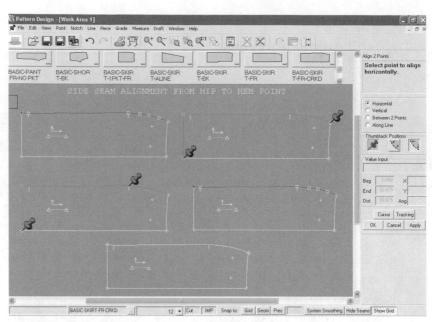

Figure 10.17 Hem notch aligned to hip notch and hem point.

8. A user input box states: "Position thumbtacks to define range or left click to continue." To move the thumbtacks, left click on the thumbtack, move the mouse to place the thumbtack at the location you want, and left click again to set down the thumbtack. Left click to continue. We opted to move the waist thumbtack to the hip notch so that the curve above the hip is not affected, as shown in the top right and bottom left skirts in Figure 10.16.

9. A user input box states: "Select the reference point." Left click to select the point. We selected the notch at the hip, as shown on the bottom right skirt in Figure 10.16. Since there are more areas to align, we did not cancel the function. The side seam does not look straight because the hem notch is not aligned yet; the hip notch was aligned to the hem point, not the hem notch.

10. Make sure the option selected in the user input box is appropriate for the next alignment. We chose **Between 2 Points** because we are aligning the hem notch to the hem point and the hip notch so that it falls in line with both.

11. A user input box states: "Select point to move." Left click to select the point to move. We selected the hem notch (see Figure 10.17).

12. A user input box states: "Position thumbtacks to define range or left click to continue." To move the thumbtacks, left click on the thumbtack, move the mouse to place the thumbtack at the location you want, and left click again to set down the thumbtack. Left click again to continue. We opted to move the waist thumbtack to the hip notch, as shown on the top right skirt in Figure 10.17.

13. A user input box states: "Select first location to align point to." Left click to select the point. This is one of the two points to which the moving point is aligning. We selected the point at the hem first, as shown on the bottom left skirt in Figure 10.17.

14. A user input box states: "Select second location to align point to." Left click to select the point. This is the other point to which the moving point is being aligned. We selected the notch at the hip as shown in the bottom right skirt in Figure 10.17. Notice how the points are lined up in the skirt at the bottom center

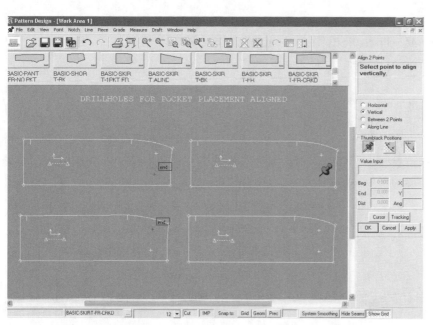

Figure 10.18 Pocket placement drill holes of a skirt are vertically aligned.

of the figure. There is one more area to align, so we still do not exit the function. We will align the drill holes used for pocket placement next.

15. Select the appropriate option in the user input box. We selected **Vertical** since the drill holes need to align vertically in this case.

16. A user input box states: "Select point to align vertically." Left click to select point. We selected the drill hole closest to the center front (see Figure 10.18).

17. A user input box states: "Position thumbtacks to define range or left click to continue." Move the thumbtack or left click to accept its current location. We left clicked to continue and accept the location. The top right skirt in Figure 10.18 shows the thumbtack.

18. A user input box states: "Select the reference point." Left click to select the point. This is the point to which the moving point is aligning. The function restarts for the next area that needs to be aligned. If no other areas need to be aligned, exit the function by right clicking and selecting **Cancel.** We selected the drill hole closest to the side seam, as shown on the

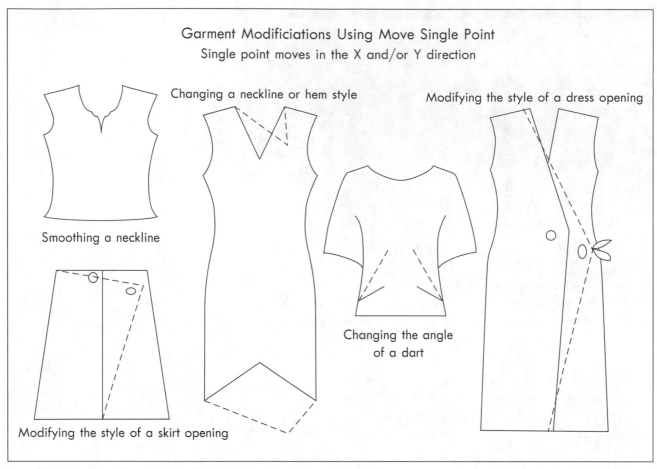

Garment Modifiations Using Move Single Point
Single point moves in the X and/or Y direction

Changing a neckline or hem style

Modifying the style of a dress opening

Smoothing a neckline

Changing the angle
of a dart

Modifying the style of a skirt opening

Figure 10.19 Examples of how the Move Single Point function can be used to modify garments.

bottom left skirt in Figure 10.18. Since there are no more areas to align, we canceled out of the function. The trued up skirt is the skirt shown on the bottom right of the figure.

19. Save the pattern to keep your changes. It is highly recommend that you save as you make changes with which you are satisfied. For instance, some users save after steps 5, 9, and 14, but saving at the end is fine, too.

Move Single Point

The Move Single Point function allows you to move an individual point. The point may move along the X and Y axes vertically or horizontally. For instance, after drafting in a piece, many new users usually ask why the neckline or the armhole or really any curved line has bumps in it. Although usually the bumps occur because of human error, it may also be because the actual pattern is not smooth at these locations. This function lets you fix these bumps by letting you move each point that is creating a bump into a position that creates a smoother line.

This function also comes in handy when you are working with darts. As you may remember, when a dart is created using the Add Dart function, it is created perpendicular to the point or line on which it is created in a pattern. When darts are rotated or distributed, the angle of the dart is generally directed toward the rotation/pivot point. If the angle of the dart created after using any of these functions is not satisfactory to your needs, use the Move Single Point function to change the angle to the location you want. Figure 10.19 shows a few garments where you may use the Move

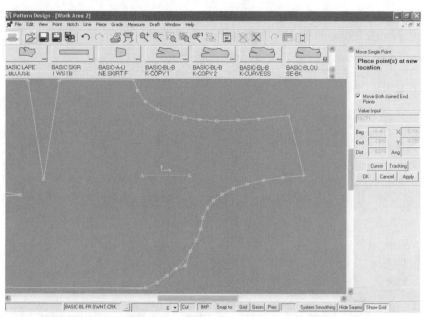

Figure 10.20 The point is moved to create a smooth neckline using the Move Single Point function.

Single Point function to modify the garments. The dashed lines represent how the garment may be changed.

The Move Single Point function lets you move a point while keeping the points before and after in place, regardless of whether it is an intermediate point or endpoint. Figure 10.20 shows a sweetheart neckline with the intermediate points displayed (View>Point>Intermediate Points). We turned on the intermediate points so you could see how the point moves and how the points before and after it are held in place. You may consider this the range or region within which the point will move horizontally or vertically.

Procedure for Move Single Point

1. Select **Point>Modify Points>Move Single Point.**

2. Check the box next to **Move Both Joined End Points** in the user input box if you want the lines attached to the point to move with the line. If this option is not checked and you select an endpoint, the point will slide along one line. Try selecting an endpoint with this option checked and then with it unchecked and you will notice the difference immediately.

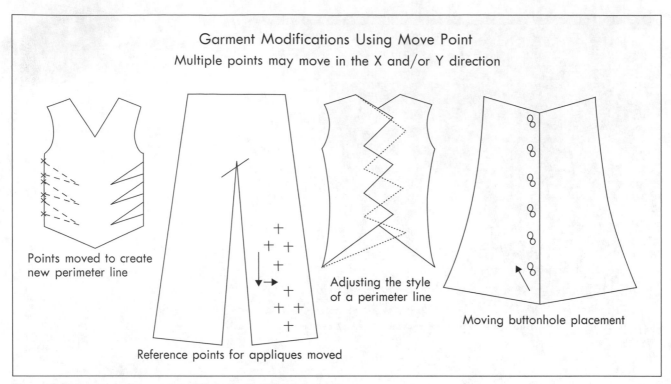

Garment Modifications Using Move Point
Multiple points may move in the X and/or Y direction

Points moved to create new perimeter line

Reference points for appliques moved

Adjusting the style of a perimeter line

Moving buttonhole placement

Figure 10.21 Examples of garments modified using the Move Point function.

3. A user input box states: "Select point to move." Left click to select point to move. The point moves along with mouse. Left click to set down the point at the location you want. If there is a specific distance the point needs to move, perform a popup or change from Cursor Mode to Value Mode. We selected a point on the neckline and moved it to create a smoother line in Figure 10.20. Notice that there are two lines where the point is being moved. When the point is set down, it displays one line with the point in its new position.

Move Point

The Move Point function allows you to select one or more points at the same time rather than one single point. While the examples to explain how this option could be used to change perimeter or internal style lines can be endless, the garments in Figure 10.21 can give you ideas of where this function may be applied.

We will use the bodice on the far left of Figure 10.21 as the garment to be modified during the

explanation for the Move Point procedure. The bodice we started with in Figure 10.21 was plain without the style lines shown in the drawing. The X's on the side seam, seen in Figures 10.21 and 10.22, are mark points we added by using the Add Point Line function, discussed earlier in the chapter. These points were moved with the Move Point function to create the triangular shapes on the side seam. The space created may be left alone or filled in with a contrasting fabric or color.

Procedure for Move Point

1. Select **Point>Modify Points>Move Point.**

2. Make your selection for the box next to **Move Both Joined End Points** in the user input box.

3. A user input box states: "Select point(s) to move, end selection to continue." Left click on the points you want to move, which highlights them in red. Right click to continue. The points moves along with the mouse. Left click to set down the points at the locations you want. If there is a specific distance the points

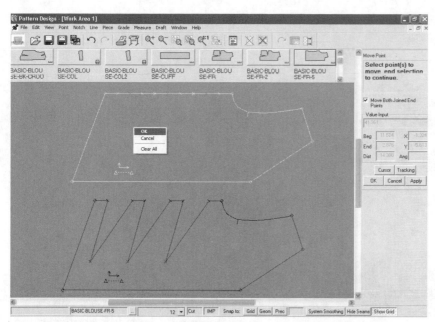

Figure 10.22 The Move Point function is used to move the mark points on the side seam for a new look.

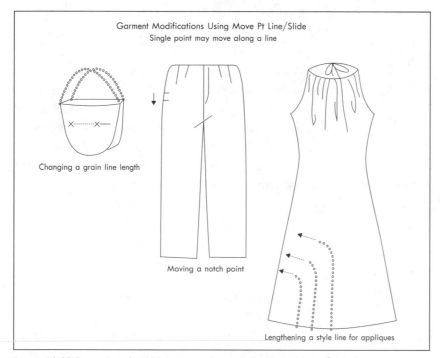

Figure 10.23 Examples of modifying garments with the Move Pt Line/Slide function.

Move Pt Line/Slide

The Move Pt Line/Slide function is used to slide a point along a line. This point may slide only along the line on which it exists if it is an intermediate point. If a hip notch is seven inches below the waist on a skirt, but needs to be eight inches below the waist, this function lets you slide the point down one inch along the line. When you move a notch on a curved line and change its shape as a result, an intermediate point remains in its place.

If you slide an endpoint, it is technically attached to two lines. Therefore, the point will slide along the line selected in the **Move Along Line** option of the user input box. Grain lines, style lines, match lines, and pattern placement lines may be shortened or lengthened with this function; the system tries to retain the original shape or angle of the line. For example, look at the style lines of the dress in Figure 10.23. When using this function on the top endpoint of the style line, the curve becomes more pronounced because the point is drawing related points toward the left. In this case, it is much like driving on a road that starts curving left. We will use this dress as the example to explain the procedure for Move Pt Line/Slide.

Use the Move Pt Line/Slide function to

need to move, perform a popup or change from Cursor Mode to Value Mode. We selected several points on the side seam of the bodice shown in Figure 10.22 and moved them as displayed.

- lengthen or shorten a grain line to keep it inside a pattern piece or to make it more noticeable.

- lengthen or shorten a style line.

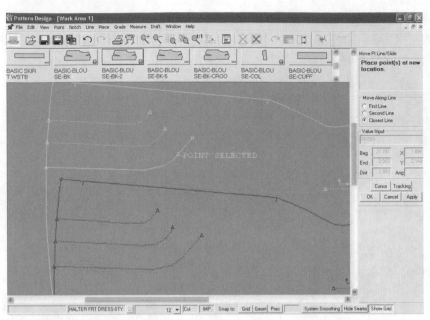

Figure 10.24 Endpoint of style line is extended using the Move Pt Line/Slide function.

the desired location. The point is moved to its new location. If there is a specific distance the point needs to move, perform a popup or change from Cursor Mode to Value Mode. The **Beg** and **End** fields represent measurements from the beginning and end of the line on which the point is currently. If you wish to move the point a specific distance from where it originally was, then enter a measurement in the **Dist** field. We moved the point to a place where it was more visually appealing, about two inches longer. The result is shown in the bottom half of Figure 10.24.

- lengthen or shorten a match line used to match stripes or plaids.
- move a notch point on a hip or an armhole.

Available Options for Move Pt Line/Slide

These options apply when selecting a point that is connected to two lines such as an endpoint.

First Line Select this option to move the point along the first line that the point hits going clockwise.

Second Line Select this option to move the point along the second line the point hits going clockwise.

Closest Line Select this option to move the point along the line closest to the point.

Procedure for Move Pt Line/Slide

1. Select **Point>Modify Points>Move Pt Line/Slide.**

2. A user input box states: "Select point to move." Left click on the point to slide. The point moves along with mouse. We selected the endpoint of the style line of the dress in Figure 10.24.

3. A user input box states: "Place point at new location." Left click to set down the point at

Move Point Horiz

The Move Point Horiz function allows a point to be moved horizontally, otherwise known as moving along the X axis. You may move more than one point at the same time. The point you select may move in a positive or negative direction while holding the previous and the next point in place, regardless of whether it is an intermediate or endpoint. The area from the previous to the next point may be considered the range or region within which the point may move horizontally. The points will be turned on for this example so you can visualize it more clearly.

Figure 10.25 displays several examples of garments that may be modified as shown with the dashed lines using the Move Point Horiz function. Keep in mind that the points before and after are always held in place, so if a point does not exist in the area you wish to hold, you may need to add a point using a function such as Add Point. The skirt on the far left of Figure 10.25 originally had a straight hem. To create the look displayed, points were added to the hem with the Add Points Line function from the Point menu. Since the skirt is made up of two layers, we created a copy of the skirt using the Copy function and added three

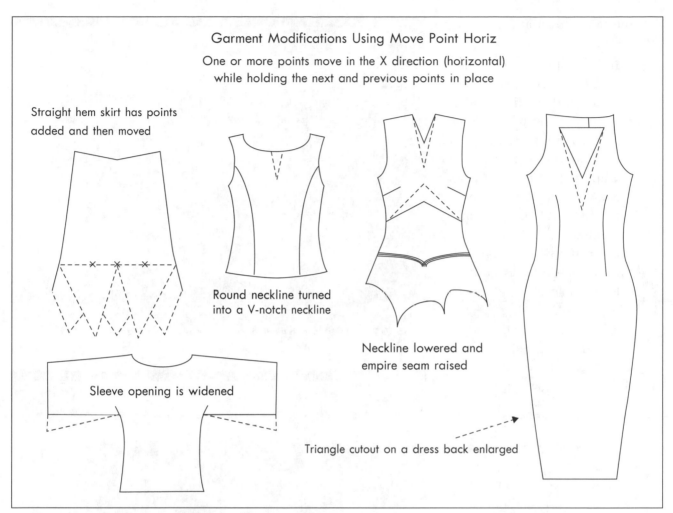

Garment Modifications Using Move Point Horiz

One or more points move in the X direction (horizontal)
while holding the next and previous points in place

Straight hem skirt has points
added and then moved

Round neckline turned
into a V-notch neckline

Neckline lowered and
empire seam raised

Sleeve opening is widened

Triangle cutout on a dress back enlarged

Figure 10.25 Garments modified using the Move Point Horiz function.

points to one skirt copy and five points to the
other copy.

Procedure for Move Point Horiz

1. Select **Point>Modify Points>Move Point
   Horiz.**

2. A user input box states: "Select point(s) to
   move, end selection to continue." Left click on
   the points you want to move. Right click to
   continue. The points move along with the
   mouse. Left click to set down the points at the
   location you want. If there is a specific distance the points need to move, perform a
   popup or change from Cursor Mode to Value
   Mode. Only the **X** field will be available since
   this point can move only in a horizontal direction. We selected several points on the hem of

the skirt shown in Figure 10.26.

3. A user input box states: "Place point at new location." Left click to set down the point at the location you want. If there is a specific distance the point needs to move, perform a popup or change from Cursor Mode to Value Mode. Only the **X** field will light up, since the point can move only in a horizontal or X direction with this function. We moved the selected points 15", as shown in Figure 10.26. Since we are doing two layers and the function restarts at Step 2, we continued for the creation of the skirt as shown in Figure 10.25.

4. A user input box states: "Select point(s) to move, end selection to continue." Left click to select points to move. We selected several points (see Figure 10.27) to create the second layer of this skirt.

5. A user input box states: "Place point at new location." Left click to set down the point at the location you want. We moved the points 15" as shown in Figure 10.27.

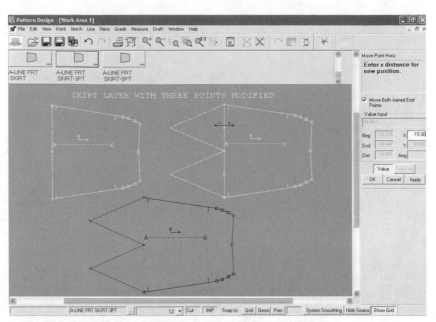

Figure 10.26 First skirt layer is modified with the Move Point Horiz function.

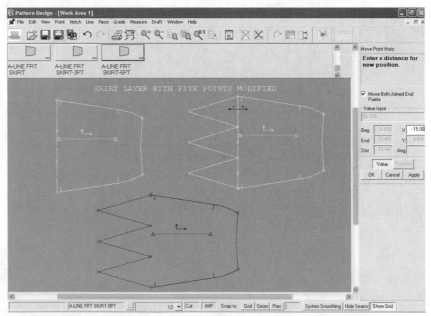

Figure 10.27 Second skirt layer is modified using the Move Point Horiz function.

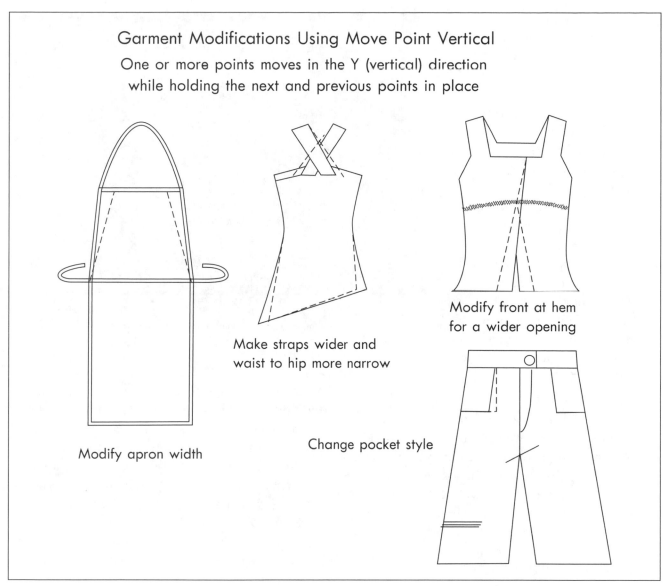

Garment Modifications Using Move Point Vertical
One or more points moves in the Y (vertical) direction while holding the next and previous points in place

Modify apron width

Make straps wider and waist to hip more narrow

Change pocket style

Modify front at hem for a wider opening

Figure 10.28 Garments modified using the Move Point Vert function.

Move Point Vert

The Move Point Vert function works the same way as Move Point Horiz, but it works vertically or along the Y axis. This gives users optimal control for pattern modification. You may move more than one point at the same time and in a positive or negative direction while keeping the previous and next point in place. We will be using the bodice with the square neckline in Figure 10.28 as an example. Notice that the adjacent lines of the point being moved are straight lines and there are therefore no intermediate points.

Figure 10.28 displays several examples of garments that may be modified, as shown with the dashed lines by using Move Point Vert. The drawings are shown upright, but remember that when they are laid out on a table or on-screen, they are horizontal if they are cut on the grain. Examples of garments that are laid out crossgrain, or perpendicular to the grain, are dancewear leotards or swimsuits.

Procedure for Move Point Vert

1. Select **Point>Modify Points>Move Point Vert.**

2. A user input box states: "Select point(s) to move, end selection to continue." Left click on the points to move. Right click to continue. The points move along with the mouse. Left click to set down the points at the location you want. If there is a specific distance the points needs to move, perform a popup or change from Cursor Mode to Value Mode. Only the **Y** field will light up since the point can move only in a vertical or Y direction with this function. We selected the point on the hem of the bodice that intersects the center front in Figure 10.29.

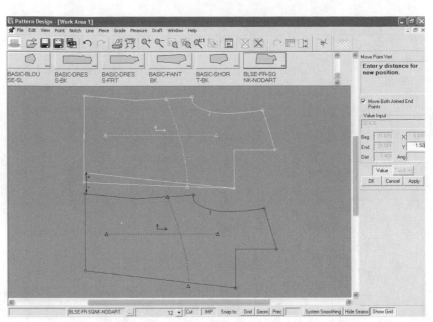

Figure 10.29 Bodice front opening is widened at the hem using the Move Point Vert function.

3. A user input box states: "Place point at new location." Left click to set the point down at the location you want. If there is a specific distance the point needs to move, perform a popup or change from Cursor Mode to Value Mode. Only the **Y** field will light up since the point can move only in a vertical or Y direction with this function. We performed a popup and entered 1.5 inches for the point to move as shown in Figure 10.29. The bodice displayed at the bottom of the figure is the modified piece.

Move Smooth

The Move Smooth function lets you move one or more points along the X and/or Y axes horizontally or vertically, much like the Move Point function. The main difference is that with Move Smooth the region from the previous to the next point may be much larger because it ranges from the last endpoint to the next endpoint.

When moving a point with the Move Smooth function, the adjacent lines are moved along with the point and are laid down as close to the original shape and as smooth as possible. The system tries to keep the lines attached to the point smooth. In the skirt in Figure 10.30, the point moved is attached to the hem and side seam. When the point is moved, the lines are not distorted.

Likewise, when a point is moved within a line segment, all the points are picked up and laid back down as smoothly as possible to the point's new position. For example, look at the angled hemline of the dress in Figure 10.30. A point in the middle of the line has been moved and while the shape is now different it is still curved but more pronounced. Now notice how the neck width of the bodice with the sweetheart neckline in Figure 10.30 has been widened. The point that hits the neckline and shoulder was moved. This point was laid back down to remain on the angle of the shoulder while the aim was to keep the neckline intact.

We will use the skirt in Figure 10.30 as an example to explain the procedure for the Move Smooth function. The skirt is made up of two layers. Many times in the industry, a garment of this nature is modified by laying out all the pieces on-screen for accuracy. Therefore, we have laid out both layers on-screen to create this scenario. Only the top layer will be modified during the explanation of the procedure for Move Smooth, but the same pro-

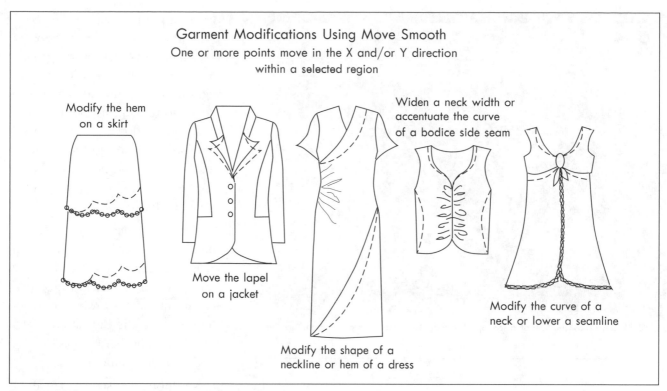

Figure 10.30 Garments modified using the Move Smooth function.

cedure can be applied to the bottom layer to achieve the look of the skirt in Figure 10.30.

Available Options for Move Smooth

Thumbtack Positions There are three icons displayed under Thumbtack Positions in the user input box, but the two right-hand icons represent available choices. The first box with the thumbtack represents that a selection between these two options will be activated.

- If the middle box is selected, thumbtacks are placed on the adjacent points, regardless of whether they are intermediate points or endpoints.

- If the box on the far right is selected, thumbtacks will be placed on the adjacent end points only—this is the widest range available to move the selected point. The thumbtacks may be moved to select a narrower region.

Procedure for Move Smooth

1. Select **Point>Modify Points>Move Smooth.**

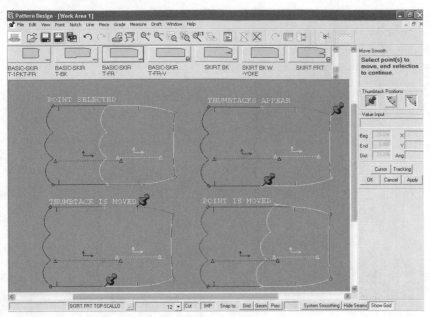

Figure 10.31 Steps show the hem of a scalloped skirt angled using the Move Smooth function.

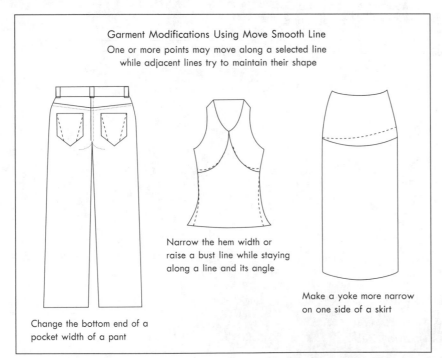

Figure 10.32 Garments modified using the Move Smooth Line function.

2. Select from the two **Thumbtack Positions** in the user input box. Since we wish to move the thumbtacks, we opted for the end point to end point option on the far right, as seen in Figure 10.31.

3. A user input box states: "Select point(s) to move, end selection to continue." Left click on the points to move. The points will turn red. Right click to continue. The points move along with mouse. Left click to set points down at the desired location. We selected the point that intersects the hem and the side seam of the skirt, as shown in Figure 10.31.

4. A user input box states: "Position thumbtacks to define range or left click to continue." Move the thumbtack or left click to accept its current location. We moved the thumbtack to the hip notch so that everything before it is not modified. See Figure 10.31.

5. A user input box states: "Place point at new location." Left click to set down the point at the location you want. The point is moved to its new location. If there is a specific distance the point needs to move, perform a popup or change from Cursor Mode to Value Mode. The **X** and **Y** fields light up, since the point can move in both horizontal/X or vertical/Y directions with this function. We moved the point as shown in Figure 10.31 to create an angled hem rather than a straight scalloped hem.

Move Smooth Line

The Move Smooth Line function is used to move a point along a line while keeping the line as smooth as possible. More than one point may be moved at the same time. Use it to make modifications on garments such as the ones shown in Figure 10.32. Notice how the pockets on the pant have been made narrower. The bottom corner point was moved along the

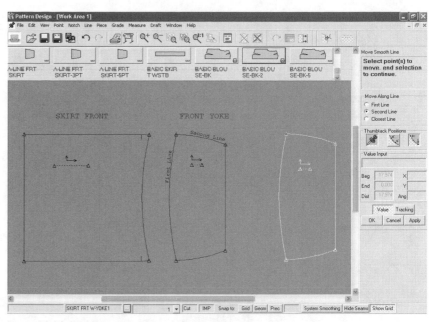

Figure 10.33 Skirt yoke shows lines defined; point selected to move.

bottom seam of the pocket to create a more angled look for the pocket. Now look at the halter top in the middle of Figure 10.32 and notice how the seam under the bust is a little higher on the side seam. Thumbtacks may be placed to hold a section of the line in place when moving a point.

We slid the yoke on the skirt in Figure 10.32 higher on the side seam to create an angled yoke rather than a curved one. Since it is a true yoke, it is constructed with two pieces. Both pieces would have to be changed to modify the pattern properly. We will be changing the yoke only for the procedure shown, but the same steps may apply to the skirt front to make sure the pieces sew together properly.

Available Options for Move Smooth Line

These options apply when selecting a point that is connected to two lines, such as an endpoint.
First Line Select this option to move the point along the first line the point hits going clockwise.

Second Line Select this option to move the point along the second line the point hits going clockwise.

Closest Line Select this option to move the point along the line closest to the point.

Procedure for Move Smooth Line

1. Select **Point>Modify Points>Move Smooth Line.**

2. Select one of the three available options under the **Move Along Line** area of the user input box. We selected **Second Line** since the side seam is the second line the point hits going clockwise.

3. Select one of the two **Thumbtack Positions** available in the user input box. We selected the box on the farthest right to select a specific region.

4. A user input box states: "Select point(s) to move, end selection to continue." Left click on the points you want to move, which highlights them in red. Right click to continue. We selected an endpoint on the yoke (see Figure 10.33).

5. A user input box states: "Position thumbtacks to define range or left click to continue." We moved the thumbtacks to protect the part of the curve on the side seam that we do not want to have modified, as shown in Figure 10.34.

6. A user input box states: "Place point at new location." The point(s) moves along with

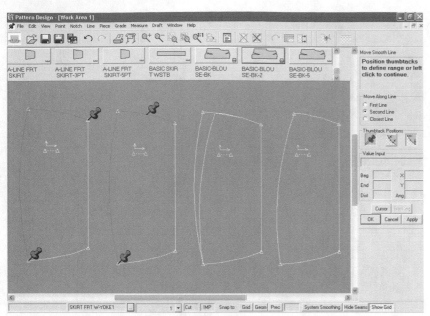

Figure 10.34 The point on the yoke is slid on the second line using the Move Smooth Line function.

mouse. Left click to set the point down at the location you want. If there is a specific distance the point needs to move, perform a popup or change from Cursor Mode to Value Mode. The **Beg** and **End** fields represent measurements from the beginning and end of the line on which the point is currently. We moved the point as shown in Figure 10.34.

Move Smooth Horiz

The Move Smooth Horiz function is used to move a point along the X axis. You may move more than one point at the same time. As in all the Modify Point menu functions, the points selected may move in the positive or negative directions. As with the Move Smooth Line function, there are two thumbtack positions available. The thumbtacks may be placed from the previous to the next point or a region may be selected from the previous endpoint to the next endpoint for a larger range.

This function is comparable with the Move Point Horiz function except for the two available thumbtack positions. Since the thumbtacks may be moved from endpoint to endpoint, there is a larger region available that you can modify; the system

picks up all the points within the region when you move a point and lays them all back down in the new location. If you know you are making several modifications on a garment in a horizontal direction from the previous point to the next point, use the Move Point Horiz function since it is actually available for this reason. The points will be turned on in the example we use so you can visualize this more clearly.

The examples shown in Figure 10.35 are some examples of how garments may be modified using the Move Smooth Horiz function. Remember that when you move a point, it stretches the adjacent lines to which it is attached, as in the skirt shown in Figure 10.35. Likewise, if you move a point within a line, the whole line or region you choose to move stretches to the new location, as in the waist modification made on the bodice located second from the left in Figure 10.35 or in the hem modification on the bodice located third from the left in the same figure.

The front of the bodice with the spaghetti straps in Figure 10.35 is made up of two pattern pieces. We will only be modifying the top front of the bodice. The bottom front will not be affected by the modification we are illustrating during the procedure, but if you wanted to modify the hem of the bodice as shown in Figure 10.35, you could use the Move Smooth Horiz function to do so.

Procedure for Move Smooth Horiz

1. Select **Point>Modify Points>Move Smooth Horiz.**

2. Select one of the two **Thumbtack Positions** available in the user input box. We selected the box on the far right to select a specific region.

3. A user input box states: "Select point(s) to move, end selection to continue." Left click on the points to move, which highlights them in

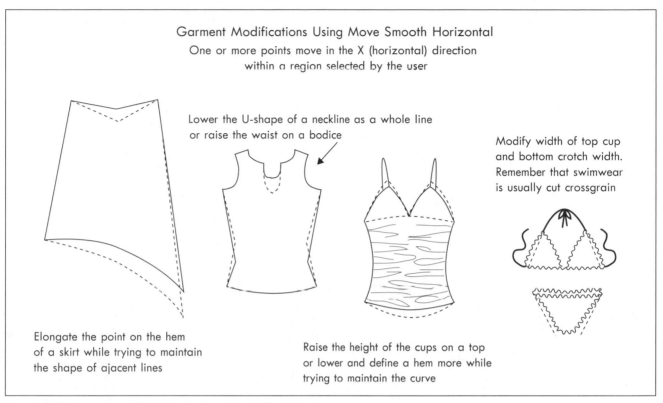

Garment Modifications Using Move Smooth Horizontal
One or more points move in the X (horizontal) direction
within a region selected by the user

Lower the U-shape of a neckline as a whole line
or raise the waist on a bodice

Modify width of top cup
and bottom crotch width.
Remember that swimwear
is usually cut crossgrain

Elongate the point on the hem
of a skirt while trying to maintain
the shape of ajacent lines

Raise the height of the cups on a top
or lower and define a hem more while
trying to maintain the curve

Figure 10.35 Garments modified using the Move Smooth Horiz function.

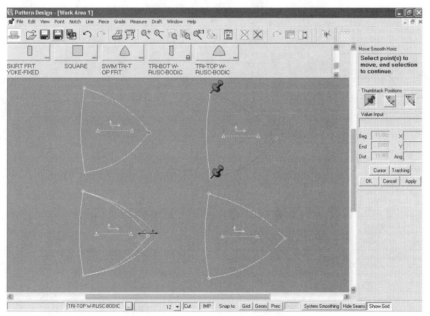

Figure 10.36 The top of a bodice is made longer using the Move Smooth Horiz function.

red. Right click to continue. We selected the point on the apex of the triangular top (see Figure 10.36).

4. A user input box states: "Position thumbtacks to define range or left click to continue." Move the thumbtack or left click to accept its current location. We left clicked to continue and accept the location shown in Figure 10.36.

5. A user input box states: "Place point at new location." The points move along with mouse. Left click to set down the points at the location you want. For a specific distance, perform a popup or change from Cursor Mode to Value Mode. Only the **X** field is available since this point moves horizontally for this function. We performed a popup to add 2" to the length of the top in Figure 10.36. Notice how the adjacent lines move along with the point.

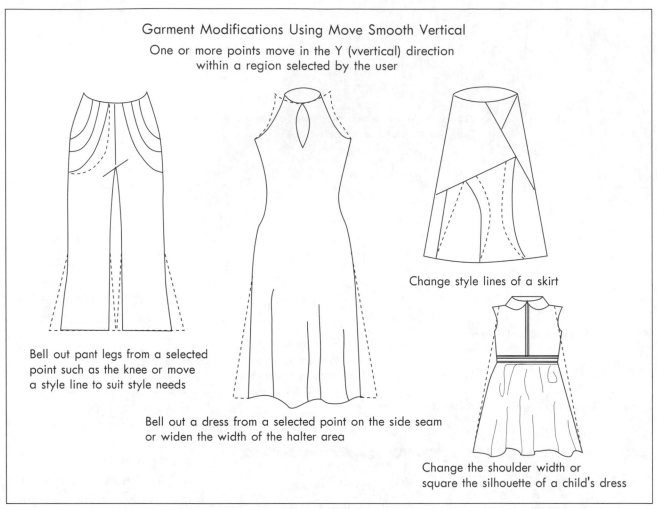

Garment Modifications Using Move Smooth Vertical
One or more points move in the Y (vvertical) direction
within a region selected by the user

Bell out pant legs from a selected
point such as the knee or move
a style line to suit style needs

Bell out a dress from a selected point on the side seam
or widen the width of the halter area

Change style lines of a skirt

Change the shoulder width or
square the silhouette of a child's dress

Figure 10.37 Garments modified using the Move Smooth Vert function.

Move Smooth Vert

The Move Smooth Vert function works the same as
the Move Smooth Horiz function, except that it
moves vertically along the Y axis. As stated earlier,
you can move points in both X and Y directions to
let you have optimal control of pattern manipulation. Figure 10.37 displays a few garment modifications created using the Move Smooth Vert function.
All the garments shown are laid out on the grain,
so the pattern will lay in a horizontal direction on-
screen when being modified. As in other examples
shown in this chapter, the pant leg has been copied
each time after it has been manipulated to display
the steps in one viewing.

Procedure for Move Smooth Vert

1. Select **Point>Modify Points>Move Vert.**

2. Select one of the two **Thumbtack Positions** available in the user input box. We selected the box on the far right to select a specific region.

3. A user input box states: "Select point(s) to move, end selection to continue." Left click on the points to move, which highlights them in red. Right click to continue. We selected the point on the leg opening (see Figure 10.38).

4. A user input box states: "Position thumbtacks to define range or left click to continue." Move the thumbtack or left click to accept its current location. We left clicked on the thumbtack to pick it up and move it to the knee point, as shown in Figure 10.38.

5. A user input box states: "Place point at new location." The point moves along with mouse. Left click to set down the point at the location you want. For a specific distance, perform a popup or change from Cursor Mode to Value Mode. Only the **Y** field is available, since this point moves in that direction for this function. We performed a popup to add 1.5" to bell out the pant leg, as shown in Figure 10.38. Notice how the adjacent lines move along with the point while the thumbtack locations remain in place. To bell out the pant leg on both sides, repeat Steps 3 through 5.

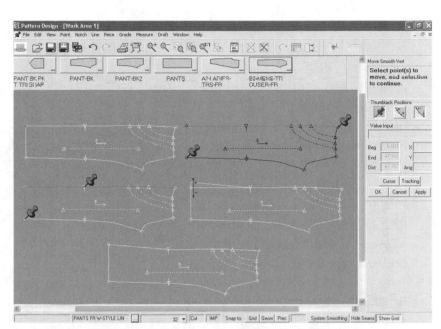

Figure 10.38 Steps involved in belling out a pant leg by using the Move Smooth Vert function.

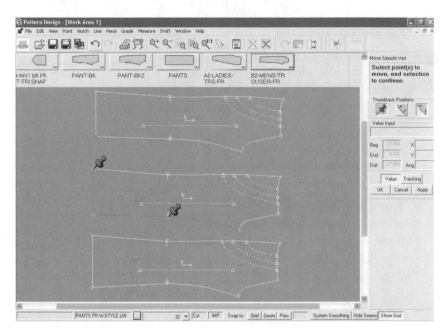

Figure 10.39 The other side of the pant leg is belled out using the Move Smooth Vert function.

6. A user input box states: "Select point(s) to move, end selection to continue." We selected the point on the other side of the leg opening (see Figure 10.39).

7. A user input box states: "Position thumbtacks to define range or left click to continue." We

moved the thumbtack to the knee point again, as shown in Figure 10.39.

8. A user input box states: "Place point at new location." We entered 1½" on this side of our pant leg to keep the piece balanced.

Armhole/Sleeve Cap

The Armhole/Sleeve Cap function is used to modify the front, back, and sleeve pattern at the same time when making changes to the armhole. This allows for an accurate modification and saves time, since each piece is not being modified individually. The points may be moved along the X and Y axes. The direction may be defined by selecting them in the **Armhole** and **Sleeve Cap** options in the user input box (see Figure 10.40).

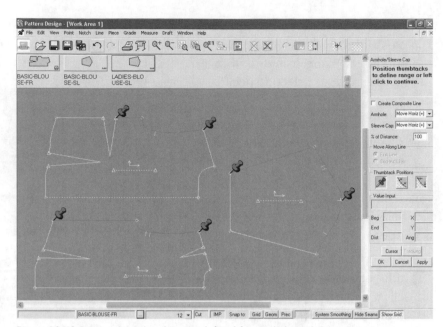

Figure 10.40 Points selected and region defined for armhole and sleeve cap move.

We suggest you lay out a front, back, and sleeve on-screen and follow the procedure closely at first so you can understand this function. Once you have followed the procedure and have a better understanding of the function, select different points for modification. For example, select the top of the shoulder on both the front and the back patterns along with the top of the sleeve cap. Select **Move Horiz (+)** in both the **Armhole** and **Sleeve Cap** fields. Enter 200 in the **% of Distance** field and notice how the top of the sleeve cap moves twice as much as the shoulder points.

Procedure for Armhole/Sleeve Cap

1. Select **Point>Modify Points>Armhole/Sleeve Cap.**

2. Select direction for **Armhole** movement in the user input box. We selected **Move Horiz +,** as shown in Figure 10.40.

3. Select direction for **Sleeve Cap** movement in the user input box. We selected **Move Horiz (+),** as shown in Figure 10.40.

4. Select one of the two **Thumbtack Positions** available in the user input box. We selected the box on the far right to select a specific region.

5. A user input box states: "Select point(s) to move on armhole piece, end selection to continue." We left clicked to select the point that intersects the armhole and the side seam on the front bodice first.

6. A user input box states: "Position thumbtacks to define range or left click to continue." We left clicked to accept the location of the thumbtacks, as shown in Figure 10.40.

7. A user input box states: "Select point(s) to move on armhole piece, end selection to continue." We left clicked to select the point that intersects the armhole and the side seam on the back bodice next.

8. A user input box states: "Position thumbtacks to define range or left click to continue." We left clicked to accept the location of the thumbtacks, as shown in Figure 10.40.

9. Right click to end the selection of armhole points.

10. A user input box states: "Select point(s) to move on sleeve cap, end selection to continue." We left clicked to select the intersection of the sleeve cap and underarm seam.

11. A user input box states: "Position thumbtacks to define range or left click to continue." We moved one of the thumbtacks to the top of the sleeve cap, as shown in Figure 10.40.

12. Right click to end selection of sleeve cap points.

13. A user input box states: "Place point at new location." The points on all the selected pieces move along with the mouse. Left click to set them down at the location you want. If there is a specific distance the point needs to move, perform a popup or change from Cursor Mode to Value Mode. We performed a popup and entered –1" for Figure 10.41. Since the move was horizontal, only the X field was available.

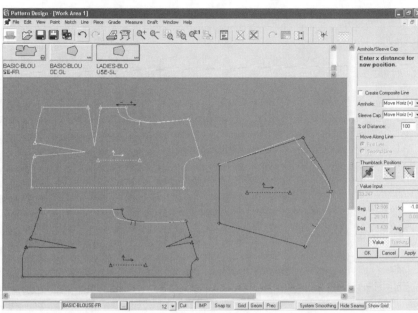

Figure 10.41 All armhole pieces selected are modified at the same time.

Reshape Curve

The Reshape Curve function is utilized to modify the shape of a curve that is created when several patterns are sewn together. For example, look at Figure 10.42. The front armhole in the bodice shown is created when the front yoke, center front, and side front are sewn together. This function lets you modify the curve as one line segment rather than each line individually. Therefore, this helps you visualize the final results of the curve when it's sewn, and helps with styling the shape of the curve. Notice that the neckline of the bodice in Figure 10.42 is also made up of more than one pattern. The Reshape Curve function may also be applied when modifying the neckline in this scenario.

To modify the armhole curve on the bodice in Figure 10.42, we placed all the pieces that make

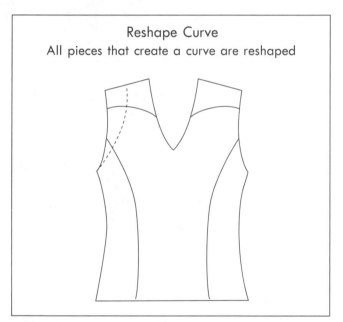

Figure 10.42 Armhole curve is reshaped on all pieces with the Reshape Curve function.

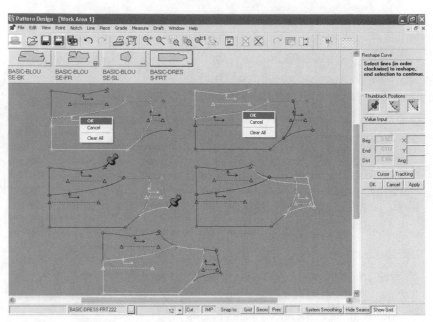

Figure 10.43 Steps show armhole made up of three patterns being reshaped.

up the armhole next to one another, as shown in Figure 10.43, as they would be if they were sewn together. The pieces do not have to be this close together to use this function, but we have done it so you can visualize the shape of the curve as it is being modified.

Procedure for Reshape Curve

1. Select **Point>Modify Points>Reshape Curve.**

2. Select one of the two **Thumbtack Positions** available in the user input box. We selected the box on the far right to select a specific region.

3. A user input box states: "Select lines (in order clockwise) to reshape, end selection to continue." Left click to select all the lines that will move and make up the curve, which highlights them in red. Right click to continue. We selected all the lines that make up the armhole, as well as the shoulder line in Figure 10.43 since it will need to be modified as well.

4. A user input box states: "Select point(s) to move, end selection to continue." Left click to select points to move, which highlights them in red. Right click to continue. We selected the intersection point between the shoulder and the armhole line, as shown in Figure 10.43.

5. A user input box states: "Position thumbtacks to define range or left click to continue." We left clicked to accept the location of the thumbtacks, as shown in Figure 10.43.

6. A user input box states: "Place point at new location." The points together with lines, move along with the mouse. Left click to set the points down at the desired location. A specific measurement may be entered in the **X** and/or **Y** fields if the mode is changed to Value Mode or a popup is performed. We moved the armhole visually in Cursor Mode with no specific measurement, as shown in Figure 10.43.

Test Your Skills

Use a basic bodice front like the one shown in Figure 10.44 to complete this section. A one-dart basic bodice may work as well. This section takes you through some of the functions discussed in this chapter. The letters will be used during the exercise to help reference lines in the pattern.

1. Place the piece on-screen.
2. Use the Add Point function to add a bust point if one is not drafted into the basic bodice.
3. Use the Add Point function to add four points for the pocket placement of a small pocket wherever you wish to place it.
4. Use the Align 2 Points function to align the points added for pocket placement in the last step. You will need to use the Horizontal and Vertical options for this step.
5. Use the Add Point function to add a point halfway between points D and E.
6. Use the Delete Point function to delete the pocket placement points.
7. Using the Move Single Point function, angle the point K dart. Notice the point can move in the X and Y directions.
8. Undo the last step by clicking the undo icon or by selecting Edit>Undo.
9. Turn on the intermediate points by selecting View>Intermediate Points.
10. Using the Move Point function, move a point on the armhole between points F and H. Now select more than one point and move them with the same function. Using the same function again, move point H. Notice that the points can move in the X and Y directions.

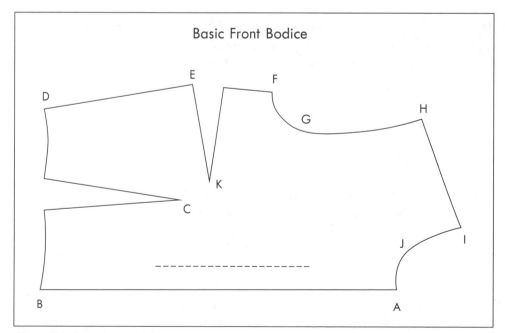

Figure 10.44 Basic front bodice.

11. Undo three times to undo the armhole modifications in the last step.

12. Use Move Smooth to move any point in the armhole. Accept the default thumbtack locations on both ends of the line. Notice how the whole line moves between the thumbtacks to follow the point being moved in the X and Y directions.

13. Using the Move Smooth option again, widen the neckline by moving point I. Select the thumbtacks at the default locations at H and A. Set the point down so that the neck width is wider, but keep the point on the same shoulder angle. Notice how point I moves while holding points H and A in place.

14. Using Move Point Vert, move point D. Notice how the last intermediate point is held in place.

15. Undo the last function.

16. Use the Move Smooth Vert function to move point D again and notice the difference. Leave the thumbtacks at the default locations. If the difference is not too noticeable to you, move point H with Move Point Vert and then again with Move Smooth Vert and note the difference.

17. Undo the last modifications.

18. Move the notch in the armhole, point G, using the Move Pt Line/Slide function. Press down both mouse buttons to perform a popup. Enter 0.5 ($\frac{1}{2}$") in the Dist field. Use the same function to shorten the grain line.

19. Move the notch point again, but this time use Move Smooth Line and note how the whole line moves.

20. Undo the last function.

21. Use the Move Point Horiz function to move the center front, point A. Notice how the whole neckline does not move.

22. Undo the last step.

23. Use the Move Smooth Horiz function to drop the neckline 1", point A. Accept the thumbtack locations that happen by default at the previous point and the last endpoint. Notice how the whole neckline moves this time. Repeat the function, but now move the thumbtack from point I to J. Notice the difference.

24. Undo twice to undo the neckline modifications.

25. Use Line>Modify Lines>Move Offset to extend the center front, point A to B, by 1". This gives you the width to place buttonhole points in the next step.

26. Using the Add Drills function, add five buttonholes for the center front and inset them $\frac{3}{4}$" from the center front. The first point should be $1\frac{1}{2}$" from the top and the last point should be 3" from the bottom. Place points at both end points by selecting the option Both under Ends to Receive Points in the user input box.

27. Undo the last step.

28. Using the Add Drills Dist function, add buttonholes for the center front and inset them $\frac{3}{4}$" from the center front again. The first point should be $1\frac{1}{2}$" from the top and the last point should be 3" from the bottom. Select

appropriate option from Ends to Receive Points to place a point at the first location. For example, for the bodice shown in Figure 10.44, we would select the option First. See how many points are placed for button placement.

29. Undo the last step.

30. Using the Lines>Create Lines>2 Point-Curve, create a curved line from point G to J.

31. Use the Add Points Line function to add five mark points along the line created in the last step. Select the option None under Ends to Receive Points.

32. Undo the last step to delete the points added to the line. We want to keep the curved line for the next step.

33. Use the Add Points Line Dist function to add mark points along the line created between points G and J. Select to place them with two inches of separation. Select the option None under Ends to Receive Points. See how many points are able to be placed with these parameters.

34. Undo once to delete the points added in the last step. We want to keep the curved line for the next step.

35. Now we are going to split the bodice along the curved line by using Piece>Split Piece>Split on Line. Check only the option that states: "Delete Original Piece." Now two pieces will be on-screen, without seam allowance and without the original whole piece.

36. Using the Reshape Curve function, reshape the neckline. Place both pieces next to each other as if they were sewn. Select the neckline on the yoke and then the neckline on the front/bottom pattern so you can modify them. Leave the thumbtacks in place. Move the point where the pattern is split in two pieces on the neckline. Notice how the lines move together.

37. Undo the last two functions until your piece is one whole piece again.

CHAPTER ELEVEN

Grading for Computerized Patterns

Objective

Grading is the process that creates smaller and larger sizes from a base size pattern, which is the pattern input into the system. This pattern is given a base size name in the Rule Table Editor, such as size 8 or Medium. When using grading in PDS, it is assumed that the user has knowledge of grading. Remember that a CAD system facilitates normal everyday tasks to let you accomplish more during a working session than you would if you were working manually. The system does not make you a patternmaker, but it does help a patternmaker work faster. Likewise, the system does not teach you grading, but it facilitates the grading process and allows accurate results.

The basics of grading manually are briefly discussed in this chapter to help you understand computerized grading. For example, the motion of the **gradeometer** is discussed to define how the X and Y coordinates are used to create grade rules. The three available computerized methods are defined by comparing them with how the industry grades from a base size.

When you are finished reading this chapter, you should understand how to create grade rules and apply them to patterns as well as how to modify existing grade rules. You should also understand the grading methods used in the industry. You should feel refreshed in geometry too, since X and Y coordinates and their quadrants are widely used in computerized grading and discussed throughout the chapter. Fractions and decimals are commonly

used in grading as well, so you will notice the use of both throughout the chapter. So, pull out your C-Thru ruler and start grading!

Please remember that not all functions available in this menu are covered in this chapter. Some functions may be much more advanced than basic grading so we cover the functions that may be covered in a limited class curriculum. Furthermore, many of the other options listed may be used by Microdynamics users rather than Gerber users. Microdynamics was a company that also manufactured a computerized system and was later bought by Gerber Technology. Features from both systems were merged and some options in the system are included to help Microdynamics users work with functions that are familiar to them from their former work environment. If you want advanced training, contact Gerber Technology.

This chapter allows you to gain skills in the following areas:

- The X and Y quadrants
- Drafting in pieces in the correct layout for grading
- Grading methods
- Rule Table Editor
- Edit Delta
- Create Delta
- Edit Offset
- Create Offset
- Change Grade Rule

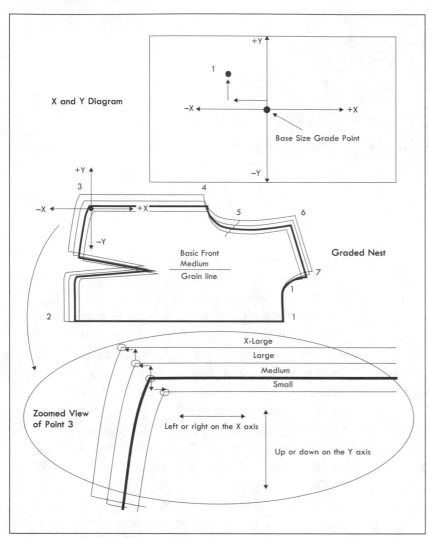

Figure 11.1 Display of X and Y grade movements on a graded nest.

- Change Base Size
- Change Base Dimensions
- More/Fewer Size Steps
- Redistribute Growths
- Edit Break Sizes
- Rename Size
- Assign Rule Table
- Create Nest
- Line
- Export Rules

The X and Y Quadrants

Grade rules are created based on X and Y coordinates. They may move in positive and negative directions. Together, these coordinates are known as a grade rule in the grading process. The points labeled with numbers on the graded nest shown in Figure 11.1 illustrate how points may move on a graded piece. Every corner of a piece has a grade rule. A grade rule is expressed as a coordinate (X, Y). If a point does not move, its coordinates are (0, 0). Any point that needs to be controlled as it moves, such as a notch, may have a grade point added as well. A point that grades, or one that has a grade rule applied to it, is referred to as a **grade point.**

The center point in the X and Y diagram shown in Figure 11.1 represents the base size at each point that should be graded. So, at each point that grades, lay out an imaginary X and Y diagram to determine the direction the point moves. Look at how we laid out an X and Y diagram on point 3 of the graded nest shown in Figure 11.1. A **graded nest** is a pattern that is graded and shown with all of its sizes. Normally, a graded nest is plotted to check that the grading is done properly on a pattern. When the pattern is cut for production or to create a sample, each size will be cut out on its own.

- Add Grade Point
- Copy Table Rule
- Copy Grade Rule
- Copy X Rule
- Copy Y Rule
- Copy Nest Rule
- Copy Nest X
- Copy Nest Y
- Flip X Rule
- Flip Y Rule
- Copy Size Line

Test Your Skills—X and Y Quadrants

Look at the graded nest shown in Figure 11.1. Test your knowledge by trying to determine in which direction each numbered graded point is moving. Each point that grades is assigned a numeric grade rule number. Write in either positive or negative for each X and Y. Write in 0 if it does not move in either direction. Rule #1 has been filled out. Since it does not move, its coordinates are (0, 0) and the X and Y are neutral, neither positive nor negative. Rule number 1 is commonly reserved as a No Growth rule consisting of X and Y coordinates (0, 0) because you will come across a point of no growth at some point in a pattern and rule number 1 is simply an easy rule number to remember.

The answers are listed at the end of the chapter. Do not peek at the answers—test your knowledge and grade yourself later.

Rule #1: _0_ X _0_ Y   Rule #5: ____ X ____ Y

Rule #2: ____ X ____ Y   Rule #6: ____ X ____ Y

Rule #3: ____ X ____ Y   Rule #7: ____ X ____ Y

Rule #4: ____ X ____ Y

Drafting in Pieces in the Correct Layout for Grading

You should lay out all pieces that belong to a garment in the same direction when you are set to draft them into the system (see Figure 11.2). If you do not lay out the pieces in the same direction, you have to create more grade rules, thereby creating more work for the grader. Each point that grades is assigned a numeric grade rule number. For example, assume grade rule 2 in Figure 11.1 has X and Y coordinates of ($-\frac{1}{2}$, 0).

When pieces are laid out in the same direction, grade rules can be copied from one piece onto another if they grade the same at that point. For example, notice how rule numbers in Figure 11.2 are the same on the front and back pattern pieces when the patterns are laid out facing the same direction. Now notice that the front and back pieces in the incorrect layout do not share the same rule numbers. They cannot share the same rules because the X and Y coordinates of the front pattern are going in the opposite direction of the back pattern. For example, if point 2 was moving in the negative X direction to get longer on the front pattern, point 2 on the back pattern should

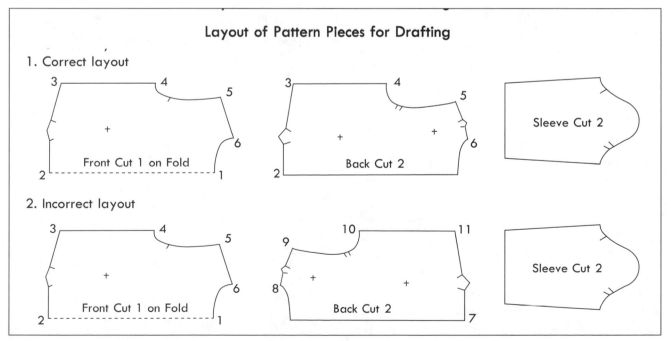

Figure 11.2 Correct and incorrect layouts for pattern pieces drafted into the system.

also move in the negative X direction so that they may sew together properly. When the back is flipped in the opposite direction, as shown in the incorrect layout, the X is positive to make the garment longer, and therefore a new rule number has to be created.

A grade rule is a movement. It does not have to specifically belong to the armhole or the neckline. If the X and Y coordinates of a grade rule in the armhole are the same for a pant at the waist, this rule may be applied to the pant as well. This allows grade rules to be minimized in the Rule Table so that you do not have to search through thousands of rules, although if you wish, you may enter up to 9,999 rules per table.

Grading Methods

When setting up the User Environment Table, you may have noticed that there were three available options for the grading method. The grading method chosen in this table determines how you set up the X and Y coordinates of each grade rule and how the system reads these rules. Each method is described below to help you understand the difference among them. All the methods you use recognize the base size that is determined in the Rule Table Editor, also discussed later in the chapter. When describing the methods available, we refer to the graded nest shown in Figure 11.3. The base size is a medium and displayed with a thick line. The size line is small to extra large. The **size line** is defined as the range of sizes available for a pattern.

The first grading method is *base up-down incremental*. As the name states, the grade rules created are based on how the points move from the base size up for a larger size and from the base size down for the smaller sizes. Look at grade points 2 and 3 on the graded nest in Figure 11.3. If point 2 moves only ½" only on the length, for each size, and point 3 also moves ½" on the length but also

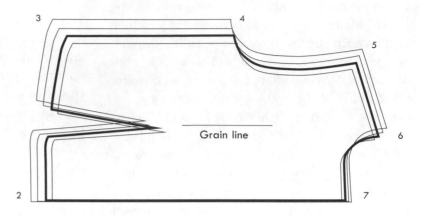

Graded Nest with Grade Rule Numbers

Grain line

Figure 11.3 Graded nest shown with grade rules.

moves ¼" on the width for each size, then the rules for these two points would be set up as displayed in Table 11.1.

Note how the positive and negative signs change at the base size. Most graders grade patterns manually from the base size up and from the base size down. For this reason, this method

Table 11.1: Two rule examples for the Base Up-Down Incremental grading method

Rule #2

Size	X	Y
M–S	+ 0.500	0
*M–L	− 0.500	0
L–XL	− 0.500	0

* Denotes the base size

Rule #3

Size	X	Y
M–S	+ 0.500	− 0.250
*M–L	− 0.500	+ 0.250
L–XL	− 0.500	+ 0.250

* Denotes the base size

is most similar to the manual grading basics taught in school.

The second grading method is *base up-down cumulative*. This method is also similar to some manual grading practices. The total amount a point grades from the smallest to largest size is known as the cumulative amount. This cumulative amount is then evenly divided and distributed among the available sizes in the size line. The grade rules for points 2 and 3 in the graded nest in Figure 11.3 would be set up as displayed in Table 11.2.

The third and last method is *small-large incremental*. This method is highly recommended because it has the lowest possibility of human error and is the simplest to set up. The other two methods work closest to the way patternmakers or graders work in manual environments; therefore, their comfort levels are higher with these methods until they realize the ease of using the small-large incremental method.

Look at the graded nest in Figure 11.3 again and ask yourself: "What direction is the point moving toward—negative or positive on the X and Y—to make the next larger size?" Forget that the base size is medium; simply answer the question moving from the smallest size in the size line. The grade rules for points 2 and 3 would be set up as displayed in Table 11.3.

Notice that all the positive and negative signs are the same throughout all the sizes from the smallest to largest. You may be thinking that X moves in a negative direction from medium to small. While you are correct, given the base size of medium, the system knows to move in the negative direction— the opposite direction of the larger sizes—to create the small size. Once again, all you need to think of is how to get larger—negative or positive on the X and Y—and the system takes care of the rest. It helps minimize the thinking process in this area so you can focus on other major tasks.

Rule Table Editor

The Rule Table Editor is the table where you set up all the rules for a pattern. It is also the place where you name the base size and determine the size line. A rule table is usually set up for several styles. It is not common practice to set up a rule table per style because if there were a thousand styles, there would be a thousand rule tables to set up. A rule table is set up for several styles whose base sizes and size lines are the same. For example, a rule table may be set up for Juniors, Misses, or Men's. Keeping this in mind will help you to name the Rule Table Editor as well.

Table 11.2: Two rule examples for the Base Up-Down Cumulative grading method

Rule #2

Size	X	Y
M–S	+ 0.500	0
M–XL	– 1.000	0

* Denotes the base size

Rule #3

Size	X	Y
M–S	+ 0.500	– 0.250
M–XL	– 1.000	+ 0.500

* Denotes the base size

Table 11.3: Two rule examples for the Small-Large Incremental grading method

Rule #2

Size	X	Y
S–M	– 0.500	0
*M–L	– 0.500	0
L–XL	– 0.500	0

* Denotes the base size

Rule #3

Size	X	Y
S–M	– 0.500	+0.250
*M–L	– 0.500	+0.250
L–XL	– 0.500	+0.250

* Denotes the base size

The Rule Table Editor is at least two pages long. The first page, called the Rule Table, is where the sizes, base size, and size breaks are set up. The second page, called Rules, is where the grades rules are input with the correct X and Y coordinates per size.

Opening the Rule Table Editor

The Rule Table Editor may be accessed in one of three ways: through the Gerber Launch Pad, AccuMark Explorer, or PDS. PDS would be used to open a Rule Table for convenience because you may already be working in PDS and want to refer to the Rule Table.

Procedure to open the Rule Table Editor using the Gerber Launch Pad

1. Select the **Pattern Processing, Digitizing, PDS** button (see Figure 11.4).

2. Select the **Grade Rule Editor** icon to open the Rule Table Editor.

Procedure to open the Rule Table Editor using AccuMark Explorer

1. Select the **AccuMark Explorer** icon from the desktop or from the Start menu (see Figure 11.5).

2. Double click on a storage area to open it. The Rule Table Editor will be created in this storage area.

3. Select **File>New>Rule Table** to open the Rule Table Editor.

Procedure to open the Rule Table Editor while using PDS

1. PDS should be open.

2. Select **File>Open** or the open folder icon.

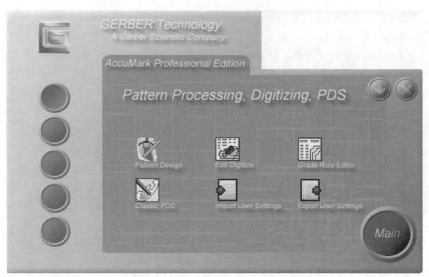

Figure 11.4 Use the Gerber Launch Pad to open a Rule Table Editor.

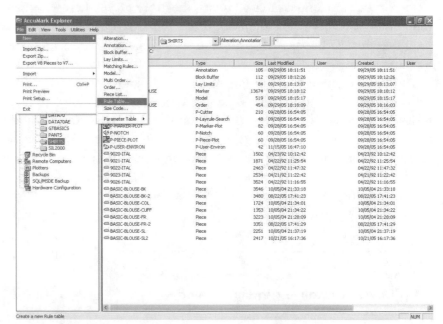

Figure 11.5 Use AccuMark Explorer to open a Rule Table Editor.

3. Right click on the white area (see Figure 11.6).

4. Select **New>Rule Table** to open the Rule Table Editor.

Numeric Versus Alphanumeric— The First Page of the Rule Table Editor

There are two types of tables from which to choose: **Numeric** and **Alphanumeric.** A numeric Rule Table is used for a numbered size line such as 1, 3, 5, 7, 9

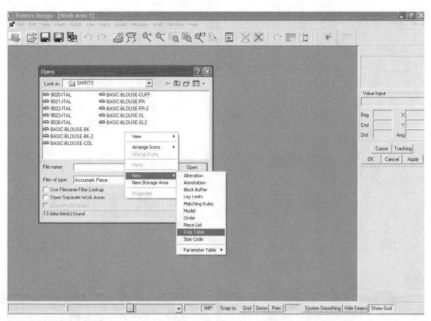

Figure 11.6 Use PDS to open a Rule Table Editor.

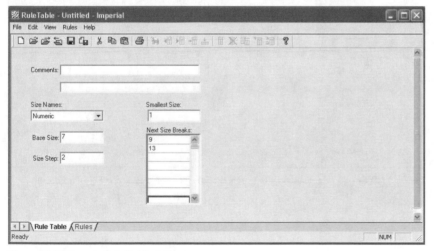

Figure 11.7 Numeric Rule Table Editor.

or 2, 4, 6, 8, 10 (see Figure 11.7). Notice that in each size line, the sizes grow by two; this is known as the **Size Step.** A size line that has consecutive sizes, such as 26, 27, 28, 29, 30, 31, 32, has a size step of one. A size step is used only when setting up a numeric rule table. Described below are the fields found in a numeric rule table. Refer to Figure 11.7 to see where these fields are located.

Comments Use this field to write in any information about the Rule Table that needs to be

referenced in the future. You may place up to 40 characters on each line.

Size Names Select from the two available options: **Numeric** or **Alpanumeric.** This determines which type of Rule Table is being set up. Select **Numeric** for numbered sizes that have a consistent size step. Select **Alphanumeric** for sizes that are numbered, lettered, or both and that do not have a consistent size step.

Base Size This field is used to type in the name of the base size. The piece drafted into the system is considered the base size.

Size Step This field is available only for a numeric Rule Table. Type in 1 if the sizes are consecutive, such as 26, 27, 28, 29, 30, 31, 32. Type in 2 if the sizes jump by two, such as size line 2, 4, 6, 8, 10.

Smallest Size Type in the smallest available size in the size line.

Next Size Break A break size is the point at which the amount a point grades changes. For example, if rule 2 grades 0.500 (½") from sizes 1 to 7, but changes to 0.750 (¾") from sizes 9 to 13, then size 9 is the break size. The last available size in a size line should also be included as a size break. We included size 13 as a size break in Figure 11.7 because it is the last size available in the size line. You are not limited to the number of fields shown on-screen. To add more sizes, use the scroll bar or the up and down arrow buttons.

The **Alphanumeric** Rule Table is used for sizes that are named with letters and/or numbers (see Figure 11.8). For example, size lines S, M, L, XL or 1X, 2X, 3X would require that an Alphanumeric Rule Table be set up for grade rules. Size lines that are numeric but do not have a consistent size step also need to be set up in an Alphanumeric Rule Table. For example, size lines 28, 30, 32, 33, 34, 35, 36 have inconsistent size steps because they change from one to two.

The fields for an alphanumeric table are all the same except that the **Base Size** field is not included. The field **Next Size Break** differs for an alphanumeric rule table.

Next Size Break No size step is required for an alphanumeric table; therefore, all available sizes in a size line, from the next size after the smallest size to largest size, including the base size, must be typed into this area. As stated previously, you are not limited to the number of fields shown on-screen. To add more sizes, use the scroll bar or the up and down arrow buttons.

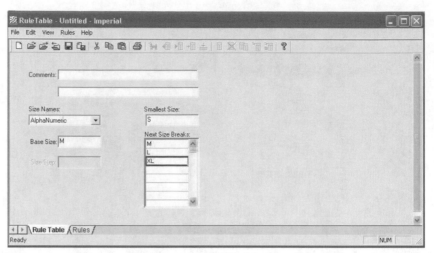

Figure 11.8 Alphanumeric Rule Table Editor.

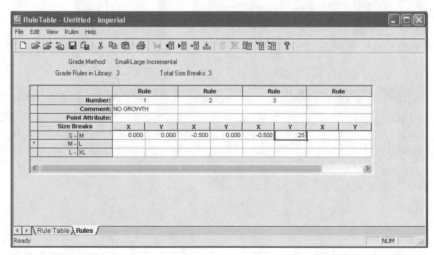

Figure 11.9 Grade rule numbers are entered on the second page of a Rule Table Editor.

Input of Grade Rules—The Second Page of the Rule Table Editor

Now that we have described the difference between an Alphanumeric and a Numeric Rule Table Editor, notice that at the bottom of the editor in Figures 11.7 and 11.8, there are two tabs. The highlighted tab says **Rule Table.** The tab next to it says **Rules.** Select the Rules tab to get to the second page of the Rule Table Editor (see Figure 11.9). Notice that this is the second page of the alphanumeric Rule Table from Figure 11.8. Described below are the fields displayed on the second page of the Rule Table editor.

Grade Method Displays the current grading method chosen.

Grade Rules in Library Displays the number of existing rules input into the table.

Total Size Breaks Displays the *number* of size breaks.

Number Lets you enter the number of the grade rule. Rule numbers need to be entered consecutively. For example, Rules may be input as 1, 2, 4, but not 1, 4, 2. You can see four rules at one time. To enter more rules, use the scroll bar seen at the end of the fields. Remember, you may enter up to 9,999 rules.

Comments This optional field lets you enter a comment about the grade rule. For example, we entered No growth for rule 1 in Figure 11.9.

Point Attribute Point attributes, such as notches, smoothing, non-smoothing, lifting and plunging, or stacking, among others, may be entered in this field. Do remember that if you reuse this rule on several patterns, it will apply these attributes.

Size Breaks The size breaks listed on the first page are listed in this field in two columns.

X and Y Enter the amount the point moves for each size under the appropriate column. If the rule is the same for all sizes in the size line, enter only the first line and the system will copy it to the rest of the sizes. For example, in Figure 11.9, notice under rule 3 that we entered -0.500 (½") and 0.250 (¼") in the first line for size break S–M. The system will copy this amount to the next two size breaks when the next rules are entered.

Saving the Rule Table Editor and Process Recap

When you are finished entering rule numbers, it is time to save the Rule Table. Save the rule table by selecting **File>Save** or **File>Save As.** Save as is recommended because it ensures that your edits are saved in the correct storage area. Select the correct storage area, type in a name for the Rule Table, and click **Save As.**

Procedure to create a Rule Table.

1. Open **Rule Table Editor.**
2. Select **Size Names**: Numeric or Alphanumeric.
3. Enter any comments you may have in the **Comments** field.
4. Enter base size name in the **Base Size** field.
5. Enter a **Size Step** if you are creating a numeric Rule Table.
6. Enter the **Smallest Size** in the size line.

7. Enter all sizes in a size line for an alphanumeric table. Enter the size breaks for a numeric table in the **Next Size Break** field.
8. Select **Rules** tab.
9. Enter all the grade rules.
10. Select **File>Save As** to save the Rule Table.

Drop-Down Menus and Right-Click Options in the Rule Table Editor

The drop-down menus in the Rule Table are similar to other menus already discussed or just very straightforward. Therefore, we will describe some of the functions that are unique to the Rule Table Editor only.

Rule Table Editor—View Menu Functions

Figure 11.10 shows the View menu functions displayed in the Rule Table Editor.

Toolbar Takes the toolbar with icons displayed on or off the screen.

Status Bar Takes the status bar on or off the screen.

Grade Options Allows you to select from three available grading options discussed earlier in the chapter.

Preferences Allows you to view or modify the preferences from the User Environment Table.

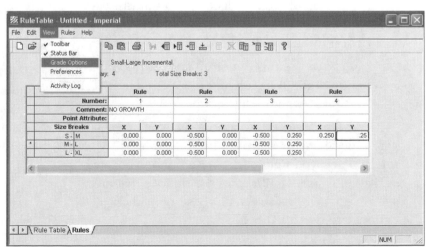

Figure 11.10 View Menu in the Rule Table Editor.

Activity Log Allows you to access and view the activity log.

Rule Table Editor—Rules Menu Functions

Figure 11.11 shows the Rules Menu functions found in the Rule Table Editor.

> *Go to Rule* Use this option to view a specific rule. It is quite helpful when there are numerous rules.
>
> *Go to Size* Use this option to view the rule of a selected size. It is quite helpful to use when reading a rule among many sizes.
>
> *Search* Allows you to search for a duplicate rule. You must select the rule as shown in Figure 11.11 for this option to be available.
>
> *Insert Rule* Use this option to insert a rule between two existing grade rules such as 2 and 4. You must select the rule as shown in Figure 11.11 for this option to be available.

Delete Rule Use this option to delete the selected grade rule altogether. You must select the rule as shown in Figure 11.11 for this option to be available.

Copy Rule Use this option to copy a rule number. It is useful in copying more complicated rules that require a lot of typing.

There are other useful options available to you when modifying grade rules. If the X or Y is selected and you right click, these options become available. Figure 11.12 shows the options that are available when X is selected. These right-click options are described below.

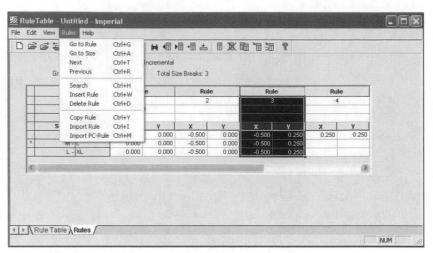

Figure 11.11 Rules Menu in the Rule Table Editor.

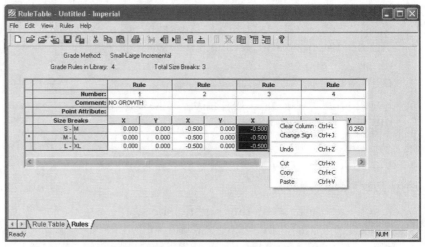

Figure 11.12 Right click options for the Rule Table Editor.

Rule Table Editor—Right-Click Menu Options

Clear Column Clears the selected column. Selecting this option for the example in Figure 11.12 would clear the X rule.

Change Sign Changes the sign of the selected column. Selecting this option for the example in Figure 11.12 would change the sign from negative to positive.

Undo This option undoes the options performed within this right-click menu.

Cut, Copy, and Paste Used to cut, copy, and paste the selected rule, which in Figure 11.12 is the X rule.

Test Your Rule Table Skills

Create a Rule Table Editor using the following guidelines:

1. Create an Alphanumeric table with a size line of S to XL.
2. The base size is Medium.
3. Create six rules with the following X and Y growths:
   a. (0, 0)
   b. (−0.250, 0)
   c. (−0.250, +.250)
   d. (0, +0.250)
   e. (+0.250, +.500)
   f. (+0.500, +0.125)
4. Name the table Women-Tops.
5. Create a Numeric table with a size line of 1 to 7.
6. The base size is 3.
7. The size break is 5.
8. Below are two groups of growths per rule. The second growth is meant for the size break (5) to the larger sizes. Create six rules with the following X and Y growths:
   a. (0, 0)   .(0, 0)
   b. (−0.250, 0)   .(−0.375, 0)
   c. (−0.250, +0.250)   (−0.375, +0.375)
   d. (0, +0.250)   .(0, +0.375)
   e. (+0.250, +0.500)   (+0.375, +0.750)
   f. (+0.500, +0.125)   (+0.750, +0.250)
9. Name the rule table Junior-Tops.

Create/Edit Rules

The Create/Edit Rules menu is used to create new grade rules and modify existing grade rules. The X and/or Y coordinates of a grade rule may be created from scratch while in PDS and later exported to the appropriate Rule Table Editor. Likewise, existing coordinates may be modified and later exported. Grade rules may be created or modified from a point or line segment.

The Create/Edit Rules menu is a great way to modify grade rules because it makes it more visual for the grader. Grade errors may be seen more rapidly when viewed on-screen and fixed in a more efficient manner.

Described below are some of the options and fields found in the user input box that are repeatedly seen in the available functions of the Create/Edit Rules menu. Some of these options are included because an endpoint is technically attached to two lines. AccuMark graders commonly select Always Both so that a grade rule is attached to both endpoints of an intersecting corner. A couple of options show (MK/V8) next to them so that MicroMark and AccuMark users with version V8 know this option is available to them.

Apply Offsets (or Rules) to Joined End Pts

Individual (MK/V8) Applies grade rule change to one endpoint of the two lines an endpoint is attached to as stated above.

Both if Same (MK/V8) Applies grade rule change to both lines attached to the endpoint if the original rule was the same in both lines.

Prev/Next You may view grade rules from the previous and next rules. Create Offset makes the previous and next offset, the X and Y, an available field for input.

Always Both Applies grade rule changes to both endpoints of an intersecting corner regardless of whether the original rules were the same.

Maintain Growths Applies growth only to the sizes that are larger than the one you are modifying. The smaller sizes are not affected.

The following options or fields are also seen repeatedly in the functions under the Create/Edit Rules menu. These are mainly located in the windows that appear when the functions are performed.

Window Form Options and Fields

Piece Name of the piece you are editing.

Grade Line The main grain line on a piece is labeled G0. This is the default grain line. Sometimes grading is based on an alternate grain line. An alternate grain line is labeled G1 and if alternate grain lines exist, they would be labeled G plus the next available consecutive number. To select an alternate grain line, select the drop-down menu to view the other choices and select one.

Point This field lists a reference number if one exists. As a refresher, when a piece is digitized or drafted into the system, a reference point is automatically attached to endpoints or grade points in a sequential order. You may change these numbers to reference alterations done on a piece. For example, a pant leg opening may have points moving for a shorter or longer length for each size to create sizes such as 26A, 26R, 26L.

Grade Rule # Defines the current rule number attached to the point if one exists.

Break Lists the break sizes for the pattern. Alphanumeric size lines list every size as a break. Numeric size lines list break sizes for where the grade changes in growth.

Previous Select this option to view the previous grade point and its rules and other pertinent information.

Next Select this option to view the next grade point and its rules and other pertinent information.

Update Select this option to immediately view grade rule changes on the screen.

Print Select this option to print the window with the current grade rule information on-screen.

OK Exits the window.

Cancel Cancels the function.

Edit Delta

The Edit Delta function may be used to edit the X and/or Y coordinates of a grade rule. The X and/or Y may be cleared for all sizes and recreated. For example, the X rule may be changed for all sizes of a pattern with a size line of 0 to 14. When modified, the rule may be updated so that the new change may be seen immediately on-screen. This new rule may then be sent to the appropriate Rule Table Editor using the Export Rules function, discussed later in the chapter. The X and/or Y coordinates of an individual size range may also be modified. For example, the X rule for sizes 8 through 10 may be changed from 0.250 (¼") to .075 (¾"). Once again, it may then be exported to the Rule Table Editor.

A point on the piece may be selected instead of modifying the **Edit Grade Point** form. You may move the point on-screen as though you were using one of the modifying point functions. If you select this option, the system automatically updates the grade rule to match the new growth for the location where the point is placed. If you wish to edit the grade in this manner, select the point on the piece to move when you are prompted: "Select point on nest or edit form." You will notice that it moves with the mouse so you may place it in a new location. You cannot modify the base size. You can move only the graded sizes.

If you need to move the Edit Grade Point window, hold down the left mouse button on the blue bar and drag the window to a different location. Release the mouse button when you are done.

Procedure for Edit Delta

1. Select **Grade>Create/Edit Rules>Edit Delta.**

2. Select your desired options in the user input box.

3. A user input box states: "Select piece to edit." Left click to select the piece.

4. A user input box states: "Select point on nest to edit." Left click to select the point you want to edit.

5. The **Edit Grade Point** window appears and the prompt states: "Select point on nest to edit or edit form" (see Figure 11.13). Change the grade amount on the form or left click on the point again to move the point on-screen. Select **Update** to view the change. We selected **Clear Y** to clear the Y column and enter 0.375 in its place (see Figure 11.14).

6. Export the rules to a selected Rule Table Editor and save the piece to keep your changes.

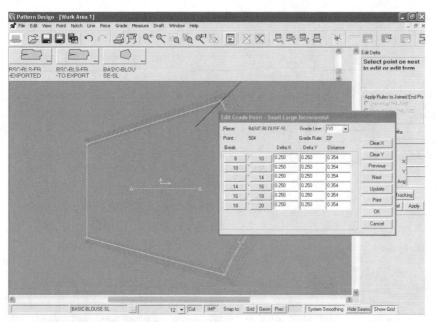

Figure 11.13 Edit Grade Point form appears with current grade rules.

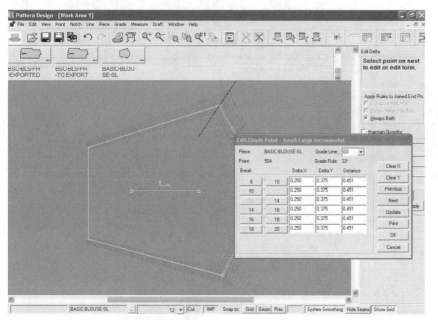

Figure 11.14 The Y portion of a rule was cleared and a new amount was entered in the window displayed.

Note: Repeat Steps 3 through 5 until you have made all your necessary modifications for your work session.

Described below are the available options found in the **Edit Grade Point** window, as seen in Figure 11.13 and 11.14. These options may be used when editing the form itself or when moving a selected

point. Options that are listed but not described below were described at the beginning of this section under Create/Edit Grade Rules.

Edit Grade Point Window Options

Delta X Use this column to edit a grade rule for the X growth.

Delta Y Use this column to edit a grade rule for the Y growth.

Dist Straight measurement from one size to the next size at the current grade point displayed.

Clear X Select this option to clear the X column and input a new amount. The X rule is erased for all sizes. For example, if the X rule is 0.250 (¼") as shown in Figure 11.13 and you want to change it to 0.500 (½"), input 0.500 on the first row/size range so the system copies this amount to all the other sizes when you update them. To edit the X rule on only one size, simply type over the old amount in that size and click on the **Update** button to see the change.

Clear Y Select this option to clear the Y column and input a new amount. It works the same way as Clear X but in the Y direction.

Create Delta

The Create Delta function is used to input new grade rules in the X and/or Y direction. It is meant to create grading on a piece that does not contain any grading, but it may be used on a piece that

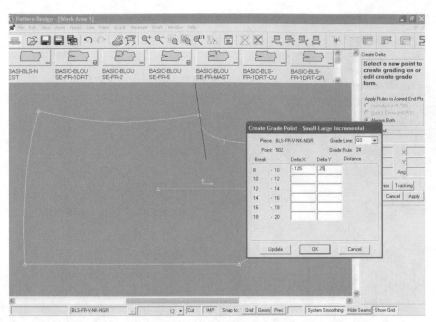

Figure 11.15 Point selected on blouse to create grading. Enter the grade rule in form.

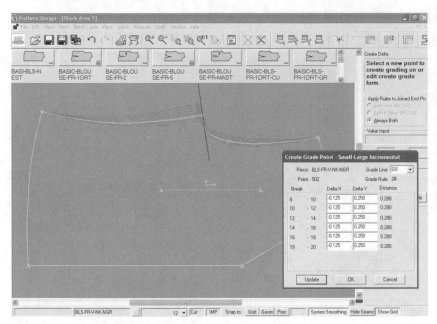

Figure 11.16 Grade rule entered is updated. Grading is seen on-screen immediately.

When entering a rule, only the first line with the first size break needs to be entered if the growth is the same for all the sizes. The system copies this rule for the rest of the sizes when the form is updated (see Figures 11.15 and 11.16). If the rule changes at a later size break, enter the amount at the same time. For example, look at the form in Figure 11.15 and notice the growth that has been entered. If that growth changes from size 14 to 20 to 0.250 for the Delta X and 0.375 for the Delta Y, then enter these amounts in the form and then select update at the end. The rule from sizes 8 to 14 will have 0.125 in the X and 0.250 in the Y entered automatically by the system. Then 0.250 and 0.375 will be entered for sizes 14 to 20.

The piece must have a size line so you can use this function. If it does not have a size line, use an option such as Assign Rule Table or Copy Size Line, both discussed later in the chapter, to apply a size line to the pattern piece.

Procedure for Create Delta

1. Select **Grade>Create/Edit Rules>Create Delta.**

2. Select options you want from the user input box.

3. A user input box states: "Select a point to create grading on." Left click to select a point. We selected the corner of the armhole and side seam, as seen in Figure 11.15.

4. The **Create Grade Point** window appears and the prompt states: "Select a new point to create grading on or edit create form," as shown in Figure 11.15. Enter a grade amount on the form in the **Delta X** and/or **Delta Y.** Select

does have existing grade rules. It is not recommendable to use this function on a piece that already has grading because we find that the Edit Delta function is more appropriate for it. Edit Delta displays the point's current growth and Create Delta does not display any growths. No growths are displayed in the form used during Create Delta so that a clean slate is offered.

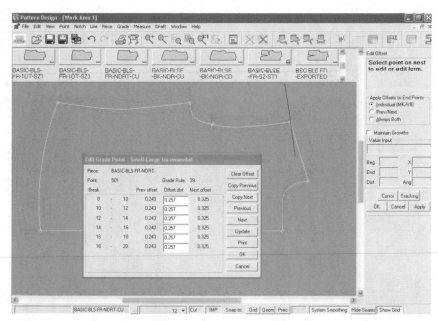

Figure 11.17 Point selected on bodice to modify its offset distance using Edit Offset.

Update to view the change. If you select **Cancel,** you exit the function without applying the grade. See the values we entered in the X and Y columns in Figure 11.15; the updated piece is seen in Figure 11.16.

5. Save the piece to keep the new grade rule changes.

Note: Repeat Steps 3 and 4 to continue creating grade rules on other points. Always select Update on the form to select another point in the piece. If you select **OK,** the last rule entered is processed but you also exit the function.

Described below are the available options found in the **Create Grade Point** window as seen in Figures 11.15 and 11.16. These options may be used when editing the form itself. Options that are listed but not described below were described at the beginning of this section under Create/Edit Grade Rules.

Create Grade Point Window Options

Delta X Use this column to enter a grade rule for the X growth.

Delta Y Use this column to enter a grade rule for the Y growth.

Dist Straight measurement from one size to the next size at the current grade point displayed.

Edit Offset

The Edit Offset option is used to modify rules on a pattern piece. The rules entered are based on a perimeter line versus the X and Y of a grade point. It is comparable with using a ruler to plot where the next line should be located and blending it to the previous or next endpoint.

The best way to illustrate this function is to try the following exercise. Bring two copies of a piece on-screen. Select a point on one piece to edit with Edit Offset. Select the same point on the second piece and enter the same amount, but use the Edit Delta function. This will help you understand the difference between grading off of a grade point using the X and Y growth versus grading off of a perimeter line. A base size may not be modified using Edit Offset.

Procedure for Edit Offset

1. Select **Grade>Create/Edit Rules>Edit Offset.**

2. A user input box states: "Select piece to edit." Left click to select the piece.

3. A user input box states: "Select point on nest to edit." Left click to select the point to modify. We selected to edit the offset of the armhole and shoulder grade point (see Figure 11.17).

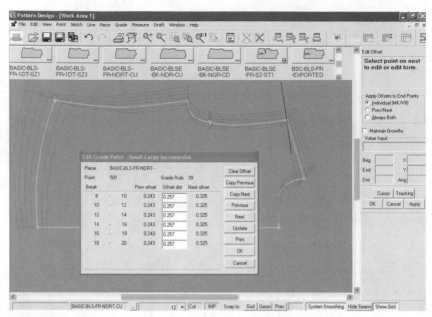

Figure 11.18 Distance from the next offset is copied using Edit Offset.

4. The **Edit Grade Point** window appears and the prompt states: "Select point on nest to edit or edit form." Left click to select another point to modify or edit the form to modify the current grade point and its offset. Click **Update** to see the changes. We selected to edit the form by copying the distance of the next offset as seen in Figure 11.18. Look at the two columns on the right to notice the change.

5. Save the piece to keep the new offset changes.

Note: Repeat Steps 3 and 4 to continue modifying the offset values on other points. Always select **Update** on the form to select another point in the piece. If you select **OK,** the last rule entered is processed but you exit the function.

Described below are the available options found in the **Edit Grade Point** window, as seen in Figures 11.17 and 11.18. These options may be used when editing the form itself. Options listed and not described below were described at the beginning of this section under Create/Edit Grade Rules.

Edit Grade Point Window Options

Prev Offset Displays the offset of the previous point.

Offset Dist Displays the offset distance from one graded size to the next at the selected point.

Next Offset Displays the offset of the next point.

Clear Offset Clears the offset value currently in the grade form.

Copy Previous Copies the previous offset amount into the **Offset Dist** column.

Copy Next Copies the next offset amount into the **Offset Dist** column.

Create Offset

The Create Offset function is used to create rules on a pattern piece based on a perimeter line versus the X and Y of a grade point. It is similar to Edit Offset, but Create Delta is a clean slate meant for pieces with no grading, although it may be used on pieces that have grading already. You cannot alter the base size with this function.

Described below is the only other option found in the Edit Grade Point window not described earlier at the beginning of this section under Create/Edit Grade Rules.

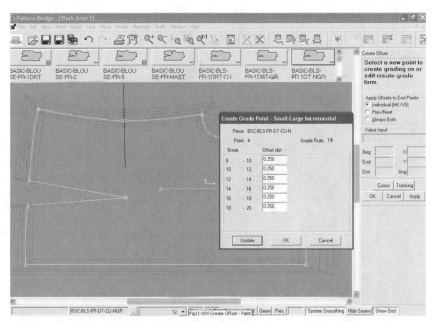

Figure 11.19 Waist area has grade point added with a ¼" offset using the Create Offset function.

Create Grade Point Window Options

Offset Dist Enter the distance to offset the selected point.

Procedure for Create Offset

1. Select **Grade>Create/Edit Rules>Create Offset.**

2. A user input box states: "Select a point to create grading on." Left click on a point on the piece to create grading. We have selected the waist area of the side seam (see Figure 11.19). Neither a grade point nor an endpoint existed in this area, so the system created a grade point.

3. The **Create Grade Point** window appears and the prompt states: "Select new point to create grading on or edit create grade form," as shown in Figure 11.19. Left click to select another point on which to create grading or enter a value in the **Offset Dist** field. Select **Update** to see the grade. We entered 0.250 in the form as seen in Figure 11.19. The grade is now 0.250 (¼") at this point.

Modify Rule

The Modify Rule menu is used to edit rules on an existing piece. You may change grade rule num-

bers and add grade points. You can copy portions of a grade rule or a complete rule from one piece to another. You may even flip and view grade rules on-screen to verify they are correct. Overall, this menu lets you modify rules while viewing the changes on-screen.

Described below are some of the user input box options that will be available during the use of the Modify Rule menu. Remember that an endpoint is technically attached to two lines. AccuMark graders commonly select Always Both.

Apply Rules to Joined End Pts

Individual (MK/V8) Applies grade rule change to one endpoint of the two lines to which an end point is attached.

Both if Same (MK/V8) Applies grade rule change to both lines attached to the endpoint if the original rule was the same in both lines.

Always Both Applies grade rule change to both endpoints of an intersecting corner regardless of whether the original rules were the same.

Change Grade Rule

The Change Grade Rule function is used to change a grade rule number on a pattern piece.

For example, it may be used if an incorrect number was entered previously. It may also be used to apply a grade rule number to a piece after it has been drafted into the system. When a piece is drafted into the system, a No Growth rule, grade rule number 1, is attached to each point the system assumes will grade, so Change Grade Rule is used to enter the appropriate rule number so that it grows properly.

If a piece is created from scratch and the piece has not been assigned a Rule Table or a size line, several warning prompts appear. These prompts include: "PDS not found on disk" and "Grade number not in library." Both these prompts appear because the piece does not have a Rule Table assigned to it nor a size line applied. The system searches for the available Rule Tables in the storage area and then prompts you to select one so that it may read the rule entered from that rule table. The prompt "Library and piece do not have the same number of size breaks" appears next. This occurs because even though it knows which Rule Table to read, that rule table and size line still have not been applied to the piece. Use the function Assign Rule Table or Copy Size Line to resolve this issue.

The grade rule number may also be changed on a pattern by right clicking on the screen when you are out of a function and selecting the Edit Point Info function.

Procedure for Change Grd Rule

1. Select **Grade>Modify Rule>Change Grd Rule.**

2. A user input box states: "Select point(s) with left button." The **Tracking Information** window appears at the same time as the prompt (see Figure 11.20). Left click to select the points to change. If you select more than one point at the same time, all of them will receive the same rule number. The fields

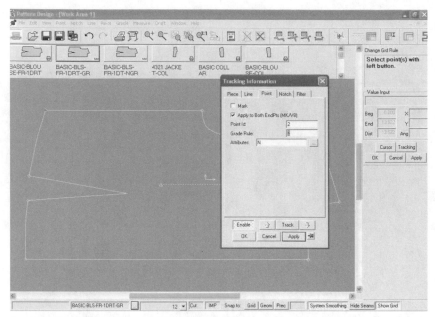

Figure 11.20 Using the Change Grade Rule function to change a grade rule.

become highlighted and available, as shown in Figure 11.20.

3. Type in the new grade rule number in the **Grade Rule** field. Click **Apply** to apply the new rule number to the piece. Click **OK** to exit the window.

4. Save the piece to keep the changes.

Add Grade Point

The Add Grade Point function is used to create a grade point on a pattern piece where one does not exist. Add a grade point at a location where you wish to control the way a point moves. For example, if the notch on a sleeve cap or an armhole is not moving in an acceptable manner, then add a grade point to the notch. You may then use a function such as Edit Delta to change the grade to your liking. Keep in mind that the way a point moves as it grades may affect the overall shape of the line.

Procedure for Add Grade Point

1. Select **Grade>Modify Rule>Add Grade Point.**

2. Select an option under the **Apply Rules to Joined End Pts** area of the user input box. **Always Both** is selected in Figure 11.21, but it

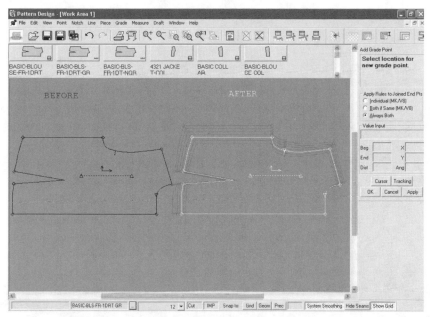

Figure 11.21 Grade point is added to armhole notch using the Add Grade Point function.

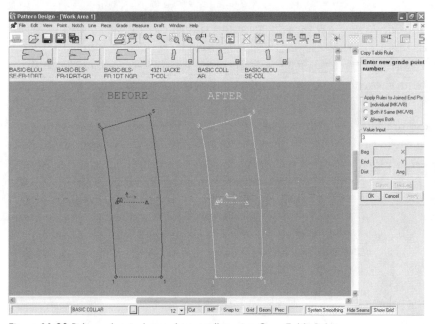

Figure 11.22 Rule number is changed on a collar using Copy Table Rule.

point to the armhole notch, as shown in Figure 11.21.

Copy Table Rule

Use the Copy Table Rule function to enter a rule number for a point on a piece. The system finds the grade rule and its coordinates from the Rule Table that is applied to the piece. This function ensures that a rule is applied from the Rule Table, not from a rule that may exist on the piece. For example, when using the Copy Grade Rule function, discussed in the next section, you may copy a grade rule straight from one piece to another without referencing a Rule Table. The Copy Table Rule function, however, does reference the Rule Table that is applied to the piece.

If the piece is new and does not have a Rule Table applied to it, use the Assign Rule Table function to apply a Rule Table to the piece. If a Rule Table is not applied, a rule will not be applied and the prompt "Size lines do not match" appears.

The example used in Figure 11.22 shows a collar with the grade points turned on so you can see the change. We displayed the grade points by selecting View>Point>Grade Rules.

Procedure for Copy Table Rule

1. Select **Grade>Modify Rule>Copy Table Rule.**

2. Select an option under the **Apply Rules to Joined End Pts** area of the user input box. We selected **Always Both** for the example in Figure 11.22.

3. A user input box states: "Select point(s) to grade, end selection to continue." Left click to

does not matter in this case because the point selected is not an endpoint.

3. A user input box states: "Select location for new grade point." Left click on the location on the piece where you want to add the point. The point may be selected on any size other than the base size. We selected to add a grade

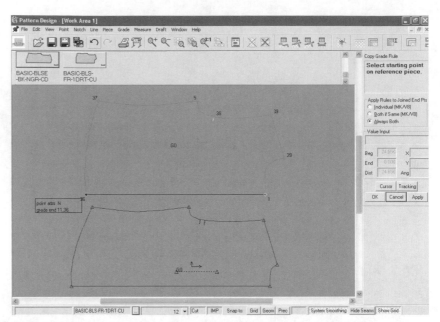

Figure 11.23 Start point selected on front pattern to copy grade rules to a back pattern.

select the point(s) that will receive a grade rule, which highlights them in red. Right click to end selection and continue. We selected the point highlighted in red on the collar shown in Figure 11.22.

4. A user input box states: "Enter new grade point number." Enter the grade rule number under **Value Input.** Press **Enter** on the keyboard or click **OK** when you are done.

Copy Grade Rule

Copy Grade Rule is used to copy a grade rule from one piece to another. It may also be used to copy a grade rule from one point to other points within the same piece. This function is very useful when copying grade rules that are shared from one pattern to another such as a front and back (see Figure 11.23). It saves time since you may copy many points at one time instead of having to change each grade point individually.

Procedure for Copy Grade Rule

1. Select **Grade>Modify Rule>Copy Grade Rule.**

2. Select an option under the **Apply Rules to Joined End Pts** area of the user input box. We selected **Always Both** for the example in Figure 11.23.

3. A user input box states: "Select reference point or piece." Left click to select a point or piece. We selected to copy the grade rules from the front piece shown in Figure 11.23.

4. A user input box states: "Select starting point on reference piece." The reference piece is the pattern with the existing rules you want to copy. Left click on the point from which the system starts copying. We selected the point with grade rule number 36 as shown in Figure 11.23.

5. A user input box states: "Select starting point on target piece." Left click to select the point to which the system starts copying on the target pattern. We selected the same point on the back pattern.

6. A user input box states: "Select 1 point(s) on reference piece to ignore, end selection to continue." This prompt appears only because there are more grade points on the front piece than there are on the back pattern. Left click on the point for the system to ignore. We selected the point in the armhole (see Figure 11.24). The grade rules are copied as shown in Figure 11.25.

Note: This prompt does not appear if the grade points are equal on the reference and target piece.

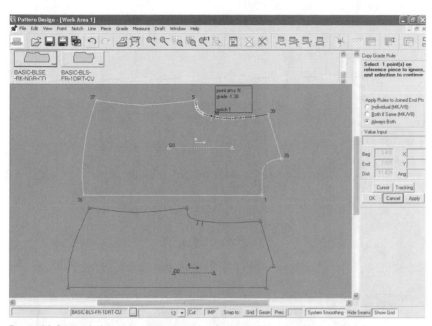

Figure 11.24 Armhole notch point selected to be ignored on the displayed bodice.

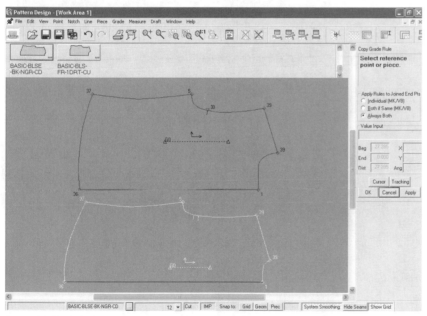

Figure 11.25 Grade rules are completely copied from the front to the back pattern.

Copy X Rule

Use the Copy X Rule function to copy the X rule portion of a grade rule from one point to another. The X rule may be copied from a point on one piece to one or more points on another piece. Figure 11.26 shows a front pattern before and after copying the X rule from one point to another. We copied the X rule from the hem/side seam to the center front at the hem.

Procedure for Copy X Rule

1. Select **Grade>Modify Rule>Copy X Rule.**

2. Select an option under the **Apply Rules to Joined End Pts** area of the user input box. We selected **Always Both** for the example in Figure 11.26.

3. A user input box states: "Select reference point or piece." Left click to select a point or piece, which highlights the point in red. We selected the hem/side seam corner point, as shown in Figure 11.26.

4. A user input box states: "Select target point(s) to assign growth(s) from reference point, end selection to continue." Left click to select the points on the target piece, which highlights them in red. Right click to continue and end the selection. The X rule is copied. We selected the center front/hem corner point, as shown in Figure 11.26.

Copy Y Rule

The Copy Y Rule function is used to copy the Y rule portion of a grade rule from one point to

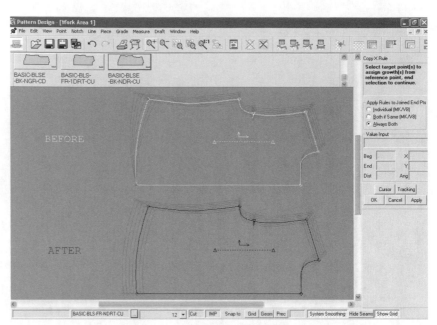

Figure 11.26 The X portion of a grade rule is copied from one point to another.

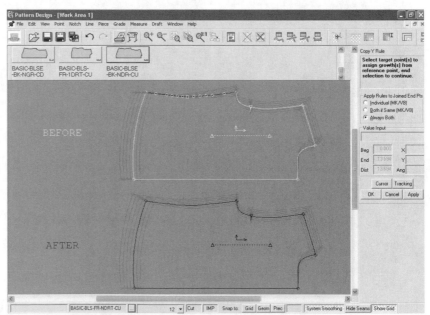

Figure 11.27 The Y portion of a grade rule is copied from one point to another.

another. The Y rule may be copied from a point on one piece to one or more points on another piece. Figure 11.27 shows a front pattern before and after copying the Y rule from one point to another. We copied the Y rule from the armhole/side seam corner point to the hem/side seam corner point.

Procedure for Copy Y Rule

1. Select **Grade>Modify Rule>Copy Y Rule.**

2. Select an option under the **Apply Rules to Joined End Pts** area of the user input box. We selected **Always Both,** as shown in Figure 11.27.

3. A user input box states: "Select reference point or piece." Left click to select a point or piece, which highlights it in red. We selected the armhole/side seam corner point, as shown in Figure 11.27.

4. A user input box states: "Select target point(s) to assign growth(s) from reference point, end selection to continue." Left click to select a point on the target piece, which highlights it in red. Right click to continue and end the selection. We selected the side seam/hem corner point, as shown in Figure 11.27.

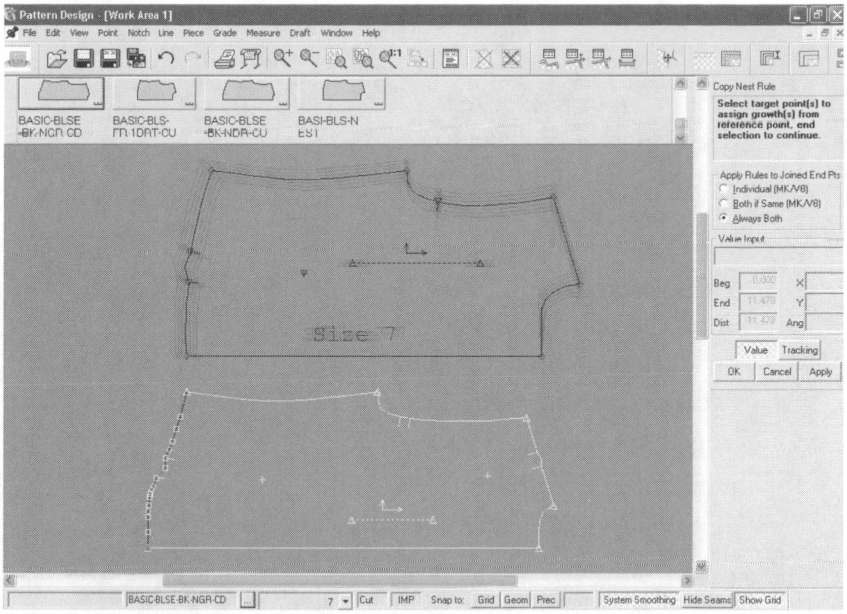

Figure 11.28 The X and Y rule from a nested front pattern is selected to be copied to a back pattern.

Copy Nest Rule

The Copy Nest Rule function is used to copy the X and Y rules from patterns in a nest. The patterns may have been created as a nest using the Create Nest function, discussed later in the chapter, or the patterns may have been stacked using a stacking point. (A stacking point is created on a piece by giving it an F attribute using the Edit Point Info function.)

Procedure for Copy Nest Rule

1. Select **Grade>Modify Rule>Copy Nest Rule.**

2. Select an option under the **Apply Rules to Joined End Pts** area of the user input box. We selected **Always Both** (see Figure 11.28).

3. A user input box states: "Select reference point." Left click to select a point on the piece with the nest you want to copy, which highlights it in red. We selected the point at

the center front on the hem, as shown in Figure 11.28.

4. A user input box states: "Select target point(s) to assign growth(s) from reference point, end selection to continue." Left click on the points to receive the new rule from the nest. Right click to end selection and continue. We selected the point on the center back at the hem as shown in Figure 11.28. The rule is copied (see Figure 11.29).

Note: Repeat function to continue copying grade rules from the nest. Save the pattern pieces to keep your changes.

Copy Nest X

The Copy Nest X function works the same way as Copy Nest Rule, but it copies only the X portion of a grade rule from a graded nest instead of the X and Y.

Procedure for Copy Nest X

1. Select **Grade>Modify Rule>Copy Nest X.**

2. Select an option under the **Apply Rules to Joined End Pts** area of the user input box. We selected **Always Both,** as shown in Figure 11.30.

3. A user input box states: "Select reference point." Left click to select the point on the nested piece with the X rule you want to copy, which highlights it in red. We selected the point at the armhole and shoulder corner, as shown in Figure 11.30.

4. A user input box states: "Select target point(s) to assign growth(s) from reference point, end selection to continue." Left click on the points

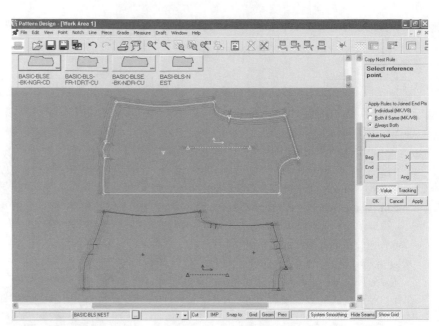

Figure 11.29 Copy Nest Rule function is completed and the rule is copied from the nested pattern.

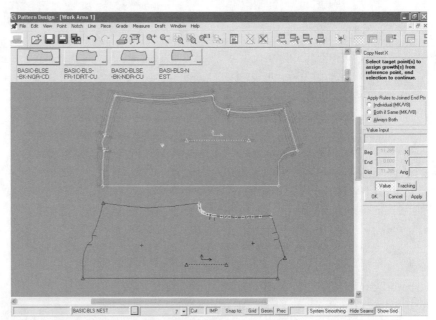

Figure 11.30 The X rule from a nested front pattern is selected to be copied to a target piece.

to receive the new rule from the nest. Right click to end selection and continue. The X portion of the grade rule is copied. We selected the point at the armhole and shoulder of the back pattern, as shown in Figure 11.30. The rule is copied (see Figure 11.31).

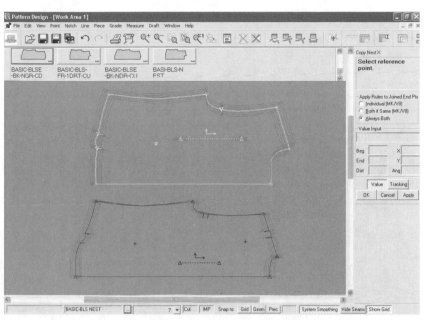

Figure 11.31 Copy Nest X is completed and the rule is copied from the front to the back pattern.

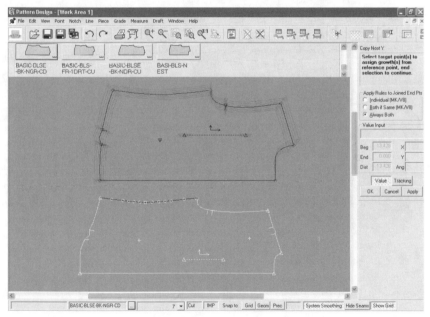

Figure 11.32 The Y rule from a nested front pattern is selected to be copied to a target piece.

Note: Repeat function to continue copying the X rule portion of another grade rule from the nest. Save the pattern pieces to keep your changes.

Copy Nest Y

The Copy Nest Y function works the same way as Copy Nest X, but it copies the Y portion of a grade rule from a graded nest.

Procedure for Copy Nest Y

1. Select **Grade>Modify Rule>Copy Nest Y.**

2. Select an option under the **Apply Rules to Joined End Pts** area of the user input box. We selected **Always Both,** as shown in Figure 11.32.

3. A user input box states: "Select reference point." Left click to select the point on the nested piece with the Y rule you want to copy, which highlights it in red. We selected the point at the armhole and side seam corner, as shown in Figure 11.32.

4. A user input box states: "Select target point(s) to assign growth(s) from reference point, end selection to continue." Left click on the points to receive the new rule from the nest. Right click to end selection and continue. The Y portion of the grade rule is copied. We selected the point at the armhole and side seam of the back pattern, as shown in Figure 11.32. The rule is copied (see Figure 11.33).

Note: Repeat function to continue copying the Y rule portion of another grade rule from the nest. Save the pattern pieces to keep your changes.

Flip X Rule

Use the Flip X Rule function to change the direction the point is moving on the X. For example, if the X is moving in a positive direction, Flip X Rule will flip it to move in the negative direction. This is the equivalent to changing the sign for the X column in the Rule Table Editor, as discussed earlier in the chapter.

Procedure for Flip X Rule

1. Select **Grade>Modify Rule>Flip X Rule.**

2. Select an option under the **Apply Rules to Joined End Pts** area of the user input box. We selected **Always Both** (see Figure 11.34).

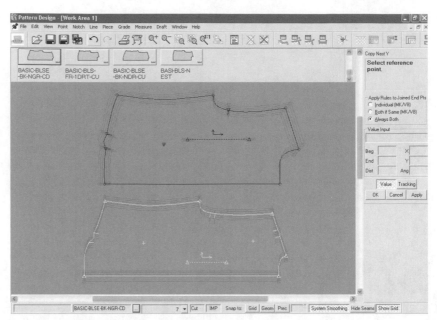

Figure 11.33 Copy Nest Y is completed and the rule is copied from the front to the back pattern.

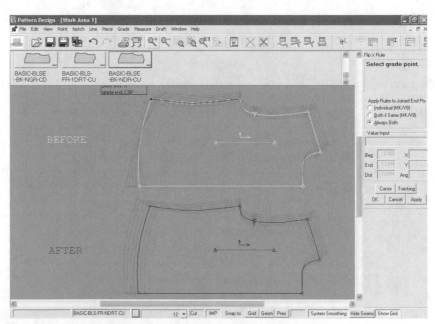

Figure 11.34 The X rule is flipped on the hem of a front pattern that is incorrect.

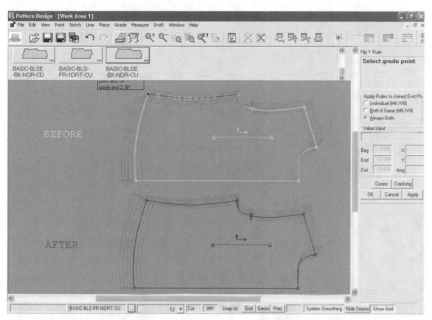

Figure 11.35 The Y rules are flipped on the side seam of a front pattern growing the wrong way.

3. A user input box states: "Select grade point." Left click on the point to change on the base size. The X Rule is flipped. We opted to flip the X rule on the hem as shown in Figure 11.34, where it was obviously incorrect in the "before" version.

Flip Y Rule

The Flip Y Rule function works similar to the Flip X rule function. If the Y is moving in a positive direction, the Flip Y Rule function flips it to move in the negative direction. It is equivalent to changing the sign for the Y column in the Rule Table Editor.

Figure 11.35 shows a front that has a side seam growing in the wrong direction. The small sizes are getting larger and the bigger sizes are growing smaller. We changed the Y rule on the side seam corner grade points so that it grows in the correct direction.

Procedure for Flip Y Rule

1. Select **Grade>Modify Rule>Flip Y Rule.**

2. Select an option under the **Apply Rules to Joined End Pts** area of the user input box. We selected **Always Both,** as shown in Figure 11.35.

3. A user input box states: "Select grade point." Left click on the point to change on the base size. The Y Rule is flipped. We selected the armhole/side seam corner first and repeated the function on the hem/side seam corner, as shown in Figure 11.35.

Copy Size Line

Use the Copy Size Line function to copy the size line from one piece to another. As a reminder, a size line is made up of all the sizes available for a pattern such as XS to XXL or 0 to 14. The size line may also be copied to several pieces at a time. After drafting a few pattern pieces into the system or creating new pattern pieces on-screen from scratch, use this function to give the new patterns a size line. Now that the patterns have a new size line, the next step may be to input the correct grade rules by using the Change Grade Point function or to create new grade rules using the Create Offset or Create Delta functions.

Procedure for Copy Size Line

1. Select **Grade>Copy Size Line.**

2. A user input box states: "Select the reference piece from which to copy the size line." Left

click on the piece that has the size line to be copied. We selected the front pattern in Figure 11.36.

3. A user input box states: "Select the target piece(s) to receive the size line, end selection to continue." Left click on the pieces to select, which highlights them in red. Right click to end the selection and copy the size line. We selected the pocket in Figure 11.36.

Note: You can verify that the size line has been copied by selecting View>Grade>Show Selected.

Edit Size Line

The Edit Size Line menu is used to make modifications on a pattern's existing size line, all the sizes available for a pattern. You may change a base size to a different size, add or delete size steps and add or delete break sizes.

Change Base Size

Use the Change Base Size function to change the current base size of a pattern to another size from its existing size line. A window labeled **Change Base Size** appears during the function and displays the piece's current size line (see Figure 11.37). The new base size is selected from this window. You may need to change the base size so you can perform other functions that do not allow you to modify the base size (Edit Delta), because of preference, or because of an error.

Procedure for Change Base Size

1. Select **Grade>Edit Size Line>Change Base Size.**

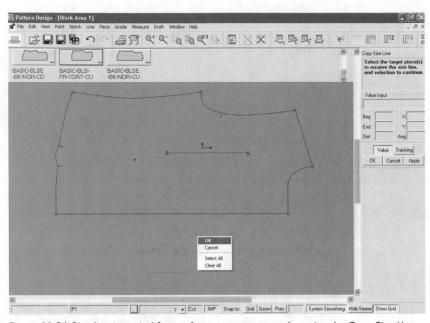

Figure 11.36 Size line is copied from a front pattern to a pocket using the Copy Size Line function.

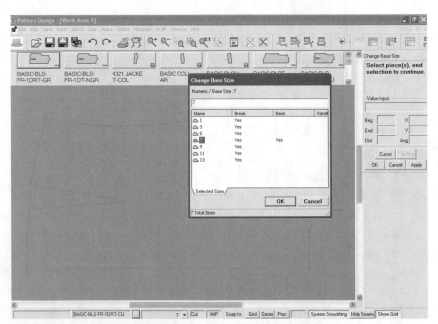

Figure 11.37 Base size is displayed while using Change Base Size function.

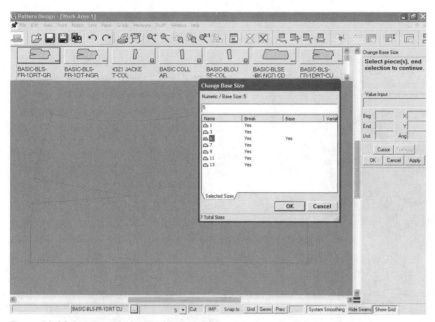

Figure 11.38 Base size is changed on a pattern.

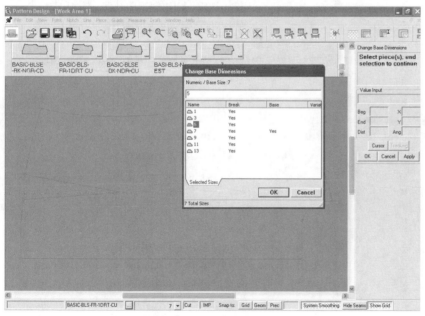

Figure 11.39 Base size 7 is being changed to base size 5.

2. A user input box states: "Select piece(s), end selection to continue." Left click to select the pieces you want to change, which highlights them in red. Right click to continue. Look at the selected piece in Figure 11.37. Notice that at the bottom of the window, next to the piece name, the piece's base size 7 is displayed.

3. The **Change Base Size** window appears. Left click on the size to make it the new base size. Click **OK** to finish. Notice the size has changed at the bottom of the window. We selected to change the base size to 5 (see Figure 11.38).

Change Base Dimensions

The Change Base Dimensions function is used to change the base size to another size's dimension or size. The base size name remains the same, but its size changes. If you have a pattern with a size line of 1 through 13 and a base of 7, and you want to change the base size to look like a 5 but still call it a 7, this function lets you do it.

Procedure for Change Base Dimensions

1. Select **Grade>Edit Size Line>Change Base Dimensions.**

2. A user input box states: "Select piece(s), end selection to continue." Left click to select pieces to change the base size dimensions, which highlights them in red (see Figure 11.39). Right click to continue.

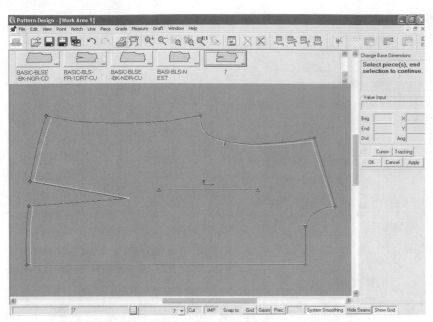

Figure 11.40 Comparison of the old and new base size 7 with size 5 dimensions.

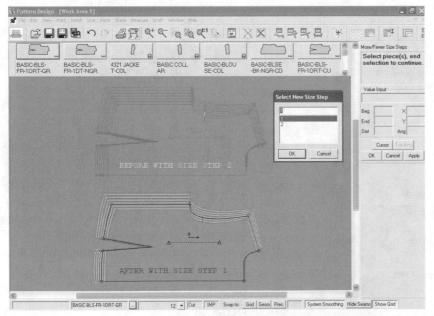

Figure 11.41 Note the difference in patterns when size step is changed from 2 to 1.

dimensions, as shown in Figure 11.39. See Figure 11.40 for a comparison of the old size 7 and the new size 7 with size 5 dimensions, highlighted in white.

More/Fewer Size Steps

Remember that a Numeric Rule Table requires you to have a size step. The More/Fewer Size Steps function allows you to change the size step selected in the current Rule Table to the alternate choice. For example, if the Rule Table you created had a size step of 1, you may change it to 2 withthis function. Alphanumeric Rule Tables do not have a size step so this function cannot be applied to them. The original sizes and dimensions of the patterns remain the same even when you apply this function. This function comes in handy when you need to add in-between sizes. For example, instead of having sizes 2, 4, 6, 8, and 10, you can also have the in-between sizes of 3, 5, 7, and 9.

Procedure for More/Fewer Size Steps

1. Select **Grade>Edit Size Line>More/Fewer Size Steps.**

2. A user input box states: "Select piece(s), end selection to continue." Left click to select the pieces for which you want to change size steps, which highlights them in red. Right click to continue.

3. The **Change Base Size** window appears. Left click on the size with the dimensions you want for the base size. Click **OK** to finish. The base size's dimension changes, but the label is still the same. Notice the size has not changed at the bottom of the window. We selected to change the base size 7 dimensions to size 5

3. The **Select New Size Step** window appears (see Figure 11.41). Select the new size step: 1 or 2. The current size step is highlighted in blue on the first line. Click **OK** to finish. We changed the size step from 2 to 1. Figure 11.41 shows the pieces as a graded nest to display the difference.

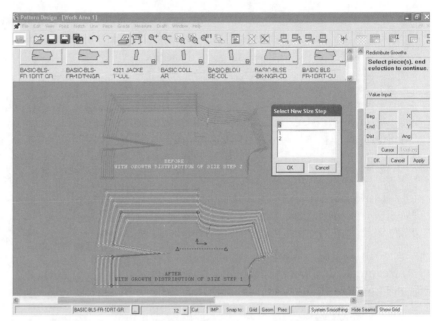

Figure 11.42 Note how the pattern grows twice as much with the displayed redistributed growths.

Redistribute Growths

The Redistribute Growths function is used to change the size step of a pattern by changing the X and Y growths. All sizes are changed except the base size. For example, if the size step is 2 and it is changed to 1 with this function, the sizes will grow twice as much (see Figure 11.42). The reverse would happen if the size step were changed from 1 to 2; the sizes would grow half the amount.

Procedure for Redistribute Growths

1. Select **Grade>Edit Size Line>Redistribute Growths.**

2. A user input box states: "Select piece(s), end selection to continue." Left click to select pieces to change size steps as seen in Figure 11.42. Right click to continue.

3. The **Select New Size Step** window appears, as seen in Figure 11.42. Select the new size step: 1 or 2. The current size step is highlighted in blue on the first line. Click **OK** to finish. We changed the size step from 2 to 1. Figure 11.42 shows the pieces as a graded nest to display the difference.

Edit Break Sizes

Use the Edit Break Sizes function to add or delete size breaks in a pattern. Remember that in a numeric Rule Table, a size break is the size where the growth changes and for an alphanumeric Rule Table, every size is considered a size break.

Since break sizes are different for alphanumeric and numeric Rule Tables, let's use the following numeric and alphanumeric grade rules, each in a separate pattern, as examples.

Table 11.4 shows a grade rule of a front pattern with an alphanumeric size line. We need to add a larger size: size 2XL. Therefore, we need to add a size break to this size line. When 2XL is added, it

---

Table 11.4: Example of an Alphanumeric size line for a grade rule on a front pattern

Rule #2

Size	X	Y
XS–S	+0.125	0
S–M	+0.125	0
M–L	+0.250	0
L–XL	+0.250	0

will take the grading growth of the previous size break. After 2XL is added to the size line, the rule will now have the following growth added:

XL-2XL   + 0.250   0

If a size break needs to be deleted for an alphanumeric size line, highlight the size and select **Delete Break.** The deleted size is no longer be available for ordering and the remaining sizes keep their original dimensions.

Table 11.5 shows a grade rule of a front pattern with a numeric size line. We need to add a smaller size to this size line, size 0. Size 0 takes on the growth of the next size—in this case, the growth of size break 2 to 6. Since this function adds or deletes size breaks, size 0 is considered a new size break in the size line. After size 0 is added to the size line, the rule will now have the following size break and growth added:

0-2   + 0.062   0

As in example 1, if a size break needs to be deleted from a numeric size line, highlight the size and select **Delete Break.** Still using the rule shown in example 2, if size 10 is deleted, the system calculates the average of size breaks 6 to 10 and 10 to 14 and the rule would show the size break as follows:

6-14   + 0.188   0

After adding or deleting a size break using Edit Break Sizes, if the new growths in the rule are not correct for the style, then use a function such as Edit Delta to modify the rule. If **Cancel** is selected in the **Edit Break Sizes** window, the changes entered will not be processed. Remember to save pieces that have been modified to keep your changes.

Procedure for Edit Break Sizes

1. Select **Grade>Edit Size Line>Edit Break Sizes.**

2. A user input box states: "Select piece(s), end selection to continue." Left click to select the pieces for which you want to change size steps. which highlights them in red (see Figure 11.43). Right click to continue.

3. The **Edit Break Sizes** window appears as seen in Figure 11.43. Add or delete a size break.

   To **Add Break:** Type in the new size break to add and press the Tab key on the keyboard. The new size break appears in the **Size** column. Click **OK** to finish process.

   To **Delete Break:** Highlight the break size you want to delete. Select **Delete Break** option. Click **OK** to finish process.

Table 11.5: Example of a Numeric size line for a grade rule on a front pattern		
Rule #2		
Size	X	Y
2–6	+0.062	0
6–10	+0.125	0
10–14	+0.250	0

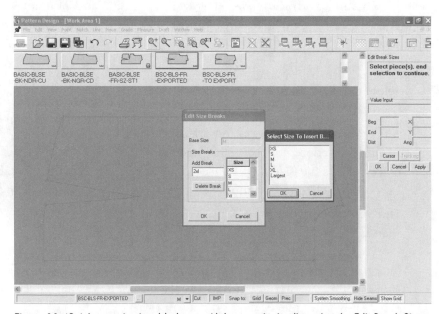

Figure 11.43 A larger size is added to an Alphanumeric size line using the Edit Break Sizes function.

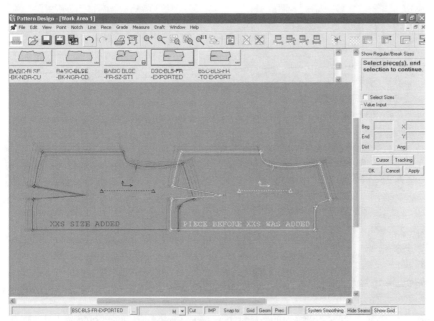

Figure 11.44 Pattern shown before and after largest size 2XL was added with Edit Break Sizes.

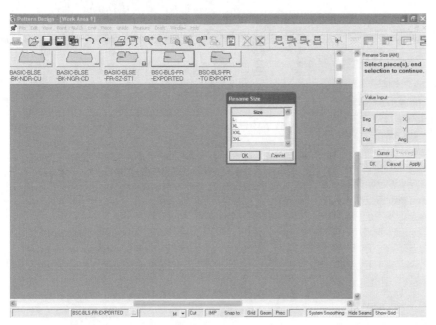

Figure 11.45 Size 2XL was renamed in this pattern's size line to XXL using Rename Size.

Figure 11.44 shows the pattern piece before and after so you can note the difference.

Note: You may use the Show Regular/Break Sizes function to view the new size breaks.

Rename Size

The Rename Size function may only be used to rename a size in an alphanumeric size line. For example, it may be used to rename size 2XL to XXL (see Figure 11.45).

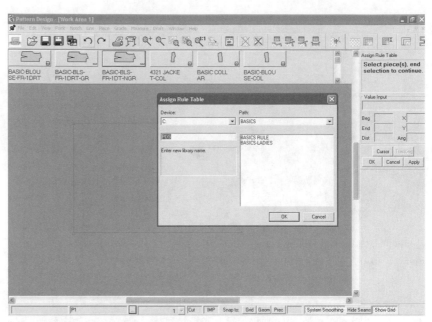

Figure 11.46 A Rule Table is applied to a new piece using Assign Rule Table.

Procedure for Rename Size

1. Select **Grade>Edit Size Line>Rename Size.**

2. A user input box states: "Select piece(s), end selection to continue." Left click to select the pieces for which you want to rename the size as seen in Figure 11.45. Right click to continue.

3. The **Rename Size** window appears. Left click to highlight and select a size to rename, which highlights if in blue. Type in a new size name. Click **OK** to finish.

4. Save the piece to keep your changes.

Assign Rule Table

The Assign Rule Table function is used to apply a new Rule Table to a piece. The piece may be a newly created piece or an existing piece. When the Rule Table is applied, the piece will assume the base size and size line from the Rule Table.

Notice that in Figure 11.46 on the left-hand side under the Device field, it states PDS. This is because a Rule Table is being assigned to a new piece. If the piece already has a Rule Table assigned to it and this function is being used to assign a new Rule Table, the existing Rule Table applied to the piece appears in place of PDS. If an existing piece is assigned a new Rule Table and the grade rules on the piece do not exist in it, the points with these rules will not have any growth. Change the grade rules or create new grade rules to resolve this issue.

Procedure for Assign Rule Table

1. Select **Grade>Assign Rule Table.**

2. A user input box states: "Select piece(s), end selection to continue." Left click on the pieces you want to select, which highlights them in red. Right click to end selection and continue.

3. The **Assign Rule Table** window appears as does the prompt: "Enter new library name," as shown in Figure 11.46. Left click to highlight and select the Rule Table to apply to the piece and click **OK** to finish.

Create Nest

The Create Nest function is used to create a nest from a pattern of different individual sizes. Say you have a blouse pattern that has seven different sizes for the front, the back, and the sleeve. Since all the

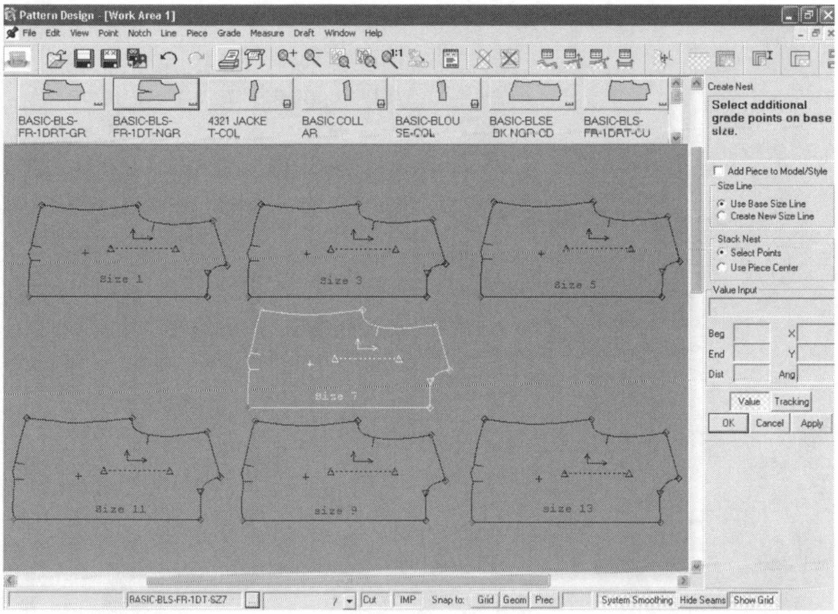

Figure 11.47 Base size and stack points selected to create a nest of all the patterns using Create Nest.

pieces are separated, there is no nest. Look at Figure 11.47, which shows a pattern for a front in seven different sizes. We annotated each piece in this example for educational purposes using the Annotate Piece function. We placed the base size in the center. The Create Nest function may be used to place all these pieces in a nest and grade rules may be created from the nest later using functions such as Copy Nest, Copy Nest X, or Copy Nest Y.

Procedure for Create Nest

1. Select **Grade>Create Nest.**

2. Select the options you want in the user input box.

3. Check the box next to **Add Piece to Model/Style** if you want to add the nested piece to a selected model.

4. In the **Size Line** area, select from one of the two available options.

    Use Base Size Line is selected so that the nest will be created using the size line that exists on the base size.

    Create New Size Line is selected to create a new size line for the newly created nest

piece. The size line may be alphanumeric or numeric.

We selected **Use Base Size Line** in Figure 11.47.

5. In the **Stack Nest** area, select from one of the two available options.

    Select Points is used to allow a point to be selected on each piece as the stacking point. We selected the hem/center front corner as the stacking point on each size in Figure 11.47.

    Use Piece Center is used when you want all selected pieces for the nest to stack at the piece's center point.

6. A user input box states: "Select base size for nest." Left click on the piece to be used as the base size. We selected the center piece—annotated size 7—in Figure 11.47 as the base.

7. A user input box states: "Select point of piece to build nest from for break size.1." The end of this prompt states 1 because it detected that our size line begins with size 1. This prompt is repeated for each size in the size line when using the option **Use Base Size Line** or for each size you entered if using **Create New**

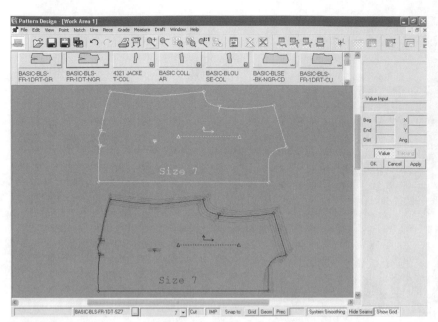

Figure 11.48 Nest created from separate patterns shown with and without the nest of all pieces.

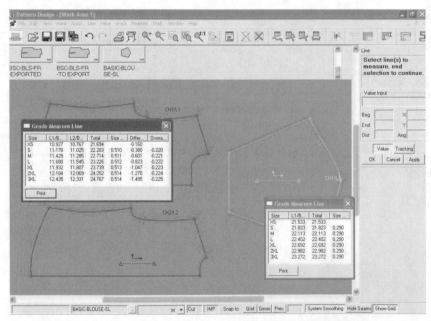

Figure 11.49 Line function is used to measure sleeve cap against front and back armholes for comparison.

Size Line. Left click to select the point on the size stated in the prompt. We selected the hem/center front corner point on each piece, as shown in Figure 11.47.

8. A user input box states: "Select additional grade points on base size." Left click on any points you wish to be shown as grade points. We selected the armhole notch as an additional grade point (see Figure 11.48). Right click to end the selection. The nest piece is created and attached to mouse. Left click to set down the piece.

9. A user input box states: "Enter piece name." Enter a name for the new nest and click **OK** or press **Enter** on the keyboard.

Note: For Figure 11.48, we displayed the nest using the Show All Sizes function.

Measure

The Measure submenu has five options used to measure a pattern. Most of these functions also exist in the main Measure menu in the PDS function bar. Therefore, all the functions have been previously discussed in Chapter 3 except the Line function. This function is unique to this menu and described below.

Line

The Line measure function is used to measure one or more lines. One or more lines may be selected on one pattern piece and compared with another set of selected lines on a second pattern. For example, a sleeve cap may be selected to be measured and compared with the armhole front and back that it will sew into eventually (see Figure 11.49). This function is an excellent way to see how these lines measure in each graded size. It lets you assess the situation and make any necessary pattern or grading modifications.

The fields seen in the **Grade Measure Line** window that appears when performing this function are described below.

Grade Measure Line Window Columns

Size Displays graded sizes for the selected pattern piece.

L1/(Name of Piece) Displays the measurement of line 1 plus the name of the piece on which it is selected. If more than one line is selected, another column appears with the line number. For example, if a second line is selected, the column is titled L2/(Name of the Piece).

Total Displays the length of the selected line. If more than one line is selected in a group, the total of all lines combined is displayed.

Size Difference Group 1 The difference of the line length between the sizes is displayed for each group selected.

Difference Between Totals This column appears if more than one group is selected. It displays the difference of the totals of one group with the totals of another group.

Overall Size Difference This column displays if more than one group is selected. It shows the difference of the line length of the groups.

Use the Line function to

- see the measurement of a line for each graded size. For example, view the measurement of a sleeve cap in each graded size.

- see the measurement of one line compared with another line in each available graded size. For example, compare the front pant inseam with the back pant inseam.

- compare one line to several other lines for each graded size. For example, measure the sleeve cap against the front and back armhole.

Procedure for Line

1. Select **Grade>Line.**

2. A user input box states: "Select line(s) to measure, end selection to continue." Left click

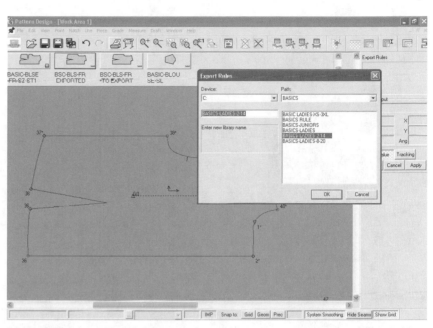

Figure 11.50 Rules displayed on the pattern piece are exported to the selected Rule Table.

to select lines, which highlights them in red. Right click to continue. The **Grade Measure Line** window appears with line measurements. We selected the sleeve cap and right clicked to view its measurements in the displayed chart. Since we want to compare it with the front and back armhole, we repeated this step. We selected the front and the back armhole and then right clicked to select them as the second group and another chart appeared with measurements, as seen in Figure 11.49.

Export Rules

Grading is modified quite often on-screen. Many times it is much easier to grade on-screen because it is more visual. After changes have been made to an existing grade rule, the rule appears with an asterisk next to it to represent that it has been modified. Export Rules may be used to send these new rules to a selected Rule Table Editor. The Rule Table Editor they are being sent to must have the same size line and base size. This prevents you from having to type each one of these rules into the Rule Table Editor. The system automatically assigns the next available rule numbers to the piece. For example, the Rule Table to which we

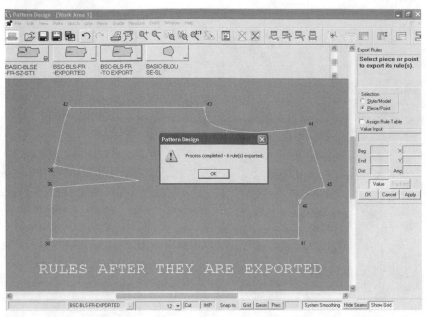

Figure 11.51 Rule numbers are assigned new rule numbers after being exported.

exported the rules in Figure 11.50 had 40 rules. Therefore, the system assigned rule numbers 41 to 46 to the six new grade rules.

Procedure for Export Rules

1. Select **Grade>Export Rules.**

2. The **Export Rules** window appears, as seen in Figure 11.50. Left click to select the name of the Rule Table to which you want to send the new rules and click **OK** to enter.

3. A user input box states: "Select piece or point to export its rule(s)." Left click on the point which you want to export or left click on the piece to have all the points exported, which highlights them in red. Right click to continue. We selected to export all the rules on the piece. Figure 11.51 shows the piece after the rules have been exported. Notice the numbers changed and we are informed of the number of rules that were exported successfully.

Test Your Knowledge

Select the correct answer from the word bank to fill in the blanks.

Word Bank

Add Grade Point	Negative
Change Base Size	Positive
Change Grade Rule	Rename Size
Copy Grade Rule	Rule Table Editor
Copy Nest Rule	Shared
Create Delta	Size Break
Edit Delta	Size Line
Edit Break Sizes	Size Names
Export Rules	X
Grading Methods	Y
More/Fewer Size Steps	

1. Grade rules are created using _____ and _____ coordinates.

2. The X and Y growths of a grade rule may move in a _____ and/or _____ direction.

3. Pattern pieces should be laid out in the same direction—for example, all necks on the right side—so that grade rules may be _____.

4. Small to Large Incremental, Base Up-Down Incremental, and Base Up-Down Cumulative are all known as _____.

5. Where are all grade rules set up for a pattern?
   _____

6. A Rule Table Editor is at least _____ pages long.

7. A _____ is the size where the growths of a grade rule changes.

8. A Rule Table is set up as a Numeric or Alphanumeric table in the _____ field of the Rule Table Editor.

9. The available sizes or size range of a pattern is known as its
   _____.

10. Existing grade rules may be modified on a piece by using the _____ function. Either the form that appears may be changed or a point on the nest may be moved as if though modifying points.

11. Grading may be created on a piece using a blank slate form and based on X and Y growths by using the _____ function.

12. A grade rule number may be changed or applied to a pattern piece using the _____ function.

13. If a grade point is needed in an area where the movement or growth of a point needs to be controlled, such as an armhole notch, use the _____ function.

14. The _____
function may be used to copy one or more grade rules from one pattern
piece to another.

15. The X and Y growths of a grade rule may be copied from a graded nest
to another piece by using the
_____ function.

16. The base size determined in the Rule Table Editor may be changed on a
pattern piece in PDS by using the
_____ function.

17. The size line of a pattern is 26, 28, 30, 32, 34, and 36. You need to add
some in between sizes, so you use the
_____ function to
accomplish this task.

18. The _____
function may be used to add or delete a size break.

19. _____ may be used to rename a size
in an alphanumeric Rule Table.

20. The _____ function is used to send
new or modified rules from PDS to a selected Rule Table Editor.

True or False

1. A Rule Table Editor should be set up per style or model. TRUE or FALSE
2. Every size in an Alphanumeric Rule Table is considered a size break.
   TRUE or FALSE
3. Grading may be created or edited based off of perimeter lines versus X
   and Y grade points using the Edit Offset or Create Offset functions. TRUE
   or FALSE
4. A size line may be applied to a pattern piece by using the Assign Rule
   Table or Copy Size Line functions. TRUE or FALSE
5. Part of a grade rule, such as the X growth, may not be copied from one
   pattern piece to another. TRUE or FALSE
6. The direction a grade rule is growing, negative or positive, may not be
   changed once it is created. TRUE or FALSE
7. The dimensions of a base size may be changed using the Change Base
   Dimensions function. TRUE or FALSE
8. The More/Fewer Size Steps function may be used to change the size steps
   of an Alphanumeric table. TRUE or FALSE
9. The Rename Size function may be used to rename a size in a numeric size
   line. TRUE or FALSE
10. The Line function in the Measure submenu is used to see the length of one
    or more lines on all the graded sizes. TRUE or FALSE

Answers for Test Your Skills—X and Y Quadrant

Rule #1: <u> 0 </u> X <u> 0 </u> Y   Rule #5: <u> + </u> X <u> + </u> Y

Rule #2: <u> − </u> X <u> 0 </u> Y   Rule #6: <u> + </u> X <u> + </u> Y

Rule #3: <u> − </u> X <u> + </u> Y   Rule #7: <u> + </u> X <u> + </u> Y

Rule #4: <u> − </u> X <u> + </u> Y

CHAPTER TWELVE

Marker Making

Objective

Marker Making is the process in which pattern pieces are positioned in the best possible way to save fabric. This layout is then plotted out on plotter paper and placed on top of the fabric to be cut. A fully automated company, however, does not have to do this because the image of the layout is transmitted electronically through network cables directly to an automated cutting machine.

Marker Making is equivalent to the manual process of laying out pieces to cut out a shirt or sample garment. Students generally try to maximize their fabric to economize on materials, time, and money. Students try to save a couple of yards of fabric in the same way a company tries to save an inch or more per layer. If a company saves 3 inches on one marker, those 3 inches are multiplied by the number of fabric layers, or **ply,** laid out to be cut. Therefore, if a company saves 3 inches on 50 ply of fabric, then they save 150 inches (3 times 50), which translates to more than 4 yards of fabric. Saving money on the cost of fabric makes a garment profitable because it brings down the manufacturing costs.

When you are done reading this chapter, you should understand how to create an order for a marker, process it, and create a marker using basic Marker Making functions. You should also have an understanding of the tables that are used to create the order for the marker. Please remember that not all functions available within the tables and editors and Marker Making software are discussed in this chapter.

This chapter allows you to gain skills in the following areas:

- Preparation prior to the creation of a marker
- Interpret a Model Editor for a marker
- Annotation Editor for markers
- Block Buffer Editor
- Lay Limits Editor
- Order Editor
- Processing the order
- Activity Log
- Marker Making, opening a marker
- The marker-making screen display
- Placing pieces in a marker
- Marker Making Toolbox
- File menu
- Edit menu
- View menu
- Piece menu
- Bundle menu
- Marker menu
- Tools menu

Preparation Prior to the Creation of a Marker

There are a few tables you need to create or that must already exist before you can create and process a marker. Once you have set up these tables you can create an order, known as the

Order Editor, for the marker. Figure 12.1 shows the two-page Order Editor that requires you to fill in mandatory information so you can process a marker. This order includes essential information for a marker, such as the model and sizes to be cut and the fabric width. Some of the fields are mandatory and others are optional, which is explained throughout the chapter. Then you process the order using the **Order Process Form,** which lets you open the marker in Marker Making, provided you made no errors.

You need to set up the following tables before you can order a marker:

- *Model Editor:* Lets you list pieces needed to create a garment or style.

- *Annotation Editor:* Lets you give titles to the marker and label individual pieces.

- *Block Buffer Editor:* Lets you protect pieces that you are cutting. This is an optional table.

- *Lay Limits Editor:* Lets you determine the layout of pieces and fabric.

You can access all four of these tables through the Launch Pad by selecting the Marker Creations, Editor button or through the AccuMark Explorer File>New menus when a storage area is selected.

The following tables and functions are used to place an order and process a marker:

- *Order Editor:* Lets you determine elements of a marker such as the marker name, marker width, and which of the tables listed above will be used for a marker. See Figure 12.1 for an example of a blank Order Editor.

- *Order Process* or *Generate Marker:* Lets you process an order, checks for errors, and sends the information to Marker Making software.

- *Activity Log:* Lets you log errors and activity.

All of these tables are discussed in this chapter in more detail, except for the Model Editor and the

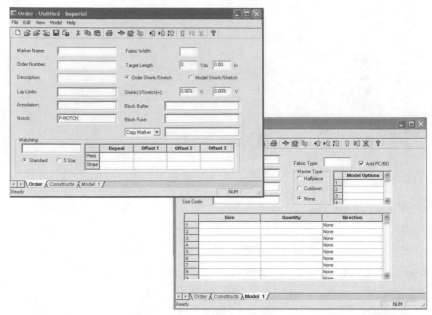

Figure 12.1 The order and model page of an Order Editor are each opened side by side for display.

Annotation Editor, which have already been discussed in previous chapters. Review those chapters to refresh your memory.

How Is a Model Editor Interpreted for a Marker?

The **Model Editor** may be considered a computerized cutter's must because it lists all the pattern pieces used to create a model/style. The Model Editor is one of the tables you input into the Order Editor. If you do not list a model in the order, then no pattern pieces will exist when you create a marker; therefore, you must create a Model Editor.

Look at Figure 12.2 to familiarize yourself with the model and the pattern pieces required to make 3400 Blouse. Then look at Figure 12.3 and notice that two blouses have been laid out in a marker. One set is labeled A and the other is labeled B: These are bundle codes. While this is not the best layout for this marker because we could lay out the pieces better to save fabric, it serves for a visual of how the pattern pieces in a Model Editor will appear in a marker. For example, the back pattern is a mirrored piece, "cut on the fold," and that is why we need to cut out only one for this blouse, as stated in the Model Editor. Notice in Figure 12.3 that this piece is opened to create the blouse properly. You are probably accustomed to folding your fabric and cutting this piece on the fold, as shown on the top left of Figure 12.3; but in a production setting, the fabric is usually laid out open as shown on the right side of Figure 12.3 and therefore the pieces are laid out opened.

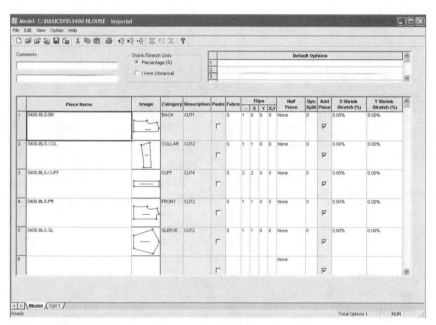

Figure 12.2 Model Editor for a blouse.

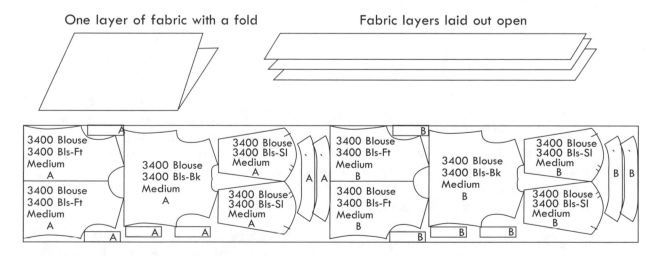

Figure 12.3 A marker layout of two blouses.

Test Your Model Editor Skills

Let's create a model using pieces that are currently in your storage area. You should have a basic sloper drafted into the system that includes a front, back, and sleeve pattern. Open these pieces in PDS and save them with the following names so that it duplicates each piece with a different name:

1. 123 Blouse Front
2. 123 Blouse Back
3. 123 Blouse Sleeve

If you do not have an existing collar or cuff in the model, then:

1. create a collar in PDS using the Collar function.
2. create a Cuff in PDS using the Rectangle function.
3. apply a size line to the new collar and cuff so that they match the other pattern pieces' size lines.
4. add appropriate grading to the collar and the cuff.
5. Name the collar 123 Blouse Collar.
6. Name the collar 123 Blouse Cuff.

Create a model named 123 Blouse using the pattern pieces as we have named them above. Use Figure 12.2 as a guide for filling out the columns under the Flips area.

Note: If you do not have an existing sloper, use the model named Ladies-Blouse in the DATA70 storage area. Follow the instructions above to recreate the pattern pieces with the new names and the 123 Blouse model. Make sure to save them in your storage area.

Annotation Editor for Markers

Chapter 7, the chapter on plotting, discussed the Annotation Editor because it was one of the tables needed prior to plotting pattern pieces. The Annotation Editor is used along with other tables to set up the order to create a marker, but it has additional information included in it that is com-monly directed to markers. The Annotation Editor is also used prior to plotting a marker, so it is used in the Marker Plot form as well, discussed later in the chapter. The following are some of the things to keep in mind when you create an Annotation Editor for markers:

Marker Heading This usually includes the marker name, model length, and width.

Pattern Piece Information You might plot information on pieces in a marker that is different from information you plot on a sample or when you verify pattern modification. Patternmakers and designers are usually the only ones that see the pattern for a plotted sample garment. On the contrary, when you lay out a marker the people who lay out the fabric and marker, sort the pieces, handle quality control, and more see the patterns, too. A sleeve pattern may obviously be a sleeve to a patternmaker, but may not be that obvious to someone else in the production of the garment. Since a pattern for a marker may pass through many hands, it is important that certain vital information is included in each piece to prevent sorting or sewing errors. For example, a bundle code may be plotted in each pattern piece to prevent losing a piece by placing it in the wrong group; all patterns with bundle code A create one blouse and those with bundle code B create another blouse. Information annotated in patterns may prevent unnecessary questions that lead to lost production time. Typical annotation for a piece in a marker may include a model name, piece name, size, and bundle code.

Figure 12.4 shows an example of an Annotation Editor set up for a marker order, marker plotting, or both. Let's review what each line states under the Category and Annotation columns for this example.

Line 1 The **Default** line is used to enter information that needs to be plotted inside each pattern piece. Therefore, each piece of information is listed on a separate line including

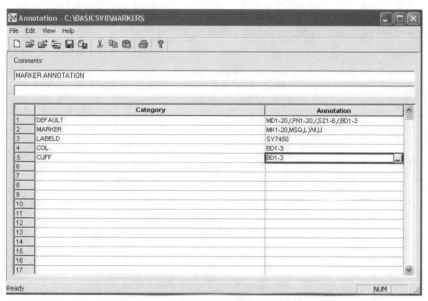

Figure 12.4 Annotation Editor set up for a marker.

the model name first, the piece name second, the size third, and the bundle code last.

Line 2 The **Marker** line is set up for the marker heading. Several markers are commonly plotted at the same time, then rolled up and set aside until the fabric is laid out for the marker to be cut. The marker heading may be plotted at a selected location so that when the roll is picked up and ready to be laid out, you can tell which marker is which without having to open everything up. This is handy when the marker is several yards long.

Line 3 In this case, the **Label** line refers to points labeled D commonly used for drill holes. The drill hole may be used for pattern placement. It is typical for a company to decide whether a drill hole is actually drilled.

Lines 4 and 5 The categories of pieces are listed in each of these lines. We are opting to plot only the bundle code in these pieces because the information to be plotted on all other pieces is too much to fit into the size and shape of these pattern pieces. If you consider the **Default** line as the rule for all pieces that are plotted with this annotation, then lines 4 and 5 serve as exceptions to that rule.

Test Your Annotation Editor Skills

1. Set up an Annotation Editor for makers using the same information shown in Figure 12.4.
2. Name the table Marker Annotation.

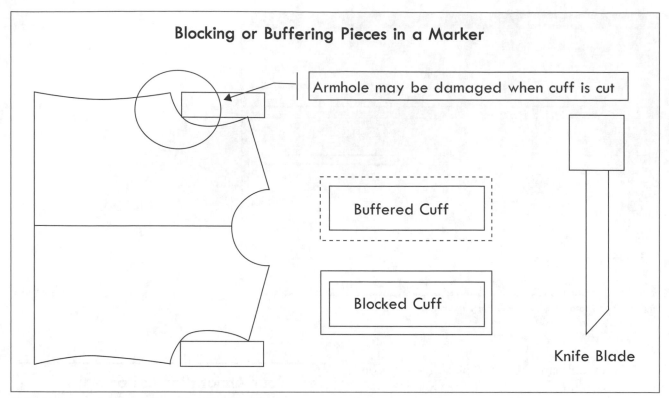

Blocking or Buffering Pieces in a Marker

Armhole may be damaged when cuff is cut

Buffered Cuff

Blocked Cuff

Knife Blade

Figure 12.5 Example of a cuff that is blocked and buffered.

Block Buffer Editor

Create the **Block Buffer Editor** to protect pieces during the cutting process. When a piece is laid close to another piece, as the cuff is to the armhole in Figure 12.5, the armhole may possibly be slit past the seam allowance and will damage the pattern piece. Notice that the knife blade displayed in Figure 12.5 has width. This knife width may cut into another piece even when you try to be extra careful cutting a tighter layout.

Blocking and buffering may be applied to selected pieces or all pieces in a marker. The amount to block or buffer pieces is set up as rules in the Block Buffer Editor, similar to setting up rules for grading in a Rule Table Editor. These rules are then generally applied and further defined to target selected pieces in the Lay Limits Editor. There is a column for blocking or buffering in the Lay Limits Editor section of this chapter.

A piece may either be buffered or blocked. Buffering is the more commonly used option when you simply want to protect a piece. A piece that is buffered has invisible space around it to protect it from getting too close to another piece. Figure 12.5 shows a buffered cuff; the dashed line represents the area that is buffered around it. You won't be able to place another piece in this invisible space. The dashed line around a buffered piece appears when you place it in a marker; the cutter cuts the original perimeter of the piece in marker making but not when it plots.

Unlike with a buffered piece, a blocked piece has a solid line around it to define the area that is to be protected when you cut it. Blocking is commonly used for pieces that are die cut or pieces used in a marker with matched pieces. When you are making a marker using blocked pieces, the solid line around it remains, and both the original perimeter line and the block line appear during the cutting process, if you opt for the block to appear.

Blocking and buffering may be set up as static or dynamic (see Figure 12.6). When static blocking

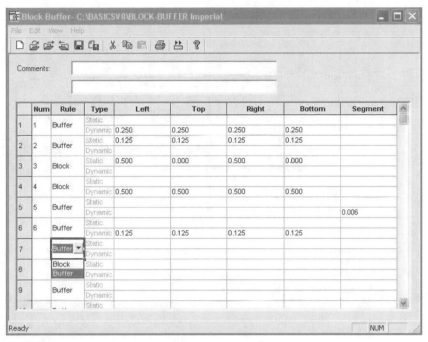

Figure 12.6 Example of a Block Buffer Editor.

and buffering is used, blocking/buffering is automatically applied to the pattern pieces in Marker Making. When dynamic blocking and buffering is used, blocking/buffering may be applied as needed during marker making using the Marker Making toolbox. If it is important for a piece to be blocked or buffered or you want to prevent the marker maker from forgetting to apply it, you should set it up as static. If you want to add blocking or buffering on a piece or pieces during marker making when you notice the need to protect the pieces, then set up a dynamic blocking or buffering rule. There is ample space to create rules in a Block Buffer Editor so that different amounts may be set up for any situation you encounter. If you run out of space for rules—an unlikely scenario—you can create another table to accommodate more rules.

The columns and fields found in the Block Buffer Editor are described below.

Comments Any information about the table may be input in this field as a reference or reminder.

Num Each rule is assigned a consecutive number.

Rule Select from **Block** or **Buffer** in this field by using the drop-down menu that appears when you click into the field as shown in row 7 of Figure 12.6.

Type Select from **Static** or **Dynamic** in this field.

Left, Top, Right, Bottom Blocking and buffering may be applied to the left side, right side, top, and/or bottom of a piece. The left, right, top, and bottom are determined according to the way the piece was drafted/digitized into the system. Enter the amount desired to buffer or block the pattern piece under each column. All columns may be filled out as in rules 1, 2, 4, and 6 of Figure 12.6, or specific sides of the pattern may be blocked or buffered as in rule 3.

Segment This field is not filled out along with the left, right, top, or bottom fields. This field is used when B and Q attributes have been applied to points on a piece to designate a segment of a pattern to block or buffer. For this scenario, you would create a separate rule and fill in only the segment column with the amount you want to block or buffer, as seen in rule 5 of Figure 12.6.

The first rule listed in the Block Buffer Editor in Figure 12.6 is a dynamic buffer in the amount of a quarter of an inch. This means you can buffer a pattern piece if necessary at the time of marker making. If the cuff is buffered with this rule, there will be a quarter inch between the cuff and the front pattern. If this buffering rule is applied to the front and the cuff in Figure 12.5, then there will be a half inch buffer between the pieces. Therefore, if you want a buffer of no more than a quarter inch between two pieces that are bumped up next to each other, where both may be buffered, you may want to consider applying a rule for one eigth of an inch.

When you are finished filling in the Block Buffer Editor with the necessary rules, save it using File>Save As. Rules may be added or deleted as needed. You may apply more advanced blocking and buffering features to patterns, such as protecting an area of a piece from one point to another, referred to as *segment* blocking or buffering. Segment blocking or buffering allows you to protect only a specific area, such as an armhole. The beginning point of the segment would have a B attribute added to it and the end segment would be labeled with the Q attribute.

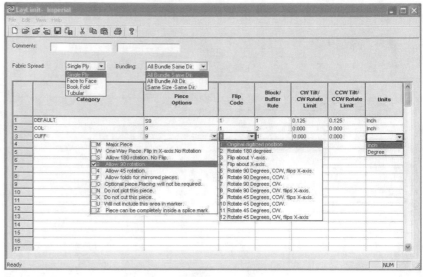

Figure 12.7 Lay Limits Editor with all multiple choice fields displayed.

Test Your Block Buffer Editor Skills

1. Set up a Block Buffer Editor using the numbers shown in Figure 12.6.
2. Name the table Block Buffer.

Lay Limits Editor

Use the Lay Limits Editor to set up parameters for pieces when you lay them out on fabric and to determine how you will lay out the fabric before cutting. For example, will the fabric be cut face up/single ply or face to face? A Lay Limits Editor must be selected and entered into the Order Editor to order a marker, so it is mandatory to set up a table. The screen shot has all multiple selection fields exposed in this figure for reference.

The Lay Limits Editor consists of 10 data input fields. Below are brief descriptions of each area so you can get a general feel of what this editor is used for in the marker making process (see Figure 12.7).

Comments Any information about the table may be input in this field as a reference or reminder.

Fabric Spread Used to determine how fabric will be laid out to be cut on the cutting table.

Bundling Used to describe the direction that each bundle will face.

Category Piece categories are listed per row after the default row. Selections across the row will be applied to pieces with the listed category.

Piece Options Determines what can be done to a pattern piece while you are laying it out in a marker. For example, it may be rotated or flipped.

Flip Code Used to have pattern pieces display in a different direction from the original drafted/digitized one.

Block/Buffer Rule Blocking and buffering rules are entered in this field to be applied to pattern pieces in Marker Making.

CW Tilt/CW Rotate Limit and *CCW Tilt/CCW Rotate Limit* Sets the limit on how much pattern pieces may be tilted off the grain.

Units Sets the unit of measure for the tilting columns mentioned above.

The first item that needs to be discussed and set up is the **Fabric Spread** field seen in the top left of the Lay Limits Editor. You may refer to this as

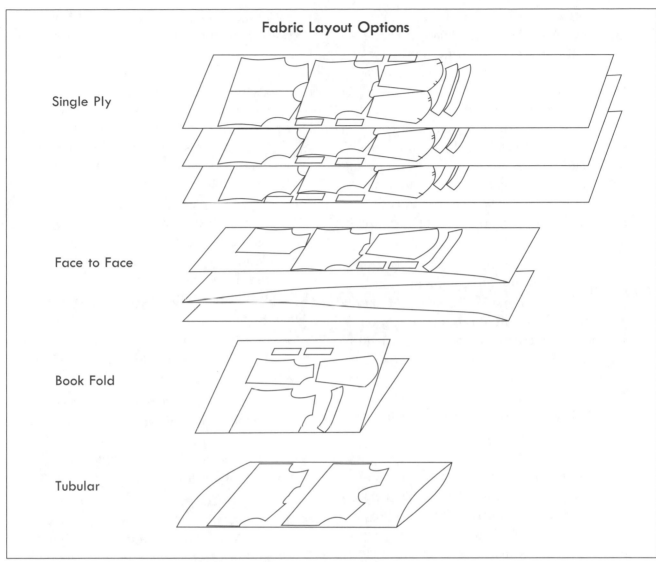

Fabric Layout Options

Single Ply

Face to Face

Book Fold

Tubular

Figure 12.8 Fabric spread options for the Lay Limits Editor.

the fabric layout and direction. This will be determined according to the type of fabric that is going to be cut. For example, due to the nap in the fabric, velvet would be laid out with the fabric spread in a single-ply fashion. Muslin, on the other hand, may be laid out with any of the first three Fabric Spread options because no nap exists (if it has a print, the selection may be narrower). Flipping or rotating pieces should be of no concern at this point since those parameters will be determined in the **Piece Options** column of this editor.

There are four options to select from in the **Fabric Spread** field. These are described as follows (see Figure 12.8).

Single Ply Using this option means that you plan on laying each fabric ply face up or face down. Figure 12.8 shows a Single Ply layout using the pieces from the Model Editor in Figure 12.2. Notice that every left and right piece listed in the "--" and "X" columns of the Model Editor is laid out on the top layer. Each continuing layer consists of the pattern pieces to create an additional garment. As shown in Figure 12.8, three blouses will be made since there are three layers.

Face to Face When this option is selected, a garment is made using two plies of fabric.

Figure 12.8 shows a Face to Face layout using the pieces from the Model Editor in Figure 12.2. Notice that only the pattern pieces considered left pieces in the "--" column of the Model Editor are laid out on the top layer. The right pieces will automatically be cut out of the layer underneath. For example, two sleeves are needed for this blouse but only one is laid out. The second sleeve will be cut out in the second layer. There are four plies of fabric laid out in Figure 12.8 for the Face to Face illustration; therefore, two blouses will be made.

Book Fold This selection is most similar to the way students are used to cutting out pattern pieces in the education environment. Industry professionals may use this option to cut out a sample garment. A garment is made using two plies of fabric when using this selection. Once again, we are using the Model Editor in Figure 12.2 to show how pieces would be laid out when using this option. Since the back pattern is mirrored, the fold may be used for greater fabric utilization.

Tubular This option is used for all the garments that are seamless, such as spandex tops and underwear. Figure 12.8 illustrates how a front and back pattern can be laid out in a tubular fabric. Tubular fabrics come in different widths just like other fabrics.

Look at the first row in the **Category** column in Figure 12.7. Notice the first row states Default. Now notice that a selection is made for each column thereafter in that same row under Piece Options, Flip Code, Block Buffer Rule, CW Tilt/CW Rotate Limit, CCW Tilt/CCW Rotate Limit, and Units. All selections in this row will apply to all the pattern pieces when creating a marker. This is similar to the Annotation Editor default row that we referred to as "the rule" earlier in the chapter and shown in Figure 12.4.

Any exceptions to the default row or "the rule" as we like to refer to it, should be listed on the following rows. For example, Rules 2 and 3 in figure 12.7 have Col and Cuff listed as categories. Any

piece with the category Col or Cuff will have the selections shown on that row applied when being placed in a marker. The category of the piece must match the category input into the Lay Limits Editor or the selections will not apply; instead, the selections of the default row will be applied. For example, if the category of a collar being laid out is Collar when using this editor, it will not be considered an exception. This is one of the reasons why we stress the importance of consistency in the naming of pattern pieces.

The **Piece Options** column lets you choose from 11 different options that may be applied to pattern pieces when you are making a marker. You may choose more than one option at a time. The selections available in the Piece Options field are defined below.

M Major Piece is applied to a piece to differentiate it from a small piece when it is cut with an automated cutter.

W Use this option for one-way pieces that you cannot rotate but may flip over the X axis. For example, if a fabric has a one way print such as sailboats, then it cannot be rotated because they will be upside-down.

S Pattern pieces may be rotated but not flipped. Rotating a pattern keeps the piece face up. When you flip a piece on a single-ply fabric spread/layout where the left and right of a pattern are laid out, it will result in two lefts or two rights.

9 This option allows you to rotate a piece 90 degrees.

4 This option allows you to rotate a piece 45 degrees.

F This option allows a mirrored piece to be folded on a fabric spread with a fold such as the Book Fold or Tubular spreads.

O Apply this option to pieces that are not required to finish a marker. Sometimes you cut out extra pattern pieces to fill empty spaces in a marker and or in case sewing mistakes are made.

N Apply this option to a piece so that it does not plot.

X Apply this option to a piece so that it does not cut.

U Apply this option to a piece so that it is not included in the area calculation of a marker.

Z Apply this to a piece so that it may be completely placed inside a splice mark. A **Splice Mark** is used on fabric spreads to show where fabric needs to be laid if the roll of fabric runs out or is damaged.

The Piece Options applied to pattern pieces are not only determined by the fabric spread you select but also by the actual fabric and the quality desired as well. For example, the proper way to lay out velvet is as a single-ply spread. You are not allowed to flip or rotate pattern pieces in this case and therefore options W and S would both be selected together. Notice that the last statement on each of the options is No Rotation and No Flip, respectively.

The **Flip Code** column is used to have a pattern display in a direction different from the original drafted/digitized direction in a marker. For example, if a patternmaker drafted/digitized all patterns with the necklines on the right but the marker maker prefers them on the left, option 2 may be selected to rotate all the patterns 180 degrees. When Marker Making is opened, the pattern appears with the necklines on the left. The grading remains on the piece as entered. When there is a time crunch and quality is not extremely affected, a company may opt to rotate the pieces to accommodate the design of the garment. The 12 available options are illustrated in Figure 12.9.

Flip Codes	Original Direction	Flip Code Applied
1. Original Digitized Direction		
2. Rotate 180 degrees		
3. Flip about Y Axis		
4. Flip about X axis		
5. Rotate 90 Degrees, CCW, flips X axis		
6. Rotate 90 Degrees, CCW		
7. Rotate 90 Degrees, CW		
8. Rotate 90 Degrees, CW, flips X axis		
9. Rotate 45 Degrees, CCW, flips X axis		
10. Rotate 45 Degrees, CCW		
11. Rotate 45 Degrees, CW		
12. Rotate 45 Degrees, CW, flips X axis		

Pattern right side up   Pattern wrong side up

Figure 12.9 Flip Codes illustrated.

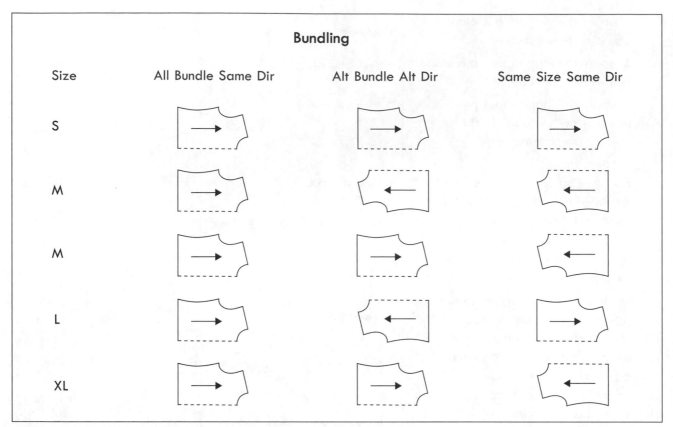

Figure 12.10 Bundling selections illustrated.

The **Block/Buffer Rule** column is used to enter the rule number you need to apply to pattern pieces. The system will reference the selected Block Buffer Editor input into the Order Editor. If a Block Buffer Editor is not selected in the Order Editor, then this column is simply ignored and no blocking or buffering will be applied or available.

The next two columns of the editor are used to set the tilting limits for pattern pieces during marker making. Pattern pieces may be tilted off the grain, up to the limits set in these columns. The **CW Tilt/CW Rotate Limit** column is used to set the limit on patterns rotated or tilted in a clockwise direction and the **CCW Tilt/CCW Rotate Limit** column sets the limit for the counterclockwise direction. The last column, **Units,** determines the unit of measure for these two columns. The unit of measure may be in inches, degrees, or centimeters.

As students you may be appalled to hear the question from an industry professional, "How much do you want to tilt off the grain?" Time and time again you may have been told never to tilt off the grain. While tilting off the grain may alter the quality of a garment, a small amount may be unnoticeable and beneficial when placing a piece for the express purpose of saving fabric. This is common practice in the industry. The tilting limit depends highly on the type of fabric being laid out and its print.

The **Bundling** field selections determine how bundles will be set up in Marker Making. The best way to define this field is by illustrating it (see Figure 12.10). We listed a size line to illustrate how pieces will appear according to the bundling selection made. Notice how the pieces in All Bundle Same Dir all face one direction. When Alt Bundle Alt Dir is selected, the next bundle, regardless of the size, is rotated in the opposite direction. Same Size Same Dir alternates the direction of the next bundle unless it is the same size, as shown in

Lay Limits Name	Spread	Fabric Example	Situation	
Single Ply 1Way	Single Ply	Velvet, corduroy One-way print/motif	One side of the nap is used. Sailboats that all face up.	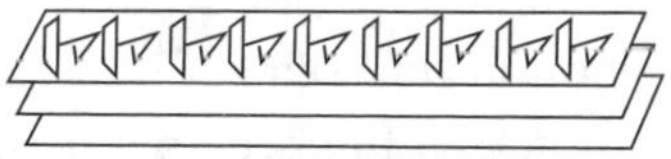
Single Ply 2Way	Single Ply	Poplin, percale Corduroy Two-way print	No nap/one-way print/motif. Both sides of nap are used. Sailboats face up and down.	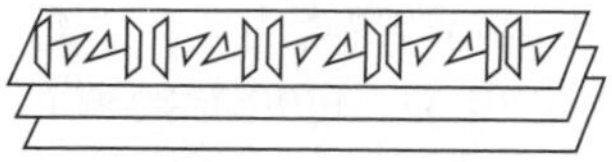
Single Ply All Way	Single Ply	Plastic, fusible Plastic with print	Fabrics without a grain line. Scattered print such as dots.	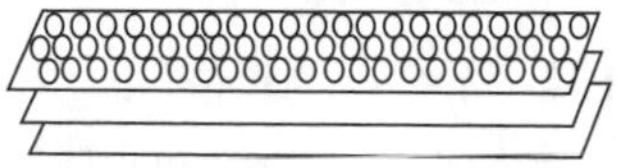
Face to Face 2Way	Face to Face	Jean, Satin, Damask	Fabric does not have a shine or nap to be concerned with when pieces are rotated. Prints are not one way.	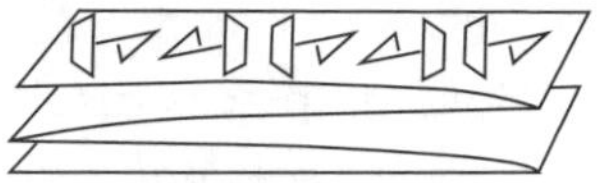
Book Fold 2Way	Book Fold	Poplin, Satin, Jean	Same as above. Mirrored pieces may fold.	
Tubular 1Way	Tubular	Tubular fabrics One-way print	Tubular goods have spandex. No rotation on one-way print. Stretch may limit rotations. If rotated 90 degrees, stretch may be different. Undergarments, seamless tops.	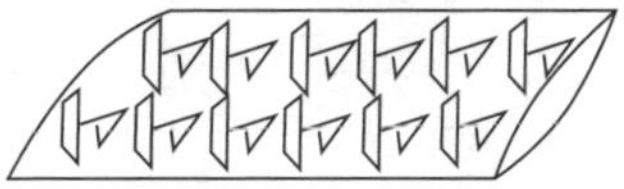

Figure 12.11 Common industry Lay Limits Editor examples.

Figure 12.10 (medium size). The Settings function in Marker Making offers you two options for how to display pattern pieces. The Icon menu option displays the pattern pieces as icons and the Piece View option display the pieces where you will be able to note their direction.

When you are finished filling in Lay Limits Editor, save it by going to File>Save As. Changes may always be made to the table by opening it up again and saving it once more to keep the changes. The editor may be saved using the Save option, but we like to recommend the Save As option so that you are always aware of where the editor is being saved. One Lay Limits Editor should be set up for each different fabric layout situation. For example, create a Lay Limits Editor for fabrics that are spread single ply and that have a one-way print or nap (see Figure 12.11).

Test Your Lay Limits Editor Skills

Set up three Lay Limits Editors with the following information and refer to the Block Buffer Editor that we created in the previous Test Your Skills. Check your answers at the end of the chapter when you are done creating the editors.

Lay Limits Editor #1

1. Name the table Single Ply 1Way.
2. All pieces may not rotate or flip, unless otherwise noted.
3. Have all pieces display flipped 180 degrees from the original digitized direction, unless otherwise noted.
4. Allow $\frac{1}{4}$" buffering for all pieces at the time of marker making, unless otherwise noted.
5. All pieces with the category Col must be automatically buffered $\frac{1}{8}$".
6. No pieces are allowed to be tilted off the grain.
7. All bundles should face the same direction.

Lay Limits Editor #2

1. Name the editor Single Ply 2Way.
2. Allow all pieces to be rotated 180 degrees during Marker Making, unless otherwise noted.
3. All pieces may be buffered $\frac{1}{8}$" at the time of marker making, unless otherwise noted.
4. Display pieces in the original digitized direction.
5. Allow all pieces to be tilted $\frac{1}{4}$" in a clockwise or counterclockwise direction, unless otherwise noted.
6. Pattern pieces with the category Col may be rotated 90 degrees or 180 degrees.
7. Pattern pieces with the category Col must be blocked on the left and right side $\frac{1}{2}$" automatically.
8. Pattern pieces with the category Col may be tilted up to $\frac{1}{8}$" clockwise or counterclockwise.
9. Pattern pieces with the category Cuff may be rotated 90 degrees or 180 degrees.
10. Allow bundles to alternate in different directions.

Lay Limits Editor #3

1. Name the editor Face to Face 2Way.
2. Use all the same information listed for Lay Limits Editor #2. The spread will be the only difference.

Lay Limits Editor #4

1. Name the table Single Ply All Way.
2. Allow all pattern pieces to rotate 180, 90, or 45 degrees.
3. Leave all pieces in the original digitized direction.
4. No blocking or buffering will be allowed or applied for any pieces.
5. The tilting limit is one degree for all pieces.
6. Allow bundles to alternate in different directions.

Order Editor

The Order Editor is used to place an order so you can create a marker. All the editors we have discussed in this chapter play a role in the Order Editor. To recap, these editors include the Model Editor, the Annotation Editor, the Block Buffer Editor, and the Lay Limits Editor. Think of them as a library of editors available to you when you are ready to create markers. If an editor does not exist to fill in the parameters or specifications needed for a marker, you may edit an existing one or create a new one.

The Order Editor in Figure 12.12 has a data field for each of the editors we have mentioned, except the Model Editor because it appears on another page of the Order Editor. Since there may be several selections for each field from which to choose, a browser button will appear on the right of each field when it is selected, as shown in the Lay Limits data field in Figure 12.12. Left click to select the browser button. The current options will be displayed in a separate window (see Figure 12.13). Notice there are four Lay Limits Editors available in Figure 12.13, but only one may be selected to encompass the needs for the marker you want to order. Make your selection by highlighting the

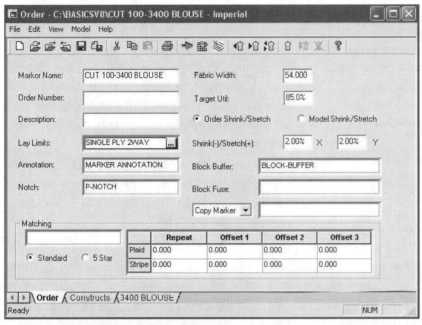

Figure 12.12 First page of the Order Editor displayed.

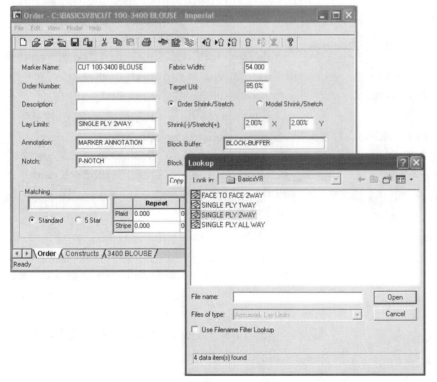

Figure 12.13 Order Editor with browser window displayed for the Lay Limits field.

name of the editor needed and then selecting the Open button or simply by double clicking on the editor's name.

You may open the Order Editor through AccuMark Explorer or the Gerber Launch Pad just like the other editors we have discussed and as described earlier in the chapter. Once the Order Editor is completed, it is processed using another option or a form named **Order Process**. The Order Editor has at least two pages that you must complete for it to be processed successfully. Not all the fields are mandatory. The order cannot be processed if you don't fill in all the mandatory fields. As a matter of fact, the Order Editor may not be saved if these fields are incomplete. A prompt appears stating: "Mandatory field, entry required."

Look at Figure 12.12 again. Notice that on the bottom left-hand side, there are three tabs. These tabs represent the available pages. Left click on a tab to display the page you want to view. The tab labeled Order is the first page, as shown in Figure 12.12. The tab labeled 3400 Blouse is the second page of the Order Editor (however, when a blank one is first opened, it is labeled Model 1). Although not all the fields in these two pages are mandatory, make sure to complete the mandatory fields to process the order properly. Since more than one model may be ordered to place in a marker, multiple Model pages may be created. The tab shown called Constructs is an optional page used to designate repeat motifs or repeat flaws on a fabric.

The commonly used fields for the first two pages of the Order Editor are described in the next two sections. Blank fields in the Order Editor have Mandatory or Optional next to them as a quick reference. Since alterations, matching, and constructs are not fully discussed in this book, we don't describe them here to prevent any confusion.

Order Editor's First Page—Order Tab

Refer to Figure 12.12 to see the fields listed for the Order tab.

Marker Name (Mandatory Field) Enter the name of the marker. The Marker Name and the Order Name are the same. We recommend that the Marker Name include a cut or lot number and the model's name. A cut or lot number is commonly used in the industry as a tracking number for orders and/or markers.

Order Number (Optional Field) Use this field as an extra field to track orders. For example, if a master marker is used often and does not contain a lot/cut number in the name, this field may be used to track the order number, much like an invoice number.

Description (Optional Field) Use this field to further describe the marker. For example, enter that it is a plaid or striped marker.

Lay Limits (Mandatory Field) Select the appropriate Lay Limits Editor.

Annotation (Mandatory Field) Select the appropriate Annotation Editor.

Notch (Mandatory Field) The P-Notch parameter table is selected by default. If you need to use a different notch table, then select the appropriate table.

Fabric Width (Mandatory Field) Enter the width of the usable fabric. **Selvage** is usually considered a nonusable part of a fabric. If selvage is used, then include it in the fabric width.

Target Length and Target Utilization (Optional Field) A Target Length or Target Utilization

may be set by selecting the option desired under the View menu of the Order Editor. Target Length is used to set the goal for the fabric limit length, for example, no more than 7 yards. Target Utilization is used to set the goal for fabric utilization, for example, an average goal of 85 percent so that you waste only 15 percent fabric.

Order Shrink/Stretch (Optional Field) Select this option to apply the shrink/stretch amounts, entered in the Shrink (–)/Stretch (+) option, to the marker as a whole.

Model Shrink/Stretch (Optional Field) Select this option to apply the shrink/stretch amounts entered in the Model Editor.

Shrink (–)/Stretch (+) (Optional Field) Enter an amount in the X and/or Y fields to shrink or stretch the marker as a whole. Sometimes fabrics stretch or shrink after they are laid out in the cutting table. The percentages are calculated and entered in this field. If the Order Shrink/Stretch option is selected, the amount in this field will be applied. If left blank, no shrink or stretch will be applied.

Block Buffer (Optional Field) If blocking or buffering needs to be applied to a marker, select the appropriate Block Buffer Editor. The rules listed in the Lay Limits Editor selected will be referenced from the selected Block Buffer Editor.

Copy Marker (Optional Field) To copy the placement of pieces from another marker, select the name of the marker to copy in this field.

Order Editor's Second Page—Model Tab

Refer to Figure 12.14 to see the fields for the Model tab.

Model Name (Mandatory Field) Select the name of the Model Editor to be used. If you don't have a model, there will be no pieces to place in the marker. If more than one model needs to be selected for a marker, select

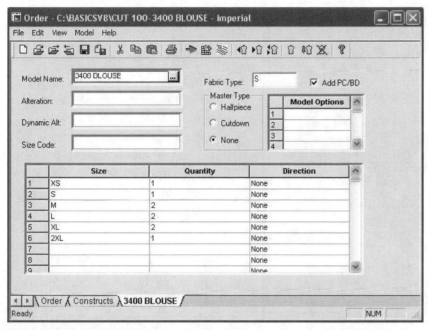

Figure 12.14 Order Editor's Model tab is shown and replaced by the Model selected.

Model from the drop-down menu. The available options allow you to add a new model page, as well as copy or delete one.

Fabric Type (Mandatory Field) Enter the fabric type to be ordered. You may list up to four fabrics to be ordered. The fabric type should match the letter or number listed in the fabric column of the Model Editor. For example, enter S to order the pattern pieces for self or F to order the patterns that need to be cut for fusible.

Add PC/BD Check this box to have the option to add a piece or bundle to the marker at the time of Marker Making without having to change the order. Only the model and pieces originally ordered may be added.

Size (Mandatory Field) Enter the size that needs to be ordered; it must be one size per row.

Quantity (Mandatory Field) Enter the number of bundles to order for the size listed. One bundle is defined by the pieces listed in the Model Editor. Usually, one bundle is one garment.

Direction Select one of the three available options to set the direction of the bundles.

- *None* This is the default selection. Select this option and the Flip Code column of the Lay Limits Editor selected will be referenced.

- *Left* Select this option for the bundles to display in the original digitized direction, which overrides the Flip Code of the Lay Limits Editor selected.

- *Right* Select this option and the bundles will display at a 180-degree rotation from the original digitized direction, which overrides the Flip Code of the Lay Limits Editor selected.

When you complete the Order Editor with the necessary information, you must save it. Select **File>Save As** to save the order with the selected file name. Changes may always be made by opening the Order Editor again and saving it once more to keep the new changes.

Processing the Order

Processing an order sends the information from the Order Editor to the Marker Making portion of the

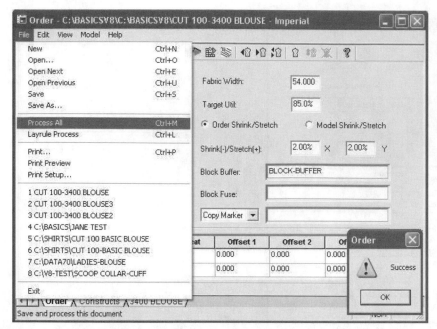

Figure 12.15 Processing an order through the Order Editor.

Figure 12.16 Order processed using AccuMark Explorer. The windows shown appear during the process.

software. An order may be processed in several ways, including from the Order Editor itself, from AccuMark Explorer, or from the Gerber Launch Pad. The Order Process form found in the Gerber Launch Pad is useful when processing several orders at one time. Each process is described below.

Processing an order through the Order Editor

1. Order to be processed must be opened.

2. Select **File>Process All** (see Figure 12.15). A prompt appears stating: "Success" if it was successful. If it is not successful, a prompt appears stating: "Error processing, Missing Components."

Processing an order through AccuMark Explorer

1. Open **AccuMark Explorer**.

2. Double click on the storage area where the order exists.

3. Highlight the order and right click to access a menu (see Figure 12.16). Select **Generate Marker** to begin processing the order, as shown at the bottom right of Figure 12.16. We created this screen capture to display all the windows at once.

4. The order is processed as seen in the **Processing Results** window in Figure 12.16. If successful, results appear in the **Success** box. If it is not successful, an error message will appear in the **Failure** box.

Processing an Order through the Gerber Launch Pad

1. From the **Gerber Launch Pad,** select the second radio button, **Marker Creation, Editors.**

2. Click the **Order Process** icon. The **Order Process** form displays (see Figure 12.17).

3. Select the storage area where the order exists in the **Location** field by clicking the browser button.

4. Select an **Order Name** by left clicking on the browse button, as seen in the first row in

Figure 12.17. Left click on the order name to highlight and select it.

5. The **Marker Name** is normally the same as the Order Name, so unless it is different, there is no need to fill in this field.

6. The **Destination** column is used to send the generated marker to another storage area in addition to sending it to the current storage area. Leave it blank if another destination is not needed.

7. Select **File>Process All** to process the order. The Processing results display in the **Status** column.

If an order cannot be successfully processed, errors must be fixed. The order will not be processed until errors are corrected. After the errors are corrected, the order needs to be processed again. View the **Activity Log,** discussed in the next section, to view error messages and figure out the errors to be corrected.

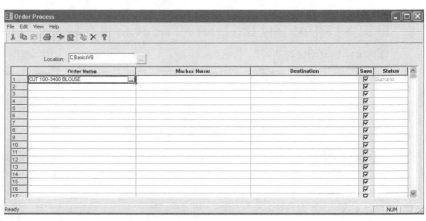

Figure 12.17 Process an order using the Order Process form.

Figure 12.18 Example of an Activity Log.

Activity Log

The Activity Log is used to view activity that has been processed such as plotting pieces, plotting markers, and processing markers. Use it to determine errors that may have occurred during marker processing. Figure 12.18 displays an example of activity that is automatically tracked and logged in the Activity Log. The Activity Log may be opened through the View menu in the Order Editor or in AccuMark Explorer. It may also be opened through the Gerber Launch Pad by selecting the fourth radio button, AccuMark Explorer Utilities, and then selecting the Activity Log icon.

Look at Figure 12.18 to see the notations from Order to Finished Processing Order. This is an example of the activity for the processing of one marker, in this case named Cut 100-3400 Blouse. This marker was not processed successfully. If you read the information carefully, you will notice that the log states the marker will be deleted because it encountered some errors when processed. The error in this case is that the Lay Limits Editor named Single Ply 2Ways does not exist. When entering data into the Order Editor data fields, or any other editor or table, make sure to take advantage of using the browse buttons whenever they are available. Clicking the browse button displays

Table 12.1 Activity Log Error Messages and Solutions

Error Message	Solution/Areas to Revise
The lay limit library X does not exist.	Make sure item exists. Check spelling of name.
Note: This may appear for a Model, Annotation, Block Buffer, Notch or other editor, table, or form listed.	
Piece X does not have size X available.	Make sure size exists. Check for typographical error.
No pieces were ordered for the marker.	Sizes were not listed in order. Model Editor was not completed. Check fabric type in order and model.
Marker X already exists or No Override	The Override Marker option in the User Environment Table is set to NO.

the available editors or tables as they were saved and, by selecting them in this manner, you will avoid typographical errors; in turn, the possibilities for errors when processing a marker will be minimized.

Table 12.1 lists some of the common errors that may be encountered when processing a marker and the possible solutions to reprocess the marker successfully. The X represents the name of the item listed or a size.

Once the order is successfully processed, you may open a marker in Marker Making so that you may lay it out. Remember that the editors or tables created serve as a library of tables to suit the needs for the specifications of a marker.

Test Your Order Editor and Process Order Skills

Using the information provided, create an order for a marker. Follow through by processing the marker. Use the editors we have created in this chapter to fulfill the parameters specified and create the order. Check your answers at the end of the chapter when you are done.

1. Name the order Lot 100-123 Blouse.
2. The fabric width is 55".
3. The model is 123 Blouse.
4. The fabric is being placed face up.
5. Pieces may rotate 180 degrees.
6. Pieces may be tilted up to $1/4$".
7. The collar and the cuff may rotate 90 or 180 degrees.
8. Pieces may be buffered $1/8$" at the time of marker making, except for the collar which should be blocked.
9. Use the appropriate Annotation Editor set up for markers.
10. Your target utilization is 88 percent.
11. The fabric being laid out and cut is the Self fabric.
12. Select four sizes from the size line; the quantities should be 2, 4, 4, and 2. For example
    - Size 3........2
    - Size 5........4
    - Size 7........4
    - Size 9........2
13. Pieces or bundles may be added to the marker.
14. Process the order and fix any errors that you encounter.

Marker Making

The Marker Making portion of the AccuMark program is used to lay out pattern pieces in the most efficient manner. At this point, editors and tables have been created through AccuMark Explorer, pieces have been entered, modified, and saved through PDS and now the last step is to lay them out efficiently in Marker Making. The marker is then plotted on paper and laid out on top of the fabric laid out on the table to be cut. Some fully automated manufacturing facilities do not even plot the marker on paper because they are networked to transmit the file directly to an automated cutter where the marker is then cut.

Opening a Marker

Marker Making may be opened using one of the several ways listed below (see Figure 12.19).

1. **Gerber Launch Pad:** The second radio button displays the icons for marker creation, including the Marker Making icon used to open the program.

2. **AccuMark Explorer:** You may select a specific marker to be opened in Marker Making when using this route. Right click on the marker to open, select **Open> Marker Making,** as shown in Figure 12.19.

3. **Marker Making** icon: This is a shortcut created on the desktop. Double click on the icon to open Marker Making.

4. **AccuMark V8** icon: Use this icon to open all AccuMark V8 programs. A shortcut icon can be created for Marker Making using this route.

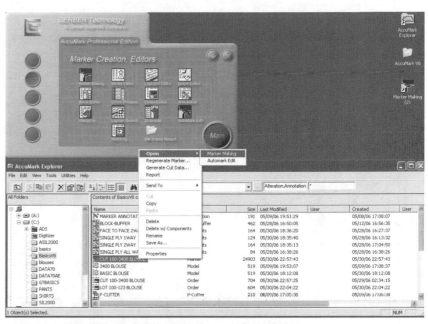

Figure 12.19 Several ways to open a marker.

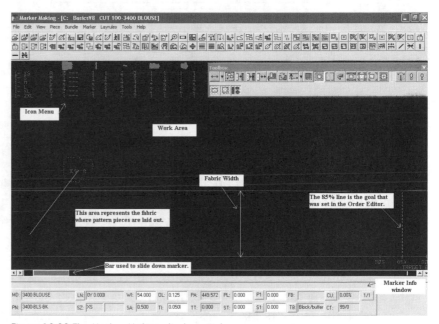

Figure 12.20 The Marker Making display window.

The Marker Making Screen Display

When Marker Making is first opened, if a specific marker was opened using AccuMark Explorer, the display will appear as shown in Figure 12.20. Look at the display areas shown in Figure 12.20. If the program is opened using any of the other three

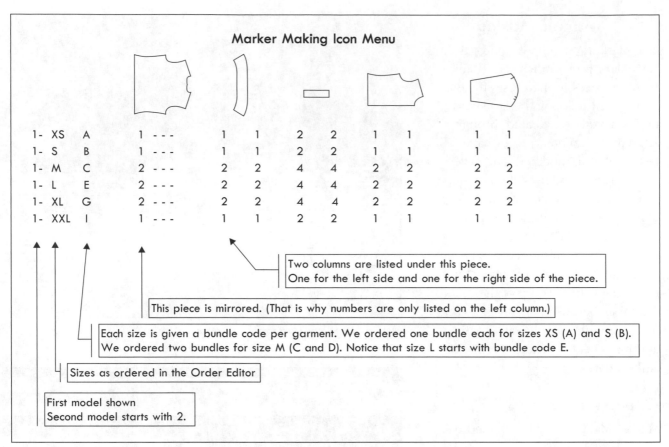

Figure 12.21 Marker Making Icon menu.

ways mentioned in the section above, Marker Making will open without showing the pieces. If any of these three ways are selected, you will need to open a specific marker by selecting File>Open.

At the top of Figure 12.20 is an area of nine drop-down menus. Below these menus are icons for many of the functions listed in these menus known as the Icon Toolbar. These icons are short-cuts to functions. Placing the mouse over the icon will display the name of the highlighted icon. The Toolbox shown displays other functions that will be described later. Figure 12.20 also details the fabric representation. The Icon menu seen in Figure 12.20 is detailed in Figure 12.21.

Marker Info Window

The Marker Info window is located at the bottom of the Marker Making screen display when you first open it. It contains information about the marker that is currently opened, so it serves as a quick reference. It also lets you edit settings such as the increments for tilting or overlapping a piece while making a marker. If you do not wish to see this area displayed, go to View>Marker Info. To display it again, return to the function. It is highly recommended that you keep this window displayed. The fields are described below and seen at the bottom of Figure 12.20.

Marker Info Window Fields

MD Displays the name of the model that is currently open.

PN Displays the name of the piece that is currently highlighted.

LN Displays the current length of the marker.

SZ Displays the size of the piece currently highlighted.

WI Displays the width of the marker. This was set in the Order Editor. Sometimes you need to change a width because the fabric received was wider or narrower than anticipated when the order was created. If it is changed, it will only be changed for the marker and not the actual Order Editor. If it needs to be changed, do the following:

1. Left click in the **WI** field.

2. Type in the new width.

3. Left click on **OK.**

SA Displays the seam allowance that will be added to pattern pieces when they are split in Marker Making. This amount was determined in the Seam Allowance field of the User Environment Table.

OL When patterns are overlapped, they will overlap by the amount shown in this field. Industry professionals sometimes overlap a piece into the seam allowance of another piece, where it is not critical to save fabric. If the amount needs to be changed, do the following:

1. Left click in the **OL** field.

2. Type in the new overlap amount.

3. Left click on **OK.**

TI This is the increment in which a pattern will tilt. For example, if the increment is set to $1/8''$ and a piece may be tilted up to $1/4''$, then the tilting option may be applied twice. You are not allowed to tilt a piece past the tilting limit set in the Lay Limits Editor unless you overwrite it in the Marker Making toolbox. If the amount needs to be changed, do the following:

1. Left click in the **TI** field.

2. Type in the new tilting increment.

3. Left click on **OK.**

PA Displays the area measurement of the currently highlighted pattern piece.

TT Displays the total tilt area of the currently highlighted piece.

FB Function displays when using a function box to make a marker.

TB Displays the option currently being used in the Marker Making toolbox. Left click on TB to hide or show the toolbox in the Marker Info window. The toolbox is displayed in Figure 12.20.

CU Displays the utilization for a marker in four different selections.

- *CU:* This option displays the current utilization of the marker, which is determined by comparing the area measurement of the placed pieces with the total area of the marker. You want this number to be as high as possible because the higher the number, the less fabric you waste.

- *TU:* This option displays the total marker utilization, which is determined by comparing the area of the ordered pieces, not placed pieces like the option above, with the total area of the marker.

- *CW:* This option displays the current amount of wasted fabric. The wasted amount of the placed pieces is compared with the total area of the marker.

- *TW:* This option displays the amount of the total waste of the ordered pieces in comparison with the total area of the marker.

CT Displays the number of unplaced pieces versus the number of placed pieces in the marker. It is quite useful when trying to make sure all the ordered pieces were placed. If a piece or bundle is added, the number increases to reflect the additional pieces.

1/1 Displays the number of piece icon pages. If the amount of pieces ordered does not fit in one page, a second page will be created to hold the pieces and this number will display as 1/2; for 1 of 2 pages. Left click on the number to toggle through the pages.

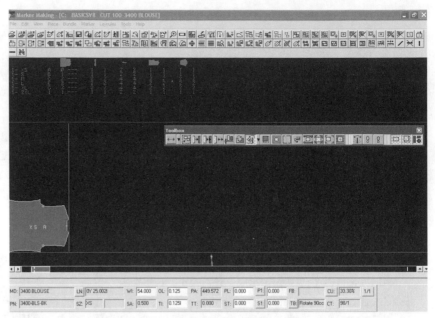

Figure 12.22 Piece placed in Marker Making and displayed after using the Big Scale function.

Placing Pieces in a Marker

Pattern pieces are dragged or slid into the marker. The reason we refer to placing pieces in this manner is because that is what you are actually doing with the mouse when placing the piece. It has become common to hear people in the industry say, "Drag the piece in." Follow these directions to place a piece in a marker. We recommend you try this a few times until you are comfortable with placing the pieces.

1. Left click on the piece desired and release. The piece will display as a dashed-pink colored piece that moves along with the mouse. Move the piece toward the area where it is to be placed, as seen in Figure 12.20.

2. Hold down the left button and drag the mouse. A vector line appears and moves with mouse. Direct the vector toward the desired direction—usually the bottom left when you start.

3. Release the left button to place the piece, which will appear in color, unless you opted for no color to fill in the pieces.

When you place the pieces, always try to get close to the area into which you are trying to place the piece to facilitate the marker making experience. When a piece is placed, it bumps up to the closest piece perimeter. Keep in mind that a piece cannot always slide through another piece to get to its destination.

Marker Making Toolbox

The Marker Making Toolbox is used for functions such as tilting, overlapping, rotating, and flipping. The Toolbox may be displayed or hidden by selecting the TB button in the Marker Info window (see Figure 12.22). It may also be accessed from the View menu or the shortcut icons at the top of the Marker Making window. The Toolbox in Figure 12.22 displays. The Auto Slide and Rotating/Tilting functions are displayed along with their additional options.

The Toolbox is set up as two separate sections: one sect of functions and one of modifiers. Functions may be applied to a piece by right clicking on the piece to perform the function. For example, if a piece needs to be rotated 90 degrees, perform the following steps:

1. Left click on the rotating function: CW or CCW.

2. Right click on the piece to rotate.

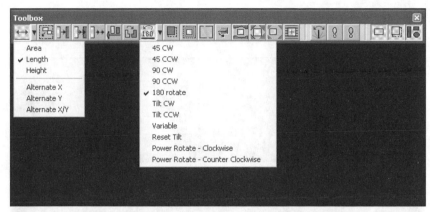

Figure 12.23 The Marker Making Toolbox with the multiple selection options.

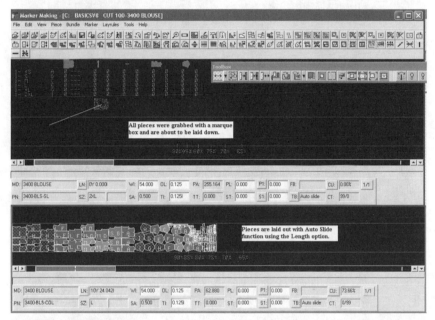

Figure 12.24 Pieces ready to be automatically slid in top window and placed on the bottom window.

when using the Rotating/Tilting function, but with the Free Rotate modifier, a piece may rotate freely with no specific increment. Other modifiers include overriding functions that were not specified in the Lay Limits Editor selected for the marker order.

Place the mouse over the function to see the function's name. The functions and modifiers will be described below from left to right (see Figure 12.23).

Toolbox Functions

Auto Slide Use Auto Slide to slide a group of pieces into the marker at the same time. Select the group using a marquee box and then drag it in with the left mouse button. The system places the pieces as best as it can, following the selections you made. The pieces may be placed or unplaced pieces (see Figure 12.24).

- *Area* Places the pieces with the largest area measurements first.
- *Length* Places the longest pieces, the X axis, in first.
- *Height* Places the tallest pieces, the Y axis, in first.
- *Alternate X* Alternates the sliding pieces flipped in the X axis direction with those in the original digitized direction.
- *Alternate Y* Alternates the sliding pieces flipped in the Y axis direction with those in the original digitized direction.
- *Alternate X, Y* Alternates sliding pieces flipped in the X, Y axes directions with those in the original digitized direction.

For faster results on several pieces or a group that needs to have a function applied, select the function and create a marquee box around pieces. Create a marquee box by performing the following steps:

1. Right click and drag the mouse to create the box around the group of pieces. Make sure all the pieces are inside the box.

2. Release the right button to apply the function.

Modifiers take the functions to a different level. For example, there are specific rotating limits listed

Group Slide Use this function to grab a group of pieces using a marquee box while keeping their current placement. It creates a temporary marriage among the pieces so that they may be moved as a group. Create the marquee box around the group, move it to the desired location, and left click to drag it into place (see Figure 12.25). For example, you may want to move a group of pieces from the beginning to the end of the marker, without losing the piece placement.

Butt When a piece is slid in, it seems to hit the perimeter of another piece in two locations. Butt may be used to direct a piece toward another piece or edge without hitting two perimeter lines. Figure 12.26 shows a cuff that is going to be butted up to the edge of the fabric using this function. To use this function do the following:

1. Right click on the piece. Move the mouse and a vector appears.

2. Direct the vector toward the location you want.

3. Left click to butt the piece.

Overlap Use this function to overlap a piece with another piece. The overlap amount is determined by the amount entered in the OL field Found in the Marker Making info window. It may also be accessed from the Edit menu. Bump up a piece next to the piece it is going to overlap to see the results. The same steps used in the Butt function can be applied

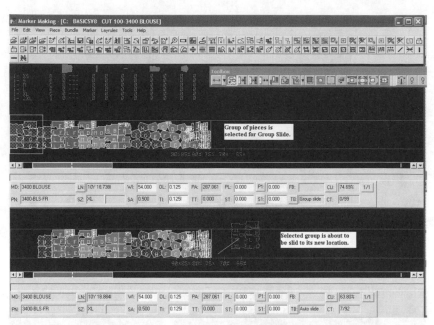

Figure 12.25 A group of pieces is moved to the end of a marker using Group Slide.

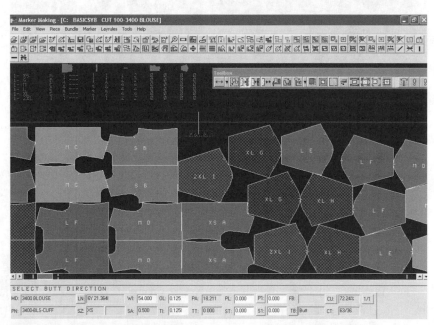

Figure 12.26 A cuff is butted up to the edge of the marker using the Butt function.

to this function. If the vector is directed away from an intended piece, it may also act as a way to create a buffer. See Figure 12.27 for an example of a piece that has been overlapped.

Step Piece Use this function to move a piece in a selected direction by small increments. The amount is entered in the Step amount field of the Settings table found under the Edit menu in Marker Making. To use this function do the following:

1. Right click on the piece. Move the mouse and a vector appears.

2. Direct the vector toward the location you want.

3. Left click to step the piece.

Align Use this function to align a piece to a stationary piece. Pieces that are buffered, blocked, married, or matched cannot be aligned (see Figure 12.28). Perform the following steps to align two pieces:

1. Right click on the stationary piece.

2. Left click on the piece you want to align. Move the mouse and a vector appears.

3. Direct the vector toward the stationary piece to which you want to align.

4. Left click to align the piece.

Flip Use this function to flip a piece. Remember that if you flip a piece that is face up it will be face down. Pieces may be flipped according to the limits set in the Lay Limits Editor selected for the order. You may override these limits by using one of the overriding modifiers, but it will be logged in a marker report. When using this function on a piece that is allowed to rotate you may notice that it rotates by 180 degrees instead of flipping it.

Rotate Use this function to rotate or tilt pieces. Pieces may rotate or tilt according to the limits

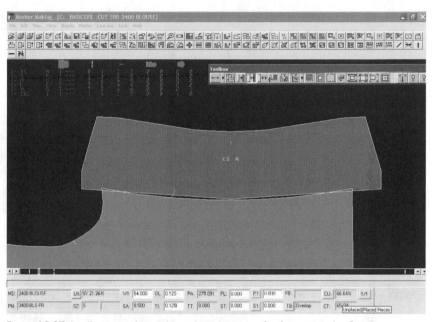

Figure 12.27 A collar is overlapped into the side seam of a front using the Overlap function.

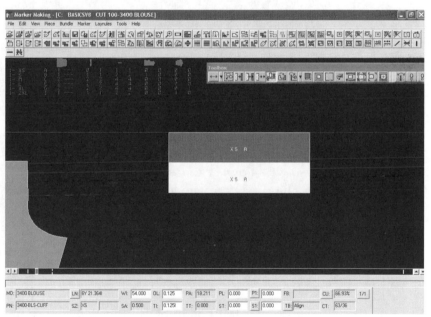

Figure 12.28 Two cuffs are shown aligned.

set in the Lay Limits Editor selected for the marker order. You may override these limits by using one of the overriding modifiers (see Figure 12.23).

- *45 CW* Right click on the piece to rotate it 45 degrees clockwise.

- *45 CCW* Right click on the piece to rotate it 45 degrees counterclockwise.

- *90 CW* Right click on the piece to rotate it 90 degrees clockwise.

- *90 CCW* Right click on the piece to rotate it 90 degrees counterclockwise.

- *180 Rotate* Right click on the piece to rotate it 180 degrees.

- *Tilt CW* Right click on the piece to tilt it clockwise.

- *Tilt CCW* Right click on the piece to tilt it counterclockwise.

- *Variable* Right click on the piece to tilt it clockwise or counterclockwise.

- *Reset Tilt* Right click on the piece to reset it to its original state.

- *Power Rotate—Clockwise* Right click on the piece to rotate it clockwise using a rotation point.

- *Power Rotate—Counter Clockwise* Right click on the piece to rotate it counterclockwise using a rotation point.

Place Use this function to place a piece exactly on a location of your choice. You won't be able to place the piece if it overlaps another piece. Right click on the piece to place it.

Block/Buffer Use this function to block or buffer pieces according to the limits set in the Lay Limits Editor selected for the marker order. Right click on the pieces to block or buffer. When a piece is blocked or buffered during marker making, a "BU" for Buffer or "BL" for Block, appears in the Marker Making window next to the size of the highlighted piece.

Split Use this function to split a piece that has a piecing line. A piecing line is a predeter-

mined split line that was digitized/drafted in with the piece and labeled "P" for piecing line. When a piece is split, the seam allowance entered in the User Environment Table is applied to the split pieces. Right click on the piece to split it.

Fold Mirrored pieces that are allowed to fold may be folded for a Book Fold or a Tubular fabric Spread. This is set up in the Piece Options column of the Lay Limits Editor. Right click on the piece to fold it.

Center Use this function to center a piece in an area. Right click on the piece to center it.

Fit Piece Use this function to fit a piece into a tight and difficult area in the marker. Right click on the piece to fit it into an area. It is highly recommended that the piece be close to the area into which you want to fit it.

Float Piece Use this function to move a piece away from another piece. The float amount is entered in the Float amount field of the Settings table found under the Edit menu in Marker Making.

Matching Allows matching to be changed on a piece that has matching applied to it by opening a matching toolbox.

Toolbox Function Modifiers

Described below are additional modifiers that are available to enhance the functions available in the Toolbox.

Free Rotate Allows a piece to rotate freely when you slide it into a marker. This function should not be used on pieces that must follow a grain line. It is a great function when you are trying to place patterns in the best possible ways, with no worries about how they lay, such as a plastic fabric, which has no grain.

Global Override This function allows you to override functions all at once. This function remains on until you turn it off. Be careful when using this modifier since it may override parameters from the lay limits that you should not override.

Toolbox Override This modifier may be used to override one function at a time. When any piece is placed or if another function is selected, this modifier turns itself off.

Unplaced When using a marquee box for a function such as Auto Slide, unplaced pieces will not be selected if this modifier is not activated.

Placed When using a marquee box for a function such as Auto Slide, placed pieces will not be selected if this modifier is not activated.

Icons When using a marquee box for a function such as Auto or Group Slide, the icon menu and the pieces left in it will not be selected if this modifier is not activated.

File Menu

The File menu, one of the Marker Making drop-down menus, is used to perform routine operations, such as opening, saving, printing, or plotting markers. Many of the functions may be accessed from the Icon Toolbar.

Open

Select this function to open a marker. A marker may be opened from a selected storage area.

Open Next Made

Select this function to open the next made or partially made marker listed. This function will not work unless there is a marker currently open on-screen.

Open Next Unmade

Select this function to open the next unmade marker listed. This function will not work unless there is a marker currently open on-screen.

Open Next

Select this function to open the next marker listed regardless of whether it is made or unmade. This function will not work unless there is a marker currently open on-screen.

Open Previous

Select this function to open the previous marker listed regardless or whether it is made or unmade. This function will not work unless there is a marker currently open on-screen.

Open Original

Select this function to retrieve the last saved version of the marker currently opened. A prompt appears asking whether you are sure you want to proceed.

Default Destination Area

Select this function to allow new imported markers to be sent to a default storage area of your choice.

Save

Select this function to save the currently opened marker into the original storage area from which it was retrieved.

Save As

Use this function to save the current marker with the option to name the marker and place it in the storage area of your choice.

Save Temporary

Use this function to temporarily save a marker quickly. A marker that is saved temporarily is tagged as a Needs Approval marker. This marker cannot be plotted nor cut until it is saved with one of the other saving functions. It may be used as a precaution when you need approval for a marker.

Print

Use this function to print the currently opened marker on a printer.

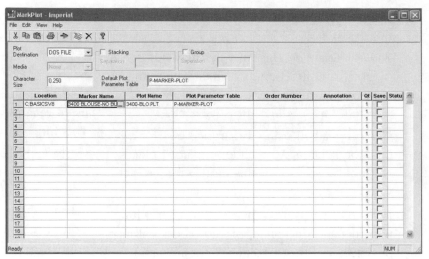

Figure 12.29 Marker Plot Form appears when sending a marker to plot from Marker Making.

Send to Plotter

Select this function to send a marker to be plotted. A form appears titled MarkPlot, also known as the Marker Plot form (see Figure 12.29). The columns filled in with a location, marker, plot name, and Plot Parameter Table name are completed by default according to the marker that is opened. The information on the form may be changed to suit the needs of the marker that needs to be plotted.

Generate Cut Data

Use this function to convert the information for a marker into information for an automated cutter to receive and understand. A Cut Data Generation Form appears with information filled in by default based on the currently opened marker.

Exit

Exit lets you closes out of an opened marker.

Edit Menu

The Edit menu is used to undo functions that you've processed and set up limits for other available functions such as overlap and tilt increments. Many of these functions may be accessed from the Icon Toolbar.

Overlap Amount

The amount a piece may overlap when using the Overlap function in the Toolbox is set up with this function. This amount may also be entered in the OL field located in the Marker Info window, as discussed earlier in the chapter. As mentioned previously, a piece may be overlapped into the seam allowance of another piece, where it is not critical, in order to save fabric.

Tilt Amount

Use this function to set the increment in which a pattern will tilt. This amount may also be entered in the TI field located in the Marker Info window. As a reminder, a piece is not allowed to be tilted past the tilting limit set in the Lay Limits Editor unless you override it with one of the overriding modifiers available in the Marker Making toolbox.

Settings

The Settings function is used to establish preferences for piece and marker display as well as other general settings. A window, titled Settings, appears when the function is selected. There are several areas listed with options provided for your preference.

Global

The Global area is used to enter settings for the functions it lists, as described below.

> *Delete Attach* One or more markers may be attached together to form one marker. For example, marker Cut 100-3400 Blouse may be attached to marker Cut 101-3400 Pant. After they are attached to form one marker, this marker may be given a new name, such as Cut 102-3400 Set. The function to attach markers is found in the Marker menu. When using the Attach function, one of the options listed below will be activated.
>
> > • *Yes:* When this option is selected, the original markers, prior to being attached, will be deleted automatically.

> > • *No:* When this option is selected, the original markers, prior to being attached, will be kept in the storage area automatically.
> >
> > • *Prompt:* When this option is selected, you will be prompted to decide to keep or delete the original markers before they are attached.
>
> *Step Amount* Enter the amount a piece should move when using the Step function in the Toolbox.
>
> *Float amount* Enter the amount a piece should move when using the Float function in the Toolbox.

Piece Display

This area is used to set up preferences for the displayed pieces.

> *Filled Placed Pieces* Check this box to fill in pieces with a color. The color is different for each bundle.
>
> *Notch* Check this box to show existing notches on pieces. When the piece is zoomed, notches appear according to the depth set up in the Notch Parameter Table. All notches in Marker Making appear as Slit notches, regardless of the notch type. For example, a V-notch and a T-notch both appear as Slit notches.
>
> *Orientation Symbols* Check this box to display the orientation symbols for pieces.
>
> *Piece Highlighting* Check this box so that a piece is highlighted as soon as you approach it with the mouse cursor. If it is not checked, only the perimeter of the piece appears highlighted.
>
> *Folding Adds Piece (Recommended)* Check this box to fold mirrored pieces that are added to the marker. It is highly recommended that you check this box.
>
> *Internals* Select one of the options listed below to see internals on-screen. Drill holes are examples of internals.
>
> > • *Off:* Internals will not appear at all.

- *Default:* Internals will appear when pieces are placed or unplaced. Internals will not appear when the piece is being moved.
- *Full:* Internals will appear when placed, unplaced, or moved.

Annotation Select one of the options listed below to see annotation, inside pieces.

- *No:* Annotation is not displayed.
- *Default:* Annotation is displayed.
- *Full:* Annotation, including shared sizes, half piece and cutdown sizes, and fused block annotation, are displayed.

Marker Display

This area is used to set up preferences for the marker display.

Icon Menu Check this radio button to display the pattern pieces in the Icon menu format. Look back at Figure 12.28. The sizes, bundle codes, and quantities for the left and right of each piece are listed.

Piece View Check this radio button to display small-scale versions of the pattern pieces ordered.

Icon Colors Check this radio button to color code the bundles listed when pieces are displayed in an icon menu.

Bundles By Select one of the options listed below for the bundle labeling of a marker. Consider that markers may have multiple models to be placed in one marker.

- *Marker:* Select this option so that when multiple models exist in a marker, they each have a unique bundle code.
- *Model:* Selecting this option restarts the bundle codes for each model that is included in a multiple model marker. If a marker has a pant and blouse, the pant and blouse will each start with bundle code A.

Colors By Select one of the options listed below to determine how pieces are filled in with color.

- *Bundle:* Select this option so each bundle will have a unique color.
- *Piece ID:* Select this option so all pieces of the same category will have the same color. For example, all sleeves will be purple.
- *Size:* Select this option so all bundles of the same size will be filled in with the same color.

OK Closes the Settings window.

Cancel Does not keep any changes made to the Settings window.

Save Keeps any changes made.

Default Changes all the options to the default setting that the system has archived.

Undo (Move/Flip/Place)

Undo restores any changes that were last made to a piece during marker making that include moving, flipping, or placing. For example, if a piece was flipped, undo flips it back.

View Menu

The View menu is utilized for general viewing tasks. For example, display the marker in different views, refresh the display, view the Activity Log, and hide or display marker info or the Toolbox. Many of these functions may be accessed from the Icon Toolbar.

Next Icon Page

Use this function to view the next page of icons when multiple pages are included in a marker. When several models are included in a marker, those that do not fit in the first page work area are displayed in other pages. This function may also be accessed by using the **1/2** button displayed at the bottom of the Marker Info window. This function is also available in the Icon Toolbar.

Zoom

Apply this function to an area of the marker that needs to be enlarged for better viewing. Figure

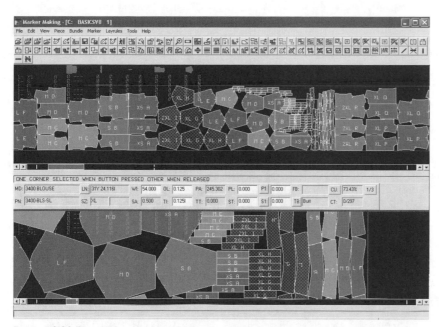

Figure 12.30 Two marker windows displaying an area of a marker selected for a zoomed view.

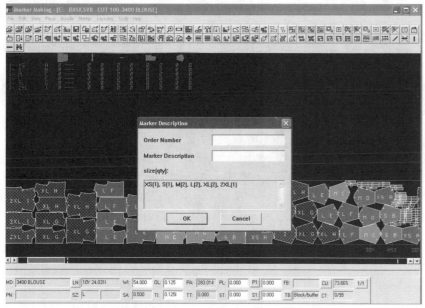

Figure 12.31 Marker Properties window is displayed and ready for input.

12.30 shows an area of a marker selected for zooming and its zoomed view below. Reuse the function to zoom in a selected area even more. This function is also available in the Icon Toolbar. The following steps let you zoom in on an area:

1. Left click and drag the mouse to create a marquee box around the area you want to enlarge.

2. Release the left button.

Full Length

Apply this function to view the whole marker in one screen view. The larger the marker, the smaller the pieces appear. This function is also available in the Icon Toolbar.

Big Scale

Apply this function for a quick zoom view of the marker. This function is also available in the Icon Toolbar.

Refresh Display

Utilize this function to refresh the display when there are leftover particles or graphics on the screen.

Toolbox

Select this function to toggle the Toolbox on or off in the marker work area. This function is also available in the Icon Toolbar and in the Marker Info window as **TB.**

Marker Info

Select this function to toggle the Marker Info window on or off at the bottom of the marker work area. This function is also available in the Icon Toolbar. Refer back to Figure 12.20 to see the Marker Info window.

Marker Properties

This function allows an Order Number and Marker Description to be entered for the current marker opened (see Figure 12.31). The sizes and quantities of the marker are also displayed.

Zoom Window

The Zoom Window option displays a separate window with the marker displayed in full length; the pieces may be moved in the zoom window as well (see Figure 12.32).

Preferences

The User Environment Table preferences appear on-screen and may be edited when using this function.

Activity Log

Use this function to display the Activity Log.

Piece Menu

The Piece menu includes functions that may be performed on pieces, such as marrying, blocking, or buffering. Pieces ordered for the marker may be added, deleted, or split according to the settings entered for them in the Model Editor. You may also use this menu to return pieces to the Icon menu.

Add Piece

The Add Piece function is used to add a piece to a marker. The only pieces that may be added are the ones ordered for the current marker. Figure 12.33 shows the prompt that appears when Add Piece is selected. When the piece is added, it is displayed at the top of the marker, starting from the left side.

Add a piece to a marker by taking the following steps:

1. Select **Piece>Add Piece.**

2. When the prompt appears, left click to select the piece you want to add.

3. Select **OK** in the **Add Piece** window to stop adding pieces.

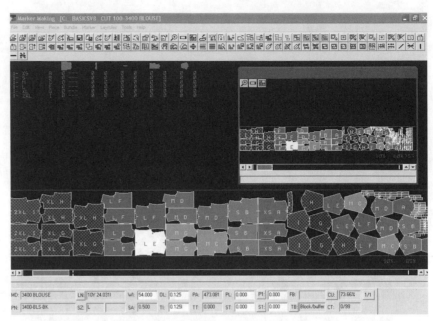

Figure 12.32 Marker with a zoom window opened.

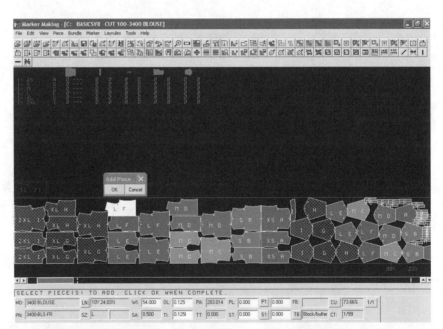

Figure 12.33 Add Piece function is used to add a piece. Added pieces appear on top of the marker.

Delete Piece

Delete Piece is used to delete a piece or pieces that have been added to a marker using the Add Piece function just described. Only pieces that have been added with the Add Piece function may be deleted. Pieces from the original marker order may not be deleted.

Delete a piece added to a marker by taking the following steps:

1. Select **Piece>Delete Piece.**

2. When the prompt appears, left click to select the piece you want to delete.

3. Select **OK** in the **Delete Piece** window to stop deleting pieces.

Return

This function is used to return pieces to the Icon menu or Piece Display menu. Sometimes it gets a little messy when you are making a marker and are moving pieces in and out trying to find the best placement. This function helps keep the work area clean and your brain clear as well. Use one of the listed options in this menu, and described below, to return a specific group of pieces or an individual piece.

All Return all pieces, placed or unplaced, to the menu. A prompt appears to make sure you want to follow through with the request. This option may also be accessed from the Icon Toolbar.

Unplaced Returns pieces that have not been placed or slid into the marker back to the icon menu automatically. This option may also be accessed from the Icon Toolbar.

Bundle Returns a selected bundle of pieces to the icon menu. Left click on one of the pieces that belongs to the bundle and all the pieces that belong to that bundle return. This option may also be accessed from the Icon Toolbar.

One Piece Returns a selected piece to the icon menu. Left click on the piece you want to return to send it back to the menu automatically.

Unplace

This function is used to unplace pieces in a marker. The system considers all pieces in a marker Small by default. If you have applied an "M" for Major in the Lay Limits Editor's Piece Options column for any pieces, then those pieces will be considered major pieces versus small pieces. If this situation exists, then a difference will be noted between the two options listed for this function.

All This option unplaces all pieces, whether they are small or major.

Small This option only unplaces the small pieces of a marker. These options may also be accessed from the Icon Toolbar.

Marry

The Marry function lets you unite selected pieces into what is known as a marriage, so you may move them as a group as many times as you need. Unlike the Group Slide function found in the Toolbox functions, a marriage is not temporary. If you need to move a piece from the marriage individually, you may modify the marriage. Multiple marriages may exist in one marker. Figure 12.34 shows a group of married pieces being slid into a marker.

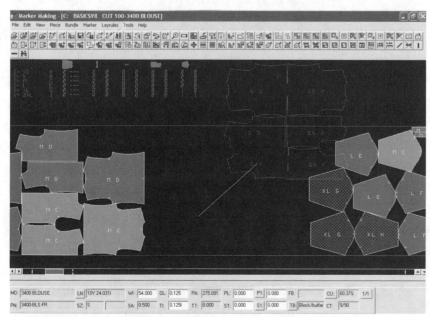

Figure 12.34 A group of married pieces are slid into a marker.

The options for this function are listed below. The latter three will not work if a marriage has not been created. These options may also be accessed from the Icon Toolbar.

Create Use this option to marry pieces (see Figure 12.35). Follow the steps below.

1. Select **Piece>Marry> Create.**

2. A prompt states: "Select piece(s). Click **OK** when done." Left click to select the pieces you want to include in the marriage, which highlights them in blue. Click **OK** in the displayed prompt to marry the pieces.

Modify Use this function to add or delete pieces from an existing marriage. Follow these steps to modify a marriage.

1. Select **Piece>Marry>Modify.**

2. A prompt states: "Select marriage to modify. Click **OK** when done." Left click to select the marriage you want to modify. Do not click **OK** yet.

3. Left click on the pieces to add and/or delete, which turns the pieces back to their original color.

4. Click **OK** when done to modify the marriage.

Delete Select this option to delete a selected marriage from the marker.

Delete All Select this option to delete all marriages that exist within a marker automatically.

Block

The Block functions are used to block pieces that have dynamic blocking applied in the Lay Limits Editor selected for the marker order. Figure 12.36

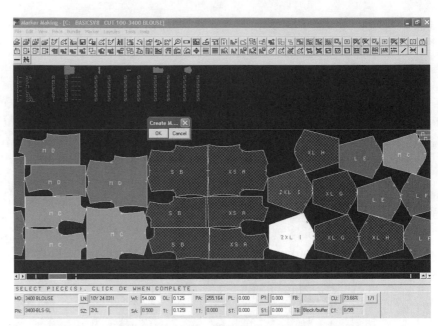

Figure 12.35 Pieces included in the marriage are shaded in the darker color.

shows two collars that are the same size. The collar on the left is not blocked and the collar on the right has been blocked; note the difference in size due to the block. Also notice that "BL" is in the field to the right of the size field in the Marker Info window. This appears when the highlighted piece has blocking applied to it.

The options for this function are specific to all pieces or small pieces. As a reminder, all pieces are considered Small by default unless otherwise noted in the Lay Limits Editor as a Major piece.

Block All All pieces will be blocked, whether they are small or major.

Block Small Only pieces considered small will be blocked.

Unblock All Blocking will be removed from all pieces, whether they are small or major.

Unblock Small Blocking will be removed from all small pieces.

Buffer

Like the Blocking functions, the Buffer functions are used to buffer pieces that have dynamic buffering applied in the Lay Limits Editor selected for the

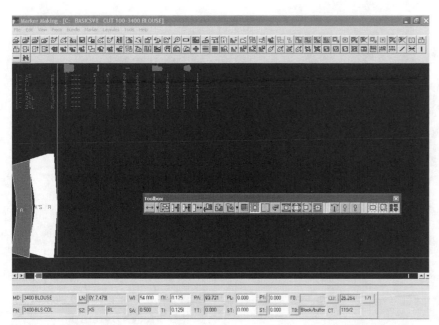

Figure 12.36 Two collars are displayed: one without blocking and one blocked.

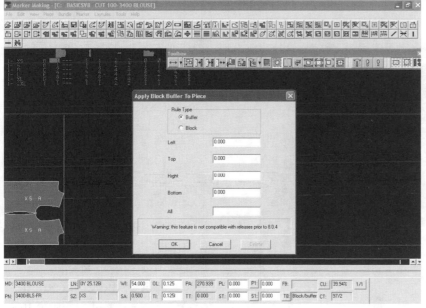

Figure 12.37 Form where you enter blocking or buffering for a selected piece.

Buffer Small Only small pieces will be buffered.

Unbuffer All Buffering will be removed from all pieces, whether they are small or major.

Unbuffer Small Buffering will be removed from all small pieces.

Block/Buffer Override

Use this function to add blocking or buffering to a piece that does not have any blocking or buffering applied to it in the Lay Limits Editor. It may also be used to change the current blocking or buffering amount on a piece. See Figure 12.37 to view the window that appears for this function and allows for blocking/buffering to be entered.

Follow these steps to block or buffer a piece:

1. Select **Piece>Block/Buffer Override.**

2. A prompt states: "Select Piece." Left click on the piece to select it, and the **Apply Block Buffer to Piece** window appears.

3. Enter the rule type and the amount needed for each field. The piece is blocked or buffered.

marker order. When a piece is buffered, BU appears in the Marker Info window when the piece is highlighted. Again, as in the Blocking options, the following listed options are specific to all pieces or small pieces.

Buffer All All pieces will be buffered, whether they are small or major.

Dynamic Split

A piece may be split while creating a marker if it was allowed in the Model Editor. Look back at the Model Editor shown in Figure 12.2. The Dyn Split column is used to enter the number of times each listed piece is allowed to split during marker making. If it is left blank, the piece will not be able to

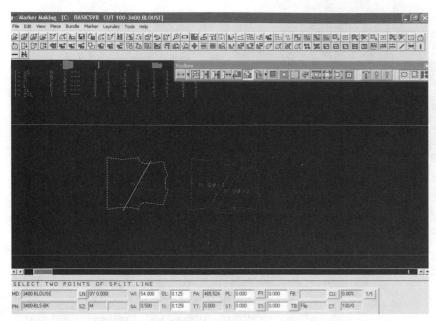

Figure 12.38 Piece is split dynamically using the manual option.

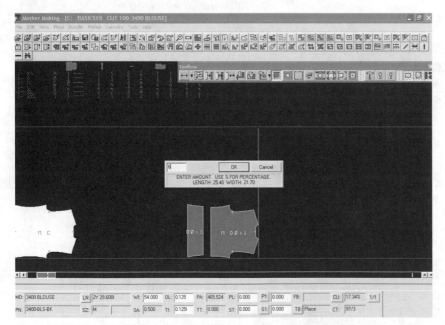

Figure 12.39 Dynamic Split Left is used to split a bodice, as shown.

split during the marker making process. Sometimes pieces are split during marker making to get better placement of the pieces. Ever noticed the seam on the back of underwear or a bathing suit? Although a split is not always visually appealing, it saves fabric and the seam may be camouflaged with extra stitching for a more professional and visually

appealing style. Sometimes splitting a piece not only saves fabric but also creates a new style. See Figure 12.38 to see a piece that has been manually split. The blouse on the left shows the line created with the Manual Split option. The blouse on the right displays the split piece.

Manual Use this option to split a piece in a direction other than horizontal or vertical. Diagonal cuts may be created with this option.

Follow these steps to split a piece manually:

1. Select **Piece>Dynamic Split>Manual.**

2. A prompt states: "Select piece to split. Click OK when Done." Left click to select the piece to split. There is no need to click **OK.**

3. A prompt states: "Select two points of split line." Hold down the left mouse button from the first point to the second point. Make sure the line intersects two perimeter lines or it will not split.

4. Release the left mouse button to split the piece.

Left Use this option to create a vertical split in the garment. The amount entered will measure from the outermost left point of the piece (see Figure 12.39).

Follow these steps:

1. Select **Piece>Dynamic Split>Left.**

2. A prompt states: "Select piece to split. Click **OK** when Done." Left click to select the piece to split. There is no need to click **OK.**

3. A prompt appears stating: "Enter Amount. Use % for percentage." Enter the amount to

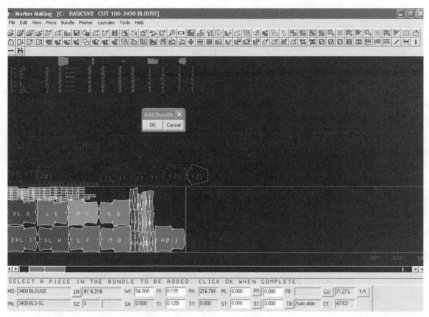

Figure 12.40 A bundle as it is added to a marker.

measure from the left and click **OK** to split the piece.

Top Use this option to create a horizontal split in the garment. The amount entered will measure from the outermost top point of the piece.

Right Use this option to create a vertical split in the garment. The amount entered will measure from the outermost right point of the piece.

Bottom Use this option to create a horizontal split in the garment. The amount entered will measure from the outermost bottom point of the piece.

Join Use this option to join pieces back together after they are split.

Bundle

All pieces listed in a Model Editor may be considered a bundle. Therefore, a bundle may be a blouse, a pant, or a pant and jacket set. If only one piece is listed in a Model Editor, then that one piece is considered a bundle. Use the Bundle menu to add, delete, return, unplace, or flip a bun-

dle. The menu is used to handle a bundle versus individual pieces. Many of these functions may be accessed from the Icon Toolbar.

Add

The Add function is used to add a bundle to a marker. It works much like Add Piece in the Piece menu, with the exception that this function adds a whole bundle versus one piece at a time. Only bundles originally ordered with the marker may be added with this function. For example, if the marker contains only blouses, a pant bundle cannot be added to the marker. To add a pant model, the Order Editor would need to be edited and processed again.

See Figure 12.40 to see an added bundle. Notice the bundle is placed on top of the marker.

Add a bundle to a marker by taking the following steps:

1. Select **Bundle>Add.**

2. A prompt states: "Select a piece in the bundle to be added. Click OK when complete." Left click to select any of the pieces in the bundle you want to add. Click **OK** when you are done adding the bundles you need.

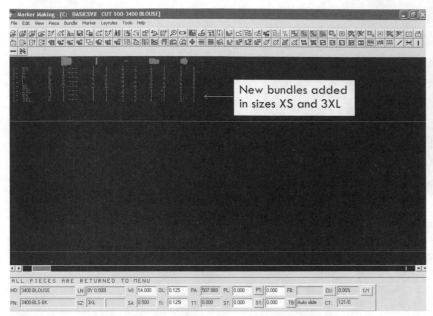

Figure 12.41 Sizes XS and 3XL are added to the marker shown.

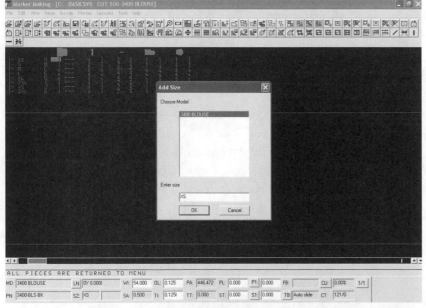

Figure 12.42 Add Size window appears so you can select a model and enter a new size.

Add New Size

Use this function to add a bundle in a size that was not ordered for the marker. For example, if the marker has a size line of XS to 3XL and only sizes XS to 2XL were ordered, use this function to add 3XL to the marker. It may also be used to increase the quantity of a bundle one at a time, since only one is added when performing the func-

tion. For example, if one XS was ordered but two are needed, use the Add New Size function to add another XS. When a new size is added, the bundle is placed in the Icon menu of Marker Making (see Figure 12.41).

Add a new size to a bundle taking the following steps:

1. Select **Bundle>Add New Size.** If you don't place all the pieces in the marker, a prompt appears stating: "Not all pieces are placed, are you sure you want to store?" Click **OK** to store or click **No** so it will not store.

2. The **Add Size** window appears (see Figure 12.42). Left click to highlight and select the model displayed in the window. Enter the new size to be added. Click **OK** to add the new size.

Note: If an error occurs, it should be handled in the same way that an error is handled when an order is processed. A prompt appears stating: "Error updating marker, view activity log?" Click Ok to view the log immediately. The Activity Log may also be viewed from the View menu in Marker Making.

Delete

Use this function to delete a bundle that has been added to a marker using the Add function. Pieces from the original marker order may not be deleted.

Delete a bundle that was added to a marker by taking the following steps:

1. Select **Bundle>Delete.**

2. A prompt appears stating: "Select a piece in the bundle to be deleted. Click **OK** when complete." Left click to select any of the pieces in the bundle you want to delete. Click **OK** when you are done deleting the bundles.

Return

The Return function is used to send a bundle back to the Icon menu. Return a bundle by taking the following steps:

1. Select **Bundle>Return.**

2. "Select a piece from the bundle to return." Left click to select a piece from the bundle and all pieces from that bundle will be returned.

Unplace

Select this function to unplace a selected bundle that is placed in the marker. After a bundle is un-placed, you may move each piece individually from the marker or you may use the Return Unplaced Pieces function to return them to the Icon menu. Unplace a bundle by taking the following steps:

1. Select **Bundle>Unplace.**

2. A prompt appears stating: "Select a piece from the bundle to unplace." Left click to select a piece from the bundle and all pieces from that bundle will be unplaced.

Flip

Use the Flip function to flip a whole bundle in a marker over the X or Y axis, one bundle at a time. If you notice that a bundle needs to be flipped, use this function to flip all the pieces of the bundle no matter where they are in the marker.

1. Select **Bundle>Flip.**

2. A prompt appears stating: "Select a piece from the bundle to flip." Left click to select a piece from the bundle you want to flip and all pieces from that bundle will flip.

Select

Use this function to select a bundle from the Icon menu instead of selecting each piece individually from the menu, which is faster and more efficient. The bundle is laid out on top of the marker so that they may be placed in the marker.

Select a bundle by taking the following steps:

1. Select **Bundle>Select.**

2. A prompt appears stating: "Select a bundle to be retrieved." Left click on one of the numbers listed in the bundle's row size to retrieve the bundle.

Return Orientation

Bundles that have been tilted, flipped, or rotated may be restored to their original orientations with this function. It is great to use when a bundle should not have been modified or if it has been modified and you are unsure of the changes that were made.

Marker

The Marker menu is used to manipulate markers as a whole. Utilize the menu to copy, attach, split, or flip markers among other options. Many of the functions may be accessed from the Icon Toolbar.

Return All Pieces

Use this function to return all pieces in the work area, whether they are placed or unplaced, to the Icon menu. When the function is selected, a prompt appears to make sure you are certain that all the pieces should be returned to the Icon menu. Use this function when you want to start a marker from scratch.

Copy

Use this function to copy the layout of pieces from another marker. It saves you time when you are making a marker. This function works best when you are copying the layout of a marker with similar pieces. The sizes do not have to be the same, but similarity in the patterns and their limits does help. When the marker is copied, some pieces may not be placed if it finds an overlap. In this case, you would need to slide the unplaced pieces into the marker to compete the piece placement. Copying a marker may also be accomplished by using the Copy Marker field in the first page of the Order Editor as discussed previously in this chapter; this route will display the marker already copied when it is opened in Marker Making.

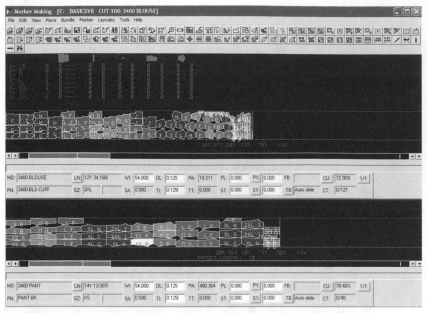

Figure 12.43 Two separate markers are displayed before they are attached.

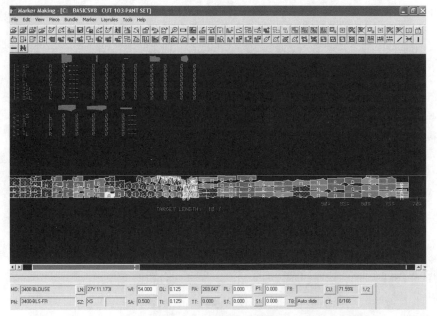

Figure 12.44 Pant and blouse markers were attached to create a marker.

Copy a marker in Marker Making by taking the following steps:

1. Select **Marker>Copy.**

2. The **Lookup** window appears. Select the marker from which to copy from the list of markers displayed. Click Open to copy the marker.

Attach

The Attach function is used to bring one or more markers together and attach them to create one marker. For example, marker Cut 100-3400 Blouse may be attached to marker Cut 101-3400 Pant. After they are attached to form one marker, this marker may be given a new name such as Cut 102-3400 Set. Use Delete Attach, in the Settings window, to determine how the original markers should be handled; they may be deleted or kept. Either one of the selections made will automatically happen when this function is used.

Figure 12.43 displays two markers: one of a blouse and one of a pant. Figure 12.44 displays these two markers attached.

Attach markers together by taking the following steps:

1. Select **Marker>Attach.**

2. The **Open** window appears. Select the marker(s) you want to attach to the marker that is open from the list of markers displayed, and select **Open.**

3. The **Save As** window appears. Enter a name for the new marker. Select Save when you are done to attach the markers (see Figure 12.44).

Split

Use the Split function to split a marker anywhere along the length. For example, use this function when pieces need to be placed in the middle of a marker. Splitting a marker can be used to create an opening for other pieces to be placed. A piece is selected as the guide for the location to split, which splits the marker from that piece to the end of the marker. All the pieces from the split to the end of the marker will be unplaced. If the pieces in the unplaced portion of the marker need to remain in their layout locations, then move them as a group by using the Group Slide function or create a marriage. See Figure 12.45 for an example of a marker that has been split.

Split a marker by taking the following steps:

1. Select **Marker>Split.**

2. A prompt states: "Select piece to start split." Left click on the piece to select as the start to split.

Flip

Flip is used to flip the marker as a whole. It is similar to flipping a piece, but in this case, the whole marker is flipped. This function may come in handy when a fabric roll is laid out the wrong way. When attaching two markers together, flipping one marker before attaching it to another marker may allow for better fabric utilization. A marker may be flipped in any of the directions listed below.

On X Axis Use this option to flip the marker over the X axis (see Figure 12.46). Look at the pieces at the beginning of each marker shown to see the difference.

On Y Axis Use this option to flip the marker over the Y axis.

X, Y Axis Use this option to flip the marker over the X axis and then over the Y axis.

Material Attributes

The options listed for this menu are used to change items such as the width of the fabric or the matching plaid/stripe repeats and offsets. Since the scope of this book does not encompass matching, only the first option is listed below.

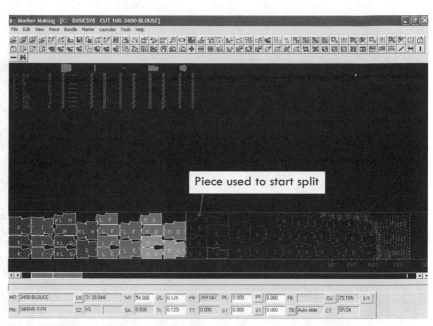

Figure 12.45 Marker split using the Split function.

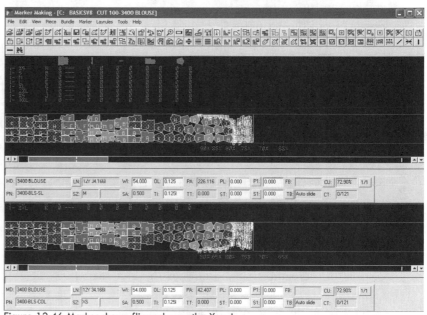

Figure 12.46 Marker shown flipped over the X axis.

Width Use this function to change the width of the marker. This amount is set in the Order Editor. Sometimes a width needs to be changed because the fabric received is wider or narrower than anticipated when the order was created. If it is changed, it will only be changed for the marker and not the actual

Order Editor. This function may also be accessed by selecting WI in the Marker Info window.

Tools Menu

The tools menu is used to make some marker making tasks more efficient. A **scoop** is a layout of pieces in selected sizes that are placed in a selected order for the marker. This scoop may be used to lay out pieces in a marker when there are numerous pieces of the same pattern to place. **Bump lines** are lines created in a marker that may be used to align pieces along a straight edge more efficiently. Many of the functions may be accessed from the Icon Toolbar.

Scoop

Use the Scoop function to create a layout of pieces for the system to retrieve and copy. The layout and the sizes included in the scoop are copied when using the scoop for the remaining pieces you need to place. When no pieces in the scoop remain, the system notifies you that it is an incomplete scoop. This function is quite useful when a marker has multiple pieces for example, 600 collars. Instead of laying out each pattern piece individually, patterns may be laid out in a placement of your choice. A scoop is then created that memorizes the layout of the pieces and their sizes so the pieces can be retrieved from the icon menu to duplicate the scoop created. Only one scoop may be created and used at a time, so if you need another one delete the original one first. See Figure 12.47 to see a scoop that has been created and a scoop that is going to be placed in the marker.

Create Use Create to select the pieces you want to include in the scoop you are going to create. Create a scoop by taking the following steps:

1. Select **Tools>Scoop>Create.**

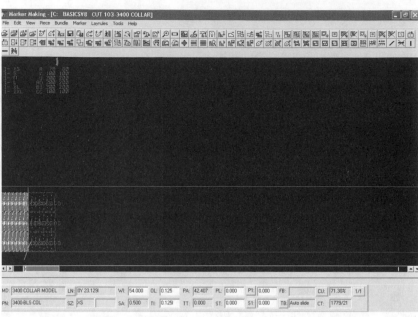

Figure 12.47 A scoop has been created for a marker and is applied to place pieces in the marker.

2. A prompt states: "Select piece(s). Click OK when done." Left click on each piece to include them in the scoop. Click **OK** when you are done. The Scoop may now be used by clicking the **Apply** icon in the function toolbar or by selecting Tools>Scoop>Apply.

Modify Use this option to add or delete pattern pieces from a scoop.

Delete Use this function to delete a scoop.

Apply Select this option to use a scoop that has been created. After selecting this function, the scoop is placed in the next available space in the marker, as seen in Figure 12.47.

Bump Line

Bump lines are created as lines to which pattern pieces may be bumped up and with which they can be aligned. Multiple bump lines may be created at one time. For example, multiple lines may be created to designate areas in the marker where pieces should not be placed due to a flaw in the fabric.

When using the available options for creating bump lines, a prompt appears where you can enter

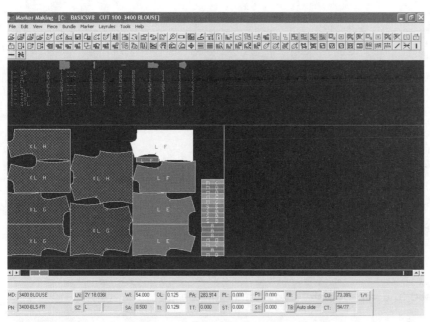

Figure 12.48 Marker shown with a vertical bump line used to align cuffs.

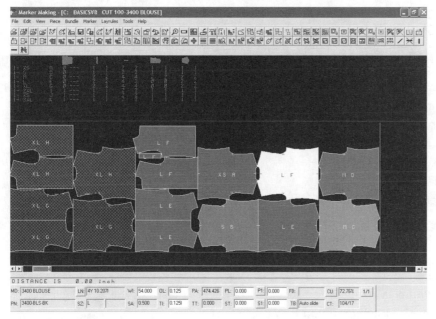

Figure 12.49 Piece to Piece option in the Measure menu is used to find the distance between pieces.

the location of the bump line. Listed below are the available options:

> *Vertical* Creates a vertical bump line across the width of the fabric (see Figure 12.48).

> *Horizontal* Creates a horizontal bump line along the length of the fabric.

Manual Allow for a freehand creation of a bump line. For example, use the Manual function to create a horizontal or vertical bump line while determining the length of the line with the mouse.

Annotate Use this option to annotate a bump line. This may be used to plot information on a marker that needs to plot.

Delete Use this option to delete a bump line.

Measure

The Measure functions are used to determine the distance from a piece to another piece or to the edge, or to measure from one point to another. Many of the functions may also be accessed from the Icon Toolbar. All measurements display in the Marker Info window (see Figure 12.49).

> *Piece to Piece* Use this option to measure the distance between two pieces. For example, use it to confirm the buffer between two pieces.

> *Piece to Edge* Use this option to find the measurement between a piece and an edge. For example, use this option to determine the length of a marker from the beginning edge of a marker to the selected piece.

Point to Point Use this option to find the measurement between two points on a piece or pieces. For example, you can determine the approximate measurement of a bodice center front.

Test Your Skills

Use the marker that was processed earlier in the chapter in the Test Your Order Editor and Process Order Skills section and the appropriate Toolbox functions to test your skills.

Change the Lay Limits Editor selected in the Order Editor and save the order under a different name. Process the new order so that a new marker may be generated. Open the newly generated marker and note the difference in the limits placed on pieces and the pattern distribution in the Icon menu. Since four Lay Limits Editors were created, you should have four Order Editors to process and four markers with which to practice functions and pattern placement.

Test Your Knowledge

Answer the following questions:

1. Name at least two tables you need to complete before you can create an order for a marker.
2. What is the visible difference between the options to block or buffer a piece?
3. What are blocking and buffering generally used for in the industry?
4. What is the difference between Static and Dynamic when buffering or blocking a pattern piece?
5. Why is a Model Editor needed for the Order Editor?
6. Does an Annotation Editor have to be included for the Order Editor?
7. What is the purpose of a Lay Limits Editor?
8. When should a Lay Limits Editor be created? Should one be created per storage area?
9. How many pages long is the Order Editor?
10. Why is an Order Editor created?
11. If errors are encountered when processing a marker, where can errors be viewed?
12. If a marker is not processed successfully, can the marker be seen in Marker Making?
13. How are pieces placed in a marker?
14. Where are pieces displayed in Marker Making?
15. Where is general marker and piece information found in Marker Making?

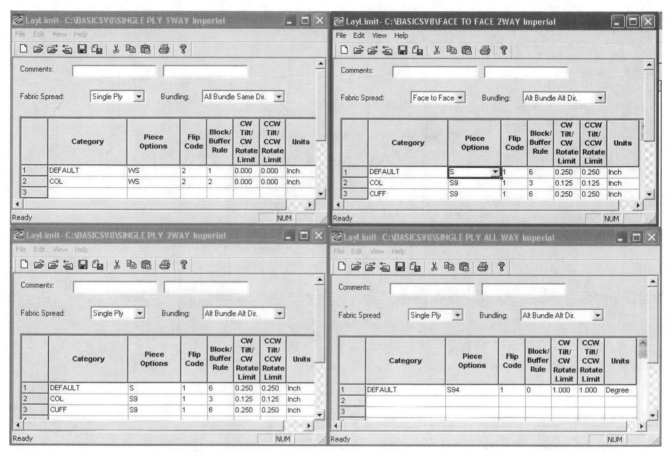

Figure 12.50 Test Your Skills answers for Lay Limits Editor.

Test Your Lay Limits Editor Skills Answers

The four tables that you created for the Test Your Lay Limits Editor Skills section are displayed scaled down in Figure 12.50.

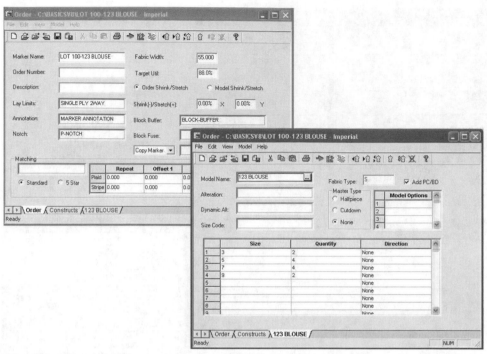

Figure 12.51 Test Your Skills answers for the Order Editor and Process Editor.

Test Your Order Editor and Process Order Skills Answers

The Order Editor pages that should have been completed to finish the Test Your Order Editor and Process Order Skills section are displayed in Figure 12.51.

Glossary

AccuMark Explorer software used to manage data such as pieces, models, parameter tables, and editors and may be used to link to PDS, Marker Making, and plotting.

AccuMark Find function used to search for data items in the AccuMark program

Activity Log function used to view activity that has been processed such as plotting pieces, plotting markers, and processing markers. The system automatically logs this information for reference.

Alphanumeric Rule Table Rule Table that consists of sizes with letters and/or numbers or a Rule Table with an inconsistent size step

Annotation Information about a piece, model, or marker that may plot inside or outside of pattern pieces or markers

Annotation Editor editor used to determine the annotation that should plot on pieces and markers

Base Size original size at which a pattern is initially created and used as a basis to grade smaller and larger sizes. It is the size drafted/digitized into the system.

Block Buffer Editor editor used to input blocking and buffering rules for use in marker making.

Blocking method used while creating a marker to protect the pieces during the cutting process and commonly used when fusing and matching pieces. This method draws a solid line around the pieces at an amount which is specified in the Block Buffer Editor.

Box Pleat combination of two folds that face opposite directions; two knife pleats folded in opposite directions create a box pleat

Break size the size where the grade rule changes to a different increment

Browse button small square that commonly appears adjacent to a selected data field. It is used to view available files from which to select.

Buffering method used in Marker Making that leaves a specified space between patterns in a marker that protects them from being nicked during the cutting process; the amount is specified in the Block Buffer Editor

Bump lines vertical or horizontal lines created in a marker that may be used to align pieces along a straight edge more efficiently.

Bundle term used in marker making that refers to all pieces listed in a Model Editor

Copy Data function used to copy data from one area to another, such as copying a model from one storage area to several storage areas

Create Piece function used after drafting a piece to change a draft piece into a valid AccuMark piece. To make the pattern a valid piece, you select all the perimeter lines that are displayed at one time, and then you select internal lines and points.

Cursor Mode this mode lets you move the cursor along a point, line, or piece during a function and is found in the User Input box; Value Mode is the alternative mode

Dart Apex term used to refer to the depth of a dart when using the Dart menu in PDS

Data Field area used to enter or select data from a list of data items

Delete Data function used to delete data from one or several storage areas at once; deleted items go to the Recycling Bin in AccuMark Explorer unless you select the option to permanently delete items

Descriptive Data is made up of the Piece Name, Piece Category, and Piece Description and used to label pieces; you save them along with every pattern

Digitize method used to input patterns into the system using a digitizer table

Draft method using a pen/stylus to input patterns into the system using a drafting table

Draft Scale used prior to drafting a pattern, this function places the drafting table area and the PDS screen in a 1:1 ratio

Draft Trace function used after drafting a piece to change a draft piece into a valid AccuMark piece. It lets you select perimeter and internal lines so you can trace them; this is highly recommended for beginners.

Drop-down arrow arrow displayed in a field that lets you from select a list of options

Endpoint the beginning or end of a line segment that may or may not include a grade rule; diamonds (and triangles) represent endpoints in PDS

Gerber Launch Pad found on the desktop, the launch pad gives you quick access to other programs, tables, editors, or other forms

Graded Nest a stacked display of all available sizes for a pattern that may be used to verify grading on a stack of all available sizes or break sizes

Grade Point an intermediate or endpoint that has an X and/or a Y movement determined by an applied Grade Rule number

Grade Rule the X and Y direction and amount applied to an intermediate or endpoint to create grading on a pattern piece

Gradeometer a machine used by patternmakers and graders in the fashion industry to aid in the grading process of a base size pattern. The gradeometer mimics the movements of the X and Y directions of computerized grading. You can move the gradeometer to the specific distance necessary to make a pattern larger or smaller.

Grading the process used to create smaller and larger sizes from a base size

Grain line refers to the lengthwise and crosswise threads that run through fabric. The crosswise grain runs perpendicular to the fabric selvage. The lengthwise grain runs parallel to the fabric selvage.

Icon menu bank of pieces available for selection; PDS and Marker Making each has an icon menu at the top of the screen

Intermediate Point point that lies between the beginning and the end of a line segment. Points create the shape of a line and may contain grading. A square or an upside down triangle symbol represents an intermediate point in PDS.

Knife pleat folds of fabric, usually narrow, that all face one direction and usually have a sharp folded appearance. Tennis and cheerleading skirts have knife pleats all around.

Lay Limits Editor editor used to establish the fabric spread and the limits for laying pieces in a marker. Among other selections, it includes single-ply or face-to-face fabric spread selections and several rotating, flipping, and tilting options.

Line/Curve Drafting Method method and function used to draft pattern pieces into the system; points are selected to create the shape of a pattern much like a connect-the-dots game

Line segment determined by the beginning of one endpoint to the next endpoint

Line label name or label applied to a line to distinguish it from other lines. Some lines have a system defined label; for example, grain lines have the label "G" automatically applied to them when created.

Marker Info Window area in Marker Making that contains information about the marker and open pieces, such as the piece name and size, model name, and marker length and width

Marker Making AccuMark program used to place pattern pieces in a marker

Model a garment with a style name, such as a pant, skirt, jacket, suit, or bathing suit; an example of a blouse's model name is 3400 Blouse

Model Editor used to list all the pattern pieces needed for the creation of a garment or style; very similar to the cutter's must in manual production

Move Data function used to move data items out of one area and into another area

Notch a small cut within the seam allowance of a pattern piece used as a reference for sewing; available notch types include Slit, V, T, and Castle/Clicker notches

Notch Table used to enter the values for notches in a storage area and referenced when pieces are plotted

Open End available in the Pleat and Fullness menu functions; it refers to the end of a created line segment whose width can open so you can insert a pleat or fullness

Order Editor form you fill out to place an order to create a marker; other components such as the Model Editor, Annotation Editor, Lay Limits Editor, and the Notch Table must exist to create the order

Orientation Symbol symbol displayed to show the original direction or orientation of a pattern when it was first drafted/digitized into the system and that appears on all valid AccuMark pieces

Parallel Fullness fabric width added to a garment needs to have fullness in the width or length; equal fullness is added to both ends of the slash lines created to spread the garment for added fullness.

Piece Name name used to save and locate pattern pieces. Every pattern piece must have a Piece Name when saved. The name is commonly created using the style name along with the pattern piece type (e.g., 3400 Side Front); there is a 20-character limit.

Piece Category name used to specify a part of a garment (e.g., Center Front or Side Front); the category has a 20-character limit and is mandatory for every saved piece. We recommend that you not include a style name.

Piece Plot Order form used to place an order for pieces or models to be sent to a plotter to plot

Piece Plot Parameter Table table used to define options for plotting pieces or models such as scale, point numbers, Grade Rule numbers, annotation location, and sizes to plot

Pen/Styles pen-like instrument used to draft a pattern into the system

Pivot End available in the Pleat and Fullness menu functions, it refers to the end of a created line segment with a pivot point; it's the side of the line that will not receive any growth or be opened

Pleats fabric folds that usually run lengthwise on a fabric and are used for decoration or to take in excess width of a garment. There are several kinds of pleats used in the fashion industry, including knife and box pleats.

Pleat Lay Side refers to the side of the piece that knife pleats will face.

Pleat Open Side refers to the side that is opposite of the lay side

Ply refers to a layer of fabric

Point Numbers consecutive reference numbers automatically applied to a pattern piece's end or grade points; these points may be changed to reference alteration or matching point locations

Point Attributes label attached to a point to define its traits, such as *N* for a non-smoothing point or *S* for a smoothing point.

Popup used to enter into Value Mode so that a measurement may be entered while performing a function; technique is performed by pressing both the left and right mouse buttons together and releasing them at the same time

PDS acronym for Pattern Design System. The AccuMark program is used to create pattern pieces from scratch and or manipulate them as you would in manual production.

Recycling Bin area where deleted items in AccuMark are sent. It may be found in the AccuMark Explorer application

Rule Table table used to define the X and Y growth amounts for the grading of patterns

Rotation Point this point is equivalent to the pivot point or point to cut or slash to in manual patternmaking when manipulating darts, fullness, and pleats.

Scoop a layout of pieces in selected sizes that are placed in a selected order for a marker: a scoop may be used to lay out pieces in a marker when there are numerous pieces of the same pattern to place, such as collars.

Seam Allowance excess fabric added around a pattern piece to guarantee specs remain correct when you sew one pattern piece to another. If seam allowance is not added, the garment specs will be smaller all around.

Selvage raw edge of the fabric that is not necessarily used for the creation of a garment

Sketch Drafting Method method and function used to draft pattern pieces into the system. Typically used with hard patterns made out of oak tag or Mylar, this method allows patterns to be traced with a pen/stylus. If you use this function be sure the pattern is well-cut.

Size Break the size in a size line where the grading growth amount changes

Size Line the size range of a pattern from the smallest to the largest available size

Size Step Size Step is only seen in Rule Tables that are set up as numeric rule tables. It is the difference from one size to the next in a numbered size line; for example, size line 28, 29, 30, 31 has a size step of 1 and size line 28, 30, 32, 34 has a size step of 2.

Splice Mark a marking used on fabric spreads to show where fabric needs to be laid if the roll of fabric runs out or is damaged

Storage Area used to store your pieces, markers, and general piece information; it is similar to a file folder in a word processing program

Symbols geometry, including a square, a diamond, a triangle, a circle, and an upside-down triangle, to define points on a pattern piece

Tapered Fullness added fabric width to a garment created with fullness at only one end of the garment (the other end stays at the same width)

Tapered Pleat a pleat that has width on one end and none on the other

Toggle/Rotary Field field that contains a list of predetermined options provided by Gerber Technology for selection. Left click repeatedly in the field to view available options: other options may not be typed in by the user.

Track used to track points, lines, or pieces within selected Edit Menu functions. When track is selected, the system momentarily stops at each point around the piece clockwise while displaying that point, line, or piece information.

User Environment Table table used to set up preferences such as decimal precision, metric/imperial measure mode, and grading method; it should be completed after the creation of a storage area since it sets important parameters for the storage area

User Input Box area found on the right side of the PDS screen that displays prompts and value inputs during functions; it may be moved to another area of the screen

Valid AccuMark Piece A valid AccuMark piece may be manipulated using all PDS functions; you may convert a draft piece into a Valid AccuMark Piece by performing the Draft Trace or Create Piece function

Value Mode Mode used to enter a specific amount to move lines, points, or pieces, Cursor Mode is the alternative mode

Index